NOTE

In May 1974 the Twenty-seventh World Health Assembly, after reviewing the Fifth Report on the World Health Situation,[1] requested the Executive Board to consider the question of rationalizing the collection and summarizing of information on the health situation in the various countries, including the intervals at which the information should be published. It also requested the Director-General to continue, pending the Board's recommendations, his preliminary work on preparation of a sixth report on the world health situation, and to present a progress report to a subsequent World Health Assembly.[2]

At its fifty-fifth session, in January 1975, the Executive Board requested the Director-General to study ways of applying, in the preparation of the sixth report on the world health situation, the suggestions he had made in a report to that session, taking into account its discussions on the subject, and to present his proposals to the Board's fifty-seventh session.[3]

After reviewing those proposals, in January 1976, the Executive Board recommended that the future reports on the world health situation should continue to comprise a global analysis and country reviews published by WHO headquarters; should be published every six years, in accordance with the major programme cycle of the Organization (the general programmes of work), with the exception of the sixth report, which should cover the five years 1973–1977, corresponding to the Fifth General Programme of Work; and should be published without prior review by the World Health Assembly.[4]

The Twenty-ninth World Health Assembly, held in May 1976, concurred in those recommendations, and recommended further that the future reports on the world health situation should, at a subsequent Health assembly, be the subject of discussion bearing particularly on their methodology and content.[5]

The present report is in two volumes. Part I contains the global analysis, with an introduction and chapters on background, health status differentials, health action, research, and the outlook for the future; and Part II the review by country and area, with the additions and amendments submitted by the governments, and an addendum for later submissions.

---

[1] WHO Official Records, No. 225, 1975.
[2] Resolution WHA27.60.
[3] Resolution EB55.R18.
[4] Resolution EB57.R46.
[5] Resolution WHA29.22.

CONTENTS

Preface vii

Summary 1

Chapter 1. Introduction 5

Chapter 2. Background 8
  General considerations 8
  Population 9
  Food and nutrition 18
  Education 19
  Social changes 22
  Economic trends 23
  Employment 25
  Poverty 26
  Health-related behavioural factors 28
  Evaluation of development progress and data needs 33
  Policy issues 34

Chapter 3. Health status differentials 37

Chapter 4. Health action 51
  Health policy 51
  National health planning and country health programming 54
  Health legislation 57
  Health care delivery systems 63
  Primary health care 78
  Disease prevention and control 82
X Environmental health 118
  Family health 124
  Nutrition 142
  Health education 144
  Health of the working population 146
  Mental health 153
  Prophylactic, therapeutic and diagnostic substances 168
  Accident prevention and control 173
  Disasters and natural catastrophes 178
  Health resources 179

Chapter 5. Research 206
  Introduction 206
  Global health research development 207
  Implications for the future of world health 223

Chapter 6. Outlook for the future 227
  Introduction 227
  Demographic prospects 228
  Social and economic aspects 234
  Health status trends 237
  Health manpower supply and demand 242
  World health policies 243

  Annex tables and figures 245
  Index 279
  Corrigendum to Part II 285

Preface

The Sixth Report on the World Health Situation covers the years 1973–1977, a period in which the international social and political climate underwent dramatic changes. The clarion call for a new economic order and for social justice has been the most articulate expression of the search for a new code of conduct in international relations in response to the steadily increasing demand for a thorough appraisal of past national and international development goals and strategies. A fundamental reorientation in our thinking and action has thus taken shape. Development goals are no longer defined exclusively in terms of economic growth. Today development is interpreted as a process aiming at the promotion of human dignity and welfare and at the radical elimination of poverty as the greatest obstacle to national and international progress and peace. Development policies and priorities are currently being reformulated so as to meet the basic human needs of all mankind within the shortest possible period and to promote social and economic equity and the attainment by all of fundamental human rights.

This new approach constitutes a unique opportunity and challenge for national health authorities as well as the World Health Organization. A series of steps have accordingly been initiated at the national as well as the international level, the most significant development undoubtedly being the positive response of the health sector to its moral and professional obligations. The quinquennium 1973–1977 was a period of transition, a period when by learning from past experience, from successes as well as failures, the foundation was laid for a social revolution in community health, in which governments found common ground across political frontiers in a firm commitment to making the fruits of scientific and technological progress available to all men and women, regardless of colour, religion, race, and social class. The declaration contained in WHO's Constitution, now almost 35 years old, that "the enjoyment of the highest attainable standard of health is one of the fundamental rights of every human being" and that "governments have a responsibility for the health of their peoples which can be fulfilled only by the provision of adequate health and social measures" has thus acquired a new meaning and a contemporary significance.

However, health is not only a desirable social goal by itself; it is also increasingly being recognized as a means and, indeed, an indispensable component, if not prerequisite, of social and economic development. Consequently, there is now an ever-increasing insistence on having health policy and health strategy fully integrated with national and international development plans. Health and development are not to be viewed as unidirectional phenomena but rather as interacting ones with far-reaching implications.

The period under review also witnessed a series of grave developments and setbacks, including such disasters as the Sahel drought. These contributed to the already serious problems of food supply, famine, and starvation that constitute a serious challenge to international solidarity. Other natural or man-made disasters, often the result of ignorance or short-sightedness, added their share. Of immediate concern, however, to health authorities throughout the world is the fact that previous optimistic assumptions and hopes about a universal and uninterrupted tendency towards improvement in the health status of the world population must be reassessed in the light of recent evidence. This applies to developed as well as developing countries. The economic and social advantages of industrialization have often been accompanied by factors detrimental to health and we have become alerted to the hazards resulting from what is only too often a reckless encroachment by man on nature and his environment.

The period was also characterized by a revolution of rising expectations with regard to the fulfilment of individual and collective aspirations. It has become evident that the gap between health needs and health resources could be bridged by traditional approaches only if we were prepared to put up with delays that were socially indefensible. In the search for alternative approaches, that of primary health care re-emerged as the most important means whereby the health sector could make an effective contribution to overall socioeconomic progress.

It was also a time marked by the sober realization that there are definite limits to the contribution health services can make to health development, that the improvement of the health status of populations requires a wide range of mutually supportive policy measures and cannot be restricted to health policy in the more narrow traditional sense. The attainment of health targets is dependent on appropriately defined progress on the economic front, on social policy measures aimed at greater equity, on improvements in the physical and sanitary environment, and also on political and institutional changes enlisting the active cooperation of the public. Hence the new emphasis on health development as an integral component of national and international development strategies.

This is the background to this report, whose objectives have been expressed by the World Health Assembly in these words:

analysis and evaluation of information on the state of health of the world population and on environmental health (the preservation and improvement of which are vital to the health and life of the present generation and of future generations), with a view to identifying general trends in the world health situation and to evolving a strategy in regard to the most promising ways of developing health services and medical science.[1]

It remains for me to express my appreciation and thanks to all the Member States and Associate Members whose cooperation has made the compilation of this report possible.

DIRECTOR-GENERAL

---

[1] Resolution WHA23.59 (operative paragraph 4(*a*)), adopted by the Twenty-third World Health Assembly in May 1970.

Summary

Perhaps nothing has arisen during the period covered by the Sixth Report on the World Health Situation of more significance than the explicit recognition of the view that health development is a reflection of conscious political, social, and economic policy and planning, and not merely an outcome (or by-product) of technology. This recognition, in turn, has been reflected in the very lively discussions that have taken place, both among and within countries, about the vital links between health and development and the political, economic, and social factors involved. It is important to point out that the changing definition of development itself—that is, as something more than the mere growth of the national product—lends critical support to the view that an increase in technological and economic capacity will not automatically produce health.

At the international level, the New International Economic Order is in the vanguard of the struggle to create a more equitable relationship in the sphere of economic exchange. While obviously bound up with international issues, the New International Development Strategy tends to concentrate on matters that concern countries internally and that have a more or less direct bearing on the health sector as such, i.e., promotive, preventive, and curative health services in particular, but also such closely related areas as sanitation, housing, education, and social welfare.

The goal of "health for all by the year 2000" expresses the political commitment of health services and the agencies responsible for them to a "new health order". The most important vehicle for attaining this new health order is primary health care, which is not to be considered as something apart from the overall health care system, nor as an all-purpose miracle solution to health care problems, and certainly not as the sole prime creator of "health for all". At the very least, however, it does offer the health sector the key to the organization of more relevant and effective health care systems.

The most important social trends during the period of this report are reflected in the still low, and in some areas worsening, nutritional level of the bulk of the population. The employment situation, including access to land, has not improved in many countries and is partly, but not primarily, affected by continuing high rates of population growth, although there are signs of a slowing-down of such growth in many parts of the world. The decline of rural life in many countries has led to unacceptable rates of urbanization and social and health problems on a mass scale in the world's cities and larger towns. Although some progress has been made in reducing illiteracy, a significant proportion of children in developing countries still do not attend primary school. The needs of women are being

1

discussed to a greater extent than ever before, but there has been little practical achievement in this domain. In spite of significant economic growth in some areas, incomes in many countries remain blocked at unacceptably low levels. In addition, even when economic growth has taken place, the distribution of the resultant benefit has sometimes been such as to widen the social and health gap within countries. In such countries it is possible to see what has been termed "growth without development". In spite of some important areas of progress during the period under review, poverty remains the lot of substantial parts of the population of the Third World and it is of course this continuing poverty that is at the root of the world's most pressing health problems. Here, it is important to note that a number of developing countries have managed to reduce overall levels of poverty dramatically and improve health indices significantly, despite having per capita income levels comparable to those of other countries in the same regions, in which the health indices remain unsatisfactory.

During the period 1973–1977, some important developments, such as the oil crisis of 1973, had profound effects on the world scene, leading to a decrease in economic growth and creating social tensions in many countries, developed as well as developing. The debate on the risks of an impending "ecological crisis" centred on such matters as the squandering of non-renewable resources, the risk of certain non-ecological industrial and agricultural practices leading to a series of natural disasters (for instance the growing desertification in the Sahel zone), and the increased pollution of the environment. The result has been a thorough reappraisal of the relationship between man and his environment.

The overall picture with regard to mortality remains mixed, with a few notable cases of dramatic decline and many of continuing unspectacular decline. The latter situation applies in the great majority of countries, in many of which the rate of mortality decline seems to be slowing down. The single most striking fact about mortality today is that, despite the massive economic growth and technological progress of the period following the Second World War, the same basic complex of infectious, parasitic, and respiratory diseases, compounded by nutritional deficiencies, still accounts for most of the world's deaths.

Data on morbidity are even less reliable than those on mortality. It appears, though, that there has been a significant increase or resurgence of certain communicable diseases, schistosomiasis being an example of an increase and malaria of a resurgence. Little progress can be reported with regard to tuberculosis or sexually transmitted diseases, though the conquest of smallpox appears to have been completed during the period under review. Cardiovascular disease and cancer continue to be the greatest disease problems of the industrialized countries, with many middle-income countries moving into the same situation.

Increasing consciousness of the gap, referred to above, between the technological knowledge and capacities available for health improvement and their application has helped to focus growing attention on the problem of the development, allocation, and utilization of resources within the health sector. Questions about the use of more appropriate health technology and its equitable distribution have come very much to the fore. To answer these questions properly will require a greatly strengthened capacity for health planning in most countries. Health planning has tended in many places to be a sporadic activity, carried out without recourse to experienced social and economic planners. The domination of the health planning process by members of the medical profession, sometimes to the exclusion of others, has not been helpful.

With regard to health manpower, there is evidence of a lessening dependence on physicians in some parts of the world and a related strengthening of various paramedical and auxiliary groupings. The brain drain of physicians from developing to developed countries appears to have abated considerably as a result of new immigration policies in the latter group of countries. These new policies reflect a doubling and tripling of the intake of medical schools in many of the western industrialized countries over the last decade or two. Because personnel budgets tend to absorb one-half to three-quarters of all health sector expenditure, it is essential to find solutions to the many outstanding questions of health manpower planning, training, and management that still remain.

With regard to health care facilities, there is now widespread agreement that a better balance is needed between facilities at various levels, typically consisting of the subcentre (or clinic/dispensary), the health centre, and the district or rural hospital. In many countries, the upper end of the system is now unduly preponderant with a virtual monopoly over resources that makes the balanced development of more basic health care facilities impossible. The limited coverage offered by hospitals in any event makes it absolutely essential that a strong brake should be placed on the further development of large hospitals so as to permit the rapid expansion of a network of primary care institutions.

Although pharmaceuticals alone do not provide adequate health care, they make an important contribution to it. Of recent years there has been an explicit demand for drug policies that would reflect true health needs, and a list of essential drugs deemed adequate to deal with the great bulk of ailments has accordingly been drawn up. Considerable attention is being paid to strengthening the capacity of developing countries to deal with all aspects of the development and application of appropriate policies in the field of medical products.

It is certainly not a new idea to relate the availability of financial resources to the quantity and quality of available health care. However, what is now clear is that the availability of extensive funds for health care does not in itself ensure the existence of a system of care that will be accessible to all in keeping with priority needs, as seen both by the health workers who provide the care and those who receive it. The cost explosion in health care in a number of industrialized countries has been partly responsible for a re-examination of the relationships between the growing volume of expensive health care—particularly hospital inpatient care—and improved health indices. There is a growing consensus that additional expenditure on health care, at least in the developed countries, is not bringing about a commensurate improvement in health. It is now widely agreed that a pattern of spending that is heavily biased towards technically sophisticated inpatient care is inappropriate, even in wealthy countries with their own particular disease problems. The issue is still more clear-cut in the case of low income countries. A growing understanding of the issues involved has led to a search for ways of financing health care systems that will be more cost-effective. Studies of the financing of health care systems are being extended by examination of the relationships between particular forms of financing and the provision of care in keeping with the priority need for primary health care coverage of the whole population.

Some of the most important new health programmes are to be found in the area of family health. This is a particularly significant area because it is in the context of the family that the needs of children can best be met. A sharp decrease in the early childhood mortality rates, which are at present very high, is considered an essential prerequisite for lowering fertility rates in those areas of the world where this is considered a priority or medium-term goal. About 17 million children under 5 years of age died in 1978. If all the countries of the world had the same early childhood mortality rates as those of Northern Europe, there would have been only 2 million such deaths. The Expanded Programme on Immunization should help reduce the number of early childhood deaths, but it can be expected to do so only in the context of an improved nutritional situation for children in much of the Third World. To illustrate the situation: in the developed countries the average infant mortality is a little over 20 per 1000 and in the least developed countries over 150; in the developed countries energy consumption averages around 13.4 MJ per person while in the least developed countries it is only 8.4 MJ. In addition, in the least developed countries there is greater inequality between social groups than in the developed countries, with regard to both infant mortality rates and food consumption.

The report describes recent developments in most of the service areas within the health sector. Some of the most important of these concern mental health, sanitation and the environment, and the relationship between the place of work and health.

The overall role and importance of primary health care are stressed in many parts of this report, and there are some specific indications of ways in which primary health care activities are being integrated with the more traditional activities of the health sector. One of the major tasks facing health service planners and administrators is to strengthen links between specific disease control programmes and wider primary health care activities.

It is appropriate to close this summary of the Sixth Report on the World Health Situation on a note of at least guarded optimism, despite the comparative failure to improve health indices in much of the world in recent years, and even the possible deterioration of these indices in some places. Such optimism is encouraged by two factors. The first is the deepening understanding in so many quarters of the true social determinants of health and disease, and the second the compelling political requirement—aside from the continuing moral one—of redressing the cruel social injustices that continue to characterize life on our planet. This political requirement is made all the more urgent by the massive pressures in favour of deep-rooted social change that are being brought to bear by those most in need of such change; that is, by more than 2000 million people who have to exist on incomes of less than US $500 per year. If we are not prepared to redeem our pledge of health for all by the year 2000, it is they who will do it for us.

Chapter 1

Introduction

In addition to reporting, like its predecessors, on changes in the health status of the world's population and developments in the organization and delivery of health care, the Sixth Report on the World Health Situation attempts to bring out the main ideas on health and health care issues and how to deal with them that arose in the period 1973–1977.

The main sources of information used in the preparation of this report were:

(a) information routinely passed on by Member Governments to WHO, such as statistical data forwarded annually;

(b) country reviews specially submitted by Member Governments for the Sixth Report (these reviews are published in Part II);

(c) information routinely collected by other organizations of the United Nations system, and

(d) information for the reference period collected by WHO on an *ad hoc* basis to meet specific policy or programme requirements.

A deliberate effort was made to minimize the burden on Member countries with regard to provision of information by drawing extensively on information already available at WHO or retrievable from other organizations of the United Nations system.

It may be worth pointing out that this report has been a difficult document to assemble. The immense body of information made a selective approach inevitable. Aspects that may be of particular relevance from a regional point of view or for a group of countries may not have been given the attention they deserve. Limitations of space as well as sheer inability to compress the mass of information in a way that would do justice to the many facets of health development in the mid-1970s necessitated compromises between the desirable and the feasible. The report aims, therefore, at highlighting major developments within each area of the health sector. Inadequacies of information at the national level, as well as the continuing problem of standardizing key statistical concepts such as those relating to coverage by and utilization of health services, exacerbated by the use of heterogeneous statistics from various sources, likewise proved to be obstacles of a formidable nature. For instance, efforts to achieve uniformity of geographical presentation have been only partially successful because of differences with regard to regional groupings adopted by the various international organizations. As far as feasible, the regional classification adopted by the United Nations in its publication *Demographic yearbook* was

5

used in the presentation of statistical material, but inevitably a large part of the data available were based geographically on the six WHO regions.

There is a certain amount of overlapping in the report, but this largely involves examination of the same issues from differing standpoints.

Chapter 2 (Background) outlines the general setting in which current ideas on "social health" and their translation into an action programme have evolved. It sets forth the leading ideas and developments in the demographic, social, and economic spheres, including a consideration of health-related behavioural patterns, and the main policy issues that emerged in the period under review, including the sweeping reappraisal of the true meaning of "development" and the realization of the need for continuous monitoring of progress towards the achievement of policy goals.

Chapter 3 is devoted to an assessment of the health status of the world's population. It analyses, in concise form, differences between countries and shows how they are essentially related to the degree of socioeconomic development. At the same time, it provides evidence that inter-country differences are only part of the picture; data are available which indicate striking differences in health status within a number of countries between, for example, various socioeconomic groups, and people living in different geographical areas. To provide a wider perspective, the period covered extends beyond the reference point, going back—wherever possible—as far as the early 1950s. In principle, this chapter does not go into any detail on individual diseases and causes of death. These points are taken care of in the subsequent chapter.

Chapter 4 which deals with health action constitutes the bulk of the report. It starts with a review of trends in health policy, followed by a presentation of developments in health planning and country health programming. After discussing recent aspects of health legislation, health care delivery systems, and primary health care, specific programme areas are discussed in more detail. In each instance, a section giving statistical evidence on the extent of the particular health problem is followed by a review of the action taken to deal with it. There are also sections on the use of health resources (manpower, facilities, and funds), which review some of the most important issues now facing policy-makers and health planners.

Chapter 5 on research summarizes mainly the evolution of health research with more emphasis on the process than on substantive developments. It points out that the research resources are still highly concentrated in the developed countries and devoted to research into their own health problems, which differ considerably from the most extensive and most serious health problems facing the majority of the world population. It highlights, at the same time, changes which are taking place in the form of international research cooperation to tackle the health problems of the vast majority of the world's people and to enhance national research capabilities particularly in the developing countries. It then describes recent developments and achievements which have occurred in research in relation to a selected group of outstanding health problems. Research implications for future health care are also discussed.

Finally Chapter 6 looks at future prospects in the light of current and expected developments. It draws heavily on work carried out by other organization of the United Nations system in sectors other than that of health whereas the sections devoted to expected changes in health status and health sector requirements make use of national projections to provide an insight into the way Member countries view their future. This chapter has particular relevance as a point of factual departure for initiating strategies and tactics for the attainment of health for all by the year 2000.

The Sixth Report represents a turning-point, and it is expected that the experience gained in its preparation will be used as a starting point for the development of more effective procedures for future reports. It is to be anticipated that it will assume a crucial role in the monitoring of progress towards the goals of "health for all by the year 2000". To give a true reflection of progress towards this goal, future reports will require a stronger emphasis on socioeconomic factors than has been the case in the past and will need to pay more attention to health-related events taking place outside the health sector as such, as well as to those events within the health sector that reflect the programmes and planning priorities of Member States.

Chapter 2

Background

General considerations

The last few years have not been altogether favourable ones for world health. Droughts and severe winters have reduced harvest yields; wars and civil unrest have destroyed crops, land, and housing; the proliferation and use of newly synthesized substances has continued without adequate check. In a substantial number of developing countries, rapid population growth has become a matter of serious concern, to which close attention has to be paid in the overall task of promoting socioeconomic development. Inflation has raised costs and inhibited the development of trade.

These circumstances have all hindered health progress but may have played an important part in shaping new thinking about development. It is no longer generally assumed that economic development and social development are distinct, that economic progress should be the primary goal. The newer policies that are emerging are aimed more specifically at a form of development that will meet all basic human social needs. Although it is too early to assess the full implications of those policies, it may legitimately be hoped that health ends will in future be better served.

But the situation remains less happy than might have been expected a decade ago. About 800 million people in the developing world live in conditions of abject deprivation, with incomes too low to ensure basic nutrition and with little access to services essential to health and life. At least 450 million people have less food than is necessary for basic survival; even more lead a precarious existence on the brink of hunger. Perhaps less than about one-third of the people in developing countries have safe water and adequate sewage disposal. Housing conditions and educational opportunities in urban areas are widely unsatisfactory. The number of illiterate adults is increasing. About 300 million adults are unemployed.

Most of these data are approximations because there is a lack of basic information from a large part of the world, but they do suffice to paint a realistic picture of the enormous problems that have to be overcome if there is to be a breakthrough in efforts to improve the health status of the world's population.

In general, there is a positive correlation between socioeconomic factors, well-being, and levels of health. When a country is desperately poor and the people are individually poor, undernourished, and uneducated, and there are few public services, the health of the people is likewise poor. In the middle range, where there is enough money for countries to make decisions on how it is spent, there may be an enormous amount of variation both within and among them in the proportion of people who are underfed, the proportion of children enrolled in school, the availability of public services, and the health of the people.

The following sections highlight some of the major facts and developments that affect the health status of the world's population to a greater or lesser extent, together with both national and international efforts to cope with them.

Population

Population size and growth

The population of the world increased in the 1970s at an annual rate of 1.9% and exceeded 4000 million in 1977 as against 3600 million in 1970. By the end of the period under review, the rate of growth seems to have somewhat slowed down. The annual rate of population increase between 1970 and 1977 varied greatly between the different regions of the world. It was 2.7% in Latin America, 2.7% in Africa and 2.6% in South Asia. Northern America and Europe had rates of less than 1%.

Half of the world's population today live in four countries: China, India, the USSR, and the United States of America; a further three countries (Brazil, Indonesia and Japan) have each more than 100 million inhabitants. In 1977, the number of countries with a population of between 50 and 100 million was eight, whereas 15 countries had a population of between 25 and 50 million. The population of the world's 30 largest countries, representing more than four-fifths of the total world population in 1977, is shown in Fig. 1 on page 10.

Low rates of population growth are associated with high levels of economic development. In 1976, 22% of the world's population was concentrated in countries with low population growth and with high or moderate income levels. On the other hand, most developing countries experience a population growth of more than 2% a year, implying a doubling of their population within 30–35 years. However, the poorest countries among them are not those with the most rapid population increases. This is mainly due to high levels of mortality.

The 30 countries with the highest population growth, e.g., 3% or more, represented 8.2% of the world's population in 1976 (doubling in about 20–23 years). This group is followed by a group of 35 countries (representing 17.6% of the world's population), which had an annual population increase of 2.5–2.9% between 1970 and 1976. This group includes most of the low-income countries, as well as middle-income countries with a moderately high average income.

However, the slowing of the growth rate does not mean a decrease in absolute numbers. In the mid-1970s the world's population was increasing annually by about 80 million in contrast to 68 million a decade earlier.

The increase in the world's population per second, per day, and per year, and the components of growth,—i.e., the number of births and deaths—are shown in Fig. 2.

9

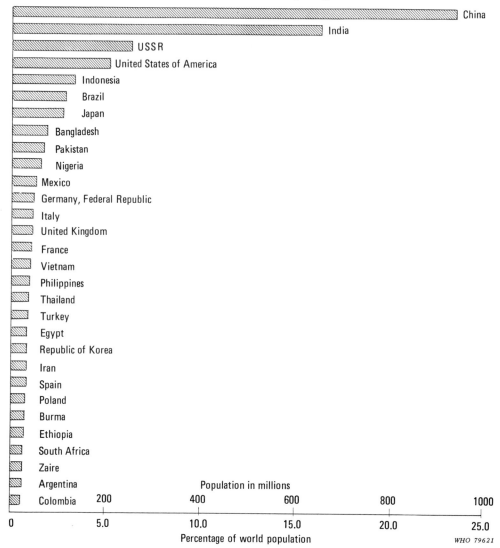

Fig. 1. Population of the world's thirty largest countries: 1977

Source: United States Bureau of the Census. *World population: 1977. Recent demographic estimates for the countries and regions of the world.* Washington, DC, 1978. p. 16.

The differences between developed and developing countries in rates of population growth reflect the differences between them in levels of fertility and mortality.

In the 1970s birth rates ranged between 26 and 49 per 1000 in the less developed regions and between 15 and 19 in the more developed regions. The death rates varied from 9 to 23 per 1000 in the less developed regions, and from 7 to 11 in the more developed regions.

Fig. 2. World vital events: 1976

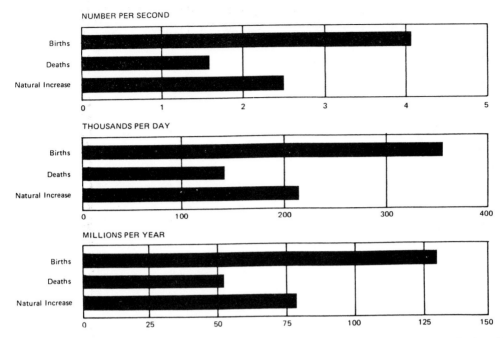

Source: United States Bureau of the Census. *World population: 1977. Recent demographic estimates for the countries and regions of the world.* Washington, DC, 1978, p. 18.

Table 1 on page 12 gives a summary of population growth and its components by continents and regions. (See also Annex, Table 1 and Figs. 1 and 5.)

The disparity between population growth and land area has been a source of increasing concern in the overpopulated less developed countries. Whereas in 1977 low population densities still existed in Oceania (three inhabitants per km^2), Northern America and USSR (11 and 12 respectively per km^2), the density of population in certain large countries of Eastern and Southern Asia was as high as 559 inhabitants per km^2 in Bangladesh, 370 in the Republic of Korea, 306 in Japan, and 190 in India. Population density was well over 100 per km^2 in Europe (excluding Northern Europe).

The distribution of population and land area by continents and population density is shown in Fig. 3 and Fig. 4 on page 13.

Population growth puts enormous pressures on many aspects of a nation's economy. A large number of infants and young children have to be fed and cared for. Later they will need to be educated or trained, and later still jobs will be needed for them as they enter the labour force. The provision of public and individual health services is only one of many competing demands. Rapid population increase often results in increases in the number of people living in poverty, the number uneducated, and the number underfed. People in these categories are usually in poorer health and have greater need of health services than those with adequate incomes, education, and food. The need for health services increases at the same time as the ability to meet that need is strained.

Table 1. Population growth, 1965–1977

Continent and region	Population 1977 (millions)	Birth rate 1965–1977	Death rate 1965–1977	Annual rate of growth[1] 1965–1977
Africa	424	46	20	2.7
Western Africa	122	49	23	2.6
Eastern Africa	121	48	21	2.7
Northern Africa	104	43	15	2.8
Middle Africa	48	44	21	2.4
Southern Africa	29	43	16	2.9
America	584	28	9	2.0
Northern America	242	17	9	1.0
Latin America	342	37	9	2.7
Tropical South America	190	38	9	3.0
Middle America (mainland)	84	42	9	3.3
Temperate South America	40	24	9	1.5
Caribbean	28	32	9	1.9
Asia	2355	34	13	2.2
East Asia	1037	26	10	1.6
China	866	27	10	1.7
Japan	114	18	7	1.2
Other East Asia	58	32	9	2.2
South Asia	1318	41	16	2.6
Middle South Asia	882	41	17	2.5
Eastern South Asia	342	42	15	2.7
Western South Asia	93	43	15	2.9
Europe	478	16	10	0.6
Western Europe	154	15	11	0.6
Southern Europe	134	18	9	0.7
Eastern Europe	108	17	10	0.6
Northern Europe	83	15	11	0.4
Oceania	22.2	23	10	2.0
Australia and New Zealand	17.4	19	9	1.8
Melanesia and	3.3	41	17	2.5
Micronesia	1.4	34	7	2.6
USSR	260	18	8	1.0
World	4124	31	13	1.9
Of which:				
More developed regions	1151	17	9	0.9
Less developed regions	2973	37	14	2.4

Source: *Demographic yearbook 1977.* New York, United Nations, 1978, p. 137.
[1] Percentage rates of population increase computed with geometric mean method. See the indicated sources in the table on p. 16.
Note: Rates for macroregions are weighted averages of regional rates and those for the world are, in turn, weighted averages of macroregion rates.

Sex and age composition

There is a marked contrast between the less developed and more developed regions of the world in the sex and age composition of the population (see Annex, Table 2).

A marked difference in the sex ratio still exists, although the gap has been decreasing. In 1975 the number of males per 100 females was 94 in the less developed and 103 in the more developed countries as compared with 91 and 105 respectively 25 years earlier. In some less developed countries, mortality rates at the reproduction ages are higher for females than for males, mainly as a result of factors conducive to maternal mortality. On the other hand, it seems that females gain more than males from general improvements in levels of mortality, the result being a tendency towards greater balance in the overall sex ratio.

Fig. 3. Population and land area by region, 1977

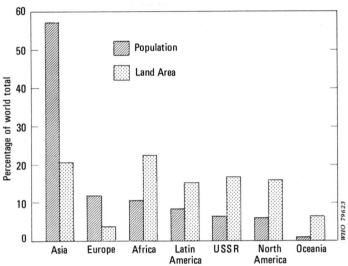

In the middle of the decade, more than a third of the world's population was below the age of 15. In the less developed countries, because of high fertility rates, the proportion was 40%, as compared with 25% for the more developed countries, indicating a widening gap (in 1950 the proportions were 39% and 28% respectively).

In recent decades the proportion of young people in the more developed countries has declined, whereas that of people over 65 years has increased. In the less developed

Fig. 4. Population density by region, 1977

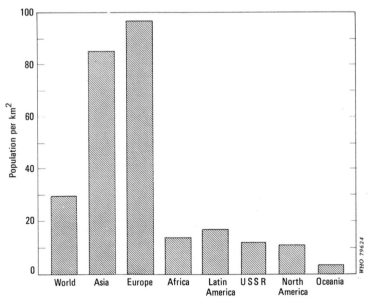

countries, the tendency was reversed. Thus, in 1975, the child dependency ratio was almost 100% higher and the old age dependency ratio nearly 60% lower in less developed regions than in more developed ones.

A picture of the differences existing in 1975 can be obtained from Table 2:

Table 2. Age distribution of population and dependency ratios, 1975

Geographical regions	Population by major age groups (%)			Dependency ratio	
	−15 years	15–64 years	65+ years	Child[a]	Old age[b]
Less developed regions	40	56	4	72	7
Africa	44	53	3	84	5
South Asia	43	54	3	80	6
Latin America	42	54	4	77	7
More developed regions	25	65	10	39	16
Europe	24	64	12	37	19
Northern America	25	64	10	40	16
USSR	26	65	9	40	14

[a] Children aged below 15 per 100 of working age (15–64 years).
[b] Persons aged 65 and older per 100 of working age (15–64 years).
Source: *Demographic yearbook 1977.* New York, United Nations, 1978, p. 139.

Urbanization

Urbanization is another important determining factor in population changes. The world's urban population more than doubled between 1950 and 1975 to reach about 39% of the total population. There is still a marked contrast in the level of urbanization between the less developed countries, with an urban population representing 27% of the total population, and the more developed countries, where the proportion is nearly 70%.

The process of urbanization has been faster in the less developed world. In the third quarter of the century, the number of urban residents increased threefold in the less developed regions, but only by 70% in the more developed regions. Nevertheless, there are still wide contrasts and extremes, as can be seen from the following table showing the proportion of urban population to total population in selected regions:

	Proportion of urban population to total population (%)	
	1950	1975
Less developed regions	16	27
Eastern Africa	5	12
Western Africa	10	18
Middle South Asia	16	21
South Asia	16	23
More developed regions	53	69
Australia, New Zealand	79	86
Northern America	64	77
Western Europe	63	77
Northern Europe	71	75

Source: See Table 3 in Annex (Population by Urban/Rural Residence, Continents and Geographical Regions, 1950, 1975, 2000).

The average annual rate of increase between 1970 and 1975 was 2.9% for the urban population and 1.3% for the rural population. In the developing world the annual rate of urban increase was over 4% in the first half of the decade, whereas in the more prosperous countries the urban population has been growing at an average annual rate of only 1.7%. Some cities are growing sufficiently rapidly to double their populations in 10–15 years.

The rural population has continued to decline in the more developed countries and to grow in the less developed ones.

Migration and refugees

Immigration caused demographic changes in only a few countries, but it is economically and socially important in a number of countries of Western Europe, Northern America, and, more recently, the Middle East. The most important movements of labour over the past decades have been the migrations from developing countries to industrialized market-economy countries. As a result of the economic difficulties of the mid-1970s, immigration rules in the latter group of countries have been tightened. Between 1975 and 1977, immigration from non-member countries practically stopped in the European Economic Community.

The ILO estimated in 1973 that there were about 11 million migrant workers in Europe, with an annual flow of 600 000 to 1 000 000, and about 4.2 million resident foreigners in Northern America. In Latin America, Argentina has perhaps 500 000–1 000 000 migrants from other countries and Venezuela 300 000–700 000. In Africa, Ghana and the Ivory Coast are estimated to have 900 000–1 500 000 migrants and South Africa and Southern Rhodesia about 300 000.

These estimates include only those migrants who have been registered as migrating for work. These probably form a high proportion of the legal migrants since work is considered as a valid reason for migrating, whereas other, more personal reasons might not be. They do not cover unregistered or illegal migration, which, in countries with long land borders and reasonable opportunities for work, may exceed legal migration.[1]

According to UNHCR, there were, in 1977, about 4 million refugees and displaced persons in Asia and about 3 million in Africa. Latin America had about 112 000, Northern America about 152 000, Europe between 560 000 and 570 000, and Australia and New Zealand about 2000. Events since then have added to the flow of people leaving their homelands as refugees.[2]

Households and families

In spite of the central role of the family and the household in society, the trends and variations in their size and structure and particularly the dynamic changes associated with the different phases of the family life cycle, as well as the factors involved in these changes, constitute a relatively new field of demography.

In numerous cases the household or family, and not the individual, is the primary unit of statistical enumeration, surveys, and analyses. The family is the basic social cell. It is the unit of renewal, through which children are brought into the world and cared for. It is in the family environment that children grow up and develop physically, psychologically, and socially. The family also has responsibility to fulfil towards its sick, dependent,

---

[1] *Migrant workers*, Report VII(1), Internation Labour Conference, 59th session, 1974, ILO, Geneva, 1973.
[2] Report of the United Nations High Commissioner for Refugees. General Assembly, Official Records: Thirty-third Session, and Addendum to the Report. United Nations, New York, 1978.

and aged members. The family or the household is the primary unit in respect of housing needs, consumption of durable goods, cost of living, savings, etc. It is also the most relevant unit on which to base planning and marketing for future needs.

Recently there has been increasing interest in interrelationships between family and the health of its members and the implications of these interrelationships for health care systems (see also Chapter 4, page 51). Important factors in the context of family health include the concept of the family as a unit, the responses of its members to symptoms, and their utilization of medical facilities. There is a constant, dynamic interplay between health and family characteristics; family structure and functions affect health and *vice versa*. Maternal and child health, all aspects of mental health, problems of the elderly and of terminal care, and the provision and use of health services are all of special relevance to family health.

In using the family as a unit in health studies, it must be borne in mind that the concept of the family varies from one culture to another and that the notion of the household is sometimes substituted for that of the family. From the health standpoint, the implications of this substitution are minimal, but since socially and economically there is a difference between the family and the household, they must be clearly distinguished.[1]

The concept of the household, particularly in developing countries, is less ambiguous than that of the family, and the household is used more extensively as the basic unit in statistical enumerations and demographic surveys, statistical data on families being relatively scarce. Moreover, household and family are virtually identical in developed countries, constituting the same unit in about 80% of cases. The brief analysis below is accordingly confined to households.

"The general trends of declining average household size are considered to be parallel to the secular declines in fertility, and broadly in association with the global process of industrialization and urbanization . . .".[2] As is shown in the following table, the estimated average size of households is substantially smaller in the more developed areas, owing to lower fertility rates and a higher proportion of nuclear families:

| | Average size of households[a] | |
Geographical region	1965	1975
World	4.5	4.3
More developed regions	3.5	3.2
Less developed regions	5.2	5.0
Major areas:		
Africa	5.0	5.0
Latin America	5.1	4.8
North America	3.4	3.0
East Asia	5.1	4.4
South Asia	5.3	5.4
Europe	3.3	3.0
Oceania	4.0	3.5
USSR	3.9	3.3

[a] Number of persons per household.

Sources: For 1965: *The determinants and consequences of population trends.* New York, United Nations, 1973, p. 337. For 1975: *The world population situation in 1977.* New York, United Nations, 1979, p. 61.

[1] For further details see: WHO Technical Report Series, No. 587, 1976 (*Statistical indices of family health.* Report of a WHO Study Group); *Health and the family. Studies on the demography of family life cycles and their health implications.* Geneva, World Health Organization, 1978.

[2] *The determinants and consequences of population trends.* New York, United Nations, 1973, p. 342.

The average size of a household in 1975 was 5 persons in the developing part of the world, and a little more than 3 persons in the more developed part. In 1965 it was estimated to be highest in Melanesia (5.9 persons), East Asia, including China and Japan (5.8) and Middle America (5.6), and lowest in Western and Northern Europe (3.0).

Between 1965 and 1975, there was a moderate increase in South Asia; however, the unchanged value in Africa and the small downward shift in the average size in other developed regions could easily be within the probable margins of error.[1] The more developed regions have been characterized by increases in the proportion of nuclear families (i.e., small households) and significant decreases in the proportion of multi-generational and extended families (i.e., large households).

The interrelationship between social and economic factors and the family or household is dynamic rather than static. The concept of the life cycle of the family, from formation to extinction, constitutes an important frame of reference.

Long-range demographic changes—e.g., lower mortality and a longer life span, earlier marriage, changes in fertility behaviour, the spread of birth control and family planning—have to a large extent altered the average age at which husband and wife reach the different stages of the family cycle. The duration of married life has become much longer, the reproductive stage shorter. The stage of bringing up children to maturity has lengthened, but in general children leave the family and become independent sooner. For parents, the period following the separation of the children from the family is much longer.

In the individual stages of married life, not only do the size and composition of families change but also objectives, needs, demands, financial situation, status, and a number of other circumstances strictly related to the typical individual phases of family life. Passage through these stages more or less determines certain changes, partly in the attitudes, roles and position of individual family members and partly in factors relating to almost every aspect of the family's social and economic status, e.g., housing requirements, consumption pattern, independent employment of wife, demands on services, leisure activities, and, last but not least, health-related problems.

Just as family patterns and changes play a determing role in the health of the individual members and their utilization of health services, health contributes significantly to changes in family organization and attitudes and in responses to such changes. Health care systems must be reoriented and adapted accordingly.

Recent studies of the cycles of family life and the different stages involved have made a valuable contribution to demographic analysis and opened up new possibilities for the investigation by sociologists, physicians, biologists, and others of the complex phenomena and correlations of family life. WHO attributes great importance to research on the family, on family size, and structure, and on the relevance of the family life cycle for health policy and strategy.[2]

---

[1] *The world population situation in 1977.* New York, United Nations, 1979, p. 60.

[2] *Health and the family. Studies on the demography of family life cycles and their health implications.* World Health Organization, 1978. See also Chapter 4, p. 51.

Food and nutrition

Malnutrition is undoubtedly a worldwide problem and one with serious consequences. Recent estimates by the FAO and the World Bank suggest that about 450 million—some say as many as 1000 million—people do not receive sufficient food. Most of these people live in the developing countries. Estimates of the number of persons with food intake below the critical minimum (excluding Asian countries with centrally planned economies) are shown in the table below:

Region	Total population 1969–71	Total population 1972–74	Percentage below 1.2 BMR[a] 1969–71	Percentage below 1.2 BMR[a] 1972–74	Total number below 1.2 BMR[a] 1969–71	Total number below 1.2 BMR[a] 1972–74
	(millions)				(millions)	
Africa	278	301	25	28	70	83
Far East	968	1042	25	29	256	297
Latin America	279	302	16	15	44	46
Near East	167	182	18	16	31	20
MSA[b]	954	1027	27	30	255	307
Non-MSA[b]	738	800	20	18	146	148
Developing countries	1692	1827	24	25	401	455

Source: *Fourth world food survey*. Rome, Food and Agriculture Organization of the United Nations, 1977, p. 63.

[a] BMR = basal metabolic rate.
[b] MSA = most seriously affected.

While malnutrition is caused by the interplay of a large number of factors, the three main ones are food production and availability, economic situation, and population, which are closely interrelated (see Annex, Table 8 and Fig. 4). In accordance with these factors, the incidence of malnutrition varies from one country to another. However, in respect of malnutrition countries fall into four distinct groups.

1. The *high-income countries*, with an annual per capita GNP of US $4500 (in 1975), comprising Japan and countries in Northern America, Europe, and Oceania, have a total population of about 1100 million. These are countries with a very low rate of population growth (0.7%) and a high level of food production. The general pattern of malnutrition is one of overeating, resulting in certain types of malnutrition, e.g., obesity (malnutrition of affluence).

2. The *middle-income developing countries* (excluding China), are found in Africa, Asia, and Latin America and have a per capita GNP of about US $950 (1975). About 800 million people live in them. This group of countries has the highest rate of population growth (about 2.8% annually) because their death rates have dropped far more rapidly than their birth rates. They have also experienced rapid economic growth and large increases in food production. However, because of population growth and poor income and land distribution, food deprivation continues in most of them, resulting in widespread malnutrition. A sizeable portion of their population (in high income brackets) also suffer from malnutrition of affluence.

3. The *poorest countries*, with per capita GNP under US $200, are spread across Asia and the middle of Africa and contain 1200 million people. These are the countries in which hunger and malnutrition are most severe. An estimated one-third to one-half of their inhabitants, especially children, are victims of malnutrition.

4. *China and other Asian countries with centrally planned economies,* with an estimated population of about 1000 million, belong to the fourth category. Their per capita GNP is probably in the lower middle-income range. There is a lack of reliable information about the incidence of malnutrition in these countries, but most observers report that overt malnutrition is not common.

The major immediate cause of hunger is poverty. Other important causes of malnutrition, such as poor environmental sanitation, infections, and infestations, are also due to poverty. The interplay of all these factors not only produces, but perpetuates, malnutrition. Poverty exists everywhere and is found on a mass scale in a considerable number of countries, especially in Asia, Africa, and Latin America. The World Bank estimates that 750 million people in the poorest nations live in extreme poverty with an annual income of less than US $75. Most of the extreme poverty is due to a low national output and income, combined with maldistribution of the income available.

Food supply and demand are critical factors in regulating per capita food availability. Between 1950 and 1975, food production in the developing countries as a whole (excluding China) expanded at the unprecedented rate of about 2.8% per year. The rate was remarkably high between 1965 and 1975, when the newer agricultural strategies were applied, leading to the so-called "Green Revolution" in certain parts of the world. In fact, the expansion was faster than that of the high-income countries (see Fig. 5). Unfortunately, the growth of population and income in the developing countries since 1960 has increased the demand for food by about 3.5% per year, more than the actual production, leaving a gap that is largely filled by grain imports. In fact, population growth has held average per capita increases in food production over the period 1960–1975 to about 0.3% per year.

For the poorest group of developing countries, the average annual increase in food production has been only 2.3% over the past 15 years. For a large number of developing countries, per capita consumption has not increased at all, and in some countries, e.g., in Africa, it has decreased. With the existing resource distribution system, this production rate leaves relatively little room for an increase in per capita food consumption leading to better nutrition.

Obviously, the developing countries need to increase food production sufficiently to balance out population increase and then make a real increase in average annual per capita food consumption. This is possible by increasing the crop area, and more important, by substantially increasing production per unit of the crop area. However, for most of the underdeveloped countries, this would demand more capital and vast improvements in skill and organization.

The problem of controlling hunger and malnutrition in the world is a difficult and complex one. Success will depend upon how effectively four major tasks are undertaken: increasing the supply of the right kind of food where it is needed, reducing poverty, improving the stability of food supplies, and decreasing the rate of population growth.

Education

During the period 1970–1975, the world total of students enrolled at primary, secondary, and higher levels of education rose from about 480 million to 557 million (excluding China). This represents an average annual increase of 2.6% which comes close to the rate

Fig. 5. Food production indices: total and per capita, 1950–1976 (1961–1965 = 100).

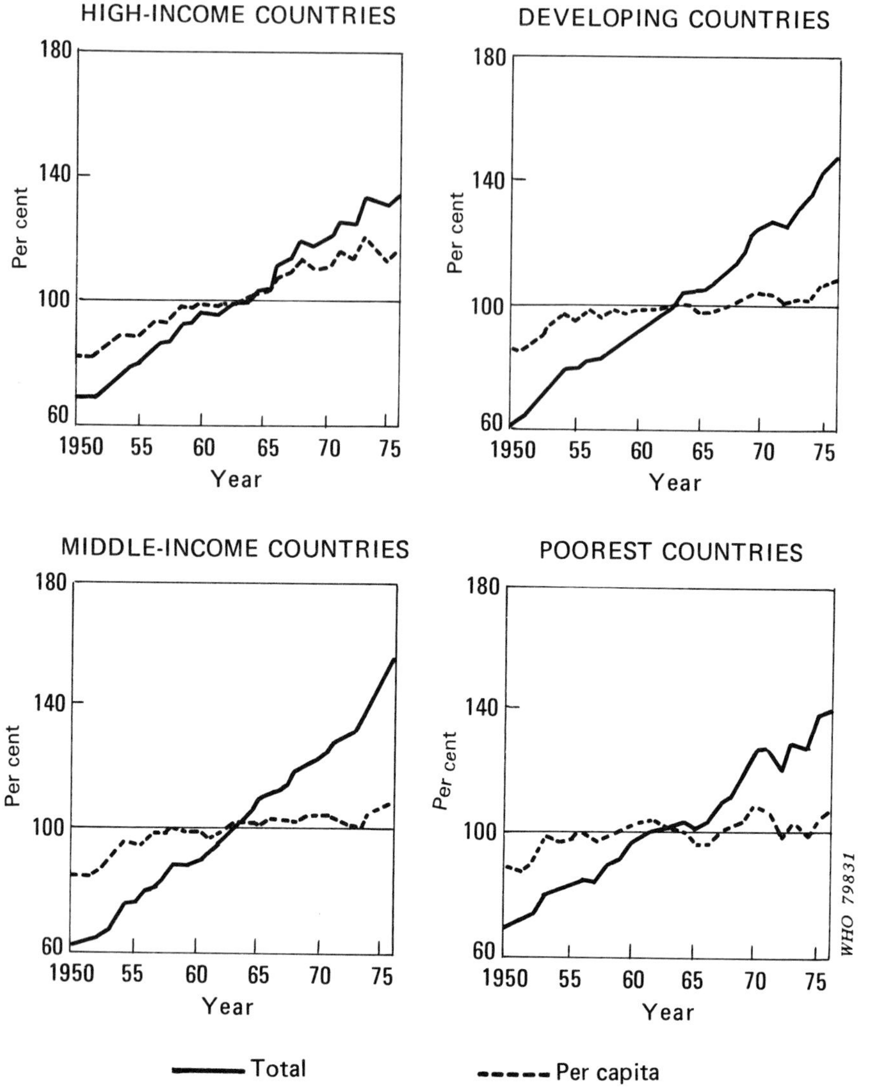

HIGH-INCOME COUNTRIES

DEVELOPING COUNTRIES

MIDDLE-INCOME COUNTRIES

POOREST COUNTRIES

WHO 79831

——— Total   ----- Per capita

Source: United States Department of Agriculture, Economic Research Service (1977).

achieved during the period 1965–1970 but which is much below the rather high growth rate of nearly 5% per annum during the period 1960–1965. This rate of expansion slowed down steadily after 1966. The deceleration reflects, to some extent, the attainment of high enrolment levels.

School enrolment at the primary level grew in the early 1970s at an annual rate of 2%. In the low-income countries, however, almost half of the children were not enrolled for primary education. In 1975 the countries that had a low enrolment ratio at the primary level (the total number of students enrolled as a percentage of the total population in the corresponding age group) were mainly located in Africa. However, some African countries plan to achieve universal primary education by 1980.

The number of pupils in primary schools has increased rapidly in Asia. However, in nearly all developing countries in the ESCAP region, the rate of enrolment at the first level was lower during the period 1970–1975 than it had been in the previous five years. Developments since 1960 are illustrated in Fig. 3 in the Annex, which convincingly demonstrates the enormous progress achieved in this area.

Enrolment at the secondary level increased at an annual rate of 3.9% during the first half of the 1970s. Between 1970 and 1975, the number of countries with a low enrolment ratio at this level decreased from 29 to 17. Particularly rapid progress in this respect was made in Africa. By 1975 two-thirds of the Asian countries and half of the Latin American countries had achieved an enrolment ratio, at the secondary level, of above 20%.

Enrolment at the third or higher level increased at an annual rate of 5.4% during the first half of the 1970s. In about half of the developing countries, the annual rate of increase was above 15% between 1970 and 1975. In most high-income countries, the third level enrolment ratio remained stable at around 20%, whereas in the low-income countries it was 0.6%. In Africa, 1.6% of the school population was enrolled at the third level in 1975, as compared with 8.1% in Europe.

In the world as a whole at mid-decade, 45% of all students enrolled at primary level were females. This represents an increase of only 1% since 1970. Equality of enrolment has already been achieved in all countries of Europe and the Americas. In Asia and Africa, female enrolment was 41% in 1975. At the secondary level female enrolment represented 43% of total secondary enrolment in the world. Female enrolment in developed countries and Latin America represented 49% and 48% respectively, whereas Asia registered 36% and Africa 34%. In Arab countries, female enrolment was 32% in 1975.

Education at the pre-primary level has also been expanding at an annual rate of 6.1% at the world level. Even countries that have not yet achieved universal primary education have established early childhood education, usually starting with 5-year-old children. Countries with centrally planned economies have high rates of growth for enrolment at kindergarten level.

Special education for children with mental, physical, or social handicaps is almost exclusively a feature of developed countries. At mid-decade, about 96% of the 4.9 million children receiving special education under educational authorities or welfare programmes were in industrialized countries. However, there is a tendency away from education in special institutions to a system of special education in ordinary schools, in order to facilitate the social integration of handicapped children.

In 1977 approximately 80% of the adult population in low-income countries were still illiterate. This represented about 800 million people, or one-fifth of the world's population; 60% of them were women. During the 1970s, only a few countries launched or renewed campaigns to reduce illiteracy. While education is frequently associated with income, it can also have an impact on health that is independent of income. This may be especially true for people at a level above that of bare subsistence who have some freedom to make decisions on the use of resources.

21

The Inter-American Investigation of Mortality in Childhood[1] showed that children who died after the neonatal period were much more likely than children who died during the neonatal period to have had mothers with no education. A study in the United States of America, in which both income and education were analysed, showed that infant mortality varied to a greater extent with material educational status than with household income.[2] A recent WHO collaborative study on perinatal mortality[3] also revealed differences according to education.

In Kerala, India, a dietary survey showed that undernutrition was inversely related to household income, being 94% in the lowest income group and 26% in the highest. Even more striking was the influence of the housewives' educational level. The proportion of people who were energy deficient varied from 94% in households where the housewives were illiterate to 9% where they had their secondary school leaving certificates. More important, there was a similar variation within each income group. When the household income was 250 to 500 rupees per month, for example, the proportion of energy-deficient people varied from 84% to 35% as the women's level of education increased (United Nations, 1975).

Both developed and developing countries are spending increasing proportions of their budgets on public education. Nevertheless, in 1975 4% of the gross national product (GNP) in developing countries compared with 6% of the GNP in developed countries was spent on education. Because incomes are so much higher in developed countries, the amount per inhabitant was US $268 in developed countries and US $19 in developing countries.

Despite the impressive growth in school enrolment, the number of children not enrolled in school was greater in 1975 than in 1970. The enormous increase in the number of children in the developing world has outpaced the increase in enrolment so that the absolute number of children who are not at school has continued to increase. Thus the number of illiterate adults will continue to increase as well, unless dynamic campaigns are launched to redress the situation.

Social changes

The social situation in most countries did not change significantly during the period under consideration.[4] However, certain trends that had emerged in recent decades came into sharper focus. The role of women in society, the family life-style, and the situation of the aged are matters of concern arising from a long process of social change.

The 1970s have witnessed the beginning of a new awareness of the rights, status, and role of women which is already deeply affecting most societies and which has resulted in greater independence for women and their greater participation in all aspects of economic, political, and social life. Although much attention has been given to the

[1] PUFFER, R. R. & SERRANO, C. V. *Patterns of mortality in childhood. Report of the Inter-American Investigation of Mortality in Childhood*, Washington, DC, Pan American Health Organization, 1973 (Scientific Publication No. 262).

[2] MACMAHON, B., KOVAR, M. G. & FELDMAN, J. Infant mortality rates: Socioeconomic factors. *Vital and Health Statistics*, Series 22, No. 14, Washington, DC, 1972.

[3] Main findings of the comparative study of social and biological effects on perinatal mortality. *World health statistics quarterly*, **31**: 74–83 (1978).

[4] See *1978 report on the world social situation*. New York, United Nations, 1979.

question of the legal rights of women, there is still much to be done to achieve *de facto* equality between men and women in most countries. Discriminatory conditions still exist in economic life, despite the fact that the principle of equal work opportunities and emoluments has now been universally accepted. A number of countries have also enacted laws to improve the rights of women within the family. Thus, the trend towards liberalization of divorce procedures and greater consideration for the rights of women has gained momentum during the 1970s.

The increasing involvement of women in economic life has, in turn, influenced the family life-style. The demand for day-care services for children is increasing, although these services still play a minor role, even in industrialized countries, except in those developed countries with a centrally planned economy. Pre-school care and education facilities are also being developed in the urban areas of some developing countries. The many changes in the structure and life-style of the family seem to indicate the emergence of a new type of family and of new types of relationship between men and women and between parents and children.

As a result of reduced fertility and increased longevity, the number as well as the proportion of people over 65 years of age has been steadily growing in Northern America, Europe, and the USSR (see Annex, Table 2). In the developing world as a whole, the proportion is only slightly increasing. The situation of the elderly in the industrialized countries is characterized by an increasing predominance of females and growing social isolation. In these countries the integration of the aged into family units is often hampered by various factors such as housing conditions, urbanization, and the social mobility of active people. Some governments have therefore stressed the provision of various forms of home help to the aged. Only a relatively small proportion of elderly people live in specialized institutions for the aged. The situation of the aged in most developing countries is different, as the coexistence of generations in a single household is still the general rule. It is, however, expected that industrialization will rapidly transform this traditional family pattern.

Developments in social security were generally characterized in the period under review by increased financial benefits, broader coverage, lower retirement ages, extended coverage by invalidity pensions, and expanded health care provision, as well as the addition of new programmes (for instance, survivor benefits). In many countries inflation and rising unemployment were among the main forces behind these changes. In many developing countries more and more industrial workers were being brought under mandatory old-age and invalidity coverage, as, for instance, in Egypt and Iraq. The extension of coverage to self-employed persons was reported from the Bahamas, Barbados, Brazil, Colombia, and Portugal. As developments in health care are being discussed elsewhere (see Chapter 4) it may suffice to mention here only a few examples, such as the adoption of a universal health service system in Australia in 1975 (with optional features added in 1976), the introduction of social insurance health care systems in Senegal and the Republic of Korea, and the institution of an employer-financed health care system in Mauritania.

Economic trends

After more than two decades of sustained economic growth the international economic environment began to change in the 1970s. The result has been a sharp discontinuity, with

earlier growth, the accentuation of already existing disparities in development performance, and the maintenance of the gap between developed and developing countries.

The sharp contrast with earlier economic growth has been particularly striking in the
developed countries with a market economy. In these countries the average growth rate of
the gross domestic product was 3.2% during the period 1971–1977, compared with more
than 5% during the 1960s. This recession was accompanied by high rates of inflation,
chronic instability in exchange markets, and serious unemployment. Whereas consumer
prices rose in the developed countries with market economies by an average 4% during
the period 1960–1973, the average increase had reached 8.6% in 1976 and 9.3% in 1977.
The continuing recession in the developed world gradually resulted in resistance to
commodity stabilization arrangements, restrictions on imports, particularly of manufac-
tured and semi-manufactured products from developing countries, and restrictions also on
the immigration of skilled and unskilled labour from developing countries. These protec-
tionist measures were also partly inspired by the increased export performances of
developing countries, which became more competitive in certain sectors.

Developed countries with a centrally planned economy continued to show relatively
high rates of economic growth in the first half of the decade. The recession, however,
started to affect these rates in the second half of the 1970s. National income increased
annually by 6.3% in 1971–1975 and by 4.9% in 1976–1977. Consumer prices were
generally kept stable, often by price subsidies.

The repercussions in the developing world differed markedly for different groups of
countries. At one extreme, in one group of 40 countries, with roughly 1200 million of the
world's population and a per capita product of less than US $200 in 1970, the annual rate
of growth between 1971 and 1975 was only 1.1%. At the other extreme, in a group of
developing countries, including a number of petroleum-exporting countries and of Latin
American countries, with roughly 256 million of the world's population and with a per
capita product in 1970 of between US $400 and US $1000, the average annual growth
rate between 1970 and 1975 was 5.1%.

A concise idea of the main economic trends can be gained from the following estimates:

	Average annual growth rate (%) *of gross domestic product (median* *values for each group of countries)*	
	1960–1970	*1970–1976*
Low-income countries	3.6	2.9
Middle-income countries	5.7	6.0
Industrialized countries	4.7	3.2
Countries with planned economies	4.3	3.9

Source: The World Bank. *World development report, 1978.* New
York, Oxford University Press, 1978, pp. 78–79.

At the same time inflation rates were increasing all over the world, making the purchase
of essentials more difficult.

Among the various trends that have emerged more clearly during the period under
review, the following may be mentioned. There has been a growing recognition in an
increasing number of countries that development cannot focus solely on economic growth
and that greater emphasis must be put on social concerns, such as the elimination of mass
poverty, the promotion of employment, and the satisfaction of basic needs for all people.

	Average annual rate of inflation (%)	
	1960–1970	1970–1976
Low-income countries	3.1	9.8
Middle-income countries	3.2	12.5
Industrialized countries	4.2	9.3
Countries with planned economies	—	—

Source: The World Bank. *World development report, 1978*. New York, Oxford University Press, 1978.

There has also been an increasing recognition of the growing interdependence of the world economy. This interdependence is not a new phenomenon, but has become more sharply evident in recent years.

Employment

Between 1970 and 1975 the world labour force increased by 137 million—an annual increase of about 1.8%—and it now amounts to some 1600 million. The fact that the employment growth rate has been slightly lower than the population growth rate is due to the decreasing proportions of both younger and older workers (through the extension of schooling and the lowering of the retirement age respectively). The labour force of the less developed regions of the world, including China, had reached nearly 69% of the world total labour force by the mid-1970s. The proportion of the world's economically active population in the developed countries with market economies has been estimated at 20% in 1975, and the proportion in the countries with centrally planned economies at 11% (see Tables 4A and B in Annex).

In 1975, the proportion of women in the total labour force was 35.5% in the developed countries with market economies and 29.3% in the developing world. In the countries with centrally planned economies it was 49.4% in 1975.

The distribution of the labour force by activity shows that in 1975 the agricultural labour force represented 10% of the total labour force in developed countries with market economies, 24% in Eastern Europe and the USSR, and 63% in the developing world, including China. The developing countries tended to rely on the growth of manufacturing activity for creating employment. The informal sector, which includes manufacturing, transport, construction, trade, and services, expanded considerably in most developing countries, thus creating employment opportunities.

During the first half of the 1970s, employment increased by 0.7% a year in the developed countries with market economies. However, in the nine member countries of the European Economic Community the level of employment decreased by 0.1% a year during the same period. This trend continued in 1976 and 1977. In the developed countries with centrally planned economies, total employment grew at 1.6% a year.

Open unemployment in developing countries at mid-decade seemed to affect approximately 5% of the labour force. According to ILO, the estimated open unemployment rates were about 4% in Asia, 7% in Africa, and 5% in Latin America.

Underemployment, or work yielding an income inadequate to meet essential needs, is much more common in developing countries than open unemployment. The extent of

25

Table 3. Preliminary estimates of unemployment and underemployment in developing countries, by region, 1975 (in millions)

Region	Unemployment[a] Total		Urban		Underemployment[b] Total		Urban		Total Total		Urban	
	No.	%	No.	%	No.	%	No.	%	No.	%	No.	%
Asia[c]	18	3.9	6	6.9	168	36.4	20	23.2	186	40.3	26	30.1
Africa	10	7.1	3	10.8	53	37.9	7	25.1	63	45.0	10	35.9
Latin America	5	5.1	5	6.5	28	28.9	14	22.8	33	34.0	19	29.3
Oceania	—	—	—	—	1	49.0	—	—	1	49.0	—	—
Total	33	4.7	14	8.0	250	35.7	41	23.3	283	40.4	55	31.3

[a] Defined as "persons without a job and looking for work". [b] Defined as "persons who are in employment of less than normal duration and who are seeking or would accept additional work" and "persons with a job yielding inadequate income". [c] Excluding China and other Asian centrally planned economies.
Source: Employment, growth and basic needs: a one-world problem. Geneva, International Labour Office, 1976.

underemployment, which is largely identified with the overall issue of poverty, is a considerable problem in these countries. ILO has estimated that in 1975 about 40% of the labour force in developing market economies was not earning an adequate income (see Table 3).

Unemployment in the developed countries with market economies increased from 2% of the labour force in 1970 to approximately 5% in the years 1975–1977. In 1975 unemployment affected about 15 million people in the member countries of OECD. Young people were increasingly affected, as well as women, poorly educated people, and foreign migrant workers.

The projected growth of the labour force will add to the difficulties of finding sufficient employment and adequate incomes.

Poverty

Poverty and its corollary, social injustice, are now generally diagnosed as the major obstacles to socioeconomic development and improvement of the quality of life.

Poverty must be understood in an absolute sense. While poverty can be socially defined and relative, social welfare systems in many developed countries do help to alleviate some of the direct effects of poverty by providing minimum incomes or services. However, very large numbers of people in the developing world live in absolute poverty. They subsist at levels shared by very few people in developed countries and, since they are residents of poor countries, there is no money for an adequate social welfare system.

The World Bank[1] estimate is that nearly 800 million people, about 40% of the population of the developing countries, are living in absolute poverty. The majority of them are in rural areas, the greatest concentration being in South Asia and Indonesia. Sub-Saharan Africa has a high proportion of its population in absolute poverty, although the number of poor people is smaller because of Africa's much smaller population.

In addition to those in absolute poverty, many other people had inadequate access to public services in the period under review. In 1975, about 1200 million people, i.e., more than a quarter of mankind, lived in low-income countries in Asia and Africa where the median per capita income was US $150. Another 900 million people lived in middle-income countries where the median per capita income was US $750.[1]

---

[1] The World Bank. World development report, 1978. New York, Oxford University Press, 1978, p. 26.

In the low-income countries, 87% of the population is rural, 77% of the adults are illiterate, 48% of the children are not enrolled in primary school, and 75% of the population does not have access to safe water.

In the middle-income countries, 57% of the population is rural, 37% of the adults are illiterate, 3% of the children are not enrolled in primary school, and 48% of the population does not have access to safe water.

There are large differences among the developing countries, but clearly most of the people in the low-income countries live in poverty—defined as inability to obtain basic services—as do many people in the middle-income countries.

In view of these shocking facts, the policies applied in the mid-1970s to reduce mass poverty and redistribute income were focused in most developing countries on fundamental economic and social changes, such as land redistribution. However, landless labourers who represent a large proportion of the population in many developing countries seem to be the least likely to benefit from land redistribution. In India, for instance, one-third of the total population, mostly in the lowest income group, is landless. During the 1970s several African countries witnessed a considerable growth in the landless population.

The United Nations 1978 Report on the world social situation contains the following statement:

> By 1978 pessimism regarding the possibilities of bringing about changes in the short term, among and within countries, in patterns of income distribution and access to opportunities for employment and consumption was compounded by the lack of transformation of the international economic order, the persistence of rapid inflation, the trade difficulties of many developing countries, the pace of economic growth in many developed market economies and serious unemployment in various parts of the world. Developing countries still face formidable problems of poverty. In the developing world the pressure for a more equitable distribution of income among nations is accompanied by calls for greater self-reliance, requiring new measures to diversify production and involve the mass of the population in more efficient, income-generating activities. The ability of many developed market economies to cope with the plight of the poorer segments of society and undertake structural change is still open to question. The centrally planned economies, more sensitive than before to external economic influences, are still struggling for increased productivity in a context of full employment and relative equality. Trends and policies for the production and delivery of social services in the world must be seen in the light of these global developments.[1]

The association between material wealth and selected health status indicators has been demonstrated time and again. Life expectancy at birth and infant mortality have in particular been shown to correlate closely with indicators of economic development, such as the per capita gross national product (GNP), i.e., poor countries have, generally speaking, a lower life expectancy and higher infant mortality at birth than those that are better-off (see Annex, Tables 5 and 6 and Figs. 2 and 6, respectively). An analysis of data from 115 countries has produced a statistically significant correlation coefficient of 0.75 between the per capita GNP and life expectancy at birth.[2] Despite certain reservations whether the association would also hold good for developed countries where—it has been argued—a better social security level and higher average cultural level may to some degree compensate for a lesser degree of material wealth, a significant correlation was also found for European countries, the coefficients being 0.55 for males and 0.79 for females. That there is a more pronounced positive correlation between per capita GNP and life expectancy in the case of females than in that of males seems to reflect the fact that females benefit relatively more from socioeconomic progress than males.[3]

[1] *1978 Report on the world social situation.* New York, United Nations, 1979, p. 30.

[2] GRANAHAN, D. V., ET AL. *Contents and measurement of socioeconomic development.* New York, United Nations Research Institute for Social Development, 1972.

[3] *World health statistics quarterly,* **31**: 160 (1978).

However, the positive correlation between income and life expectancy at birth holds good not only for countries but also within countries.

For instance, it was recently estimated that in Brazil life expectancy at birth is 49.9 years for the lower income group and 62.0 for the higher income group. Differences among subgroups are even bigger, life expectancy at birth amounting to 42.8 years for the lower income group in the country's North-East Central Region and 66.9 for the higher income group in its Southern Region. Infant mortality likewise is high where income levels are low (see below, page 47).

Because of the population-based surveys conducted by the National Center for Health Statistics in the United States of America, more data on the relationship between income and illness are available for that country than for any other. While the United States of America cannot be taken as representative of the world, it has a large enough population and sufficient economic variability for the study of differentials. For twenty years the United States Health Interview Survey has shown that people in low-income families have had more disabling illnesses, more long-term incapacity, and more short-term incapacity, including days missed from school or work, than those in high-income families. It is not simply a function of age or sex; the finding applies in all the different age-sex categories. Perhaps most important from the standpoint of policy is that it has continued to hold good despite the implementation of programmes to make medical care available to the elderly and to those living on low incomes.

Other data confirm the finding. Welfare cases and the near-poor in both urban and rural areas have a higher rate of disability than those who are not poor. Mental retardation is likewise more common among people born and reared in poverty, partly because of greater hazards associated with birth and partly because of cultural deprivation.

Health-related behavioural factors

The idea that life-style is somehow related to health and disease is not new (in the eighteenth century the Scottish physician, Cheyne, attributed increasing morbidity, and especially mental disorders, to "the rush and tear of modern life"), but attempts to translate this idea into the idiom of psychosocial research are a recent development. Life-style comprises many things, and, in the absence of an agreed definition, research into its effects on health has evolved along several different lines.

Smoking

There can no longer be any doubt among informed people that in any country where smoking is a common practice, it is a major and certainly a removable cause of ill-health and premature death.[1] Moreover the introduction and extension of the smoking habit in countries where it is not yet established will certainly be followed by similar effects there. The threat to many developing countries is immediate and serious.

In most countries of Europe more than 50% of adult males smoke cigarettes at an

---

[1] WHO Technical Report Series, No. 636, 1979 (*Controlling the smoking epidemic*. Report of the WHO Expert Committee on Smoking Control).

average rate of 15 per day. For adult women the percentage varies from as low as 10 to as high as 50, but in many countries it is higher than 30. While for males the trend in many countries is to smoke less, there is a general tendency for smoking by teenagers and women to increase. At present, the age gradient in smoking shows a downward trend, with older adults smoking less than younger ones. At older ages many former smokers have given up the habit either because their health has become impaired or because they believe it to be at risk of impairment. If, however, today's teenagers fail to overcome their addiction, the downward age gradient could become less marked and even disappear. If this happens, the overall adult smoking rate will rise. This is almost certain to happen in the case of women who have recently started smoking at frequencies and quantitative levels previously associated only with males.

In Asia, Africa, America, and Oceania it is rare to find less than 40% of males who are regular smokers. In Japan, some parts of India, South Africa, and the Philippines the smoking rate for males is higher than 70%. Female indulgence in smoking is generally lower, rarely exceeding 30%.

The impact of smoking on health has been amply documented. Deaths are uniformly higher among smokers than among non-smokers, in both sexes and whatever the age at death. The excess mortality of cigarette smokers is proportionately greater at ages 45–54 years than at younger or older ages. A smoker doubles his or her risk of dying before the age of 65.

The diseases most commonly associated with cigarette smoking are lung cancer, bronchitis and emphysema, and ischaemic heart disease and other diseases of the vascular system. They account for 80% of the excess mortality. Other diseases that are significantly commoner in smokers are cancer of the lip, tongue, mouth, larynx, pharynx, oesophagus, and bladder. Gastroduodenal ulcer occurs twice as frequently in smokers as in non-smokers.

It has been calculated that in countries where smoking has been a widespread habit, it is responsible for 90% of deaths from lung cancer, for 75% of deaths from bronchitis, and for 25% of deaths from ischaemic heart disease among men under 65 years of age. In women, the proportions may be somewhat less. Without cigarette-smoking, it is likely that the total cancer death rate could be reduced by a quarter.

Apart from its effects on the mortality rate, smoking is responsible for a considerably increased morbidity rate, resulting in loss of working days and excessive demands on medical services, both for primary and for hospital care. The cost to the community of premature death, increased illness, and loss of productive capacity due to cigarette smoking is very high in countries where the habit has been common for a long time.

Besides being a risk factor for lung cancer, cardiovascular diseases, and other smoking-related diseases in both sexes, smoking poses special health problems for women. Smoking during pregnancy is associated with lower birth-weights, shortened gestation, higher rates of spontaneous abortion, especially during the last months of pregnancy, more frequent complications of pregnancy and labour, and higher rates of perinatal mortality. The infants of mothers who smoke may face additional problems. The risk of an infant developing bronchitis or pneumonia in the first year of life is doubled if the parents smoke.

Several studies have shown that children may be harmed by the passive inhalation of cigarette smoke. The children of parents who smoke are more likely to smoke themselves, and if they do they experience more respiratory symptoms than those who do not. The earlier the age at which a child starts to smoke, the greater his or her chance of having a less healthy life and of dying prematurely.

The difference in health between smokers and non-smokers may be substantially aggravated by occupation. The combined effect of smoking and other environmental hazards, mainly of an occupational nature, results in more sickness and accidents. In a large number of studies on occupational morbidity, a very significant difference between smokers and non-smokers has been discovered.

Recently there has been increasing concern about the effects of smoking on non-smokers. Although the effects of involuntary smoking on healthy adults involve no long-term impairment of health, they are nevertheless the cause of considerable distress to individuals and may result in loss of efficiency at work. On this ground the question of "passive" smoking merits more attention from employers and the smoking public.

More attention has to be paid to the socioeconomic implications of smoking. It has to be clearly understood that smoking does not affect only those who smoke. The smoker creates expenses for his or her family, other tax-payers, and society at large. Smoking reduces a population's working capacity and thereby the gross national product because: there are more deaths before retirement age among smokers than among non-smokers; non-fatal smoking illnesses create disability; and there is more absenteeism among smokers. Smoking also generates extra demands for medical care. Such care is given and paid for at a real cost to society and cannot be recouped directly by increased tobacco taxes.

Despite mounting evidence of the health hazards of tobacco use, the world-wide growth, manufacture, and use of tobacco are increasing. In 1977 nearly 5 million metric tons (dry weight) were produced. The increase in cigarette manufacturing continues long-term trends toward more tobacco consumption, both in absolute amount (see Fig. 6) and per capita (see Table 4).

Fig. 6. World unmanufactured tobacco consumption and cigarette production, 1959–1977

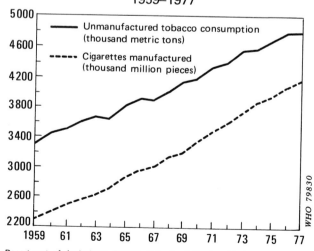

Source: United States Department of Agriculture. Foreign Agricultural Service. World tobacco supply and distribution, 1959–77. Washington, DC, 1978.

Table 4. Annual cigarette consumption per person aged 15
and over, selected countries, 1935, 1950, 1965, and 1973

	Consumption per adult*			
Developed countries:	1935	1950	1965	1973
Australia[a]	450	1280	2680	3080
Canada[a]	700	1790	3310	3450
Denmark	470	1290	1500	1850
France	530	930	1510	1920
Germany, Federal Republic of	—	630	2100	2610
Japan	880	1220	2350	3240
Sweden	380	810	1360	1580
United Kingdom	1590	2180	2680	3230
United States of America	1450	3240	3800	3850
Developing countries:				
Argentina	1060[b]	1460	1660	1940
Barbados	—	—	1110	1620
Brazil	600[c]	1140	1220	1490
Chile	—	—	1220	1320
Costa Rica	—	—	1850	2060
El Salvador	—	—	750	1020
Ghana	—	—	480	480
Hong Kong	—	—	3310	2780
India	80[d]	100	180	170
Indonesia	—	—	—	230
Jamaica	—	—	1270	1350
Kenya	—	—	390	470
Malawi	—	—	150	200
Malaysia	—	—	1440	1600
Mauritius	—	—	1610	1920
Mexico	1440	1510	1510	1360
Morocco	240	510	570	690[e]
Nicaragua	—	—	1140	1520
Pakistan	—	—	450	760
Sierra Leone	—	—	280	430
Singapore	—	—	2380	2490
Turkey	960	1220	1820	2050[e]
Venezuela	—	—	1900	2210

[a] Handrolled cigarettes not included; to do so would add about 10 per cent to total consumption.
[b] Figures are for Year 1940.
[c] Annual averages for 1935–1939.
[d] Figures are for Year 1948.
[d] Figures are for Year 1972.
* The consumption figures per adult per annum in the above table are based on the total sales of tobacco goods and the population resident in each country aged 15 years and over (except Jamaica, where the age is 14).
Source: LEE, P. N., ed. Tobacco consumption in various countries, 4th ed. London, Tobacco Research Council, 1975 (Research Paper 6).

Tobacco production is increasing more rapidly in the developing than in the developed countries. Data from FAO[1] show that tobacco production in the less developed regions of the world rose by 28% between 1969–1971 and 1977, while in the developed regions it rose by 15%. Of the world's top 10 tobacco-producing countries, 6 are in the developing world (Brazil, China, India, Indonesia, Republic of Korea, and Turkey).

The smoking habit has spread like an epidemic. Although the developing countries have not had yet time to experience the grim increase in smoking-related mortality that has taken place in the industrialized countries, they must expect it unless they halt and reverse the increase in cigarette consumption. In many less developed countries, the epidemic of smoking-related diseases is already of such magnitude as to rival even infectious diseases or malnutrition as a public health problem.

In the absence of strong and resolute action by governments, we face the serious

[1] 1977 FAO production yearbook, Vol. 31. Rome, Food and Agriculture Organization of the United Nations, 1978.

probability that the smoking epidemic will have affected the developing world within a decade and that, as a result of commercial enterprise and governmental inactivity, a major avoidable public health problem will have been inflicted on the countries least able to withstand it. Failing immediate action, smoking-related diseases will spread in developing countries before communicable diseases and malnutrition have been controlled, and the gap between rich and poor countries will thus be further expanded.

WHO has convened Expert Committees on Smoking and its Effects on Health (1974) and on Controlling the Smoking Epidemic (1978). Both committees made extensive recommendations in their reports[1,2] on action that could be taken by national governments and international agencies. The belief was expressed that the reduction of smoking to the status of a private activity confined to a minority of adults should be seen as an attainable goal within the next two decades at the latest. Nothing less would be compatible with WHO's objective of health for all by the year 2000.

Other factors

There have been several studies in which the rates for specific disorders in contrasting communities or cultural groups have been compared. For example, hypertension has been found to be much rarer in Papua New Guinea than in Australia; mortality due to cardiovascular disease higher among the Japanese in the United States of America than among the Japanese in Japan, etc. Since the whole ecology of traditional agricultural communities is very different from that of industrial or urbanized communities, it is difficult to disentangle the different causal factors involved. More specific conclusions have emerged from studies dealing with individual variables like migration and the experience of cultural change associated with it. A study in Southern Africa established that adherence to traditional beliefs and values was associated with lower blood pressure in members of extended rural families, but individuals who maintained such beliefs after moving to the city were at increased risk of hypertension. Overall rates for lung cancer have been found to be higher in first-generation migrants from rural to industrial areas than in second-generation migrants of comparable origin.

Secondly, new techniques for assessing and quantifying life stress have made it possible to study morbidity risk in relation to the "stressfulness" of the environment. Associations between measurable life stress and disease have been found in myocardial infarction, tuberculosis, depressive illness, and other conditions. At present WHO is carrying out a large-scale comparative study on the frequency and nature of stressful "life events" in different cultures and types of communities.

Thirdly, different patterns of personality and of individual behaviour have been implicated in differences between morbity rates in population groups. It has been suggested that, at least in developed countries, the majority of illness episodes of all kinds that occur in a population over a period of time tend to cluster within a relatively small proportion of individuals who may have certain psychosocial characteristics in common, for example a heightened level of anxiety. Different personality types (e.g., type A—active, aggressive,

---

[1] WHO Technical Report Series, No. 568, 1975 (*Smoking and its effects on health.* Report of a WHO Expert Committee).

[2] WHO Technical Report Series, No. 636, 1979 (*Controlling the smoking epidemic.* Report of the WHO Expert Committee on Smoking Control).

and self-punitive; and type B—passive, avoiding conflict, adaptable) appear to be associated with higher and lower risks, respectively, for myocardial infarction. The importance of alcoholism and drug abuse is discussed elsewhere in this report (see Chapter 4, pages 158 and 160).

Evaluation of development progress and data needs

Considerable emphasis is now being placed on the evaluation of development progress in general and social progress in particular. There is now a clear shift towards the measurement of social development and changes in well-being by non-monetary indicators and away from excessive reliance on such indicators as per capita gross national product.

In current work to develop yardsticks for measuring social change, ways of measuring the impact of health action on the improvement of health status are being given increasing priority. Among health status indicators, life expectancy (at birth or age 1 year) and infant mortality are often selected, together with a few other social indicators, for the construction of composite indices of social progress. However, it is clear that a multifaceted process such as development cannot meaningfully be compressed into a few figures. A selected series of indicators to measure specific aspects of health have also to be considered in the light of their relevance to conditions in each country. A global assessment of development progress should then be based on those indicators that are relevant to a large number of countries.

For the planning, monitoring, and evaluation of health action, indicators are needed of progress in health care, as well as of the health status of the population. Health care indicators provide a periodic statistical summary of information originally generated for day-to-day managerial use at all levels of the health services. Judicious use of the two types of indicators enables decision-makers to assess the effectiveness and efficiency of health action, thus contributing to the improvement of health care delivery.

Valid indicators can be derived only from reliable basic data which in turn have been generated by adequate statistical services and other information systems. In particular, the statistical services are still rudimentary in a number of developing countries and the quality of the data produced is accordingly poor. Timeliness of information is lost because of long delays in data-processing. The data often cover only a part of the country, e.g., the capital and a few large towns. Even when the whole country is covered, there may be insufficient geographical and other breakdowns of data for the detection of health and social differences between population groups.

Health-related socioeconomic statistics cover a wide spectrum of information, most of which is collected outside the health sector, often without any coordination with the health administration. Their usefulness for the health sector may therefore be limited and they may require arduous adjustment. For instance, in some countries, the socioeconomic classification used in the population census is different from that used in vital statistics, which makes it impossible to match numerator and denominator information for the calculation of meaningful rates. Another example is provided by the legal rules on the registration of fetal death; in a number of countries the registration of late fetal death is part of the birth registration system and consequently there is no item in the registration form for recording information on causes of death, which would be essential for studies on perinatal events. Health manpower data, e.g., on medical students, offer yet another example of uncoordinated and fragmented statistics, being usually collected by the Ministry of Education without adequate consultation with health authorities regarding information needs.

In addition, some of the information recorded on relevant source documents is not processed or, at any rate, not tabulated, although it would be potentially valuable. In the statistical processing of death certificates, for instance, causes of death are only rarely tabulated by marital status or by socioeconomic group.

There are often no national or international guidelines or standards on data collection procedures, classification schemes, and coding rules, with the result that statistics are heterogeneous and incompatible. For example, there is a great demand for international data on health expenditure. However, the definition of health expenditure varies from one country to another. Information from the private sector is often not available. Above all, the pattern of expenditure strongly depends on the particular health system and social policy of the country, so that meaningful international comparisons become extremely difficult.

Much thus remains to be done to improve the mechanism for data generation in many countries. As data are usually collected through the health and social services, no significant breakthrough can be expected in countries in which the infrastructure is weak. Indeed, health statistical services should be developed as an essential component of the health system of each country. At any rate, steps can be taken to produce more timely and relevant information by streamlining data collection through the careful selection of a minimum of the most essential items, the elimination of duplication, and the acceleration of data processing. Furthermore, the development and application of inexpensive information procedures adjusted to the conditions of the country will be of great value, e.g., simple and quick sample surveys, lay reporting of mortality and morbidity, and the effective use of traditional health workers for the reporting of simple data items.

Each country needs to analyse its own health situation as a basis for health planning and to monitor and evaluate development progress. It is therefore of great importance that it should improve its capability for undertaking the analysis and projection of health trends by making the best use of the data available, both from the health sector and from other socioeconomic sectors. This should facilitate overall analysis of the health situation.

Policy issues

Profound changes have taken place in international political and economic relationships. During the period under review, new realities, new perceptions, and new perspectives started to emerge in international relations, calling for political, social, and economic adjustments, for new concepts and new structures. The evolution of relations between developed and developing countries generated an unprecedented series of debates and intensive discussions in various international forums and placed the United Nations system at the centre of international cooperation. A large number of conferences convened by organizations of the United Nations system during the period 1973–1977 brought into sharper focus some of the central issues of the developmental process.

In 1974, in an atmosphere of crisis in world economic relations, and with increased recognition of the interdependence of nations, the Sixth Special Session of the United Nations General Assembly adopted the Declaration and the Programme of Action for the Establishment of a New International Economic Order. These two documents embody principles on which economic relationships should develop among all the countries of the world and define the measures which should be taken to establish "a new international economic order based on equity, sovereign equality, interdependence, common interest and cooperation among all States, irrespective of their economic and social systems which shall correct inequalities and redress existing injustices, make it possible to eliminate the widening gap between the developed and the developing countries and ensure steadily accelerating economic and social development and peace and justice for present and future generations".

In the same year, the United Nations General Assembly approved the Charter of Economic Rights and Duties of States, the essential objective of which is the establishment of a just economic order through the creation of a code to regulate economic relations among all States.

The United Nations General Assembly designated 1974 as World Population Year to focus international attention on the various aspects of the population problem. The World Population Conference (Bucharest, 1974) adopted the World Population Plan of Action, the explicit aim of which is to help coordinate population trends and those of socioeconomic development.

Also in 1974, a major effort was launched to deal with food crises that had developed in many parts of the world. The United Nations World Food Conference was held in Rome, its principal task being to develop ways and means whereby the international community could take specific action to resolve the world food problem within the broader context of development and international economic cooperation. The United Nations General Assembly was requested to establish a World Food Council and an International Fund for Agricultural Development.

The Lima Declaration and Plan of Action on Industrial Development and Cooperation, adopted by the Second General Conference of UNIDO in 1975, specified the need for a better balance in the structure of world production. It set the goal of an increase in the share of the developing countries in total world industrial production from 7% to at least 25% by the year 2000.

The Declaration and Programme of Action for the Establishment of a New International Economic Order gave the impetus to the Seventh Special Session of the United Nations General Assembly, held in 1975 and devoted to development and international economic cooperation. Notwithstanding the economically oriented nature of the session, the significance of various activities in which the United Nations system is engaged and their interrelationship with economic development were recognized throughout.

The General Assembly proclaimed 1975 as International Women's Year. The programme for that year aimed at setting in motion dynamic national, regional, and international activities to improve the condition of women and at ensuring three basic objectives—equality, development, and peace. A World Conference of the International Women's Year, convened in Mexico City in 1975, adopted the Declaration of Mexico and a World Plan of Action which can be considered as the first international instrument to contain proposals for action to make half the world's population full members of society.

Special international conferences relating to the environment included the Human Settlements Conference, held in 1976 and the Water Conference and the Desertification Conference, both held in 1977.

The United Nations Conference on Human Settlements (HABITAT), held in Vancouver in 1976, produced a programme of action to improve the quality of life in human settlements.

The United Nations Water Conference held in Mar del Plata, Argentina, in 1977, unanimously agreed on the need to implement the recommendations of the Human Settlements Conference on the provision by 1990 of adequate and safe water supplies for all people, particularly the rural communities in developing countries. It was suggested that countries should adopt detailed plans on water supply and sanitation services specifically suited to national conditions, and that the international community should adopt a more effective approach in supporting the increased national commitments of the developing countries by financial and other means. The Conference also recommended designating the decade 1980–1990 as the International Drinking-Water Supply and Sanitation Decade, to be devoted to implementing the national plans for drinking-water supplies and sanitation.

In 1976 the Tripartite World Conference on Employment, Income Distribution and Social Progress, and the International Division of Labour adopted a Declaration of Principles and Programme of Action to guide international and national development efforts towards fulfilling the basic needs of all people, particularly the elementary needs of the lowest income groups, and towards achieving full productive employment in decent working conditions.

During the 1970s the international community also took a number of initiatives in the field of human rights. In 1976, the General Assembly adopted a Programme of Action against *Apartheid*, and in 1977 the World Conference for Action against *Apartheid*, held in Lagos, Nigeria, adopted the Lagos Declaration promoting international action in support of the struggle of the South African people to eradicate *apartheid* and racial discrimination and to build a society based on the principle of equality of persons, irrespective of race, colour, or creed.

Chapter 3

Health status differentials

As defined in the Constitution of the World Health Organization: "Health is a state of complete physical, mental and social well-being and not merely the absence of disease or infirmity". Unfortunately, health status cannot be adequately measured in such terms anywhere in the world. It is still common, indeed necessary, to measure and compare health primarily in terms of the incidence and prevalence of diseases or infirmities, variations in causes of death, and according to levels and trends in mortality. For the most part the available data on health status for the less developed countries range from the extremely weak to the non-existent. Information on morbidity and cause of death is often only accurate within very broad ranges of error for the more developed countries. Similarly, both time-series data and statistics from different countries are frequently not fully comparable. Consequently, health status differentials can only be discussed in broad terms.

Crude death rates are sometimes used as though they were indicative of health status. However, they are so influenced by the age structures of populations that they are of interest primarily in relation to changes in population growth rates. In most parts of the world they have declined to low levels which, in combination with high birth rates, have been producing high growth rates. However, in recent years crude death rates in a few more developed countries have equalled or risen above birth rates, with the result (if the effects of migration are ignored) that their populations have ceased to grow or started to decline. This trend has been noted recently in Austria, Belgium, the German Democratic Republic, the Federal Republic of Germany, and all parts of the United Kingdom.

The stabilization or natural decline of populations does not, in itself, indicate increasing levels of mortality. Rather it reflects special combinations of declining birth rates, population aging, and continuing progress in reducing mortality.

The one common feature of recent health trends in all parts of the world seems to be a slow-down in progress in the reduction of mortality. In some places this is manifested by a cessation in mortality decline or even a small increase in the rate. The explanation for this development differs from one part of the world to another. In countries where mortality was already very low, the recent trend can be attributed to the difficulty of making further improvements and to normal fluctuations in a basically stable situation. It is considerably more difficult to understand the recent trend in areas where mortality remains well below the optimum level or where it can be characterized as high, except in terms of flagging determination on the part of the governments concerned and special circumstances that make further improvement in health especially difficult.

Fig. 7. Frequency distribution of expectation of life at birth, males and females, in 37 of the more developed countries around 1950 and in the 1970s

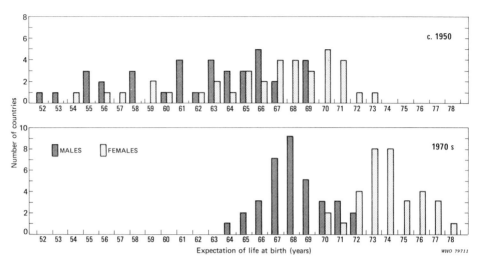

Source: *Recent levels and trends in mortality,* New York and Geneva, United Nations and World Health Organization (in preparation).

Recent developments in health, as measured by levels of mortality, are most readily discussed and understood in terms of life expectancy at birth. All of the more developed countries have recorded significant improvements in life expectancy during the past quarter of a century. Equally important, the dispersion of life expectancies about the mean has diminished during recent years, but the gap between male and female life expectancies seems to be unchanged (see Fig. 7). The most recent data available show that the life expectancy for females in the more developed countries ranged from 70 to 78 years at birth during the early 1970s. At the same time, life expectancy for males varied from 64 to 72 years, averaging six years less than corresponding figures for females. The three top-ranking countries, in terms of average life expectancy at birth during the early 1970s, were Japan, Norway, and Sweden, with male life expectancies of between 72 and 73 years and a female life expectancy of 78 years. Concurrently, the lowest life expectancies among the more developed countries (excluding Turkey) were those of Portugal, the USSR, and Yugoslavia for males, and of Albania, Northern Ireland, and Yugoslavia for females. In these countries life expectancy for males averaged 64–65 years and life expectancy for females was about 70 years.

After a thorough review of the available literature, it is still not possible to determine levels of mortality, much less trends, in Sub-Saharan Africa with any degree of confidence. However, the evidence points to life expectancies in all countries (except the small, unrepresentative islands of the Comoros, Mauritius, and Réunion) of well below 50 years at birth. On the whole, it seems that the mortality levels in Sub-Saharan Africa are still the highest in the world and that the countries in that area have made the least progress in lowering mortality during recent years. Moreover, while there is slight evidence of improvement, there is much that suggests a deterioration in health conditions over the past decade.

Table 5. Expectation of life at birth in selected Asian countries and areas, for which reasonably reliable estimates can be made (c. 1975).

Region	High mortality: e^a = less than 50 years	Medium mortality: e^a = 50–60 years	Low mortality: e^a = more than 60 years
East Asia		China Democratic People's Republic of Korea Mongolia	Hong Kong Republic of Korea
Eastern South Asia	Burma Democratic Kampuchea Indonesia	Philippines Thailand	Peninsular Malaysia Singapore
		Sabah and Sarawak	
Middle South Asia	Bangladesh India Nepal Pakistan	Iran	Sri Lanka
Western South Asia	Democratic Yemen Saudi Arabia Yemen	Iraq Jordan Syrian Arab Republic	Kuwait Lebanon

^{a} e = expectation of life at birth.

Source: *Recent levels and trends in mortality.* New York and Geneva, United Nations and World Health Organization (in preparation).

Mortality levels can be determined with a greater degree of confidence for most of Northern Africa. In all but two of the countries of the area, life expectancy currently falls in the medium range of 50–60 years at birth. The only countries in doubt are Morocco, which has an estimated life expectancy in the vicinity of 50 years and may belong in either the medium or high mortality range, and the Sudan, which almost certainly falls in the high mortality range of less than 50 years.

The mortality situation in Asia can be outlined with about the same certainty as that in Northern Africa. It may be assumed that somewhat more progress has been made in improving health in Asia than in Sub-Saharan Africa as a whole, but the data for Asia, like those for Sub-Saharan Africa and Latin America, show a slowing-down in mortality decline in recent years. Applying the criteria for high and medium mortality used above and equating low mortality with a life expectancy higher than 60 years at birth, the mortality situation in Asia in the early 1970s may be summarized as follows for those places for which reasonable estimates can be made (see Table 5). Seven relatively small countries and areas can be placed in the low mortality category: Hong Kong, Kuwait, Lebanon, Peninsular Malaysia, Republic of Korea, Singapore, and Sri Lanka. Ten appear to belong in the medium mortality range: China, the Democratic People's Republic of Korea, Iran, Iraq, Jordan, Mongolia, the Philippines, Sarawak, Syria, and Thailand. Eleven can be placed in the high mortality category: Bangladesh, Burma, Democratic Kampuchea, Democratic Yemen, India, Indonesia, Nepal, Pakistan, Sabah, Saudi Arabia, and Yemen.

Among the less developed countries, mortality conditions are best documented for those of Latin America, and all 28 Latin American countries and territories with a population of 250 000 or more can be classified with reasonable ease according to the criteria used above (see Table 6). By the mid 1970s only Bolivia and Haiti remained in the high mortality category. The Dominican Republic, Ecuador, El Salvador, Guatemala, Honduras, Nicaragua, and Peru fell in the medium mortality range, with a life expectancy of between 50 and 60 years at birth. Brazil and Colombia appear to be on the borderline

Table 6. Expectation of life at birth in Latin American countries and areas (c. 1975).

Region	High mortality: e^a = less than 50 yrs.	Medium mortality: e^a = 50–60 yrs.	Low mortality: e^a = more than 60 yrs.
Caribbean	Haiti	Dominican Republic	Barbados Cuba Guadeloupe Jamaica Martinique Puerto Rico Trinidad and Tobago
Middle America		El Salvador Guatemala Honduras Nicaragua	Costa Rica Mexica Panama
Temperate South America			Argentina Chile Uruguay
Tropical South America	Bolivia	Brazil Colombia Ecuador Peru	Guyana Paraguay Suriname Venezuela

^{a} e = expectation of life at birth.

Source: *Recent levels and trends in mortality*, New York and Geneva, United Nations and World Health Organization (in preparation).

between medium and low mortality. All the remaining areas, most notably those in the Caribbean and the three countries of Temperate South America, could be classified as low mortality areas. Within the low mortality group, most life expectancies fell within the range of those for more developed countries at the same time. In Latin America, as in Africa, Asia, and the more developed countries, there has been a marked slow-down in health progress as measured by the decline in mortality in recent years.

Among the Latin American data, those for Cuba and Argentina are especially interesting. If the figures for Puerto Rico are discounted as being inflated, Cuba currently appears to have the highest life expectancy in Latin America. In excess of 70 years at birth, it rivals that of the USA and is the third highest in the hemisphere. Cuba's achievement is especially impressive because it was accomplished in the absence of general or industrial economic development, mainly through the extension of basic medical and public health services to all parts of the country and the improvement of the basic nutritional status of all the people. In contrast, Argentina, which may have had the highest life expectancy in Latin America round about 1960, now ranks among the low-mortality countries and rather far down the list. In fact, it appears that life expectancy has declined there since 1960. In the other countries of Temperate South America also, mortality seems to have ceased declining. These recent developments have not been explained.

The health status of broad groups of populations, according to estimated life expectancy at birth, is indicated in the table opposite, which shows life expectancy in the more developed countries to be perhaps 1.75 times the average for Sub-Saharan Africa. It must be borne in mind, of course, that the figures for the less developed countries are very rough approximations. If the lowest national life expectancy were known, it would probably be found that the highest national life expectancy was twice as high.

Life expectancy at birth reflects mortality levels at all ages. Thus, in the early 1970s, mortality was, on the average, lower at all ages, in the countries of Northern and Western

	Estimated life expectancy at birth (c. 1975) (Years)
World	56–57
More developed regions	70
Northern America	73
Australia and New Zealand	73
Europe	70
Japan	74
USSR	70
Less developed regions	c. 54
Northern Africa	50–55
Sub-Saharan Africa	<50 (probably 40–45)
East Asia	50–60
South Asia	c. 50
Latin America	62

Sources: Demographic estimates and projections for the world, regions and countries as assessed in 1978 (New York, United Nations Population Division, Provisional Report, 25 January, 1979); *Recent levels and trends in mortality.* (New York and Geneva. United Nations and World Health Organization (in preparation). See also Annex, Table 7.

Europe, and in Northern America and Japan, than it was in Southern and Eastern Europe and he USSR. The greatest international variations in age-specific death rates occurred in the first year of life and in the age group 1–4 years. The range of infant mortality rates in the early 1970s among the more developed countries, was 9.1–42.9 deaths per 1000 live births for males and 7.5–37.6 for females. Sweden had the lowest rate for each sex, whereas Portugal had the highest rate for males and Yugoslavia the highest for females. Sweden also had the lowest rates for the age group 1–4 years: 0.3 and 0.4 per 1000 population at risk for females and males respectively. Romania had the highest rates: 1.8 and 2.1. In general, infant mortality rates were from 20 to 25 times as high as the corresponding childhood mortality rates, and the maximum rates for each group were on the average 5 to 6 times as high as the minimum ones.

Because the normal range of fluctuation in infant mortality rates is a wide one, it is often difficult to determine with confidence whether levels of infant mortality have really changed recently or how significant the changes may have been. However, the information available for Sub-Saharan Africa during the early 1970s offers no ground for thinking that there have been any significant improvements. At the national level, rates for all of the countries in that region must still be in the vicinity of 150–200 deaths per 1000 live births. Rates for Northern Africa can be given with more certainty. All exceed 100, but except for the Sudan they are definitely lower than 200 and probably do not come to more than 125 or 130. In both Asia and Latin America, the infant mortality rates cover a wider range. In Latin America the range is from about 30 to nearly 150, if Haiti and Bolivia are excluded, but up to 160 or 170 if they are included. However, the majority of Latin American countries and territories have infant mortality rates well below 100. In Asian countries and areas the rates range from 14–15 in Singapore and Hong Kong to perhaps 200 or more in Afghanistan and a few other areas of high mortality. In the large populous nations of Asia, infant mortality rates seem to remain well above 120.

The data for Asia, Latin America, and Northern Africa indicate that very substantial progress has been made in reducing infant mortality during the past quarter of a century, but also that the rate of improvement has slackened in recent years. In several Latin

41

Fig. 8. Annual average percentage rates of change in infant mortality, selected Latin American countries, 1950–1975

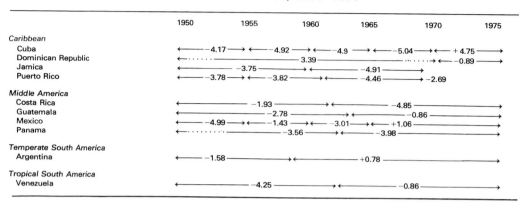

Source: *Recent levels and trends in mortality.* New York and Geneva, United Nations and World Health Organization (in preparation).

American areas the reported infant mortality rates have increased, but it cannot be determined as yet whether the increases reflect random variations within the normal range for stabilized intrinsic rates or represent secular trends (see Fig. 8). Another feature of infant mortality rates that is common to all areas where they can be measured properly is that of apparent divergencies among national levels. Generally, rates appear to have dropped faster in areas where mortality was already low than in high mortality areas.

In the less developed regions, what has been said above about infant mortality applies equally to childhood mortality rates. Infant and early childhood mortality rates for major regions of the world, estimated on the basis of the most recent data (*c.* 1970–1975), are broadly summarized below.

	Infant mortality (per 1000 live births)	Early childhood mortality (1–4 years) (per 1000 population at risk)
More developed regions		
Country range	8.3–40.3	0.4–2.0
Less developed regions		
Northern Africa	c. 130	c. 30
Sub-Saharan Africa	c. 200	>30
Asia	c. 120–130	>10
Latin America	<100 (probably c. 85–90)	c. 6.0

Sources: *Recent levels and trends in mortality*, New York and Geneva, United Nations and World Health Organization (in preparation) and WHO data.

In the more developed countries, mortality rates for males exceed those for females at all ages. During the 1970s, the least excess male mortality occurred at the youngest and oldest ages. From early childhood, the ratio of male to female mortality increased to its highest point during the young adult ages and then began to drop off. At the highest point, male mortality rates have commonly been two to three times the corresponding female rates. This pattern, based on death statistics from over 30 developed countries, is, of course, a generalized one. In individual countries the ages at which male mortality is most excessive vary from the late 'teens to the late 40s or early 50s. Data for the USA show that male mortality has been almost three times as high as female mortality in the age group 25–34 years, probably since at least 1950. Statistics from England and Wales, on the other hand, show the sex difference in mortality to be greatest between 35 and 44 years of age, while those from France indicate a maximum differential in the group 45 to 54 years of age.

The intranational variation of excess male mortality is well illustrated by the occupational data for France given in Table 7. In very general terms, it is evident from these data that excessive male mortality occurs at a later age among the occupational groups of higher socioeconomic status. Thus, among teachers, managers, and technicians, excess male mortality is greatest between the ages of 55 and 64, whereas in most of the other occupational categories its peak occurs in the age group 45–54 years of age.

In Latin America, as in the more developed parts of the world, mortality rates for males have been consistently higher than those for females at any given age. The data do not always confirm this, but, considering their quality, and the weight of all the evidence, the statement seems to be valid. In contrast, it appears that in certain age groups female mortality exceeds male mortality, both in parts of Asia and in Northern Africa. In the latter, female mortality has been consistently found to be higher than male mortality in the age group 1–4 years, for reasons that no one has yet been able to explain fully. Only four Asian countries, all in the medium and high mortality ranges, provide sufficiently reliable data to demonstrate conclusively that female mortality exceeds male mortality, and in each case death rates for females are high enough to produce life expectancies that are lower than male ones. The four countries are India, Iraq, Pakistan, and Sabah (East Malaysia). The reasons for this phenomenon remain obscure but they seem to be rooted in cultural attitudes, discrimination against females, and particular hazards of childbirth in the prevailing circumstances. In the four countries just mentioned, female mortality is higher than male mortality at most or all ages. Otherwise, however, the common feature of recent data for most of Asia and Northern Africa is an excess of male over female

Table 7. France: Index of excess male mortality[a] by social category and age (married men and women), based on a sample of individuals followed since 1954.

Occupational category of husband	Age group (years)			
	35–44	45–54	55–64	65–74
Teachers	1.45	1.55	2.18	2.15
Senior management and professions	1.18	1.85	2.16	1.67
Lower management (public sector)	1.32	1.90	2.12	1.91
Technicians	1.52	1.62	2.17	1.70
Lower management (private sector)	1.74	1.99	2.22	2.10
Farmers	1.68	1.62	1.85	1.86
Foremen	0.92	2.20	1.93	1.56
Skilled workers (public sector)	1.42	2.13	2.12	1.94
Clerical workers (public sector)	1.71	1.99	1.97	1.67
Craftsmen and tradesmen	2.25	2.14	2.18	1.63
Clerical workers (private sector)	1.71	2.12	2.28	1.75
Semi-skilled workers (public sector)	1.61	2.10	2.04	1.64
Skilled workers (private sector)	1.68	1.82	2.08	1.76
Farm workers	1.30	1.71	1.69	1.65
Semi-skilled workers (private sector)	1.85	1.98	1.91	1.75
Unskilled workers	1.68	2.11	2.05	1.65

[a] For a given age group the index of excess mortality is obtained by calculating the ratio between the gross male mortality rate in that age group and the corresponding female rate.

Source: VALLIN J. Facteurs socio-économiques de la mortalité dans les pays développés (paper prepared for an international meeting on socioeconomic determinants and consequences of mortality, Mexico City, 19–25 June 1979).

mortality like that found in the more developed countries and Latin America. This raises doubts as to the authenticity of past observations which frequently showed higher mortality rates for females than for males, both in Asia and Northern Africa. It may be that excessive female mortality occurs only in conditions of relatively high mortality; on the other hand, the earlier figures may reflect differential inadequacies in older data or, conceivably, differences in the social status of females.

Reliable information on causes of death, particularly in respect of the recent past, comes almost exclusively from the more developed countries. Nevertheless, it is possible to draw some broad contrasts between the leading causes of death reported to WHO by selected groups of more and less developed countries (see Table 8). As a whole, the figures from the less developed countries are not as reliable as those from the more developed ones. Nearly all the data for the less developed countries come from the medium-to-low mortality countries of the Caribbean and Latin America. Nevertheless, the leading causes of death in those countries do not differ from those reported by the few African and Asian countries that provide reliable statistics. Consequently, the three leading causes of death given for each age category in Table 8 may be taken as implicitly indicative of broad differences in health status between the more developed countries and the more favoured countries in the less developed regions. Health differentials are implicit rather than explicit inasmuch as differences in the mortality levels are not always indicated by the leading causes of death, especially where these are the same for both groups of countries, as in the case of the age group 15–44 years.

Where accidents are among the three leading causes of death, it is generally true that

Table 8. Leading causes of death in a more developed and a less developed group of countries, as reported to WHO, most recent data (c. 1975).

Age group	More developed countries	Less developed countries
All ages	Heart diseases Malignant neoplasms Accidents	Heart diseases Malignant neoplasms Accidents
Under 1 year	Causes of perinatal mortality Congenital anomalies Influenza and pneumonia	Causes of perinatal mortality Enteritis and other diarrhoeal diseases Influenza and pneumonia
1–4 years	Accidents Congenital anomalies Malignant neoplasms	Influenza and pneumonia Accidents Congenital anomalies
5–14 years	Accidents Malignant neoplasms Congenital anomalies	Accidents Malignant neoplasms Influenza and pneumonia
15–44 years	Accidents Malignant neoplasms Heart diseases	Accidents Heart diseases Malignant neoplasms
46–64 years	Heart diseases Malignant neoplasms Accidents	Heart diseases Malignant neoplasms Accidents
65 years	Heart diseases Malignant neoplasms Influenza and pneumonia	Heart diseases Malignant neoplasms Influenza and pneumonia

Sources: WHO Data Bank for all age groups except infancy.

Fig. 9. Estimated percentage of deaths caused by infectious and parasitic diseases by level of life expectancy at birth, selected Latin American countries, *c.* 1965.

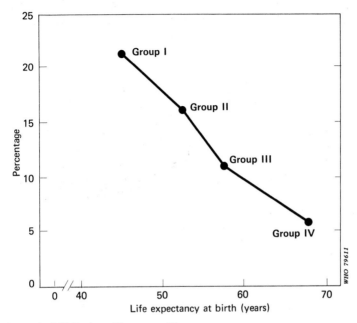

Group I: Bolivia, Guatemala, Haiti, Honduras, Nicaragua, and Paraguay.
Group II: Colombia, Costa Rica, Ecuador, El Salvador, Peru, and Dominican Republic
Group III: Brazil, Chile, and Mexico.
Group IV: Argentina, Cuba, Panama, Uruguay, and Venezuela.

Source: *Determinantes de la evolutión de la población. Mortalidad.* Santiago de Chile, CELADE, 1970.

they represent a significantly smaller proportion of all deaths in the less developed than in the more developed countries. This is because of the greater incidence of infectious, parasitic, and respiratory diseases in the less developed countries, which have been more thoroughly controlled or eliminated in the more developed ones.

The general relationship between the infectious diseases and levels of mortality may be illustrated by data for selected Latin American countries *c.* 1965 (see Fig. 9). These data show the improvement in health status, as measured by life expectancy at birth, than can be expected to accompany the reduction and control of infectious and parasitic diseases. It can be seen that as the percentage of deaths caused by these diseases diminishes from approximately 22% to 6% of all deaths, life expectancy increases from about 45 to 68 years. Obviously, other factors were also involved in the differential mortality, but the paramount fact remains that where the infectious, parasitic, and respiratory diseases are most prevalent, the health status of the population and life expectancy are lowest.

Mortality in the less developed regions is primarily associated with the excessive incidence of infectious, parasitic, and respiratory diseases. These diseases most profoundly affect the young, and one of the many disheartening features of the gap between health conditions in the more and the less developed regions is that children in the latter appear to have benefited less from general improvements in mortality than have their counterparts in the more developed regions. This is borne out by the higher mortality rates for children under 5 years of age in less developed countries as compared with rates for children of the same age in more developed countries where life expectancy at birth is the same. This difference stems from a series of poorly understood, perhaps unidentified, factors, among which the particular health risks associated with life in tropical regions undoubtedly play a major role. What we do know with a reasonable degree of certainty is that infant mortality rates in the countries of highest mortality are currently at least 20 times as high as they are in those of lowest mortality. Viewed in the light of global resources and knowledge, this is not only an unnecessary but an unpardonably disgraceful situation. It reflects a worldwide lack of commitment to the closing of the enormous health gap between the more and the less developed nations.

As regards the many diseases that plague the less developed countries, there appears to have been little or no progress in recent years in reducing either their incidence or their prevalence. This stands in sharp contrast to the apparent eradication of smallpox. To give but one example of the current states of affairs, the Bangladesh authorities estimate that 92% of the children in that country suffer from worm infestations. The threat posed by such diseases as malaria, schistosomiasis, filariasis, trypanosomiasis, leishmaniasis, cholera, and leprosy has either not lessened in recent years or has actually increased. The incidence of foodborne diseases, venereal diseases, and certain zoonoses similarly seems to be increasing. Most of these trends are discussed in some detail in other chapters. To the ravages of these diseases must also be added the debilitating and often fatal consequences of widespread nutritional deficiencies. Taken together, the malnutrition and the infectious, parasitic, and respiratory diseases that have been largely eliminated in the more developed countries are still the principal source of the suffering, disability, and death in the less developed regions. Inasmuch as the incidence of most of these conditions can be dramatically reduced at relatively modest cost, the suffering and death they cause must be accounted as unnecessary and preventable.

Perhaps the most interesting recent health trend in the more developed countries concerns the cardiovascular diseases. Of the countries for which there are time-series, these diseases appear to have increased only in Bulgaria, Czechoslovakia, Poland, and Yugoslavia, but even in these countries it is unclear just how much of the observed increases is real and how much stems from improvements in statistics on cause of death. During recent years, the general trend in the age group 35 years and over has been for mortality from cardiovascular disease to decline. The largest drop in death rates from the cardiovascular diseases occurred in Japan and the USA, in both of which the rates for males and females decreased by 17–22%. The reduction in deaths from these diseases appears to be strongly related to campaigns to alert people to their causes and to ways of preventing them. Campaigns designed to point out the dangers of smoking and improper dietary and exercise habits, and to identify and treat individuals at high risk, seem to have been particularly effective.

A discouraging feature of recent mortality data is not simply that the mortality rates for any given age cover a broad range but that the range has apparently been increasing. The international variations in infant and early childhood mortality rates are almost certainly greater now than ever before. In part, this may be because more rapid progress has been made in recent years at the lowest mortality level. In the few cases in the more developed countries in which perinatal and maternal mortality can be measured accurately, it is evident that the most rapid progress in reducing the mortality rate has also occurred in precisely those areas where it was already the lowest. The previously assumed "floor" for mortality rates is thus dropping continually, at a rather rapid pace, and the gap between the lowest and highest rates is consequently increasing. High perinatal and maternal mortality rates are, like all high mortality rates, becoming exclusively a problem of the poverty complex: they are highest among the poor, in particular high-parity, very young, or very old mothers, as a result of gestation and childbearing intervals that are shorter than optimum, and low general health and nutritional levels.

There are no discernible urban-rural differentials in mortality in the more developed countries. In the less developed countries, however, most evidence points to urban mortality being lower than rural mortality. Findings to the contrary can tentatively be attributed to either the quality of the data or lack of control for other variables. Thus, within a given level of aggregation, it would appear to be true that urban mortality is lower than rural, but if data were controlled for socioeconomic structure, different patterns might emerge. As regards the higher income groups, it may be assumed that the more ready access to health facilities enjoyed by those in urban areas gives them an advantage over their rural counterparts. On the other hand, however, it is probably true that the urban poor are worse off than the rural poor because of the higher risk of contracting disease in crowded areas and because of the notorious sanitation, health, and food supply problems in urban slums and squatter settlements.

All evidence points to urban-rural health differences being related primarily to the differing socioeconomic structure of the two types of area and to the fact that mortality levels vary inversely with socioeconomic status, the lower socioeconomic groups everywhere having the highest mortality. When urban-rural data are controlled for socioeconomic status, the urban-rural differentials all but disappear.

Socioeconomic differentials in mortality have been studied in detail in a relatively small number of countries, and there is a crying need for much more research into their determinants and consequences. Nevertheless, in very broad terms, it is clear that the relatively underprivileged in any society suffer from health risks and levels of mortality that are substantially greater than average. As may be seen in Table 8 and Fig. 9, the mortality experienced by the lowest of five socioeconomic groupings has been observed to be between about 20% and about 300% higher than that experienced by the highest-ranking grouping. These data apply to a different age groupings and cover only three "Western" countries and a combination of 12 Latin American countries. If other areas of the world could be included, it is likely that the range would be even wider. The data illustrated in Fig. 10 indicate that the greatest relative differentials in socioeconomic mortality operate during infancy. However, data from France and the USA suggest that the differentials, in relative terms are greater among certain adult age groups.

As important as the existence of differences that are often huge between socioeconomic groups within countries is the apparent recent trend in many countries for these differences to increase. In most of the developing countries where this seems to be happening, it can often be explained by class differentials in participation in medical advances and in national improvements in health services. It can also sometimes be argued that the evidence for the trend is spurious and can be accounted for by the changing quality or coverage of statistics. None of these arguments, however, can be used in such cases as those of England and Wales, France, and the USA (see Table 9 and Fig. 10, and satisfactory explanations are sorely needed. Data from France (see Table 10) clearly

Table 9. Socioeconomic differentials in selected countries: mortality of the lowest of five socioeconomic groupings expressed as a percentage of the mortality of the highest socioeconomic group

Country, age group, date	Both sexes	Male	Female
USA: Chicago (White population) Infants			
1940	(1.21)[a]	1.31	1.10
1960	(1.27)[a]	1.31	1.22
England and Wales Infants			
1949–1953	2.18		
1970–1971	2.65		
Age groups 15–20 to 64–65 years			
1949–1953		1.20	
1970–1971		1.78	
France Age group 40–55 years			
1955–1960		2.75	
1966–1971		3.27	
Age group 55–70 years			
1955–1960		1.75	
1966–1971		1.88	
12 Latin American countries First two years of life			
c. 1968–1970	*c.* 4.00		

[a] Figures in parentheses are the simple average of those for males and females.

Sources: VALLIN J. Facteurs socio-économiques de la mortalité dans les pays développés, and BEHM, H. Determinantes económicos y sociales de la mortalidad en America Latina (papers prepared for an international meeting on the socioeconomic determinants and consequences of mortality, Mexico City, 19–25 June 1979).

Fig. 10. Mortality by social class[a] and age, England and Wales, 1970–72.

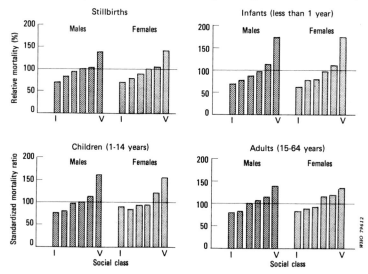

[a] Class I professional occupations; Class II=managerial and lower professional occupations; Class IIIN=skilled non-manual occupations; Class IIIM=skilled manual workers; Class IV=partly skilled occupations; Class V= unskilled workers. Ratios and proportions are based on the average mortality for each sex counted as 100.

Source: FOX, A. J. Prospects for measuring changes in differential mortality (paper prepared for an international meeting on socioeconomic determinants and consequences of mortality, Mexico City, 19–25 June 1979).

Table 10. Ratio of probability of death at 45–54 years for unskilled workers to that for senior managers, by cause of death and period, France, 1956–1960 and 1966–1971

Cause of death	1956–1960	1966–1971
Cardiovascular diseases	1.18	1.39
Cancer	1.96	2.30
Suicide	5.29	5.01
Accidents	4.38	4.38
Tuberculosis	6.50	9.41
Alcoholism and cirrhosis of the liver	8.26	10.90
Other causes and ill-defined causes	2.41	2.99
Total	2.55	3.03

Source: VALLIN, J. Facteurs socio-économiques de la mortalité dans les pays développés (paper prepared for an international meeting on the socioeconomic determinants and consequences of mortality, Mexico City, 19–25 June 1979).

indicate that changes in industrial safety have not played a part in recent trends in that country. The socioeconomic ratio for deaths caused by accidents remained constant from the late 1950s through the late 1960s. The ratio for deaths alone has declined, while those for the other causes listed have increased. It would be extremely useful to know precisely why in each instance—cardiovascular diseases, cancer, tuberculosis, and alcoholism and cirrhosis of the liver—the socioeconomic ratio of mortality has increased so significantly.

In less developed countries it is important to identify health differentials that can be reduced or eliminated by there are few countries for which this has been done with much precision. One dramatic example of relative health gaps between socioeconomic groups comes from a study carried out in Chile in the early 1970s in which an attempt was made to pinpoint specific health problem areas, (see Table 11). The data deal with post-neonatal mortality and show that what is termed "known avoidable mortality" accounts for about 75% of all deaths among children of white-collar workers and about 80% of all deaths among children of blue-collar workers. These percentages are somewhat deceptive inasmuch as they imply a relatively small socioeconomic differential. An examination of the ratio of blue-collar to white-collar death rates, however, shows that very large class differences exist. On the average, the mortality level for the blue-collar children is over three times that for the white-collar children, and the socioeconomic mortality ratio rises

Table 11. Post-neonatal mortality: Causes of death according to father's occupational group, Chile, 1972–1973

Group of causes of death	Mortality per 100 000 births among children of		
	White-collar workers (1)	Blue-collar workers (2)	Ratio (2)/(1)
Reducible mortality	937	3243	3.5
infectious etiology	385	1233	3.2
respiratory diseases	462	1683	3.6
malnutrition	41	227	5.6
accidents	49	100	2.0
Non-avoidable mortality	120	124	1.0
Ill-defined causes	136	589	4.3
Other causes	71	128	1.8
Total	1263	4083	3.2

Source: TAUCHER, E. Mortalidad infantil en Chile, tendencies, differenciales y causas, CELADE (Santiago) October, 1978.

through the infectious and parasitic diseases to reach a high point with malnutrition, the death rate for blue-collar workers from this cause being 5.6 times that for white-collar workers. A more unequivocal example of the vast inequalities in health would be hard to find.

By way of contrast, the Cuban example demonstrates how easily and quickly socioeconomic differentials (and, incidentally, urban-rural differentials) can be dramatically reduced, and perhaps practically eliminated, if the basic public health, medical, educational, nutritional, and environmental needs of all people are met. Almost all these needs can be met with modest investments if governmental priorities are set accordingly and the government's commitment is strong enough. But this may not be as easy as it seems, since individual governments are pushed and pulled in many directions by conflicting interests, many of which are not domestic but foreign. Aside from ideological and cultural forces, foreign governments, corporations, and lending institutions play a significant role in shaping domestic priorities in less developed countries through the conditions and incentives they attach to foreign trade and financial agreements and to various forms of aid, to mention only a few examples. From this standpoint, it is clear that the wealthy, more developed countries and the various institutions involved must shoulder some of the responsibility for the lack of progress in reducing levels of morbidity and mortality in the less developed countries and in reducing socioeconomic health differentials both in those countries and at home.

Chapter 4

Health Action

Health policy

Important developments in health policy and in the political climate in which health issues are being debated can be discerned in recent years. Discussion has ranged far beyond the domain of medical care, and health has come to be conceived as an essential part of human development. The subject has been debated within national ministries of health and health sectors, and in many countries the public at large has shown a growing interest in the organization of health-related matters, as have the mass media. At the international level, the debate has taken place not only in health organizations like WHO, but also within groupings of countries representing all shades of social and economic development and political opinion. These include, for example, the non-aligned countries movement, OAU, groupings of Latin American countries, the CMEA countries, the European Economic Community, and the OECD.

Health development has also been given increasing emphasis in the policies of a number of organizations and programmes of the United Nations system. One example is that of UNICEF, which has intensified its efforts in the field of health, particularly through its commitment to primary health care, and which maintains close liaison with WHO on policy issues in a Joint Committee on Health Policy. Another example is UNDP, which has shown a growing interest in health development, as has the World Bank. The latter has taken a major policy decision by agreeing to provide funds for the health component of economic development programmes, and it is giving serious consideration to extending this policy to the direct subvention of health programmes. UNFPA too has continued to recognize the importance of family health in its demographic policy. The implementation of the recommendations of the United Nations Water Conference concerning the provision of safe water supplies and sanitation for all by the year 1990 will have a profound influence on the promotion of health. The policy of UNEP for the protection of the human environment aims at promoting the quality of life of which health is an essential component and protecting the world against health hazards in the environment. The ILO programme includes promotion of the safety of the working environment and rehabilitation of the disabled, and the UNESCO programme of raising levels of literacy can have indirect but nonetheless powerful effects on the health of individuals and communities. Finally, the Economic and Social Council of the United Nations has had the opportunity of reviewing trends in health policy as they relate to policies in other social and economic sectors and as they reinforce one another in preparation for the New International Development Strategy.

In all the above forums, it has become clear that health development is not the affair of the traditionally defined health sector alone, but is closely interlinked with all aspects of social and economic development. It is now recognized that improvements in people's health status can only be reached as a result of appropriate national political will, the coordinate efforts of the health sector, and the relevant activities of other sectors concerned with social and economic development. Health development both contributes to and results from social and economic development; hence, health policies have to form a part of overall development policies, thus reflecting the social and economic goals of governments and people. It has been further understood that health programmes must then be devised to give effect to these policies and attain these goals, rather than being mere extensions of existing medical care services. Health services, in turn, have to be organized in such a way as to deliver these programmes.

The very concept of health development as distinct from the provision of medical care is a product of recent policy thinking. Through WHO in particular countries have elaborated a number of fundamental principles for health development. One is that governments have responsibility for the health of their people, and that at the same time people should have the right as well as the duty, individually and collectively, to participate in the development of their own health. Governments and the health professions also have the duty of providing the public with the information and social framework that will enable them to assume greater responsibility for their own health. These principles have led to the further principle of individual, community, and national self-determination and self-reliance in health matters. Self-reliance implies taking initiatives, determining what can be done without external resources when appropriate, and deciding when to seek external support, for what purposes and from what sources. National initiatives of this kind in health matters can lead to genuine cooperation between countries rather than dependence on the aid of others. Self-reliance is not synonymous with self-sufficiency, since no community or country can be self-sufficient as far as health development is concerned. On the contrary, an important part of recent health policy has been the realization of the interdependence of individuals, communities, and countries based on their common concern for health.

The distribution of resources affecting health has come under close scrutiny. This has led to the widespread acceptance of the need for a more equitable distribution of health resources within and among countries, including the preferential allocation of new resources to those in greatest social need so that the health system adequately covers all the population. Increasing emphasis is being laid on preventive measures well integrated with curative, rehabilitative, and environmental measures. Biomedical and health services research is undergoing critical analysis, and policies are emerging aimed at orienting such research more closely to the solution of problems that are highly relevant to people's priority needs. The importance is being highlighted of applying useful research findings as speedily as possible, since in many countries the application of existing knowledge would go a long way to improving the health status of the people. Health technology as such is undergoing critical analysis as part of a broader analysis of technology in general. The concept of appropriate technology for health has emerged, this being understood to mean a technology that is scientifically sound, adapted to local needs, acceptable to the community, maintained as far as possible by the people themselves in keeping with the principle of self-reliance, and capable of being applied with resources the community and the country can afford. Further, this technology has to be applied through well-defined health programmes delivered through a countrywide health system that incorporates the above concepts and that is based on primary health care and the support it receives from the other levels of the system. As for health manpower to plan and operate such health systems, new policies have emerged that emphasize the social orientation of health workers of all categories to serve people, and their technical training to provide people with the services planned for them.

The understanding of the broad concepts of public health outlined above, and the recognition that much more could be done to improve people's health with available knowledge and resources if only they were properly distributed, led the Thirtieth World Health Assembly in May 1977 to decide that the main social target of governments and of WHO in the coming decades should be the attainment by all the citizens of the world by the year 2000 of a level of health that will permit them to lead a socially and economically productive life. This will be remembered in the future as an outstanding decision in health policy, and as a dramatic political, social, economic, and technical challenge to mankind. The concept of social and economic productivity is based on the understanding that human energy is the most important motive force for development and that health is the key to generating the human energy required for development. The road to health and the road to development are the same.

A further landmark in the development of health policy was the International Conference on Primary Health Care which took place in September 1978 in Alma-Ata, USSR. This Conference, and in particular the Declaration of Alma-Ata which it adopted, clearly stated that primary health care is the key to attaining the target of health for all by the year 2000 as part of overall development and in the spirit of social justice. The Declaration called on all governments to formulate national policies, strategies, and plans of action to launch and sustain primary health care as part of a comprehensive national health system and in coordination with other sectors. The Declaration also called for urgent and effective international—in addition to national—action to develop and implement primary health care throughout the world.

It has become increasingly clear over these last years that health for all has meaning only *within* countries. However, international collaboration and support is needed to meet this worldwide social goal. In view of this, and in keeping with the policy of basing international action on countries' real needs, the strategies should be formulated first and foremost by the countries themselves. Each country will have to develop its health policies in the light of its own problems and possibilities, particular circumstances, social and economic structures, and political and administrative mechanisms. Among the crucial factors affecting realization of these goals are: appropriate political commitment; various social considerations, not the least of which is community participation; administrative reforms that may be required; financial implications; and basic legislation. In short, health and related reforms will be required if an acceptable level of health for all is to be achieved by the year 2000. Regional and global strategies will have to be developed by countries collectively on the basis of national strategies and plans of action, and in support of them.

In formulating and implementing strategies of health for all, technical cooperation among developing countries is an important policy factor. By means of such cooperation, countries will be able to express their self-reliance in health matters. They will be able to undertake cooperative activities and joint measures in such areas as health manpower development; biomedical and health services research, including psychosocial and economic aspects; the exchange of information and experience on health care; the production, procurement, and distribution of essential drugs and medical equipment; and the development and construction of health facilities, such as low-cost drinking water supply and waste disposal systems, health centres, hospitals, laboratories, and training institutions. Countries will have to reach agreement on policies concerning, for example, production, quality control, pricing, export, and import relating to such commodities as essential drugs, vaccines, food, prophylactic, diagnostic, and therapeutic substances, equipment, and supplies. Cooperative relationships may also have to be reached with social and economic organizations and enterprises whose activities have implications for health.

It can be seen that in recent years many refreshing health and related socioeconomic policies have been defined and adopted by people and countries, as well as internationally by WHO and other international agencies. In the process, WHO has emerged stronger than ever before as a major factor in health development throughout the world, in keeping with its constitutional mandate of acting as the directing and coordinating authority on international health work as a cooperative effort of its Member States. A start has been made in giving effect to the policies outlined above. The full implementation of these policies will help to bring about the social revolution in public health advocated by the Director-General of the World Health Organization in 1976 in his address to the Twenty-ninth World Health Assembly.

National health planning and country health programming

General considerations

Most countries now prepare national, regional, and sectoral plans covering one or several years. Although the health sections of these plans tend to concentrate upon the work of the ministries of health, other sections deal with such important health-related areas as agriculture and nutrition, water and sanitation, and education and social welfare.

Here, attention will be paid primarily to some selected planning issues in the context of the activity of ministries of health.

A special difficulty in planning the health sector has been that, while it is quite possible to measure health service inputs in terms of money, buildings, and manpower, there is as yet no convenient methodology for measuring the output of improved health itself in response to those inputs, especially in countries with weak health and other statistical systems. It then becomes necessary to make additional use of output, as measured in terms of the volume, type, and distribution of services offered and taken up, as the next best available indicator of health. This is not to say that considerations relating to the quality and effect of the health care being offered (outcomes) need be discarded, but only that the volume, type, and utilization of these services constitute the best means at present available in most developing countries for measuring at least the potential output of health itself.

Data needs

The question of improved data for planning is of great importance. If a country's health service is to be geared to serving the population as a whole, it should be developed in accordance with existing disease patterns and the possibilities for acting on them. The fact that the development of health services, and thus the health plan, should ideally be in keeping with the disease pattern of the nation does not mean that in most countries the primary data requirement for improved health planning would be additional or improved disease statistics, though these may be very useful and in some cases essential.

In contrast to the relatively large volume of work which goes into disease statistics there is the unsatisfactory situation with regard to relevant economic, financial, and health manpower data, as well as information on the utilization of health service facilities by different sections of the population.

Gaps in the disease statistics need not defer the further development of appropriate health services; in very few countries would there be so little data of this sort available as to prevent substantial progress being made with the development of reasonable and substantially improved health plans. It must be stressed that what should be aimed for are minimum levels of data, directed to the necessary prerequisites for the health plan.

Developing a country health programme

The procedure for the development of a country health programme is seen as the systematic identification of priority health and health-related problems in a country; the specification of objectives for the reduction of these problems, including the establishment of specific targets; the identification of strategies that will lead to the attainment of the objectives and the translation of such strategies into health development programmes. Particular stress is laid on the intersectoral approach to ensure that health problems are tackled with the support of, and in collaboration with, activities in other social and economic sectors. The process is a continuing one, including the implementation of health development programmes as soon as feasible, their ongoing evaluation, and reprogramming when necessary.

Finally, the close interrelationship between programming, project formulation, project management, and any health policy formulation warrants their inclusion in the country health programming process as a single continuous entity.

Current activities

Country health programming (CHP) was first introduced in Bangladesh in 1973 as a collaborative effort between the national authorities and WHO. Following the Bangladesh experience, 24 countries initiated the CHP process in the period covering 1973 to 1977. In addition, 9 countries initiated various CHP activities during 1978.

The countries listed in the following table are at various stages of the CHP cycle.

WHO Region[1]	1973	1974	1975	1976	1977	1978
Africa			Congo	Cape Verde Guinea-Bissau Nigeria Uganda	Angola Madagascar Mozambique	Gambia Namibia Upper Volta Zambia
South-East Asia	Bangladesh	Nepal Thailand	Burma		Bangladesh[a]	Sri Lanka
Europe			Algeria			Spain Switzerland
Eastern Mediterranean		Afghanistan	Sudan	Yemen	Iraq	Democratic Yemen
Western Pacific			Laos	Fiji	Papua New Guinea Samoa Solomon Islands	Philippines

[a] Second CHP effort leading to the completion of the programming phase.

[1] A process similar to, but not identical with, CHP has been conducted in many countries of the Americas. More recently, e.g., in Honduras, the process has coincided with the CHP process.

Overall assessment

Two interregional seminars (New Delhi, 1975 and Bangkok, 1977) offered an opportunity to review accumulated experience and knowledge on methods and practice of CHP in different countries. The following preliminary conclusions can be drawn.

– Health plans and programmes are now drafted as integral parts of national socioeconomic development plans. There is a growing realization in the national economic planning boards that public health benefits from, but also contributes to, overall development.

– Consequently, there is a growing tendency to plan and programme in a multidisciplinary way within the health sector and, more significantly perhaps, with the participation of other sectors. Participating sectors often include the education, public information, agriculture, public works, and water boards. During the formulation of major health programmes, it is imperative to have various ministry and agency representatives in the planning group to ensure that the health action prescribed is consistent with and supported by other development plans.

– One significant effect of this has been the growing consideration given to comprehensive packages for community development. These schemes are liable to attract considerable internal and external funding to a much greater extent than any number of isolated development projects.

– The emphasis placed on achieving self-reliance is reflected in the fact that increasingly serious attempts are made to select and adapt the local health and relevant technology that is most appropriate; i.e., inexpensive to obtain, practical to apply to great numbers, and easy to maintain.

– The application of planning methods in an objective, rational, and cohesive way may have helped some administrations to realize that this approach is needed on a periodical or continuous basis in order to assess, evaluate, and reorient all health work. The effect has been to foster sound management practices in the everyday implementation of programmes.

– Regarding organizational requirements in support of CHP, some countries have come to realize that traditional planning units should be replaced by multidisciplinary, multisectoral teams that will play an extensive managerial role in coordinating the work, assess and study the effects of planning, programming, and budgeting, and carry out programme evaluation. For this, permanent mechanisms in the form of centres for health development are being set up.

While the above features are common to a number of country health programming ventures, this does not mean that these have been identical in all countries. In fact, countries' responses have been quite dissimilar in every case. Many countries have expressed an interest in the training of their executives in CHP, and 35 workshops—the majority in countries, some in WHO settings—have been organized for the purpose. While some countries have been successful in applying the CHP approach, others have reacted rather cautiously. Countries which have traditionally been thinking along the lines of resource planning, and for which development has meant more resources of the traditional types, could not be expected to adhere overnight to the principle of management by objectives whereby the relevance of any type of resources in the face of national priorities can be objectively questioned. The CHP approach may call for changes in many aspects of ongoing activities, and not all activities and all administrations can be equally ready to sustain the challenge. Several countries are nevertheless fully at home with CHP processes with increasingly encouraging results. Countries such as Bangladesh, Burma, Nepal, and Thailand have, for instance, formulated in detail a considerable number of integrated programmes (8–12 in each case), which form the health sectors' contribution to the national development plan. These have attracted strong internal support and funding from internal sources as well as external cooperation agencies. Sri Lanka has recently engaged in a similar effort.

In the African and European Regions too, experience has been different in each case. While the methodological and training aspects are of interest to an increasing number of countries, some have only undertaken the formulation of country health plans, while others have adapted principles and techniques as seemed appropriate. Some have attempted the CHP approach in a number of major programmes (Algeria), others in provinces where the need seemed particularly great (Portugal and Spain). In Africa the approach has produced a comprehensive health plan in some places (Cape Verde, Gambia, Guinea-Bissau, Upper Volta) while in others attention and investment have been concentrated on one crucial aspect of basic health services (Nigeria).

Mention should also be made of Sudan with its integrated primary health care programme, Yemen with its health plan, and Pakistan with its population and family health programmes.

Health legislation

Interest in health legislation as one of the key elements in international and national health action is no new phenomenon; as long ago as 30 January 1909, the Director of one of WHO's predecessor organizations, the Office International d'Hygiène Publique, addressed a circular to the health authorities of the States that had signed the Rome Arrangement of 9 December 1907 requesting them to transmit to the Office copies of their laws, regulations, ordinances, decrees, and circulars dealing with the general organization of their health services, the measures they had adopted to control communicable diseases, the organization of their port health services, and the organization and regulation of urban and rural medical care. Was this interest in health legislation justified? Can any reckoning be made of the contribution of health legislation to personal and environmental health services in recent decades? These are formidable questions, if only because health legislation is no more than a tool for the realization of a given health policy; it is self-evident that the mere adoption of a law or decree will achieve nothing unless the will and resources exist to ensure its implementation. And yet a most significant response to the questions was provided in a recent editorial in one of the most respected medical journals: "Public-health legislation and related measures have probably done more than all the advances of scientific medicine to promote the well-being of the community in Britain and in most other countries".[1]

The period 1973–1977 was extraordinarily rich in developments in the health legislation field at both the international and national levels, although clearly the impact of the legislation introduced during the period on the health of the community cannot yet be calculated. Much of the legislation was of course, in such key areas as communicable disease control, sanitation and water supply, and food and drugs. Many of the developing countries do have such legislation but, because of lack of resources and an adequate infrastructure, it cannot be fully implemented.

Although each country enacts legislation in accordance with its own historical, legal, and cultural traditions, all countries face common problems in designing and drafting appropriate legislation. Implementation appears to be the single most difficult problem related to health legislation. One of the challenges of the international community in coming decades will be how to cooperate with the developing countries in seeking solutions to the problems of legislative enforcement and other problems in health legislation: the multiplicity of ministries and other agencies that may be concerned; the special difficulties that may arise in countries with a federal structure, where jurisdiction over health matters may be divided between the central government and the governments of subnational entities; the lack of sufficient trained legal draftsmen with a knowledge of the health sector; the existence of a body of health laws inherited from the colonial era that cannot be readily amended or replaced for various reasons, including the slowness of the legislative process; the lack of an adequate scientific data base for the development of environmental health legislation and standards adapted to national needs; and so on.

International aspects

It has been observed that in recent decades numerous regulatory regimes have emerged at the international level in such widely differing fields as telecommunications, aviation, health, food, and meteorology. The resultant rules and regulations are intended for application at the national level.

Can one then talk of a body of "international health law"? If "health" is interpreted in the sense understood by the framers of WHO's Constitution, the answer must today be a clearcut "yes". International health law is, of course, closely linked with the vast and rapidly growing body of international environmental law, international population law, some aspects of international law on human rights, those aspects of international labour

---

[1] *Lancet*, **2**: 354–355 (1978).

law that deal with occupational health, and the international regime for the control of narcotics and psychotropic substances.

Before turning to international legal instruments as such, it is important to stress the impetus given to national health legislation by specific resolutions of the World Health Assembly and the Executive Board. Certain reports of WHO expert committees have also had a clear impact on health legislation.

In 1976, one of the major components of what has been termed the "international bill of human rights", namely the International Covenant on Economic, Social and Cultural Rights, came into force (having received the necessary number of ratifications by Member States of the United Nations). Its Article 12, based on WHO's Constitution, prescribes that:

"1. The States Parties to the present Covenant recognize the right of everyone to the enjoyment of the highest attainable standard of physical and mental health.

"2. The steps to be taken by the States Parties to the present Covenant to achieve the full realization of this right shall include those necessary for:

(*a*) The provision for the reduction of the stillbirth-rate and of infant mortality and for the healthy development of the child;
(*b*) The improvement of all aspects of environmental and industrial hygiene;
(*c*) The prevention, treatment and control of epidemic, endemic, occupational and other diseases;
(*d*) The creation of conditions which would assure to all medical service and medical attention in the event of sickness".

Another United Nations instrument that has come into force (on 16 August 1976) is the Convention on Psychotropic Substances, 1971. The 1972 Protocol amending the Single Convention on Narcotic Drugs, 1961, entered into force on 8 August 1975. Mention should also be made of the Universal Declaration on the Eradication of Hunger and Malnutrition (endorsed by the United Nations General Assembly on 17 December 1974) and the Declaration on the Rights of Disabled Persons (proclaimed by the General Assembly on 9 December 1975). The International Year of the Child, 1979, the International Year for Disabled Persons, 1981, the current work in the General Assembly on the Draft Convention on the Elimination of Discrimination Against Women (which includes specific health-related provisions), and the continuing discussions at the Third United Nations Conference on the Law of the Sea (where a consensus now appears to have been reached on the pollution control provisions), will undoubtedly have a considerable impact on national legislation in the particular sectors covered. Certain United Nations Conferences held in recent years have called for legislative reforms at the national level. This was the case with the Stockholm Conference on the Human Environment (1972), the Bucharest World Population Conference (1974), the World Conference of the International Women's Year in Mexico City (1975), the United Nations Conference on Human Settlements (HABITAT) in Vancouver (1976), and the United Nations Water Conference in Mar del Plata (1977).

Of the various organizations within the United Nations system, ILO has continued its traditional work in the development of conventions and recommendations. Three significant new conventions are the Occupational Cancer Convention, 1974, the Working

Environment (Air Pollution, Noise and Vibration) Convention, 1977, and the Nursing Personnel Convention, 1977. UNEP has made extensive use of its mandate to develop (with the assistance of WHO and other agencies) regional activities for environmental management, including the necessary legal instruments; the entry into force (on 12 February 1978) of the Convention for the Protection of the Mediterranean Sea against Pollution and the adoption (on 24 April 1978) of the Kuwait Regional Convention for Co-operation on the Protection of the Marine Environment from Pollution testify to the success of UNEP's approach, which is now being applied in other regions, including the Gulf of Guinea, the Caribbean, and the South-East and South-West Pacific subregions. Many other environmental protection conventions have been concluded for other regions through direct cooperation between the States concerned or under the auspices of regional or other international organizations; for example, a Regional Convention on the Protection of the Red Sea and Gulf of Aden Environment is in preparation, under the auspices of the Arab League Educational, Cultural and Scientific Organization.

As regards nongovernmental organizations, the number concerned with (*inter alia*) promoting appropriate health legislation at the national level is substantial. Among the most influential are the World Medical Association (particularly in the field of medical ethics, in which it has worked in close collaboration with WHO and CIOMS), the International Planned Parenthood Federation (for all aspects of family health), the International Advisory Committee on Population and Law, the International Council of Environmental Law, Rehabilitation International (in the field of legislation for the disabled), the International Commission on Radiological Protection (whose Publication 26 will no doubt lead to significant changes in national legislation), and the newly established International Commission for Protection against Environmental Mutagens and Carcinogens.

National legislation

Significant developments in health legislation at the national level can be reported for the period 1973–1977. As health policies have changed, so (in most cases) has the corresponding legislation. As the developing countries in particular move towards the goal of health for all by the year 2000, they will increasingly find themselves in need of new legislative instruments that are in harmony with their stated programme objectives. This is equally true for legislation on pharmaceuticals, health manpower, traditional medicine, environmental health, health planning, mental health, and a number of other health-related subjects. Some of the new legislation now on the statute book or likely to be enacted in the next few years will deal with areas of preventive medicine that were not previously the concern of the legislator. Cautionary notes have been sounded as to the possible impact of such legislation on personal liberties. If the Government is too interventionist, it could be regarded as interfering with the liberty of the individual to do as he sees fit with his own life and health. If it is non-interventionist, it could be accused of dereliction of duty. The problem reflects a fundamental dilemma of democratic society. But preventive medicine has always involved some limitation of the liberty of the individual, often for his own good, often for that of the community, and often for both. For example, quarantine laws at ports of entry have been recognized and accepted for centuries.

Except possibly in such areas as road accident prevention and the control of smoking, the new types of health legislation will not—and indeed cannot—be expected to result in a dramatic reduction of mortality and morbidity, and excessive expectations as to the likely effects on the health of the community are unjustified.

The importance of health and the quality of life as national goals of prime importance is increasingly reflected in the incorporation of provisions on health and environmental protection in national constitutions. The adoption of comprehensive public health acts or codes (or the updating of obsolescent texts) is also common; thus, comprehensive laws on environmental protection are being adopted in countries at all stages of development.

While descriptive and analytical surveys of legislation on such relatively recondite issues as organ transplantation or the criteria for death are commonly encountered in the medicolegal literature, this is not the case for the core of public health, i.e., the actual organization and planning of health services and resources. And yet it is in this area that the exchange and sharing of experiences could perhaps be most fruitful. It is clear that many countries introduced substantial changes in their national legislation on health care delivery during the period 1973–1977. There are already signs of increasing attention on the part of legislators and health ministries to ensuring primary health care (backed up by appropriate referral systems), in particular for their rural populations. One frequent problem has been that of improving health services while at the same time holding down expenditure. Legislation on what is now termed "cost containment" has been enacted in a number of countries; some have, in fact, introduced stringent limits on the installation of new and costly health facilities. At the same time, there has been growing attention to disadvantaged segments of the population, such as the aged and the handicapped, as well as to the special problems of women and their dual role as providers and beneficiaries of health services. While the impact of laws on genetic counselling to prevent congenital disabilities is unlikely to be dramatic, the same is not true if and when drastic measures are taken to prevent road accidents associated with, on the one hand, alcohol and drugs and, on the other hand, failure to use (for example) seat belts or crash helmets.

The questions of disease and disability are, of course, intimately linked with social security, particularly its health insurance component. The ILO conventions on social security and, at a regional level, the European Convention on Social Security (concluded under the auspices of the Council of Europe) have certainly contributed to some harmonization of national policies in this field.

In the planning of health and, particularly, hospital services, more and more attention is being paid to the humanization of the environment in which the patient or disabled person is accommodated. The same applies to the right to die in dignity, the criteria for death, and the rights of patients (and healthy subjects) involved in biomedical and behavioural experimentation (the World Medical Association's Declaration of Helsinki, as amended by the World Medical Assembly in Tokyo in 1975, is having an increasing influence on national legislation in this field). The civil liability of physicians using new methods of treatment has also received attention, as have the special problems of research on biologicals, transplantation, and the confidentiality of medical data (a subject on which many countries are now promulgating legislation, usually designed to protect patients' rights while at the same time allowing the collection of epidemiologically significant information). It is perhaps in the fields of cancer and mental illness that the problems may be most acute.

Turning now to the field of family health, it is safe to say that attention in the medicolegal literature has tended to focus mainly on those issues that have bioethical implications rather than on the key problems of the delivery of services, although much national legislation has of course been promulgated to cope with these problems. In some countries, highly innovative approaches have been adopted. The literature on the legal aspects of such subjects as abortion, sterilization, and family planning has attained substantial dimensions and the number of national, regional, and international meetings devoted to these and allied subjects is legion. Legislation on menstrual regulation and on education on population and sexual matters has also been reviewed. In Europe, an attempt has now been made to analyse the impact of such legislation (as well as family law in general) on fertility trends. Reference should also be made in this context to the special problems that apply to children and adolescents.

In the field of mental health, reference should be made to a WHO study that has revealed the need for laws and regulations to be brought into harmony with programme objectives. Comparative studies have also been published on legislation dealing with the control of alcoholism. The whole question of the rights of mental patients, including their right to treatment, has received attention both in national legislation and in the medico-legal literature. Some comparative surveys of pharmaceutical legislation have also been published in recent years, although none presents a fully satisfactory picture of the global situation in this key area. Related to pharmaceuticals, of course, is the problem of cosmetics, to which considerable attention has been paid in recent years. Numerous countries are introducing legislation on this subject, and some uniformity of approach can now be discerned. In part of the European Region this uniformity is of course due to the promulgation by the Council of the European Communities of its 1976 Directive on cosmetic products.

Medical devices, too, have been the subject of intense regulatory activity in recent years. While classical-type regulations on poisons have continued to be promulgated in many countries, there has been a clear trend towards the regulation of a wider range of toxic and hazardous substances than in the past.

In the disease control field, regulatory action has, as in previous periods of WHO's history, been intense. A comparative survey of venereal disease legislation was published by WHO;[1] new legislation on the control of these diseases was promulgated in several countries. There was substantial legislative activity aimed at controlling the more important zoonoses. Lassa fever, Marburg disease, viral haemorrhagic fever, and certain other diseases became notifiable in a number of countries. With the final eradication of smallpox, several countries terminated or suspended their routine vaccination require-(on, for example, immunization against rubella and for rhesus incompatibility).

Cigarette smoking is still as important a cause of death as were the great epidemic diseases of the past. Many countries are responding to the challenge by introducing legislation to cope with what has been described as the "smoking epidemic".

Cancer would not appear to be the type of disease that is amenable to legislative control. Yet better data concerning its epidemiology could certainly assist in developing

---

[1] *Venereal disease control. A survey of recent legislation.* Geneva, World Health Organization. Reprint from *International digest of health legislation,* **26** (1): 1–44 (1975).

long-term strategies, if only by identifying putative carcinogens and risk factors. The classification of cancer as a notifiable disease (as has been done in several countries) may be one strategy for obtaining better statistics. An interesting example of international collaboration in the cancer control field was the Agreement Concerning Technical and Scientific Collaboration in the Field of Research on Malignant Tumours.[1]

Turning now to the human environment, it is clear that the impetus given to legislation in this field by the 1972 Stockholm Conference has been enormous. "Kogai"—the Japanese term for environmental pollution used in what appears to have been the first comprehensive law on pollution control—is now being controlled with varying degrees of vigour in developed and developing countries alike. Environmental protection has, indeed, become one of the areas in which international cooperation is most pronounced. It is not without interest that the States participating in the 1975 Conference on Security and Co-operation in Europe agreed to cooperate on the "study and development of criteria and standards for various environmental pollutants and regulation regarding production and use of various products" as well as on "legal and administrative measures for the protection of the environment including procedures for establishing environmental impact assessments". The environment has become a subject of interest to legislators and politicians—a positive development since it is they who will have to pass the requisite laws.

National legislation in many aspects of environmental protection has been greatly influenced by WHO's work as well as the activities of other organizations, notably the European Economic Community (whose environment programme for 1977–1981 calls for an ambitious legislative strategy), CMEA, OECD, UNEP, ECE (which has established a body known as the Senior Advisers to ECE Governments on Environmental Problems), and ESCAP (under whose auspices an intergovernmental meeting on environmental legislation was held in Bangkok in July 1978). Space constraints prevent any discussion of the massive amount of regulatory activity during the period 1973–1977 dealing with such problems as water, air, and soil pollution, toxic chemicals, nuclear power generation, waste management, protection against ionizing and nonionizing radiations, noise and vibrations, pesticides, the occupational environment (an area in which both ILO and WHO have been active in developing the necessary scientific and administrative framework for appropriate legislation), and the domestic environment. What is clear is that, as new data are generated, as for example by the WHO Environmental Health Criteria Programme, they will almost certainly be incorporated in national standards. Some uniformity of approach in the occupational and environmental health areas is clearly desirable, if only to prevent the "export" of hazardous industries from the developed to the developing countries where stringent standards are nonexistent or unenforceable.

Health care delivery systems

In principle, the objective of comprehensive health care delivery systems is to provide services to deal with existing health problems through the best utilization of the available

---

[1] See *International digest of health legislation*, **29**: 149 (1978).

resources. Thus national health care delivery systems should be measured against the following criteria: (i) impact on the health problems of the population; (ii) coverage of population in relationship to allocated resources; (iii) efficiency of services in attaining objectives at minimum possible cost; (iv) the effectiveness of activities that are health-related, though not carried out by the health services.

As a rule, only a small part of the overall morbidity in most countries requires the intervention of highly specialized medical care services. A somewhat larger proportion of health problems require general medical care services. The majority of prevailing health complaints can be satisfactorily dealt with through adequate primary care, supported by appropriate technology, and by people themselves through guided self-care. However, in most countries the major health care effort is still being directed towards the development of highly sophisticated medical services. This leads to a disequilibrium in the types and distribution of the services provided, with too much emphasis on acute institutional care and little on more essential care of large segments of the population, on continuing community care of the chronically ill and disabled, or on preventive and promotive services. Such a situation prevents the achievement of budgetary efficiency, as highly specialized, highly technical, and sometimes commercialized curative medical care for a small number of selected patients receives the bulk of available funds and personnel. In more affluent countries such a disequilibrium is "compensated for" by the rising cost of medical care. However, in countries with more limited resources it obstructs the development of priority areas of health care, thereby preventing the health services from making a more positive contribution to the health of the population.

With regard to the difficulties encountered in developing and operating health care delivery systems, as indicated by country reports, the following overall conclusions can be drawn.

The existing distribution of health care facilities is very uneven and, in many countries, expansion of services still goes on mainly in urbanized areas, leaving much of the population without any services or with only ineffective and inadequate ones.

The absence of regional networks with proper referral links between different-level facilities leads to underutilization at the periphery and overutilization at the centre, as the population bypasses simpler (or inadequate) levels of care in direct search of more sophisticated facilities.

Major difficulties in the functioning of health care facilities are found to arise from the lack of specific definitions of promotive, preventive, curative, rehabilitative, and supportive functions for each level of care, the resulting misuse of complex facilities for primary care purposes, and the undue fragmentation of health programmes as different teams and facilities are established for various kinds of health problems.

In staffing health care facilities the main problems seem to arise from the lack of appropriately trained personnel, aggravated by maldistribution and a combination of education and specialization that is inappropriate for the tasks to be performed.

Important difficulties arise from the general lack of encouragement for management training at all levels and the lack of a proper definition of roles and career structures.

The lack of simple, low-cost materials and methods designed for, and adapted to, local conditions aggravates present difficulties.

In the maintenance of health care facilities major difficulties are caused in some countries by the use of mixed equipment and material drawn from different sources, often without back-up or spare parts; the lack or inefficiency of repair workshops, with maintenance confined to major health care facilities and, even there, consisting primarily of emergency repair without preventive measures; and in some cases the "drain" of already insufficient technical and maintenance personnel from health to other fields offering more incentives.

Some of the main problems of economic support to health care delivery systems arise not only from limited resources but also from poor coordination of different sources of funds, inappropriate allocation of funds within the health sector, lack of incentives for cost containment and control, and insufficient attention to the interrelationship between investment and running costs, with too much emphasis on investment costs.

Growing awareness of the problems listed above is, in fact, evident among Member States; however, it is still fragmentary and often powerless against strong traditions and erroneous concepts that can lead only to costly or inadequate "solutions", and against pressure groups working to protect vested interests.

In recent years some essential steps have been taken towards a better understanding of the problems involved in developing the various components of health services and integrating them in a balanced manner, in accordance with the needs and possibilities of each country, and ways in which these problems can be solved. The organizational study on methods of promoting the development of basic health services (1973) and the joint UNICEF/WHO study on alternative approaches to meeting basic health needs of populations in developing countries (1974) were important turning-points. They showed clearly that conventional health care delivery systems, as developed in some affluent countries, are unlikely to provide a suitable model for other countries as the solutions they imply are too costly and, therefore, irrelevant. In fact, they often exacerbate existing inequities in the distribution of health services. Partly on the basis of these studies, Member States have developed a global programme aimed at the development and extension of primary health care to all populations and the simultaneous evolution of a scientifically sound technology, feasible in terms of cost, manpower, application, and local production and acceptable to the providers and to the public. The studies also drew attention to the fact that some countries have attained a more equitable distribution of less costly health services. The experiences of such countries are valuable with regard to the adaptation and wider application of appropriate health technologies and organizational solutions.

Other studies based on international comparisons have also contributed to a better understanding of the interrelationships between needs, resources, and use of health services, and their implications for the development of national health care delivery systems. More knowledge has also become available on international trends in the development of some important components of health care delivery systems, such as hospital-based medical services and maternal and child health care services. In view of the increasing concern of developing countries with building up a physical infrastructure for health care delivery, usually under the stimulus of national health planning or country health programming, a global study of the subject has been undertaken by WHO. This is based on the analysis of existing problems and a search for suitable solutions with the aim of evolving clear and practical guidelines on all phases of the provision of health care facilities in developing areas, from area-wide planning to equipment, staffing, administration, and operation. In order to rationalize economic support to health care delivery systems, WHO has also initiated a wide programme of technical cooperation, with specific provision for research and testing, in the development of national policies for the financing of health services.

In spite of encouraging signs that an increasing number of countries are beginning to realize the importance of suitable permanent structures for the delivery of primary health care to their entire population, the best ways of assisting them to do so have still to be agreed upon. Results in this area are often not easily discernible, and quick results cannot be expected because of the nature of the problems involved. The creation of a service infrastructure for the delivery of a number of health programmes of necessity takes several years, and there may be a strong temptation to try to bypass this infrastructure in the hope of speedy and dramatic results. There are many instances of early successes gained in this way which later proved only temporary. The immensity of the problem, which involves so many political, economic, and social factors, may discourage a number of Member States from grappling with it as thoroughly as they should. From country reports, it emerges that three aspects of the development of health care delivery systems are a source of particular concern. They may be broadly summarized as follows:

the *distribution* of health care, including the desire for universal coverage, and accessibility in the widest social, cultural, economic, and geographical sense;

participation, i.e., community participation in the entire development process, including attention to the perceived needs of the population, control over the allocation of local resources, and community accountability;

greater *rationality*, in the sense of relevant planning and programming, flexibility to meet changing needs and future developments, reliability and soundness of the solutions adopted and of the planning process itself, and efficiency of the system as expressed in terms of reasonable quality; the aim should be to achieve a proper balance between need and supply, centralization and decentralization, and costs and effects, and greater manageability of the whole system of health care delivery, including referral.

Organization

Major trends in national systems of health care delivery today are towards public financing and tighter organization, integration and regionalization that will reduce fragmentation and duplication in health services, and more equal access to a comprehensive range of services linked by more efficient health information systems.

(a) Integration

In recent years there has been an acceleration in the rate of organizational change in national health services. This has been accompanied by increases in the size of these services as a result of the incorporation of individual service units into the larger entity of the national health care delivery system. Furthermore, as health care systems form parts of social systems that are themselves in a state of change, concepts of health needs and demands are changing, together with the ways in which these needs and demands are met. Changes in the social system also generally lead to increased government involvement and, partly as a result of political pressures, a more careful examination of the relevance and cost of health care.

One important reason for organizing health care as a single whole is economic. The increasing financial means required to cover current expenditure and new investments now come more frequently from public sources. The allocation of funds among the functional service units involved in the health care delivery system can therefore be viewed as a single transfer payment. Health care thus becomes one sector of a whole range of collective services. The percentage of the national income that can be made available for health care comes under the pressure of governmental budgeting, and the final allocation depends on the priority given to health care within the socioeconomic policy of the country. This means that scarce health resources (scarce at least in relation to demand) come under additional pressures requiring that they be used as rationally as possible. For instance, lowering costs in the hospital services for acute care is increasingly being regarded as the most significant means of reducing the total cost of medical care. In developing countries this is most likely to mean holding the inpatient acute bed/population ratio constant. The reduction of costly inpatient services appears to be mainly a matter of substitution—for instance, the simultaneous expansion of less costly sources for extended care or for ambulatory, domiciliary, and primary health care. Recent experience shows, however, that real savings from a reduction in hospital inpatient utilization can only be achieved if these alternative forms of care not only replace some proportion of the care provided on an inpatient basis, but also if there is a simultaneous relative reduction in the available inpatient facilities. The chances of success thus increase with greater freedom to reallocate funds among the various service units that comprise the health care delivery system.

So far the initiative for changing the health care delivery system has come principally from governments. In most countries not enough effort has been made to involve consumers and health workers in the organization of health care delivery as a system. However, organizational change cannot be effected by governmental initiative alone. Although the viability of organizational change will depend upon economic and social circumstances, it also appears that the necessary initiative for it depends on obtaining sufficient cooperation between health management and policy makers, supported by a competent technical group large enough to take the initiative and shoulder the responsibility. From the longitudinal standpoint, even this seems to be insufficient. The will to change of the initiating group must be strong enough, and sufficiently widespread, for the initiative to be translated into a permanent development of the total health care delivery system.

The traditional concept of integrated health services is one in which all service units in a geographical area form a functional unity. The prevalent developmental trend of recent years, in most of the countries reviewed, is to extend the range of the service units to the extreme periphery, thus permitting full vertical integration of primary health care into the total health care delivery system. In the more affluent countries, in view of the prevailing health problems (mainly chronic conditions), high priority is being given to the integration of general hospitals for acute care with the functions of ambulatory care and institutions for extended care (both medical and social), so that a smooth patient flow becomes possible. In the developing countries, where communicable and environment-related conditions still prevail, the emphasis is on the integration of preventive programmes in existing or developing health care services. The present concept of primary health care seems to have become one of the most important positive factors in this respect.

(b) Decentralization

The development of administrative structures for the health services is currently influenced by the forces of centralization and decentralization, pulling in opposite directions. On the one hand, because of the increasing responsibility of governments for the development and financing of national health care delivery systems, it is necessary to maintain the power of policy decisions and control at the central level for all matters pertaining to planning, legislation, and allocation of resources. On the other hand, progressive regionalization of health services implies administrative and budgetary decentralization in order to make the allocation of health resources more relevant to local needs, involve communities in the development and operation of their local services, and simplify bureaucratic procedures. These trends apply in both developed and developing countries. In those countries in which an integrated health care delivery system has been long established and where legislative and administrative capabilities are strong enough, a proper balance has been achieved between the two trends. This seems to offer more favourable conditions both for the creation of well balanced national health development programmes and for their efficient execution at the regional and local levels. In those countries in which government responsibility for organizing and financing the health service system is less evident, both the initiation and execution of health-related activities remain the responsibility of local authorities or voluntary groups. The situation may result in problems of coordination or efficiency.

Countries that had been subject to foreign rule for many years usually had a highly centralized administrative system. However, this system, located in the country's administrative capital, had very little initiative as major decisions were taken in the capital of the colonial power. In many fields, but particularly in the health field, services were organized in a historically older and much more limited way than the corresponding services of the occupying powers. With independence, the central administrations of these countries continued to function within the centralized components left behind by the former rulers. Moreover, they were discouraged from change by another factor—namely, the weakness of the local authorities. Therefore, in many developing countries the local authorities continue to perform only routine duties of an elementary or traditional nature. They have been denied the financial resources and manpower necessary for the creation of local administrations capable of organizing the health services properly and preparing long-term programmes and plans. Because the administrative microstructures are weak or non-existent, the local health services are often deprived of necessary support. To solve this problem, by encouraging local initiative and responsibility in health development, Member States are now promoting primary health care, including community involvement and control. There is growing appreciation of the fact that in a number of developing countries this approach has already been successfully put into practice.

(c) Regionalization

Regional development of health care facilities is something to which health planners have aspired for many years. It is thought that, through its application, the development of hospitals, health centres, and peripheral facilities can be better fitted to the requirements of users and a more appropriate distribution of health facilities can be obtained. Health services could then be created in which care at different levels of complexity would be adapted to the needs of users, and in which the point of entry to the health care delivery system would be clearly identified. It is already widely recognized that a regionalized health service system has enormous advantages, not only from the point of view of better utilization of resources, but also in facilitating access to the most suitable level of care. Financial administration and personnel management become more efficient. Maintenance services for equipment and installations can be extended to all the health care facilities of the region (hospitals, health centres, dispensaries, etc.). Supplies of medical equipment, materials, drugs, or food can be procured in bulk with advantages in quality and cost. Even some supporting services, such as laundry or administrative accounting, may be merged for purposes of economy.

However, practical experience suggests that the introduction of the concept and mechanism of regionalization is a complex process and one not easily achieved. The setting up of a regional health system is relatively simple when all health facilities belong to the same health care provider, but this situation is rare. With the involvement of several separate agencies, it is usually difficult to attain the necessary harmony of wishes and objectives for the establishment of a genuinely unified and functional regional system. In such cases, regionalization is generally partial in that it is applied to the facilities of one particular provider, such as the Ministry of Health or the social security system. In those countries in which private commercial enterprise is predominant in the financing of hospital services, the most that can be expected is financial regionalization, whether for construction or for procurement of equipment and supplies.

From the foregoing it can be inferred that certain conditions must be met before a completely regionalized system of health services can be put into operation. Of course, it is easier to bring about regionalization of the health services in those countries that have a planned economy and a decentralized system of economic and social administration. It is also usually necessary that, at the regional level, there should be a political and administrative body with executive and coordinating authority over services, not only in the health field but also in those of education, housing, welfare, and other related areas. Even when these ideal conditions do not exist, it is possible for countries to establish a regionalized health service, provided a firm political decision is taken and is backed by legislation. Complementary measures include the adoption of uniform administrative and information methods and the establishment of joint training programmes for the directing and executive personnel of the participating institutions.

It is evident from experience in a number of countries that another important factor in the regionalization of health services is *territorial comprehensiveness,* meaning that the region should ideally comprise an urban sector, a suburban sector, and a rural sector. This is the way to achieve complete regional self-sufficiency, as the rural health services on their own cannot provide fully comprehensive care including the most highly specialized services. For economic reasons (specifically, shortage and cost of specialists and the high cost of diagnostic and treatment equipment), it appears inevitable that the most highly specialized services can be made available only at regional (or even national) hospitals that are conventionally associated with a school of medicine. Such facilities are usually reserved for the largest cities only, although their specialized services may be made more readily available to the suburban and rural centres under a system of referral and technical and advisory assistance by the larger hospitals to the less developed hospitals, health centres, and primary care services in the suburban and rural areas. Although the above patterns of regionalization are apparently becoming more frequent in almost all the countries providing information, the extent of their practical application varies very widely.

(d) Referral

A pyramidal health service structure providing for successive referral has been widely accepted as the best model for the development of national health care delivery systems. A relevant concept here is that of modules of population size in which both prevailing health problems and the content of required care could be properly balanced at various organizational levels. In general, relatively small population groups (2000–30 000 persons) generate large numbers of common problems requiring primary health care; larger population groups (200 000–500 000 persons) generate in addition enough difficult and more severe health care problems to warrant the provision of secondary or specialist care; and large population groups (1 000 000 and over) generate even more complex problems or serious illnesses so that the provision of tertiary care involving superspecialists and technologically intensive facilities becomes warranted. The first level is supported by the other two, and all three must be linked by adequate transport and communication systems. Thus a balanced health care delivery system requires appropriate combinations of personnel and facilities at all three levels of care in order to meet the needs of most of the population most of the time in the least costly manner; otherwise the system will be unbalanced with respect to coverage, benefits, or costs.

Until now only relatively few countries have achieved a reasonable balance between all levels of care. These are the countries in which systematic and unified health service planning has been well established over a period of many years (e.g., in countries with a centrally planned economy and in Scandinavia, the United Kingdom, and various others). In most other countries tertiary care predominates over the other two levels, particularly that of primary care, with predictably negative consequences.

The type of health care delivery system found in most of the industrialized countries has developed in response to the greater demands made on the curative sector and in particular the demands made on the hospitals with their advanced technology. Such development is favoured where medical care is still largely a marketable commodity. In such countries, the main step towards a change in the imbalanced health care delivery system is the organization of a regional system of hospitals for acute care according to the model described on page 71.

A second important organizational change would be the reduction of the total capacity of the acute care hospitals in terms both of their medical and technical facilities and the number of beds. A reduction in the capacity of the medical and technical facilities may be achieved by concentrating them into the largest possible units so as to achieve economies of scale, always depending on transport and referral possibilities. A reduction in the number of beds, at least in a relative sense, should be achieved by shifting acute patient beds to long-term, lower-cost facilities. A reduction in the number of beds in an absolute sense may be achieved by substituting ambulatory care for institutional care, i.e., by the introduction or extension of ambulatory facilities, mainly in support of the primary care level.

In most of the developing countries the growth of health care delivery systems has been based primarily on district community hospitals which were supposed to provide all necessary services to the population, either directly or through the satellite type of health care facility, i.e., health centres and dispensaries. So far, at least, "modern" health care delivery systems have always been initiated in the urban areas, with the expectation that increasing national income would lead to their gradual spread over the rest of the country. The fact that this has not happened is related at least partly to continuing poverty. However, there are other factors as well; for example, a "self-augmenting concentration effect", which means that scarce resources are almost always invested in the same small group of institutions. To break this vicious circle it is the express policy of most developing countries to achieve a significant extension of coverage within their limited resources. This goal can be realized only by replacing the usual hospital-oriented solutions by others requiring less financial means, as well as being socially more effective. This means that the population base for hospital care must be raised and that community-oriented health care facilities must be developed to compensate for the long distances most of the population would have to travel to hospital. Simultaneously, there must be a shift in the allocation of resources in favour of primary health care, with its preventive component, and the rural areas. This policy will have a far-reaching effect on the existing health care delivery complex and will require long and continuous organizational action. In this case, a circumstance favourable to the desired organizational change is that, in the rural areas in which extended coverage will primarily have to be achieved, the existence of voluntary agency hospitals is unlikely to prove a stumbling-block to the introduction of some form of regionalization. It appears, in practice, that such hospitals present no obstacle to the introduction of a regional approach in support of community-oriented primary care services (as, for example, in Botswana and the United Republic of Tanzania).

It follows from the above observations that within a region there must be a two-way flow of users, staff, and equipment between the various levels of care. For this to take place, a clear understanding must exist of the functions, responsibilities, and limitations of each level of care. Ideally, primary care workers will refer those patients who require more competent medical attention to the health centres or first-line hospitals, which in turn will send their patients for medical advice to the higher and more specialized health care facilities or, alternatively, will be visited periodically by medical specialists from the higher echelons and will be able to obtain diagnostic and treatment equipment on loan in order to provide better care for their patients. For their part, the regional hospitals and other specialized services will send patients back after diagnosis or treatment, with case reports, to ensure continuity of follow-up at the peripheral level. This type of organization implies a referral system that is part of a hierarchical structure of health services having built-in technical support and supervision. It has been noted, however, that for a referral system to function effectively, it is essential that professional and technical staff at all levels should belong to the regional health team.

With few exceptions the referral system described is in place in the more industrialized countries. It appears, however, from the global review that in developing countries it is more difficult to develop a referral system based on the traditional model. Although many obstacles to the development of appropriate referral systems exist in both developed and developing countries, some are aggravated in the latter: for example, physical and material constraints, such as long distances or poor roads between outposts, health centres, and hospitals, and the scarcity or cost of public transport, and also the bypass phenomenon, i.e., the effect of self-referral in which the first- and sometimes second-line facilities remain underutilized while the larger urban hospitals receive too many patients. The failure of referral systems has several negative consequences. The first is that the peripheral outposts are forced to operate without effective support. Auxiliary staff in such facilities often have to treat difficult cases themselves. A further consequence is misuse of the higher hospital facilities which begin to function largely as very expensive medical services for relatively simple complaints. The support system must reverse the flow so as to bring technical support to the periphery.

(e) The role of the private sector

Although the worldwide tendency is towards an organized health care sector of a public nature, in respect of either financing or the direct delivery of health services, a private health care sector continues to exist in most countries. It is usual to differentiate between providers of health care according to whether they are profit-making or not. The same applies to providers organized in teams (group practices), as well as to various kinds of facilities including highly specialized hospitals. The definition of the private sector within the overall health sector varies from one country to another. For example, occupational health services run by private companies (mines, factories, agricultural enterprises), health facilities maintained by voluntary agencies or private insurance companies, and various financing arrangements may be called "private", or "non-public", or "para-statal" etc.

Among the voluntary health care agencies, the most important are those related to religious missions. In many African countries they provide up to 50% of all hospital beds. These groups often operate as independent units, sometimes without the backing of government policy. In some countries (e.g., Botswana, Ghana, Lesotho, Malawi, Nigeria, and Zambia) mechanisms have been established for joint church and government planning of health services. Two of these countries have gone further by adopting a national health service plan that provides for a concerted effort by the public and private sectors to fill existing gaps in the health care network. In many areas local government health personnel are urged to join with the private sector in drawing up plans to deal with local health problems.

The relative sizes of the private and public health sectors vary widely. In those countries in which the private sector is larger than the public sector, its inclusion in overall national health planning is essential if national health policy goals are to be attained. There is a continuing worldwide debate about how far private areas of medical practice and insurance should be tolerated or even encouraged; that is, should health services be provided by a state scheme alone or by a combination of public and private activities?

Supporters of the coexistence of a private sector operating side by side with the public sector argue that it can reduce public expenditure and that it can increase the resources available for health care as a result of the demand created through freedom of choice and opportunity for spending. It also gives health personnel the incentive to extend working hours and establishes standards of comfort for the patient, which act as a spur to the State sector.

The main argument against the coexistence of a private sector is that private money should not be allowed to buy preferential medical care. Resources are always limited in terms of skilled people and costly facilities, so that the injection of more resources into the private option. Health personnel working, for example, in non-priority nursing homes, could be better employed in public hospitals serving more patients and dealing with cases of higher priority. In some countries, therefore, private practice, although tolerated, is not considered desirable. However, the very existence of higher earnings in the private sector often leads to governments' having to permit mixed private and public practice. Such a situation is the cause of many potential and actual distortions within national health service systems.

Administration and management

(a) Adoption of management techniques

There is a widespread belief among Member States of WHO that better management of health services is essential if higher standards in the national health care delivery system are to be achieved. Concern over the "big system" aspect is one of the reasons for the trend towards examination of management methods already developed to cope with similar complexities in other sectors. These methods include the systems approach of operational research; more general systems analysis; programme budgeting; management information systems; economic and other techniques concerned with the productive use of resources; and organizational and behavioural approaches relating to communications, personnel selection, training and motivation, adaption to change, the team concept, organizational design, and other factors. The need for different types of management technique varies from one country to another. Thus, in countries where health services are already extensive and complex, what is needed is probably that they should become truly comprehensive, that the massive resources the country has already committed to the health sector should make their full contribution towards the attainment of a healthy population, and that efficient choices among the wide range of options open to them should be made at all levels of the health services. In those countries whose present health facilities are more limited or even minimal, the need is rather for an adequate diagnosis of the problems deserving highest priority, having regard not only to good health as an end in itself, but also to the contribution that the reduction of disease and disability can make to overall socioeconomic development. Where the health system has few resources, the need is to establish an efficient and fair justification for more, to apply these to a relatively few high-priority objectives, and to manage their application to maximum effect. In working towards more comprehensive health services, the developing countries would do well to be extremely selective in their emulation of more developed systems. The important commitments must be chosen with an eye to efficiency and on the basis of objective evidence.

Although the need for modern management techniques differs from one country or situation to another, it is evident that the differences are not always appreciated and acted upon in practice. The perceived need is likely to be strongly influenced by what is available in the field of management, and what is available may be influenced by the demand for it. Thus, in countries where there is an established tradition for the application of operations research to management problems in private industry, the use of this technique in government services including the health services is more likely. So, too, is the perception of need in terms of problems closely analogous to industrial ones, such as that of balancing the capacities of facilities. In time closer attention may be paid to those needs that are specific to the health sector, though this is likely to happen only in response to demands arising within the health service itself. In countries where there are no local examples to follow and personnel with expertise in management techniques are not available, perception of the need for them is less likely.

It seems that some confusion has recently been created by the belief that the mere transfer of modern management techniques to health care problems will solve them automatically. This is not the case. It is increasingly evident that successful health management is essentially dependent on the existence of a potentially rational and effective health care delivery system and of the capacity for appropriate management. Thus, the mere introduction of more elaborate methods for choosing between alternatives would be futile, if steps were not also taken to ensure a fruitful range of alternatives from which to choose. Similarly, a highly developed decision process will have little effect if nothing is done to motivate those involved in implementing the decisions that flow from it. To take another example, a system of programme budgeting needs to be associated with a rational process for allocating funds to relevant programmes and a control system to see that the funds are actually used to achieve the goals intended. Thus, the value of modern health management is more likely to be seen when it is being introduced in a properly balanced sequence of steps. Each step should reinforce the others so as to generate sufficient momentum to overcome existing constraints. Recent experience has shown that the management training of health personnel requires good, convincing examples as a basis for "teaching by doing", but the examples, to be convincing, should be of problems that are of real relevance to the conduct of health services and that have been solved successfully. However such training is unlikely to be available unless there is already a sufficient number of health professionals with a good appreciation of modern management (and, of course, appropriate health sector goals); moreover, the relevant techniques and the skills needed to apply them in meeting health service needs will be developed only in response to pressure from the services themselves.

Almost all the Member States recently questioned on the subject have been involved in various activities aimed at enhancing their capacity for health management. A number of national programmes have been initiated and international collaboration in the health management field has been strengthened. It is notable that, apart from the revision of traditional programmes relating to public health administration or hospital/medical care administration, new opportunities have been made available for assessing and improving national health management systems in a number of areas, including country health programming, health services planning, health information systems, health services re-search, health facilities planning, maintenance and management, and financing of health services. To make efforts in this field more relevant to the specific situations in different countries, emphasis has been placed on national self-reliance; in addition, closer coopera-tion between countries affected by similar problems has been encouraged.

Many promotional activities relating to the improvement of national health manage-ment have recently been initiated by Member States in and through the different WHO regions. For instance, in the African Region, an intercountry project on the planning, programming, and management of health services has been developed. Consideration has also been given to developing the regional capacity for postgraduate training in public health administration and improving and modernizing health planning and management capabilities within the ministries of health of the participating African States.

In the Region of the Americas, a series of international seminars on health services administration has been organized and steps have been taken to promote the creation of national centres for training in health management as a responsibility of the governments concerned. In 1976, an analysis of 44 regular training programmes in health administration in 11 countries of the Region was initiated; this is expected to provide a basis for the reorientation and expansion of these programmes with a view to making them more responsive to health system requirements.

In the South-East Asia Region, a regional programme to strengthen health service administration through training in management has been carried out. In the European Region a number of working groups on various aspects of modern health management and of training requirements have contributed to the promotion of national programmes and international collaboration in this field.

In the Eastern Mediterranean Region, working groups on postgraduate education and training in public health administration have contributed to upgrading and expanding existing programmes in Member States.

In the Western Pacific Region, a long-term regional programme in the field of public health administration has been modified and extended, with emphasis on the development of an effective system for assessing training requirements and on the establishment of continuing education programmes to meet the varying needs of health staff in the field of health management.

(b) *Information systems*

In the health sector, national health statistical systems are expected to provide much of the information that will be used by decision-makers in establishing national health priorities and in allocating funds to implement and strengthen given programmes. In providing the flow of data sought by health planners and administrators, the assessment of health information needs and the continual evaluation of health statistical services have an important part to play. As the health sector manager, at many different levels of the system, is the primary and most important user of health statistics, the need for a close link between the health manager and the health statistical services is now clearly recognized, and statistical services in many countries have been modified accordingly.

On the other hand, recognition of health as an essential component of socioeconomic development has led to the review and reorientation of health statistical services within the framework of the overall statistical information system. Limited resources, changing health needs, and competition for available funds among important governmental programmes have resulted in increased pressure for better national planning and resource allocation, both in developed and developing countries. A national health statistical information system is now required to provide reliable multipurpose descriptive health statistics for the use of the health sector, broadly defined, and of those responsible for overall national planning, and also to meet many of the needs of government policymakers, managers of national health programmes, administrators of programme components, and medical educators and researchers. Therefore, the development of systems and services that will provide the information necessary to health management is progressively being given higher priority within national health programmes. There are, however, many countries where this does not apply; in fact, no country has yet established an ideally integrated single service to deal with all the information required by health managers at every level.

The Thirtieth World Health Assembly emphasized the importance of adequate systems and services for the generation, collection, and dissemination of statistical and other relevant information on health and socioeconomic matters as an important basis for better planned and effective health services. The main objective of the Organization's health statistics programme is to cooperate with Member States in the development of the information required for the planning, management, and evaluation of their health programmes.

However, the capacity of Member States for careful analyses of the health situation is often very rudimentary, and their statistics, if published at all, may be unreadable, inconsistent, and in a format hard to interpret by users. Such factors as a shortage of qualified personnel, a lack of coordination between producers and users of statistics, or the inadequate training of administrators and health staff in statistics still prevent many countries from developing a satisfactory health statistics system. To remedy the situation, a number of countries are developing analytical skills for the conversion of primary data into meaningful information for the monitoring and evaluation of health programmes and of their impact on the health of the population. The creation of a body of personnel versed in all aspects of health information is a high priority in most countries, training being given not only to providers of health information but also to users. Emphasis is placed on the development, adaptation, and application of the various statistical and other scientific methods that are simple in terms of cost, technique, and organization and that fit particular country situations. As many countries do not have the necessary skills or facilities, international and intercountry cooperation is being enlisted; in this area, the WHO collaborating centres have an essential part to play.

Many countries do not have health services covering all the population, and consequently there is no information, based on health service records, about this unserved population. Similarly, many countries do not have health professionals or services for such health problems as psychiatric and neurological disorders and those due to psychosocial factors. Thus no information is collected, and the result is continued unawareness of the existence of such problems and lack of planning for appropriate health care. In this connexion, the possibility of obtaining useful information from traditional health workers is being explored. Other activities include the development of health records outside hospitals, the encouragement of the better use of health record data for health management, and education in this area aimed at meeting the needs of the consumers of health information and services.

The need to bring providers and users of information generated at various levels closer together has led many countries to create various coordinating mechanisms—for example, national committees on vital and health statistics or similar coordinating or advisory bodies of official standing.

In view of the frequent scarcity of health sector resources, there is an increasing need for improved data relating to the measurement of efficiency in the allocation of these resources. Monitoring their efficient use is vital for the accomplishment of the Organization's goal of 'health for all by the year 2000'. It is to be expected that, in future, health information systems will concentrate much more fully on the relationship between particular health sector resource inputs and the corresponding outputs in terms of population coverage and efficient technological choice within the health care delivery system.

(c) Financing

To what degree the health of an individual is a collective social responsibility and, thus, to what degree health services should be financed socially is largely determined by a country's political and social philosophy. The USA can be taken as an example of a country in which private sector providers ensure the delivery of health care, the services being purchased by the customer; nonetheless, even in the USA, services for certain population groups such as the aged or the poor are financed from public funds. Different models are found in the USSR and other socialist countries, and the United Kingdom and New Zealand. In these countries virtually complete medical coverage is available for everybody through funds mainly derived from general revenues. Most Western European countries have chosen the social security system as a vehicle for the provision of medical care. In many countries of Asia and Africa and in most of Latin America, the great majority of the population cannot afford to pay for medical services either through insurance or private payments and depend on services provided directly and without charge by the government. However, the level of the services is seriously impaired by shortage and maldistribution of resources and by inappropriate technical choices which exacerbate the situation. In these countries most of the services are offered by salaried personnel working in hospitals, dispensaries, or health centres. In the larger cities, private physicians and private hospitals are available for a relatively small layer of the population. Sometimes a means test is theoretically applied to determine eligibility for public services. On a world level there seems to be a trend in all countries towards more socially organized and financed health services.

The high cost of advanced technology, the increasing number of people demanding and utilizing medical care, the measures necessary to deal with man-made health problems (air and water pollution, industrial hazards, road accidents), selected monopolistic practices on the part of the health care industry, and inflation are considered as the main causes of the increasing cost of health services. These increases, often expressed as a larger percentage of the gross domestic product, have led to a worldwide effort to contain the costs of health services. This is to be seen particularly in the industrialized countries.

There are considerable variations in the proportion of resources made available for health activities in the public sector. In some countries the budget of the ministry of health and other authorities dealing with health care has been increasing at the same rate as the overall government budget, while in others there is stagnation or even regression, particularly if the purchasing power of the currency is taken into account. In many countries the structure of the budget for the ministry of health does not lend itself to analysis and comparison with national health objectives. However, a pattern that is found almost everywhere is the use of the available funds mainly for curative services in urban areas, to the detriment of the rural areas and services other than curative, e.g., prevention or rehabilitation services. The available resources for medical care are mostly tied to the recurrent expenditures of hospitals, and only limited amounts can be reallocated to new priorities, e.g., primary health care. External assistance to developing countries does not always comply with changes in national health policy; for example, the provision of funds for new hospitals aggravates the problem of reallocating recurrent expenditures towards primary health care. In general, shortages and maldistribution of funds, lack of coordination between the sources of funding, and insufficient consideration of the cost/benefit and cost/efficiency aspects of health services remain major problems in financing and allocating resources for national health care delivery systems.

Primary health care

In the introductory paragraphs of this report it was mentioned that the period 1973–1977 witnessed a considerable amount of rethinking about what is meant by and what is involved in health development. A key event was the WHO Executive Board study on basic health services in 1973. This study focused on the deficiencies of existing health services, and on the lack of health services for the overwhelming majority of the world's population. It went beyond a mere analysis of the functioning of the basic health services to address wider issues such as the essential importance of communities participating in matters concerning their health, and the vital contribution of other sectors to health. In doing so, it laid the foundation for what was soon to be known as the primary health care approach.

The need for a "new" approach to meeting people's basic health requirements grew out of more than a simple dissatisfaction with the basic health services. There was and continues to be growing concern about the unacceptably low health status of the majority of the world's population, especially the rural poor. It was this concern, fundamentally, that led the Thirtieth World Health Assembly in May 1977 to decide that the main social target of governments and of WHO in the coming decades should be the attainment by all the citizens of the world by the year 2000 of a level of health that will permit them to lead socially and economically productive lives. The seriousness of the problem is shown by the high morbidity and mortality rates that exist among the rural and periurban populations that constitute the great majority of the world's population, including some 800 million people that still suffer from absolute poverty. Despite downward trends in mortality, such conditions as, for example, malnutrition, communicable diseases, and parasitic infestations continue to take a heavy toll of lives, especially among infants, children and other weaker groups. The poor health status of the populations affected is manifested not only in morbidity and mortality rates, but also in the incapacity of individuals and communities to develop their human potentialities and lead fully productive lives.

The lack of organized health care is a contributing factor. It is especially the people underserved in this respect who are most vulnerable to the conditions promoting and leading to ill-health. Instead of being in a position to alleviate the suffering of those most in need, the health services are, by and large, more accessible and more readily available to a small, relatively prosperous segment of the population. This gap manifests itself within as well as between countries. Within countries, it takes the form of inadequate coverage by essential health care; between countries, there are still gross disparities in the resources available for essential health care.

In the past, because of the dramatic nature of certain disease problems, programmes to tackle them have been of overriding concern to individual countries and WHO. This has meant that programmes for the provision of specific types of health service have been implemented as separate entities. Furthermore, in most countries the main aim in health services development has been to provide highly sophisticated medical services. All this has led to a disequilibrium in the types of service provided and their distribution, with most emphasis being placed on centralized, sophisticated, and costly institutional care and relatively little on the essential care to be delivered at the periphery to large segments of the population.

The resultant "health systems" are characterized by a medical orientation with no attempt to develop mechanisms and approaches that take into account the important contribution other sectors can make to health. In consequence, few ministries of health are in a position to promote health by, for example, working with their respective ministries of agriculture on improved food and nutrition programmes. Also, few ministries have the means for, or indeed are interested in, stimulating, supporting, and channelling the participation of the community, which could actively and responsibly exert the pressures necessary for essential reforms.

The situation is not, however, the same everywhere. There have always been health programmes that approach the priority health needs of a community in an equitable manner, encouraging the most effective use of available resources. Many such examples were examined in the course of the joint UNICEF/WHO study on "alternative approaches to meeting basic health needs in developing countries". This study was presented to the UNICEF/WHO Joint Committee on Health Policy in February 1975. The recommendations adopted by this Committee included principles to be followed in the reorientation and development of health services. These underlined the importance of recognizing primary health care as forming part of overall development; the need for firm policies, priorities, and plans; the need for a reorientation of all other levels of the health system to provide support to the primary health care level; the importance of involving communities in the design, staffing, and functioning of primary health care; the need for primary health care workers simply trained and selected by the community itself, when possible; and the special emphasis that should be placed on preventive measures, health and nutrition education, the health care needs of mothers and children, the utilization of simplified forms of medical and health technology, association with some traditional forms of health care and the use of traditional practitioners, and respect for the cultural patterns and real needs of the consumers in health and community development.

These principles were later to be reformulated and incorporated in the more comprehensive statement on primary health care to be found in the Declaration of Alma-Ata prepared in September 1978 at the International Conference on Primary Health Care. In many ways this Conference represented the culmination of the search initiated in 1973 for an "alternative approach" to the basic health services.

In 1975 WHO began to develop an expanded long-term programme for primary health care and to review of the experiences of health services of various countries in providing it. Countries were encouraged to train and use appropriate personnel, to foster and coordinate research in primary health care, to disseminate the information thus obtained, and to promote the active participation of different socioeconomic sectors. In the same year it was decided by the World Health Assembly to hold an international conference to exchange experience on the development of primary health care, and in 1976 the USSR's offer to be host country, and UNICEF's co-sponsorship were accepted. 1976 also saw the introduction of a programme for appropriate technology for health relating to primary health care and rural development.

Countries have responded to these formal decisions in a variety of ways, according to their understanding of primary health care and to national circumstances. Despite outstanding examples of primary health care and rural development projects, national endeavours in this direction have not always taken into account the basic tenets of primary health care. This has been particularly true in instances where needs as expressed by communities were not taken into account or where the communities were not associated with the provision of primary health care or did not take part in development activities. This situation pointed to the need for a further specification of the components of primary health care and led in 1976–1977 to the joint WHO/UNICEF study on community involvement in primary health care. Other studies—e.g., on water and sanitation in primary health care (also a joint WHO/UNICEF venture)—have been carried out to disseminate the experience gained in different countries and promote an understanding of those aspects of primary health care that are least understood.

It can be seen that, in the gradual development of primary health care, new issues have been raised and resolved. The decision to hold an international conference on the subject demonstrated the continuing need to review outstanding problems and experience in different countries. The objectives of the conference were:

- The exchange of experience and information on the development of primary health care within (1) a framework of comprehensive national health systems and services, and (2) overall national plans.
- Promotion of primary health care.
- Recommendations to governments.

Although these is universal support for primary health care, the degree to which its various aspects are being developed varies widely among countries. Some of the constraints on achieving nationwide coverage by primary health care are: implementation policies are at times poorly understood and conceived and they sometimes omit a number of the essential components of primary health care; the principles of the primary health care approach are not translated into feasible programme steps by national health planning systems; resources are scarce and those available are inadequately allocated as regards primary health care (this may point to a lack of political commitment to primary health care based on social equity); joint sectoral planning is not undertaken, owing to weak intersectoral cooperation; appropriate health technologies are not well understood or utilized; and community participation is not viewed as a "partnership" relationship between government and communities. The period under review has thus witnessed an evolution on two main fronts, i.e., promotion and development, and, in the process, a more exact recognition of existing disparities.

In practice, only a few countries have actually adopted a wider intersectoral approach to health issues. These tend to be countries with low per capita incomes and a clear commitment to the more equitable distribution of that income. They refuse to accept shortage of resources as a reason for failing to deliver health care to the population as a whole, considering rather that the technology for the delivery of health care must be adjusted to fit the resources available. They also believe that the improvement of the health status of their population requires not only the full participation of the people themselves in identifying their needs and planning to meet them, but the active involvement of all health-related ministries, agencies, and nongovernmental institutions in a collaborative effort to direct and control all factors affecting health. The limited number of industrialized countries that share these views at present do so at least partly because they are disillusioned with the outcome of their own past health policies. These countries are initiating primary health care as an integral part of overall social policy.

On the other hand, there are many countries, most—though not all—enjoying medium or high incomes, that have developed strong institution-based medical care services and are concerned with primary health care principally as a means of extending existing basic health (or medical) services. These countries do not fully appreciate the fact that primary health care requires new policies and planning processes that will reallocate and redistribute existing resources, as well as mobilizing others that were previously untapped, with emphasis on the active participation of the community in its own development, including the choice of priorities, objectives, and action to be taken for health.

What is even more serious, however, is the tendency observed in some of these countries to make health workers (known as village health workers or primary health workers) available for simple curative and preventive activities at the community level, letting them work almost in isolation from the rest of the system, which remains unchanged. Whether these activities at the community level can be truly developmental and scientifically sound or whether they will end up as "primitive" or second-rate medicine will depend on whether they were the outcome of a true commitment to primary health care at the highest policy level, whether the necessary administrative changes or reforms have occurred (e.g., decentralization and democratization) and whether the necessary logistic, managerial, and training support is provided by all the other levels. In fact, wherever primary health care has "worked" and fulfilled expectations, it is because the activities undertaken at the community level received the necessary support in the form of regular supplies (including essential drugs), equipment, spare parts, and maintenance, supervision and training, appropriate technology, and the reorientation of the other levels of the system to complement and sustain the activities undertaken at the community level.

It is thus clear that at present there is a general endorsement by all countries of primary health care. It is also clear that the practical application of the principles of primary health care as enunciated in 1975 differs significantly between countries and that there are considerable variations in the speed with which national primary health care programmes and activities are being implemented. WHO has provided countries with information on primary health care and its components and will continue to do so. For example, the twenty-first session of the UNICEF/WHO Joint Committee on Health Policy initiated a detailed study on water and sanitation as components of primary health care. In addition to a survey in depth of activities in this area, a number of case studies are to be carried out with special reference to work at the community level and the support given by the other levels.

One factor in the present renaissance of the primary health care concept has been the influence of many isolated but sometimes quite successful projects, most of them in rural communities. Although their achievements have so far been limited, others have been encouraged to emulate them with the increasing support of national or international bodies. This, combined with the fact that an appreciable number of countries have either launched primary health care programmes as part of their national health systems or incorporated the approach into their systems, has led to worldwide acceptance of primary health care, at least in spirit if not yet always in practice. The final impact of this is not yet

81

clearly visible, but the monitoring methods being devised to measure progress towards the goal of health for all by the year 2000 will help to show more clearly the commitment of governments to primary health care in spirit and reality. For example, although approximately one-third of the countries in Africa have at least partially integrated the primary health care approach into their national health care programmes and most of the rest have special budgetary provisions for primary health care, it cannot be considered as properly established if it exists only as one separate "pillar" or budget item within the overall health care system. In any event, the most difficult part of primary health care is probably the achievement of full and genuine community participation, in that communities may increasingly view "community participation" as implying "community control", thus offering a difficult choice to those now responsible for health policy in most social and political settings.

Disease prevention and control

Like other serious and continuing health problems, communicable diseases demonstrate the relationship between health and socioeconomic development; in particular, they reflect the interrelationships between infection, malnutrition, and an unhealthy environment. Thus measures for communicable disease prevention and control should form a major component of primary health care, and they are inextricably bound up with other health-related activities such as the provision of comprehensive health services, the promotion of a clean environment, and the application of appropriate agricultural and nutritional policies.

Accumulated technical information and operational experience make it possible to integrate the control of most communicable diseases of major public health importance into the existing structure of the health services. However, the challenge of applying and adapting technology known to be effective in communicable disease control has had to be met in the face of real constraints: inadequate national commitments; inadequate community understanding and involvement; weaknesses in the health infrastructure and supporting services; shortcomings in epidemiological surveillance; and lack of managerial capability to identify problems and develop the most suitable solutions at all levels of the national health services.

Although data on morbidity and mortality are deficient in many respects, sufficient information for action has been forthcoming on most of the communicable diseases of public health importance in the world. This has contributed to the establishment of priority control programmes which, in turn, have often generated improved information systems. In the period 1973–1977, action for the control of the communicable diseases was increasingly based on primary health care facilities. These facilities were often inadequate at the beginning of the period, but much has now been done to strengthen them.

Parasitic diseases

(a) Malaria

The period under review was characterized by a serious resurgence of malaria in a number of countries in South-East Asia and Latin America resulting, in some instances, in epidemics such as that in Turkey. On an average there was a 2.3-fold increase in the overall number of malaria cases reported over the five-year period, but great variations have been reported. In India alone 6.5 million cases were reported in 1976 as against 2 million in 1972, and the trend in 1976 was towards an increase. In other countries, notably in the Western Pacific Region and in Latin America, progress was slow or nonexistent. In Africa south of the Sahara, relatively few organized control activities were undertaken.

Figure 11 shows the numbers of malaria cases[1] reported throughout the world (excluding the African Region) from 1972 to 1978. Figure 11 also illustrates progress of the disease in the South-East Asia Region, and Fig. 12 presents an epidemiological assessment of the malaria situation at the end of 1977.

The resurgence of malaria is related to the decision to reduce antimalaria activities in the countries affected. This decision was due partly to the economic and energy crises and partly to the increased cost of insecticides and antimalaria drugs. In addition, technical problems in the form of resistance of vectors to insecticides and of *Plasmodium falciparum* to drugs affected 20% or more of the malarious areas in the mid-1970s as against 1.5% in the mid-1960s. Although the gains obtained in the drive to eradicate malaria in the late 1950s have been maintained in the countries where eradication had actually been achieved, the recent resurgence of the disease has increased surveillance problems even for these countries.

Between 1972 and 1977 there was a twofold increase in the number of imported cases of malaria in the malaria-free countries of Europe and Northern America.

The major resurgence of malaria occurred in the South-East Asia Region. In other WHO Regions affected by the disease, incidence increased slightly between 1973 and 1977, except in countries in the Eastern Mediterranean Region where there tended to be a decrease in the number of cases reported. However, it should be pointed out that,

Fig. 11. Malaria cases reported, 1972–1978 (excluding African Region).

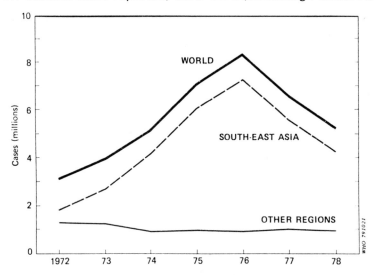

---

[1] The information requested from countries was on microscopically confirmed malaria cases.

Fig. 12. Epidemiological assessment of status of malaria, December 1977.

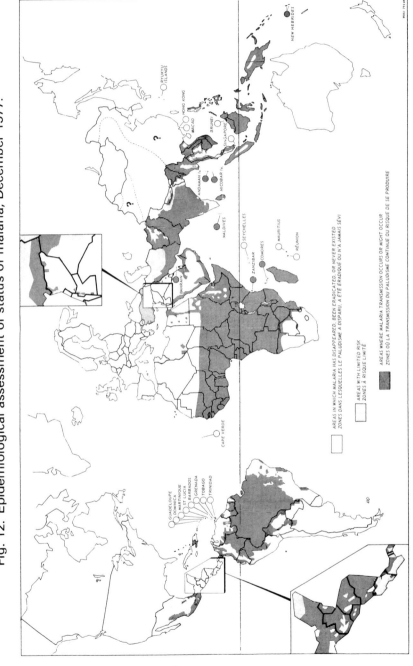

Source: *Weekly Epidemiological Record No. 22, 1979.*

84

although in certain countries (such as Guatemala and Haiti in the Americas, Turkey in the European Region, and Philippines in the Western Pacific Region) a significant increase was reported in the number of cases recorded, in other countries a considerable reduction was noted (Algeria and Mexico). In fact, in countries in which a political decision on the malaria problem had been taken rapidly, good results were immediately recorded (even for South-East Asia), as reflected in the overall flattening of the rising incidence curve in 1976–1977.

The worsening epidemiological situation in South-East Asia and in some other areas of the world provoked a strong political reaction on the part of the governments of many of the countries affected. The revised strategy adopted by the Twenty-second World Health Assembly had not been implemented, and the health administrations of many countries appealed to WHO to establish a strategy that would be applicable to the varying ecological conditions of malaria transmission.

In spite of considerable changes over the last two decades, rural areas in the subtropical and tropical areas of the world remain the same in many ways, and the sleeping habits and housing situation of the population of such areas still favour man-mosquito contact. This necessitates a very specific epidemiological approach to the control of the disease. It is an established fact that, with the tools at present available (at least as far as drugs and insecticides are concerned), transmission cannot be interrupted in the Sudan savanna areas of Africa where malaria is holoendemic. Studies carried out in Nigeria clearly indicate that each inhabitant of these areas receives between 40 and 120 infective bites per year. Therefore, in the environmental conditions mentioned above, the interruption of transmission cannot be obtained within a reasonable time nor can countries afford the expenses it might involve. As well as the epidemiological features of endemoepidemic malaria, the control strategy must take into account the level of the risk to the population, the existing structures, the manpower and financial resources available, and technical problems relating to both the vector and the parasite. For this reason, the malaria control strategy has been elaborated with four tactical variants for undertaking activities ranging from the prevention or reduction of mortality, the shortening of the duration of the disease, and the reduction of incidence and prevalence rates to a full-scale attack on malaria, including (where feasible) its eradication.

Malaria has been recognized as a major public health problem in some 70 countries around the world; in areas where epidemics occur, it is also of socioeconomic and political importance. For this reason, it is considered that, for any country to undertake a successful control campaign, the basic conditions are: a decision by the government to give malaria control major priority within the overall development programme; a commitment by the government to support control activities on a long-term basis; the inclusion of malaria control as an integral part of the country's health programme; and, finally, as a key element, community participation at the political level and at the level of execution.

To meet the challenge of malaria, the following measures must be undertaken simultaneously: the control of epidemics, the elaboration of a long-term course of action, the training of health workers, and research.

During the period under review, research was carried out on such important aspects of malaria as the phenomena involved in the intricate man-parasite-vector relationship, with the ultimate aim of developing new tools (chemical and biological) for the control of the disease; particular attention was also paid to research on the development of new drugs and a vaccine. Considerable progress has already been made in drug development and the testing of at least one chemical compound has advanced to a stage at which clinical and field trials may be started. Progress has also been made in the development of a vaccine based on work on sporozoites and merozoites as immunogenic developmental stages of plasmodia. With the successful development of a technique for continuous *in vitro* cultivation of the erythrocytic forms of plasmodia, one obstacle to the development of a vaccine has been eliminated. However, other obstacles remain, among them the development of suitable adjuvants. While research in this field continues to receive priority, it may take up to ten years actually to develop a vaccine. Extensive research, initiated by WHO, on the epidemiology of malaria in a savanna area of northern Nigeria has resulted in the development of a mathematical model that can be used by health administrators for the planning of malaria control programmes in Africa.

WHO, for its part, cooperates with Member States in evaluating and assessing individual country programmes; in preparing a plan of action; in providing specialized training for health manpower (which more recently has included in-service training in specific techniques for the monitoring of drug resistance and the application of serological techniques for epidemiological evaluation); and in disseminating information on the epidemiological situation, the geographical distribution of technical problems, and the availability of drugs and insecticides.

It has been estimated that each year at least a million children under 14 years of age in tropical Africa die from malaria, complicated by nutritional and other health problems.[1] With the resurgence of malaria in other parts of the world, there must be an increasing number of deaths among infants, if the control measures in effect from 1965 to 1968 were as effective in reducing mortality as they appeared to be. In a controlled study carried out during a spraying project in Kenya, it was shown that general mortality decreased in just two years (1973–1975) from 23.9 to 13.5 deaths per 1000 population and infant mortality from 157 to 93 deaths per 1000 live births.[2] If spraying operations can reduce mortality to that extent, the impact of the resurgence of the disease has to be carefully watched. Growing morbidity resulting from an increase in malaria incidence could have deleterious effects on certain development activities. Specific information on this question is not usually available.

(b) Other parasitic diseases

Schistosomiasis is recognized to be endemic in 71 countries and it is estimated that over 600 million people are exposed to the risk of infection; prevalence rates indicate that some 200 million are actually infected. Intestinal helminthic and protozoal infections affect many millions of people in Africa, Asia, and Latin America. Large-scale water impoundments, artificial man-made lakes, and population habits are factors favouring the transmission or recrudescence of these diseases. Field research in the major UNDP-financed project on Lake Volta, Ghana, on the epidemiology and methodology of control of schistosomiasis is providing valuable scientific information on all aspects of the disease

---

[1] WHO Technical Report Series, No. 537 (*Malaria control in countries where time-limited eradication is impracticable at present.* Report of a WHO Interregional Conference), p. 9.
[2] PAYNE, D. ET AL. Impact of control measures on malaria transmission and general mortality. *Bulletin of the World Health Organization,* **54**: 369–377 (1976).

and on the organization of appropriate services to deal with it. Large-scale control programmes have been successful when there has been a firm commitment on the part of the government, together with the necessary finance and manpower. Unfortunately, such programmes have usually been too costly to serve as models for other countries.

Filariasis due to *Wuchereria bancrofti* and *Brugia malayi* affects at least 250 million people in the developing countries. Major foci continue to exist in Africa, South-East Asia and Oceania. In the endemic foci in tropical Africa, in Yemen, and in Middle and South America, *Onchocerca volvulus* is estimated to be responsible for more than 30 million cases. The disease is relatively severe in Guatemala and Mexico, and a new focus was recently discovered among the Amerindians between Brazil and Venezuela. Onchocerciasis is one of the major causes of blindness in Africa. Control of the disease is based almost exclusively on control of the vector *Simulium* flies by the application of insecticides to their breeding-sites in fast-flowing rivers and streams. The large-scale control programme launched by WHO, in cooperation with UNDP, FAO, and IBRD, in the Volta River Basin area of Western Africa covers parts of Benin, Ghana, Ivory Coast, Mali, Niger, and Togo and the whole of Upper Volta, i.e., a total area of approximately 700 000 km^2 with about 10 million inhabitants of whom some 70 000 are blind. The project is making satisfactory progress.

African trypanosomiasis (sleeping sickness) is a permanent menace to some 35 million people, of whom 20 million are not under regular surveillance and among whom 9000 new cases occur each year. Caused by *Trypanosoma gambiense* and *T. rhodesiense*, the disease is transmitted by flies of the *Glossina morsitanas* group. At present control has to be a continuous process aimed at limiting transmission to the lowest possible level. Vector control operations are costly, and there is a serious shortage of qualified manpower. Efforts are mainly directed at the improvement of diagnosis, chemotherapy, and means and methods of vector control.

American trypanosomiasis (Chagas' disease), caused by *T. cruzi* and transmitted by reduviid bugs, is a health problem of rural areas and city slums where poor standards of housing and deficient sanitary conditions favour the establishment of the vectors. Over 10 million people are reported to be infected in Latin America. At present there is no apparent alternative to vector control, which is limited, however, by the increasing cost of insecticides and by resistance on the part of the vectors. Its future control directly depends on socioeconomic development and in particular on higher standards of housing in the endemic zones.

Leishmaniasis is found in tropical and subtropical areas all over the world. The disease is widely disseminated in South America and spreading elsewhere, notably in Africa; serious outbreaks took place in India and Kenya in 1977. The control strategy is based on control of the vector sandflies and of reservoir hosts (mainly rodents and dogs) and partly on immunization (available against cutaneous leishmaniasis only). Special attention is being paid to research on chemotherapy and new approaches in immunology, parasitology, and pathology. Community-based control activities are a distinct possibility for the future, within the framework of extended primary health care activities.

Acute diarrhoeal diseases (including cholera) and enteric infections

While the cholera situation showed a steady improvement in the period under review as regards the total number of cases reported to WHO, which decreased from some 108 000 in both 1973 and 1974 to about 59 000 in 1977, there was little change in the number of countries affected. In 1977, some 34 countries reported the disease, the same number as in 1972; the maximum number during the period under review was 36 countries in 1974. Although some countries managed to free themselves of cholera, the disease spread to 15 cholera-free countries or areas in all regions except the Americas during the 5-year period. The spread of cholera to Kiribati (Gilbert Islands) in Oceania in 1977 and its recrudescence in a number of countries in Asia and Africa that had been free for several years caused particular concern and showed that there was little hope as yet of the present pandemic coming to an end.

New knowledge resulting from extensive clinical, epidemiological, and bacteriological studies has had a considerable influence on the current attitude of the health authorities and of the public towards the disease and on practices in diagnosis and control. There appears to be less panic and less tendency to impose severe unjustified restrictions on traffic and trade. However, because of slow progress in the improvement of water supply and excreta disposal, cholera is continuing to spread in receptive areas and to become endemic, though little is known about the real situation because of the difficulties of surveillance. Countries with higher levels of sanitation and better surveillance systems have been able to avoid its spread within their territories when infection has been introduced. The Organization continued to cooperate with countries in the control of outbreaks and was gratified to note a steady decrease in the demand for cholera vaccine in such situations. No significant advance has been made in immunological control, though two aluminium adjuvant bivalent whole-cell vaccines have been found to protect children in endemic areas to a much greater extent than the vaccine generally available; they also provided about 50% protection for approximately 14 months in adults. A toxoid vaccine prepared from cholera enterotoxin was found to offer little protection in a field trial, and a combined whole cell/toxoid vaccine is now being developed.

The research effort has perhaps been most fruitful in the improvement and simplification of treatment. The understanding of the physiological basis of oral rehydration with the required salts and sugar in proper concentration, the demonstration of the effectiveness of this procedure in the treatment of dehydration due to almost all acute diarrhoeas, including cholera at all ages, the fact that it can be brought to the patient's home and administered by health workers without any formal professional training and by mothers with a little guidance, and the evidence that this method of rehydration during diarrhoea helps children to gain significantly more weight than those who are not so treated—all these factors have offered new hope to millions of children in areas where diarrhoeal diseases and cholera are endemic.

Although there is a lack of reliable information on the incidence of diarrhoeal diseases and related mortality, it has been estimated that in 1975 there were about 500 million episodes of diarrhoea in children under 5 years of age in Asia, Africa, and Latin America. These episodes, coupled with—for example—poor nutritional status, malaria, or lack of immunization, resulted in at least 5 million deaths. Most of these diarrhoeas are now known to be caused by rotavirus, enterotoxigenic *Escherichia coli*, or certain other newly recognized enteropathogens. In cholera-endemic areas, cholera constitutes only a very small proportion, probably not more than 5–10%, of all acute diarrhoeas and in more than 90% of instances is clinically indistinguishable from other acute diarrhoeas.

An interdisciplinary approach, centred upon primary health care and involving activities in the fields of water supply and excreta disposal, communicable diseases, maternal and child health, nutrition, and health education, is regarded as essential for the ultimate control of these diseases and is in fact being adopted in WHO medium-term programming. In addition, it is recognized that one critical strategy that could be applied now within available means and that should have a very significant immediate impact on a global basis is the widespread practice of oral rehydration therapy supported by education on dietetic management and personal hygiene. The significance of this development in the context of national primary health care programmes is obvious. Many countries are now using oral rehydration for the control of epidemics as well as for the routine treatment of acute diarrhoeas, including cholera; thus they are not only reaching communities that were previously deprived of such benefits but are also potentially economizing on hospitalization and costly intravenous fluids.

In 1973, typhoid and dysentery due to drug-resistant organisms caused widespread epidemics in the Americas and limited outbreaks in Asia. A WHO meeting on International Surveillance for the Prevention and Control of Health Hazards due to Drug-resistant Enterobacteriaceae held in late 1977 recommended the implementation of a system of surveillance to generate internationally comparable data so as to provide regular information and guidance to health workers and facilitate the development of national policies for the rational use, manufacture, and import of antibiotics.

Tuberculosis

The global tuberculosis situation is changing only slowly, thus reflecting not only the specific epidemiological dynamics of the disease but also the difficulties faced by many countries in the application of the available control techniques. As a result, tuberculosis is one of the few communicable diseases that has been reported by all WHO regions as one of the most important public health problems (along with the group of non-tuberculous respiratory diseases and hepatitis).

According to estimates based on data from 88 Member countries,[1] about 3.5 million people develop tuberculosis each year and more than half a million die from it. Tuberculosis occupied the fourth place among the causes of death in the South-East Asia Region, the seventh place in the Western Pacific, the ninth place in the Eastern Mediterranean, the eleventh place in the Region of the Americas, and the thirteenth place in European Region.

With the highly efficacious drug regimens that have become available, mortality has lost its importance as an epidemiological index for measuring the magnitude of the tuberculosis problem. A high mortality from tuberculosis merely signals the inadequacy of the treatment component of the national tuberculosis control programme—in particular a lack of regularity in drug ingestion. The highest mortality rate (75 per 100 000 inhabitants) was reported from the Philippines in 1974.[2] In Oceania, mortality rates ranged from 22.4 per 100 000 in the Pacific Islands in 1971 to 2.4 in New Zealand in 1975, 0.9 in Australia in

---

[1] BULLA, A. Global review of tuberculosis morbidity and mortality in the world (1961–1971). *World health statistics report*, **30**: 2–38 (1977).

[2] WORLD HEALTH ORGANIZATION. *World health statistics annual, 1977. Vol. 1: Vital statistics and causes of death.* Geneva, 1977.

1975, and 1.1 in Tonga in 1971.[1,2] Such differences between countries and areas were also observed in other parts of the world, e.g., in Africa where the range was from 32.1 in Réunion in 1971 to 3.4 per 100 000 population in Congo in 1971;[1] in the Americas, where the range was from 29.8 per 100 000 in Peru in 1972 to 1.6 and 1.5 in the USA and Canada respectively in 1974;[1,3] and in Europe, where the rates ranged from 12.8 in Poland in 1975 to 1.9 and 1.0 per 100 000 (in Denmark and the Netherlands respectively) in 1976.[2,3] In technologically advanced countries tuberculosis often caused more deaths than all other notifiable infections diseases combined.

Morbidity reports[1] differed widely from country to country, with high rates ranging from 300 to more than 500 per 100 000 inhabitants in Burma, East Timor, Macao, the Philippines, and the Republic of Korea, and rates lower than 20 per 100 000 in Australia, Canada, Denmark, the Netherlands, and the USA, where tuberculosis control programmes have been operating successfully for a long time. To improve the quality of morbidity reports, efforts were made by WHO to convince Member States that bacteriological confirmation needs to be reported separately as the only conclusive criterion of diagnosis.

Whereas mortality from tuberculosis can be lowered almost immediately by an effective treatment programme, the impact on morbidity shows only in subsequent years. This retarded impact is also usually observed with BCG vaccination programmes. Whereas immunization with a potent BCG vaccine generally prevents the development of tuberculous disease in uninfected individuals, a good treatment programme lowers the risk of tuberculosis infection in the community.

During the period 1973–1977, coverage in the BCG vaccination programme throughout the world increased substantially when the direct vaccination approach without prior tuberculin testing was adopted. For example, in 18 Latin American countries where a total of 122 million BCG vaccinations were given during a 12-month period, four countries reported reaching a coverage of 75% or more of their child population (between 0–14 years) and seven countries achieved coverages of the order of 50–74%. The direct approach also enabled more and more countries to provide combined immunization against tuberculosis and smallpox. BCG has been included with five other vaccines against childhood diseases in the Expanded Programme on Immunization (see page 93).

To evaluate the magnitude and nature of the tuberculosis problem, both in developed and in developing countries, the most relevant and practical epidemiological index is the annual infection rate, which reflects the risk of being infected (or reinfected) in a given community during a year. During the period 1973–1977, the risk of infection declined steeply (by as much as 12% each year) in some of the more privileged countries, approaching levels as low as 0.03% or even less. In developing countries, however, the risk of infection with tuberculosis was 20–50 times higher and, moreover, it often remained constant or declined only insignificantly.

Although the highly efficacious drug regimens available have made it possible to provide ambulatory treatment and also to shorten the duration of chemotherapy, this is

[1] BULLA, A. Global review of tuberculosis morbidity and mortality in the world (1961–1971). *World health statistics report,* **30**: 2–38 (1977).

[2] WORLD HEALTH ORGANIZATION. *World health statistics annual, 1978. Vol. 1: Vital statistics and causes of death.* Geneva, 1978.

[3] WORLD HEALTH ORGANIZATION. *World health statistics annual, 1977. Vol. 1: Vital statistics and causes of death.* Geneva, 1977.

not yet sufficiently reflected in the tuberculosis bed density (number of tuberculosis beds per 10 000 population) in many countries. Nevertheless, the question of beds is becoming increasingly important in a broad public health sense, since, apart from the substantial capital cost of institutional facilities, it influences both the pattern of the services rendered and the use of the resources available. The extension of efficient primary health care systems could be important in improving possibilities of ambulatory treatment for tuberculosis and of earlier case-finding.

Leprosy

Leprosy control has been accepted by an increasing number of governments as an item in overall health plans. However, the difficulties of taking operational action and the lack of training and experience of primary health care workers in leprosy control remained major problems during the period under review. Resistance to dapsone, the standard drug given against leprosy, has become quite common, reaching up to 3% per annum in groups of patients undergoing ambulatory treatment. As a countermeasure, combined chemotherapy has been advised by WHO for all multibacillary patients, with adequate supervision of the regular drug intake and adequate training of the health staff in combined drug regimens. By 1980, this training will be a prominent feature of technical cooperation. The actual number of leprosy cases requiring treatment is not known. A large proportion of the estimated 12 million cases are still detected very late or treated inadequately.

According to answers by governments to questionnaires relating to the period 1975–1977, the leprosy problem has not declined to any great extent over the past 15 years.[1] Large numbers of leprosy cases still went undetected in all regions (an estimated 700 000 in the African Region alone). Burma, Thailand, Upper Volta and some other African countries have, however, succeeded in achieving a reduction of 70–75% in the initial caseload. To obtain significant results, at least 75% of all estimated infectious cases must be treated.

In the African Region, the prevalence of leprosy ranged, in most countries, from 10 to 40 per 1000 population, the proportion of lepromatous cases being between 10% and 15%; WHO-assisted leprosy control has been integrated into epidemiological programmes and plans for the strengthening of health services. In the Region of the Americas, where some 68% of all registered cases were under surveillance and 85% of all new cases were regularly reported from five countries only, the Pan American Center for Training and Research in Leprosy and Tropical Diseases, in Caracas, has promoted the coordination of manpower training for detection and treatment. In the South-East Asia Region, where the number of leprosy cases was estimated at about four million (3.2 million in India), leprosy control was also in the process of being integrated into health programmes, and WHO assisted in the training of national staff and health education of the public. In the Western Pacific Region, because of the low priority given to leprosy control, the disease constituted a public health problem in some areas, where new cases were discovered in many communities, often at a late stage of the disease; the majority of leprosy cases have been treated on an ambulatory basis, and in 1977 a Regional Leprosy

---

[1] *Weekly epidemiological record*, **54**: 17–23 (1979).

Advisory Team undertook epidemiological and operational surveys to provide guidance on the implementation of national leprosy control programmes.

As in the case of tuberculosis and many other diseases, the strengthening of primary health care activities would permit more efficient early case-finding and less expensive ambulatory care for those who had contracted leprosy.

Cerebrospinal meningitis

During the period 1973–1977, a rise in morbidity from epidemic cerebrospinal meningitis was observed in many European countries and in Africa, Latin America, and Asia. In the early stages of epidemics, diagnosis was sometimes difficult. However, whenever large outbreaks occurred, the causative agent was usually *Neisseria meningitidis* (predominantly Group A but occasionally Group C as well, as was the case in Brazil from 1972 to 1975). During interepidemic periods, sporadic cases were associated with an increased frequency of serotype B and other microorganisms. Between 40 000 and 50 000 cases of bacterial cerebrospinal meningitis were reported to WHO annually.[1]

Mono- and polyvalent polysaccharide vaccines (A or C or A+C) were produced as a result of WHO-supported activities for the development, production, and evaluation of meningococcal vaccines. They have proved their effectiveness in epidemics in Brazil and Mongolia, and in controlled field trials in Egypt, Finland, Sudan and the USA. Mono- and polyvalent vaccines (A or C or A+C) stabilized with lactose, which facilitates transportation and conservation, were also produced.

Smallpox

The intensified programme for smallpox eradication was launched in 1967; in that year 44 countries reported smallpox, including 32 in which the disease was considered to be endemic. By the end of 1972 endemic transmission had been interrupted in all but six countries: Bangladesh, Botswana, Ethiopia, India, Nepal, and Pakistan. From 1973, the number of countries affected steadily declined. By the end of 1977, no country was reporting smallpox cases.

Smallpox was eradicated in Asia by the end of 1975, but its spread in the Horn of Africa was not checked until an intensified campaign was initiated in Somalia in 1977.

By the end of 1977, international commissions convened by WHO had certified 45 countries as free of smallpox.

During the period 1973–1977, the yearly totals reported for the world were 135 853 cases in 1973, 218 364 in 1974, 19 278 in 1975, 954 in 1976, 3234 in 1977, and 2 (both due to laboratory infection) in 1978.

The year 1973 was an important one for two reasons: the marked decrease in incidence in Ethiopia from 16 999 cases in 1972 to 5414 in 1973, and the establishment of more complete surveillance in Bangladesh, India, and Pakistan, countries that accounted for over 95% of the cases reported that year; this was organized through periodic active searches by special teams. In the same year, the need for continued surveillance in countries considered to be free of smallpox was exemplified in Botswana by the occurrence of two outbreaks in March and September. The last case in Botswana was reported in December 1973.

---

[1] *World health statistics report*, **30**: 369–373 (1977); *World health statistics quarterly*, **31**: 359–398 (1978).

The year 1974 was characterized by an increase in overall incidence, but a decrease in the geographical extent of heavily infected areas. At the start of the year, endemic smallpox was recorded in five countries: Bangladesh, Ethiopia, India, Nepal, and Pakistan. Four north-eastern states accounted for 96% of all cases in India, and thus for the overall increase in the worldwide reported incidence. A similar reduction in the areas involved occurred in Ethiopia. The last quarter of 1974 saw a marked improvement in the world situation. Pakistan was successful in interrupting transmission in October.

1975 was an historic year. Transmission of variola major, the severe form of smallpox, was finally interrupted in the world, variola minor remaining endemic only in the Horn of Africa. At the beginning of the year, smallpox was restricted to five districts in Bangladesh, three states in India, two provinces in Ethiopia, and Nepal. The last case in India occurred on 24 May, and the last in Nepal on 6 April. In Bangladesh, where the situation first deteriorated, an internationally supported emergency plan, with active searches and rewards for reported smallpox cases, led to a decrease in the number of cases which started in June and ended on 16 October when the last case of variola major in the world was recorded. In the same year, transmission of variola minor steadily declined in Ethiopia.

The major achievement of the year 1976 was the attainment of zero incidence in Ethiopia, where the final case was recorded on 9 August. For five weeks no smallpox cases were reported in the world, but, in the later part of the year, 34 cases were detected in Mogadishu (Somalia) as a consequence of importation of the disease by nomads.

In early 1977, five cases of smallpox occurred in Kenya as a result of importation of the disease from Somalia; these were to be the last cases in Kenya. In Somalia, the outbreak which had been detected in Mogadishu in late 1976 came to an end on 17 January. However, surveillance in surrounding regions detected an increasing number of cases with a peak of 1388 cases in June. An emergency operation was conducted with international assistance, and the last case of endemic smallpox in the world occurred in Somalia on 26 October 1977. By the end of 1977, worldwide interruption of smallpox transmission appeared to have been achieved, and the necessary steps were undertaken to verify eradication during the following two years.

In 1977, only 18 laboratories maintained strains of variola virus, compared with 76 in 1975. A further reduction in the number of laboratories retaining the variola virus is expected. Moreover, the virus will be retained only under conditions of maximum security.

Diseases of childhood preventable by immunization

During the period under review, WHO initiated the Expanded Programme on Immunization (EPI), with the goal of reducing morbidity and mortality from diphtheria, pertussis, tetanus, measles, poliomyelitis, and tuberculosis by providing immunization against these diseases for every child in the world by 1990. At present, fewer than 10% of the 80 million children born annually in developing countries are being fully immunized.

While the reported numbers of cases and deaths may underestimate the extent of the consequences of these six diseases, they are thought to cause some 5 million deaths among children under 5 years, while blinding, crippling, or otherwise permanently disabling an additional 5 million. Of course, as is the case with the large numbers of childhood deaths estimated to be due to, for example, diarrhoeal diseases and malaria, these deaths usually occur in the context of severe malnutrition and interacting diseases. The figures published for individual diseases usually involve considerable overlap. The leading killers are measles, pertussis, and neonatal tetanus. The first two diseases affect most unimmunized children under 5 and have case-fatality rates ranging between 1% and 10%, the higher rates being more commonly observed among younger and/or less well nourished children. Although evidence on the subject is relatively scanty, it is thought that neonatal tetanus probably affects fewer than 2% of children born to unimmunized mothers in developing countries, but 70–90% of those infected die.

The leading crippler is poliomyelitis. Virtually every unimmunized child is infected with one or more of the polioviruses, the infection resulting in paralysis in 1–2% of children under the age of 3 years and in a higher proportion of the older children infected. An ominous trend[1] is the increase in the numbers of cases of paralytic poliomyelitis recorded in developing areas during the period under review, perhaps as a result of improved reporting, but perhaps also because of improved standards of living, which, by delaying the average age of first exposure to polioviruses, may contribute to higher rates for paralytic poliomyelitis. Death may occur in 15% of paralytic cases.

Morbidity and mortality for diphtheria are less well defined than for other diseases, although over 100 000 deaths from the disease are believed to occur annually among children less than 5 years of age (for tuberculosis, see page 89).

The EPI formally started in 1974, in response to a resolution by the Twenty-seventh World Health Assembly. By the end of the period under review, 42 developing countries, in which some 57 million children are born annually, had expanded their immunization programmes in active collaboration with WHO. WHO staff for the EPI had been appointed at country, regional, and headquarters levels, and an active training programme dealing mainly with management and vaccine quality control had been started for national staff.

It is expected that it will take several years for these activities to result in increases in the proportion of susceptible children being effectively immunized and in reduced morbidity and mortality from the target diseases. In fact, experience in the early years of the smallpox eradication programme suggests that the coming five years are likely to witness sharp increases in the numbers of reported cases, resulting from improved disease surveillance. A special advantage of the EPI, as compared with the smallpox programme, is that it comes into existence at a time when there is growing understanding of the great assistance that well-structured primary health care systems can give to disease control programmes, and the potential contribution of active community participation to programmes such as the EPI. In many countries, especially those with the least material resources, the active participation of the community is likely to make all the difference to the success of national immunization programmes.

Viral diseases

The period 1973–1977 was marked by two unusual situations as far as *influenza* was concerned. An influenza A virus, A/New Jersey/76 (Hsw1N1), closely resembling the swine influenza virus of 1918, caused an outbreak among 500 persons in a military camp in the USA in January 1976. It was first feared that this might be the beginning of a

---

[1] For a detailed study of trends in poliomyelitis see: PACCAUD, M. F., World trends in poliomyelitis, morbidity and mortality, 1951–1975. *World health statistics quarterly.* **32**: 198–224 (1979).

deadly pandemic as in 1918. Governments therefore envisaged different policies, which were reviewed during a meeting in WHO, Geneva in April 1976. Some countries decided to embark on immediate vaccination, whereas others preferred to constitute emergency reserves of vaccine. However, the virus showed no great epidemic potential, and no further spread was observed in the USA, or in other countries. Another unusual situation occurred in 1977 when epidemics associated with strain A/USSR/90/77 (H1N1)—close to the viruses A(H1N1) that prevailed from 1947 to 1957—took place first in China as from May, and then in the USSR and Hong Kong as from November, before spreading to the rest of the world, concurrently with epidemics associated with variants of the virus A(H3N2)—or A/Hong Kong—already in circulation. Everywhere the disease associated with A(H1N1) was relatively mild and affected mostly groups of people below 25 years of age in schools, universities, and military formations. It largely spared persons belonging to older age groups who were born before the extinction of virus A(H1N1) in 1957. Following meetings held at WHO headquarters in early 1978, virus A/USSR/90/77(H1H1) was introduced in vaccine formulation.

A major breakthrough occurred in virology with the isolation and characterization of *hepatitis* viruses A and B, and this gave some evidence that at least a third one now existed and was associated with post-transfusion hepatitis. Immunoglobulins are now available against hepatitis A and B and a vaccine against hepatitis B is under preparation.

In 1976, sudden epidemics of *viral haemorrhagic fevers* with high fatality occurred simultaneously in the Sudan and Zaire.[1] A new virus was characterized: Ebola virus, resembling Marburg disease virus. The epidemics were caused by man-to-man transmission, and a high number of cases were of nosocomial origin. In the Sudan, there were epidemics in two townships in the southern region. The first one caused 70 cases, 33 of which were fatal, and the second 229 cases,[2] 117 of which were fatal; in the second town involved, 76 members of the hospital staff of 230 were infected and 41 died. In Zaire, the outbreak, which involved many villages in an area with a radius of 120 km, caused 318 cases involving 280 deaths.[3] WHO emergency aid contributed to the successful mobilization of all the resources needed to overcome the spread of this dangerous new virus.

Zoonoses and foodborne diseases

There have been increases in the incidence of zoonoses and in the risk factors associated with poor food hygiene. This trend was due to: increases in human populations and in the numbers of animals in contact with man; urbanization and environmental pollution; the inadequate health measures taken by uncoordinated veterinary and public health services; changing patterns of land use and agricultural practices; industrialization of food production; evolution of consumer habits involving greater collective consumption and use of processed foods; an increase in the national and international trade in foods and feeds; and the development of tourism.

Although international programmes for the surveillance and control of zoonoses and foodborne diseases were developed, the problem seems to have grown faster than the services to deal with it. To prevent and control diseases with complex epidemiological

---

[1] See *Weekly epidemiological record*, **52** 177–180, 185–192 (1977).
[2] Plus one nosocomial case in the hospital of Juba, where four patients were evacuated.
[3] *Bulletin of the World Health Organization*, **56**: 271–293 (1978).

patterns such as brucellosis, leptospirosis, salmonellosis, mycosis, and a number of parasitic diseases associated with dense populations, steps were taken to set up a network of collaborating centres to assist governments by promoting the international coordination and concentration of resources (expertise, facilities, and material). In close cooperation with FAO, the International Office of Epizootics, and regional institutions, WHO provided guidance on the promotion of legislation for the control of zoonoses, food hygiene, and the disposal and recycling of wastes from animal industries.

A start was made on the development of international guidelines, adapted to different socioeconomic conditions, concerning the prevention and control of zoonotic and food-borne diseases. Specific codes of practice are required for those working in agriculture, food-handling, and the processing of animal by-products. Intensive large-scale animal production, in particular, has contributed to an increase in health hazards for the workers concerned.

The infrastructure needed to enforce the regulations has still to be developed in many countries, notably as regards adequate cooperation between health and veterinary services. Veterinary services have to be mobilized so that they can contribute to comprehensive health plans. In rural areas veterinary services play an important part in improving health, thus contributing to rural development. Better use should be made of veterinary services in primary health care, particularly as they extend far into peripheral areas and can give valuable help with laboratory services (transport of vaccines and specimens, bacteriological work, antibiotic sensitivity testing, serodiagnosis of certain zoonotic diseases).

To reduce malnutrition and other health hazards, research should be promoted on zoonoses and other diseases of animals used for food that may reduce the availability of proteins; research should also be developed in the food production industries on ways of reducing losses of food, which sometimes reach 50%. Research in comparative medicine has led to progress in knowledge of certain diseases, such as influenza—it was found, for example, that influenza A viruses from domestic and wild animals were presenting haemagglutinin and neuraminidase antigens similar to those of recent human influenza A viruses.

It is expected that in future years the increasing populations of man, livestock, pet animals, and man-associated wildlife will cause an exponential increase of zoonotic and foodborne diseases in rural and urban areas if the development of those activities of veterinary services with a bearing on human health goes on at the present pace. A considerable effort should therefore be made to improve the situation.

Sexually transmitted diseases

The resistance of gonococcal strains to penicillin and other antibiotics continued its upward trend, particularly in areas where non-observance or absence of national drug control regulations fostered the misuse of antibiotics. The rapid shift towards drug resistance in many developing countries may entail a prohibitive escalation in the cost of treatment.

An additional complication has been the sudden emergence of penicillinase-producing gonococcal strains, totally resistant to therapeutic doses of penicillin, separately in East Asia and West Africa in early 1976. Since then these strains have been isolated in some 21 countries, a few of which provided an environment favouring their maintenance and now function as foci for their international dissemination.

Since 1975 an increasing number of countries have reported an impressive increase in syphilis transmission. This trend has been expected as a result of the universal tendency to replace penicillin by other antibiotics in the initial treatment of gonorrhoea.

The epidemic trend of gonococcal infections[1] has been declining in some countries after reaching a peak about 1974–1975, but this decline has often been more than compensated for by an increase in the incidence of nongonococcal genital infections—the latter being now more common in nearly all countries. Particular attention is being paid to certain serotypes of *Chlamydia trachomatis* which are associated with 35–50% of all cases of nongonococcal urethritis and cervicitis; there is strong evidence that some of the sequelae attributed to gonococcal infections (e.g., salpingitis, peritonitis, infertility) could also be caused by *C. trachomatis*. The perinatal transfer of this agent may cause inclusion conjunctivitis (usually self-limited) in 30–40% of infants born to infected mothers and pneumonitis in about 15% of them.

The systematic surveillance of sexually transmitted diseases in important groups such as pregnant women and in selected high-risk groups has been organized through primary health workers. These workers are being trained for diagnosis and systematic treatment, with or without laboratory assistance, so that adequate control may be obtained even in the most peripheral areas.

Endemic treponematoses

After ten years of mass-treatment campaigns against the endemic treponematoses (yaws, endemic syphilis, pinta) in most tropical countries, the prevalence of these diseases was reduced to low levels and in some areas their transmission was interrupted. Complacency after successful mass campaigns and the premature discontinuation of surveillance activities have led to resurgences of these crippling infections in a number of countries, principally in Africa. For the period 1976–1977, a number of West African countries reported increased transmission of yaws or endemic syphilis, these diseases apparently being more frequent than they were before the mass campaigns. Owing to their epidemiological pattern and the scarcity of resources in areas where they occur, endemic treponematoses may again constitute a serious health hazard in a few years if adequate measures are not organized urgently, possibly with external assistance.

Special teams may be temporarily required to control this trend, pending the development and implementation of adequate primary health care systems.

Blindness

The importance of blindness as a major health, medical, social, and economic problem is best measured in terms of morbidity and disability.

At the national and international levels, the statistical data both for morbidity and disability are very limited or completely lacking. For this reason the extent of blindness is evaluated on the basis of different estimates. Using the definition in the International

---

[1] WHO Technical Report Series, No. 616, 1978 (Neisseria gonorrhoeae *and gonococcal infections.* Report of a WHO Scientific Group).

Classification of Diseases (ICD), "less than 6/60 of visual impairment", the number of blind people in the world is estimated at 40–42 million, or 1% of the population. Using another ICD criterion "less than 3/60 of visual impairment", the number of people in this category is estimated at 28 million. The number of totally blind people in the world is estimated at 16 million, i.e., about 0.4% of the world's population. At least, two-thirds of the cases could have been prevented or could be cured.

Observations, studies, or estimates of blindness rates for different countries or regions vary considerably: from 150 to more than 1000 per 100 000 population in Africa, from 90 to 1000 per 100 000 population in the Americas, from 250 to 4000 per 100 000 population in Asia, and from 50 to 275 per 100 000 population in Europe and Oceania.[1] These figures generally apply to "total" blindness and do not include the large number of persons incapacitated by partial loss of vision.

In the Eastern Mediterranean Region, for a population of 250 million, it was estimated that there were in 1975 approximately 7.5 million blind persons (figure based on category 3 of the ICD definition, i.e., acuity of less than 3/60) or 3% of the population. The same estimate gave a higher rate (4–4.7%) for the rural population, among whom infections (i.e., trachoma) and malnutrition are relatively more prevalent because of the generally low socioeconomic level and other environmental factors.

Causes of blindness can roughly be divided into two broad categories: accidents and disease. Accidents are likely to affect all age groups. Loss of vision caused by disease may be linked to degenerative changes usually occurring late in life, e.g., glaucoma, diabetic retinopathy, and vascular disease, particularly in industrialized countries. In less developed countries, infections and malnutrition are the most important causes of loss of vision and they tend to manifest themselves during childhood or throughout the entire life span. This has an even more severe impact on the individual affected and on society, with complex public health, social, and economic implications.

As already mentioned, it has been estimated that at least two-thirds of the cases of blindness in the world could have been prevented or could be cured by the application of existing knowledge. Probably more than half of the world's blind are affected by *cataract*, which appears to occur early in life in certain parts of the developing world and which could be cured by a relatively simple operation. Among the others, an estimated 2 million cases are caused by severe *trachoma*, while an undetermined number of very young children become blind—and often die—because of xerophthalmia caused by vitamin A deficiency and linked with protein-energy malnutrition. *Onchocerciasis* is the main cause of blindness in parts of Africa, where it represents a serious obstacle to socioeconomic development. Present knowledge and methods are to some extent adequate to control these causes of blindness but further progress is hampered either by the lack of available resources or the poor utilization of those that are available, or more usually a combination of both factors.

Although, during the period under review, the control of trachoma and onchocerciasis was undertaken mostly through national or multinational mass campaigns in a number of countries, the trend is now towards a more comprehensive approach, and a blindness prevention programme has been promoted as a major priority by WHO. Primary eye care will be provided as part of general primary health care, and a strong ophthalmic care

---

[1] *WHO Chronicle*, **33**: 275–283 (1979).

structure will be developed at the intermediate and central levels to ensure adequate referral and training facilities. It is proposed, however, to start with intensive programmes whenever they are required and to use them for the training of health personnel, including primary health workers.

Cardiovascular diseases

(a) *Extent of the problem*

In developed countries, cardiovascular diseases remained the leading cause of death among men in the period under review; they were the second or third leading cause among women. In many developed countries they accounted for half the total mortality. If present conditions persist, every second person born alive will ultimately die from cardiovascular disease.

In some countries there is a noticeable tendency towards a decrease in the mortality from cardiovascular diseases owing to a reduction in mortality from stroke, rheumatic heart disease, and hypertensive disease. Certain countries have also recorded a decrease in mortality from ischaemic heart disease. Specifically, these declining trends were noted in the USA (Fig. 13). Simultaneously, in the USA, a decrease in serum lipid levels and an improvement in hypertension control were noted. Other countries, like Australia, Belgium, Canada, Japan, and New Zealand also showed declining mortality trends, but not such marked ones. In some countries, such as Finland, mortality tended to decline only for those under 60 years of age, while for those over 60 years there was no change. On the other hand, in most countries with relatively low mortality rates, such as Bulgaria, Poland, Romania, and Yugoslavia, mortality from ischaemic heart disease is tending to

Fig. 13. Mortality per 100 000 population from cardiovascular diseases, United States of America, 1968–1976.

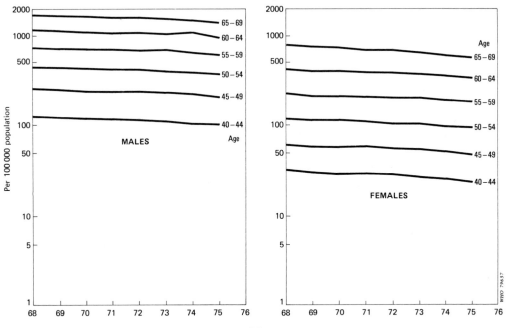

increase. In most of the remaining countries mortality rates from ischaemic heart disease remained unchanged during the period under review.

In industrialized countries, cardiovascular diseases—and notably ischaemic heart disease—rank first as a cause of premature deaths in those age groups in which productivity and social and family responsibilities are highest. This trend should eventually appear in the developing countries, too, as they proceed with their industrial development. Table 12 shows attack rates for acute myocardial infarction in the age groups 20–64 years in 21 areas studied under a WHO project,[1] which provided information on more than 10 000 cases of acute myocardial infarction occurring during a year among a study population of 3.5 million.

In some less developed countries, cardiovascular diseases have emerged rather abruptly

Table 12. Annual attack rate of acute myocardial infarction per 1000 population by age and sex

Centre	Sex	Age group						Age-standardized attack rate[a]
		20–39	40–44	45–49	50–54	55–59	60–64	20–64
Gothenburg	M	0.1	1.0	3.2	5.5	8.1	9.7	2.6
	F	0.03	0.2	0.3	0.9	2.0	3.1	0.6
Prague	M	0.3	1.8	3.4	7.5	11.5	12.3	3.5
	F	0.0	0.1	0.4	1.2	1.5	3.4	0.6
Bucharest	M	0.1	0.8	1.5	3.1	4.9	5.8	1.5
	F	0.01	0.3	0.6	0.7	1.0	2.5	0.3
Budapest	M	0.3	2.4	3.4	6.1	7.3	11.1	2.9
	F	0.1	0.4	0.7	1.7	1.7	4.3	0.8
Dublin	M	0.4	1.9	6.9	10.9	13.8	15.5	4.7
	F	0.03	0.5	1.8	2.8	3.4	5.4	1.3
Heidelburg	M	0.3	1.8	3.7	4.4	6.8	9.9	2.6
	F	0.02	0.1	0.3	0.4	0.7	2.3	0.4
Helsinki	M	0.4	4.8	9.3	14.5	21.8	26.9	7.3
	F	0.1	0.4	1.7	2.4	4.3	8.6	1.6
London	M	0.6	4.0	4.8	8.0	11.4	15.2	4.3
	F	0.03	1.1	1.3	1.1	3.5	5.4	1.2
Nijmegen	M	0.3	3.3	5.2	9.9	14.1	17.8	4.8
	F	0.1	0.5	0.4	1.3	2.4	5.7	1.0
Tampere	M	0.2	4.4	6.8	13.3	16.2	25.4	6.2
	F	0.0	0.0	0.7	1.9	2.6	7.1	1.1
Warsaw	M	0.3	2.3	3.9	5.9	8.4	10.9	3.1
	F	0.03	0.3	1.1	1.7	2.9	4.0	0.9
Lublin	M	0.2	2.2	3.1	5.5	7.2	9.2	2.6
	F	0.03	0.3	0.9	0.3	1.4	2.7	0.5
Innsbruck	M	0.2	2.0	3.7	5.6	7.3	10.2	2.8
	F	0.04	0.0	0.4	1.1	1.3	2.8	0.5
Kaunas	M	0.3	1.9	2.9	5.9	5.1	10.4	2.6
	F	0.0	0.2	0.3	0.8	1.2	2.4	0.4
Boden	M	0.2	2.6	3.3	9.0	12.7	16.0	4.1
	F	0.0	0.0	2.4	3.1	6.5	2.7	1.4
Sofia	M	0.2	0.8	3.2	2.3	4.2	7.0	1.7
	F	0.01	0.1	0.1	0.2	1.1	0.9	0.2
Perth	M	0.3	2.9	5.5	8.2	13.1	19.0	4.6
	F	0.04	0.6	1.0	2.5	4.6	6.2	1.4
Tel Aviv	M	0.2	2.2	4.5	6.8	8.2	19.1	3.8
	F	0.03	0.3	0.8	2.7	4.3	6.8	1.3
Berlin	M	0.2	1.4	3.1	3.6	9.8	8.9	2.6
	F	0.0	0.4	0.6	1.8	2.5	4.8	0.9
Erfurt	M	0.1	1.5	1.4	2.5	3.4	5.2	1.4
	F	0.03	0.1	0.5	0.2	1.1	0.9	0.3
Pasewalk	M	0.3	1.5	4.6	3.7	4.8	12.4	2.6
	F	0.0	0.0	0.0	1.1	0.7	3.8	0.5

[a] The age composition of the total population in the study areas has been used as the standard for the computation of the age-standardized rate.

[1] *Myocardial infarction community registers.* Copenhagen, WHO Regional Office for Europe, 1976 (Public Health in Europe, No. 5).

as a major public health concern, suggesting that they are becoming a problem of worldwide dimensions and one that will increasingly attract attention.

Rheumatic fever and rheumatic heart diseases are the leading cardiovascular disease category in most developing countries[1] and are prevalent in developed countries as well (see Table 13).

Prevalence rates for rheumatic heart disease give the best idea of the impact of rheumatic fever on the health of populations. They are usually based on the screening of groups of schoolchildren. This is relatively easy to perform and may yield satisfactory information on the most relevant aspect of the disease: valvular heart disease in the young. The reported prevalence rates in school-age children in various parts of the world range from very low to as high as 33 cases per 1000 (among inhabitants of slums and other underprivileged areas). Since rheumatic fever is preventable, efforts to improve the present situation should be increased, particularly in the developing countries.

Hypertension, although itself not a symptomatic disease, is one of the most important factors in the pathogenesis of stroke and ischaemic heart disease and is a direct cause of hypertensive heart and renal disease. It is prevalent among the populations of developed as well as developing countries. A graph showing the distribution of blood pressure among different populations is presented in Fig. 14. Three important facts are illustrated by the examples given in this figure: (*a*) a high proportion of people in various populations have high blood pressure; (*b*) blood pressure tends to be higher in older age groups; and (*c*) the distribution is similar in the examples from both developed and developing countries.

Stroke makes an important contribution to morbidity and mortality, particularly in older age groups, in developing as well as in developed countries. Table 14 on page 103 gives age-specific annual incidence rates for cerebrovascular attacks as observed in a WHO cooperative project involving community-based registration of all cases of stroke in various parts of the world. Although differences do exist among the populations studied, these are—on a world scale—considerably smaller than the differences in the incidence of ischaemic heart disease. Stroke is thus a worldwide health problem.

Table 13. Mortality from rheumatic heart disease and rheumatic fever in selected countries in age group 15–24 years[a]

Country	Year	Deaths per 100 000[b]	Rank among causes of deaths[b]
Bulgaria	1974	3.3	2
Romania	1973	3.8	2
Poland	1973	1.9	3
Portugal	1974	3.0	3
Italy	1973	1.7	4
Yugoslavia	1973	1.6	4
Spain	1973	1.5	5
Israel	1973	0.8	6
Greece	1974	0.8	8
Czechoslovakia	1973	0.8	9
USA	1973	0.5	11
France	1973	0.4	12
Hungary	1974	0.7	12

[a] Based on data from *World health statistics annual, 1973–1976, Vol. I. Vital statistics and causes of death.* Geneva, World Health Organization, 1976.
[b] Accidents and ill-defined conditions excluded.

[1] See *Bulletin of the World Health Organization*, **56**: 887–912 (1978).

Fig. 14. Systolic blood pressure distribution in three different populations.

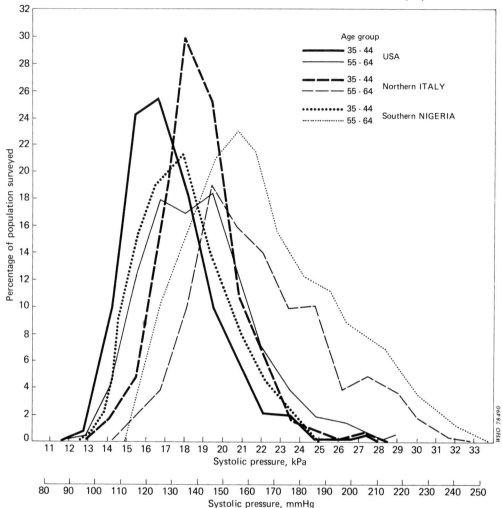

(b) *Community action*

During the period under review, the prevention and control of cardiovascular diseases at the community level have been increasingly promoted. This approach involves the integration of population-oriented public health programmes with existing health care systems. With WHO as coordinating agency, model areas have been set up in several countries, and the approach is being tested in many others. The idea is to take the results of research on the prevention and control of different cardiovascular diseases, adapt them, and apply them in the daily practice of the health services at all levels. Thus, programmes for the control of hypertension and the prevention and control of rheumatic fever have been established, as well as comprehensive control programmes dealing with several

Table 14. Annual incidence rates for stroke, per 1000 population

Centre	Sex	Age			
		45–54 years	55–64 years	65–74 years	75+ years
Gothenburg	M	0.73	2.72	0.49	
Sweden	F	0.45	1.46	0.31	
	M+F	0.62	2.05	0.39	
Copenhagen,	M	0.68	3.23	6.35	14.04
Denmark	F	0.37	1.46	3.88	12.79
	M+F	0.51	2.21	4.78	13.14
Dublin,	M	1.01	3.99	8.02	15.53
Ireland	F	0.62	2.19	6.76	17.35
	M+F	0.79	3.00	7.27	16.75
North Karelia,	M	2.12	4.34	8.92	14.06
Finland	F	0.92	3.01	7.23	14.07
	M+F	1.49	3.62	7.94	14.07
Zagreb,	M	1.31	3.82	6.33	
Yugoslavia	F	0.99	1.68	3.87	
	M+F	1.14	2.44	4.91	
Tel Aviv,	M	0.04	1.73	6.09	
Israel	F	0.01	0.60	7.24	
	M+F	0.01	1.79	6.68	
Fukuoka,	M	1.07	5.22	13.36	26.49
Japan	F	0.65	1.34	7.16	15.77
	M+F	0.84	3.55	9.92	19.47
Osaka,	M	0.47	3.82	12.28	31.46
Japan	F	0.75	2.80	7.06	20.67
	M+F	0.63	3.26	9.36	24.45
Ulan Bator,	M	1.10	3.18	4.60	3.67
Mongolia	F	1.27	2.19	3.20	3.39
	M+F	1.18	2.67	3.90	3.52
Colombo,	M	0.73	1.52	4.26	5.79
Sri Lanka	F	0.48	1.20	2.97	4.01
	M+F	0.63	1.38	3.63	4.81
Ibadan,	M	0.64	1.79	4.23	2.77
Nigeria	F	0.27	1.49	2.55	1.39
	M+F	0.49	1.66	3.46	2.12
Rohtak,	M	0.25	1.95	4.69	
India	F	0.41	1.24	1.95	
	M+F	0.32	1.64	3.50	

Source: AHO, K. et al. Cerebrovascular disease in the community: results of a WHO collaborative study. *Bulletin of the World Health Organization*, **56** (1) (1980).

cardiovascular diseases simultaneously at the community level. These are being carried out in developed as well as developing countries. For example, the programme for the comprehensive control of cardiovascular diseases is now in progress in 23 countries, 11 of which are considered as developing countries. Efforts are being made to assess the extent of the cardiovascular disease problem in each community and to assign specific roles in the prevention and control of cardiovascular diseases to each level of health personnel, who are then taught the necessary skills. Action is being taken to involve the public. Thus, in developing countries, programmes mainly for the prevention of rheumatic fever and rheumatic heart disease, the control of hypertension, and the prevention of stroke are being developed, while in industrialized countries there are programmes for the prevention and control of ischaemic heart disease, the control of hypertension, and the control of stroke. The most advanced model area is North Karelia in Finland; the project there has already been in progress for several years, and the first phase was finished in 1977. Preliminary results have shown that when intensive preventive and control measures are applied with the full participation of the community, including every sector of society, it is possible to reduce the percentage of the population with elevated blood pressure and the percentage of smokers, and consequently the incidence of stroke and myocardial infarction. However, the whole community must be mobilized and made aware of the possibilities of this approach. This is more a political action than a traditionally medical one.

The new approach stems from earlier activities in the control of individual cardiovascular diseases at the community level. Here, specific mention must be made of hypertension control, in which a significant favourable trend has been noted. As already indicated, hypertension is as frequent in developing countries as in industrialized, developed ones. Thus, a prevalence rate of about 80–150 cases per 1000 population was found in adults in parts of Africa (e.g., in Ghana and Nigeria), in South America and the Caribbean countries, and in some Asian countries (e.g., China, Indonesia, and Mongolia). Similar figures have been recorded in Europe and Northern America. In earlier studies, it was noted that half of the population with elevated blood pressure did not know about the disease, half of those who did know were not treated, and half of those who were treated were not treated properly. In countries with well established services this proportion is now changing, the percentage of those who are not aware of having elevated blood pressure is decreasing (to approximately 20–30%), and the quality of treatment is improving. Although many problems still remain, especially in long-term follow-up and adherence of patients to therapy, the effects of a more systematic approach to hypertension control are already reflected in many countries by a decrease in the incidence of stroke. Essential hypertension is, however, expected to remain the most difficult to handle of the cardiovascular diseases for many years, as knowledge about its primary prevention is very limited and much more research is needed before any definitive preventive measures can be introduced for the general population.

Cancer

(a) Extent of the problem

Until recently it was only in developed countries that cancer was a relatively serious disease in terms of morbidity and mortality. However, with the increasing control of infectious and nutritional diseases, it is rapidly becoming a major cause of morbidity and mortality and a heavy burden on health care systems throughout the world. More than half of the world's population now live in countries where cancer is among top-ranking causes of death. The annual number of deaths from cancer throughout the world was estimated at about 5 million in the mid-1970s, when the total annual number of deaths was 50 million.

Despite worldwide efforts and the allocation of substantial financial and manpower resources to cancer research and anticancer programmes, progress in the fight against the various forms of the disease has been slow. All over the developed world where comprehensive data are available, cancer is one of the leading causes of death (in the majority of countries second only to cardiovascular diseases). Under present conditions every fifth person will ultimately succumb to cancer. Among males, age-specific risks of dying from cancer have been decreasing for a few sites, such as the stomach and the oesophagus, but mortality for other sites is either stationary or continues to increase, notably as regards cancers associated with tobacco-smoking, such as lung cancer. Among males in some developed countries the increase in death rates for lung cancer has either neutralized or more than offset decreases in cancer mortality for all other sites combined. A slowing down of the rate of increase in mortality from lung cancer in males is also noticeable in some countries. Age-specific death rates from cancer in females exhibit a decline for sites such as the stomach and the cervix uteri, but the available evidence suggests a worsening of the situation for cancer of the breast, the leading cause of death among middle-aged women. Death rates for cancer of the lung in females, too, are on the increase in many developed countries.[1]

An analysis of cancer mortality in 24 countries in Europe (containing 96% of the Region's population) has shown that, in the period 1955–1974,

(a) cancer mortality in males (all sites) had been increasing statistically significantly in 20 countries, 4 countries being in the range of random variation; and

(b) cancer mortality in females declined significantly in 9 countries and increased in 5, whereas for 10 countries the results were not statistically significant.

A worldwide review of available incidence data suggests significant differences in geographical patterns and a real increase in the overall cancer risk in all developed countries with reliable registration data, this being largely due to an upward trend in the incidence of cancer of the respiratory organs. Time trends for the largest group of cancers—those affecting the digestive organs—are stable, but this is because decreasing rates for cancer of the stomach are balanced by increasing rates for cancers of the colon, rectum, and pancreas. A similar balance is found in the mean rates for cancers of the female genital organs (decreasing rates for the cervix and increasing rates for the corpus uteri and the ovary). Cancers of the male genital organs are on the increase, because of an upward trend in cancers of such common sites as the prostate. Cancer of the female breast, bladder cancer, and melanomas of the skin are increasing at similar rates. Cancers of the brain, the nervous system, and the endocrine glands, as well as lymphoma and leukaemia, show smaller increases but are less stable internationally.

There are not enough reliable statistical data, particularly in developing countries, to permit the study of time trends in relation to causes of cancer.

China and Singapore are examples of less developed countries in which the transition from the previous disease pattern, with its preponderance of infectious and parasitic diseases, towards a preponderance of noncommunicable diseases occurred very rapidly. In both countries cancer has become a prominent public health concern in less than a generation. It is therefore all the more important that steps should be initiated now to prepare health services in less developed countries for the tasks they can expect to face as infectious and nutritional diseases are brought under control.

Advances in cancer treatment have resulted in considerable improvements in survival prospects and quality of life for some cancer patients, such as children with acute lymphocytic leukaemia, chloriocarcinoma, and Hodgkin's disease. Unfortunately, there has been little, if any, improvement in the prospects for patients with the common cancers, such as lung cancer and stomach cancer, which shows the importance of efforts for primary prevention. There is an urgent need for better and more comparable data to evaluate trends and differences among, as well as within, countries.

More and more attention is being paid to the social implications of cancer. In many developed countries the disease is the leading cause of premature death during the

---

[1] Detailed reviews of trends and differentials in cancer mortality have been published in the *World health statistics quarterly* since 1975. Information on cancer incidence is published at regular intervals by IARC.

working life of females, whereas in males it is second only to cardiovascular diseases. More than a quarter of the total person-years lost during the working lifetime are lost as a result of cancer. The disease has also been shown to have a marked influence on maternal survival during the crucial infant and childhood ages. It is the principal cause of death among mothers of children and adolescents up to the age of 20.

(b) *Prevention*

The primary prevention of any cancer is never likely to be a simple matter. There may be some direct-acting carcinogens that, once identified, could be removed from man's environment, but many cancer risk factors may prove to be, for example, "normal" dietary components or "normal" cultural habits that cannot simply be removed or changed overnight. Nevertheless, it is evident that any effort at primary prevention depends on some reasonable idea being gained about the cause of a given cancer.

The one cancer for which knowledge of the cause is most certain is lung cancer. Cigarette-smoking has not only been implicated as the cause of lung cancer but is also associated with cancers of the larynx, the oesophagus and the bladder and is estimated to be responsible in the United Kingdom for over 40% of all cancer deaths in males and in France for 11–12% of all deaths. These dramatic figures could certainly be repeated in all industrialized countries, and in many developing countries increased consumption of tobacco runs parallel with or even ahead of increases in general living standards. There have been few successful efforts to reduce this major cause of mortality, much of which should be preventable—though in Finland, for instance, the incidence of lung cancer in males seems to have declined since the early 1970s (whereas the rates for females continue to rise).

Smoking is in sharp contrast to other hazards, which would probably not account for more than a very small percentage of all cancers.

Excessive exposure to sunlight is now recognized as the cause of much of the skin cancer that occurs in Caucasians, but discouragement of sunbathing is an unpopular measure.

The danger from radiation is well recognized, and stringent protective measures are enforced in those countries where nuclear power is being applied to energy production, where high energy radiation is being used in therapy and diagnosis, and where radioisotopes are being used in clinics, in industry, and for research.

Several cancer risks arising from exposure at the place of work have now been recognized, and in many countries control measures to reduce such exposure are rigorously applied although the accepted exposure levels vary from country to country. Thus, acceptable dust levels have been established for the asbestos industry, as have maximum permitted concentrations for vinyl chloride. Similarly efforts are being made to control environmental pollution by potential carcinogens.

There are some 2 million chemicals in existence, and the number increases by about 40 000 each year. Of those, perhaps 500 eventually reach the general environment of appreciable numbers of persons. In many countries, regulations provide that all new drugs and food additives must be subjected to rigorous testing for carcinogenicity. Because this is long and costly, increasing efforts are being made to establish rapid screening tests based on mutagenicity, but the problem remains that mutagenicity is not necessarily an indicator of carcinogenicity, nor is it possible to be certain that every animal carcinogen will be a human carcinogen or *vice versa*. Neither is it possible to extrapolate findings from animal dose-response experiments to man.

In this situation, which calls for much more research, some countries are inevitably taking a pragmatic but perhaps needlessly cautious approach to the problem, and some substances, e.g., saccharine and amaranth, have been made subject to—or are being considered for—regulation on very limited experimental evidence. Exposure levels or permitted concentrations of suspected carcinogens have sometimes been fixed on the basis of general rather than scientific considerations.

Considerable efforts have been put into secondary prevention, but very often without careful evaluation of their efficacy.

Intervention studies now in progress may eventually make it possible to prevent two types of malignancy. With the cooperation of the Government, it has been possible to distribute chloroquine to all the children in an area in the United Republic of Tanzania, thus lowering their risk of catching malaria. Since malaria is believed to be a joint factor in the etiology of Burkitt's lymphoma, it is hoped that malaria control will also result in the suppression of this form of cancer. In a part of Swaziland where the incidence of liver cancer is high, a project has been initiated, in collaboration with UNEP and FAO, and with the support of the Government, to improve agricultural methods, harvesting, and food storage. This should lead to a reduction in the degree to which foodstuffs are contaminated with aflatoxin, the suspected etiological factor for liver cancer, which in turn should result in a reduction in the incidence of liver cancer.

(c) Organization of cancer services

On the basis of present clinical knowledge, it is recognized that cancer therapy should be handled by a multidisciplinary team comprising as a minimum the disciplines of surgery, radiotherapy, and chemotherapy. The team approach to cancer management is mainly practised in specialized cancer institutes. General hospitals sometimes lack specialists in all of the three aspects of treatment just mentioned; chemotherapy, in particular, is often not widely available in general hospitals as a subspeciality in internal medicine. While the creation of a cancer team may be definitely less feasible in general hospitals than in cancer institutes, the approach is one that should be fostered in order to ensure the best treatment for the cancer patient.

It must be recognized that the title "cancer institute" has an ominous ring for patients and their families; this situation could possibly be completely reversed by health education. It is necessary to emphasize the potentially positive results of cancer treatment (e.g., treatment of baraliomies with a 95–99% cure, followed by a high percentage of potential cures in cancers of the cervix uteri, if treated at an early stage, etc.) and to break the myth of incurability of cancer so widely current among the general public and often in the medical community as well.

(d) Screening and early detection

Detection and screening programmes for early and precancerous lesions have continued to be the cornerstones of cancer control. The strengthening of cancer control activities at the country level has been promoted as an effective means of assisting developing countries, in particular, to prepare the way for dealing with the health problems associated with a higher incidence of cancer. In spite of weak incidence data in many areas, carcinoma of the cervix uteri continued to be considered one of the most frequent cancers in the world as a whole during the period. In most industrialized countries, cancer of the lung in males and cancer of the breast in females were the most widespread problem.

It has been suggested that screening programmes were introduced before their value had been demonstrated. Attention has focused on screening for early and precancerous lesions of the cervix uteri by means of exfoliative cytology (Papanicolaou smear). A national evaluation of cervical cancer screening programmes in Canada showed the efficacy of these programmes in reducing mortality from carcinoma of the uterine cervix to be reasonably good. Recent studies in Finland and Iceland do appear to show that total population screening for cervix carcinoma can result in a fall in mortality. However, any optimism about future trends should be tempered in the light of recent disquieting reports on the appearance during screening campaigns of dysplastic cells in younger women, including teenagers. In many countries, the incidence of cervical carcinoma had been falling for some years before the introduction of cervical cytology, and it may be that this was due to improvements in personal hygiene among women.

As regards screening for breast cancer, there has been concern about exposure to radiation from repeated X-ray mammographies and the risk of breast cancer developing as a result. Following a nationwide programme in the USA, involving the screening of 280 000 women annually for five years, using mammography, physical examination, patient history, and thermography, the routine use of mammography was discouraged for the 35–50 year age group. However, it was established that, for women of 50 years and over, the combined use of mammography and physical examination was of definite value.

Experience of screening programmes for cancers of other sites is still limited, with the possible exception of stomach cancer, for which 3 million people are screened annually in Japan by mass radiography. The mortality rate from cancer of this site in Japan has gradually declined over the past 20 years. It has been estimated that at least 20% of the decrease can be attributed to screening programmes. Studies on screening for lung cancer have so far demonstrated no tangible effect on mortality.

Anxiety has been expressed about the possible contribution of the use of steroid contraceptives to the risk of developing neoplasia of certain sites such as the breast, the uterus (endometrium and cervix), the ovary and the liver. A number of epidemiological studies on the relationship between steroid contraceptive use and neoplasia have been undertaken during the past few years. At present there is insufficient evidence on which to base recommendations of public health value.

(e) Therapy

No breakthrough has been achieved in the treatment of cancer in the five-year period covered by this report. Some improvements have been obtained in drug-combination schedules in respect of leukaemias as well as solid cancers, although the results are awaiting further confirmation. Much the same may be said of progress in radiation therapy. Surgery, one of the principal means of treatment, has reached its limits as regards organ and tissue removal, and more emphasis is being placed on treatment schedules combining surgery, radiotherapy, and chemotherapy and their sequence. The immunotherapy of cancer has not yet crossed the border of possible adjuvant therapy. In general, progress in cancer treatment is rather slow because of the present insufficient understanding of malignant growth as such, and only progress in basic cancer research may lead to the improvement of cancer therapy on a rational basis. There is of course always the possibility of a breakthrough by serendipity, but the chances of this are very limited.

The treatment results obtained at present in institutes of excellence cannot be considered as generally valid for the countries in which these institutes exist, let alone the whole world, though they may be regarded as targets. Health services should rather be concerned with countrywide averages and the difference between the results obtained in highly specialized institutes and those obtained in general hospitals. At present, comparative data of this kind are lacking, even in the literature, and the publication of such data could be a delicate matter indeed, leading to serious misunderstandings. There is still a lack of good, internationally accepted parameters for reporting results of treatment for different cancer sites. Many publications report such results, especially those that are the outcome of particular treatment strategies, but the measurement of these results is often made on an arbitrary basis.

Standardization in the reporting of treatment results would be a desirable development and one very probably acceptable to authors. Besides possibly improving the level of many cancer journals, the existence of a baseline for the evaluation and comparison of the results of treatment would be useful for the health services in many countries, including the developing ones.

(f) Information needs

Increasing attention has been paid at the national and international levels to improving information support for cancer prevention and control programmes. Recent developments point to the urgent need to integrate information from different sources so as to obtain as complete a picture of the cancer situation as possible. Statistical information in the field of cancer should contribute to a better understanding of the epidemiology of malignant disease and to the planning, implementation, and evaluation of cancer control programmes. New developments in this connexion include: projections of cancer frequency and resource requirements, the estimation of the social and economic costs of cancer as an aid in taking decisions on priorities, data collection schemes embracing surveillance, epidemiology, and end results, and the establishment of hospital-based cancer registries,[1] particularly (but not exclusively) in countries where for various reasons it is not feasible to operate population-based registries. At the instigation of WHO, standardized hospital-based cancer registries have been set up in 30 countries. A total of 65 institutions are participating in this scheme, one of whose major advantages is its potential usefulness in hospital management.

---

[1] *WHO handbook for standardized cancer registries (hospital-based)*. Geneva, World Health Organization, 1976 (Offset Publications, No. 25).

At present it is very important to interpret geographical differences more comprehensively and to organize the monitoring of trends in cancer incidence in different geographical and industrial areas. The international network for this purpose, proposed by IARC, will be of great value for cancer control, etiological studies, and prevention.

(g) Epidemiology

There is now increasing awareness of the importance of both descriptive and analytical epidemiology utilizing routine and other data to study variations in cancer distribution and identify geographical or occupational groups subject to disparate cancer risks. However, the spread of the same general cultural habits within countries and from one country to another is producing increasing homogeneity in the environments of different populations, and it is therefore becoming urgent to take advantage of the existence of any special groups whose cultural patterns are still identifiable and distinct in order to draw the maximum amount of information from any correlated peculiarities in their cancer-risk patterns.

If epidemiological studies of cancer are to be effective, it is necessary for epidemiologists to have either a population cancer registry providing morbidity data on all cancers in the community, or else access to all death certificates in order to have mortality data. Unfortunately, however, many population-based registries do not collect data on exposure hazards and specific risk factors, so that the morbidity data can be considered only as a point of departure for more detailed investigations. In many countries, the confidentiality of death certificates is such that it is impossible to have access to them; if etiological studies are to continue, it is essential to obtain authorized access to mortality information. It is realized that in an age of automatic record linkage there is legitimate public concern about the protection of privacy, but it is important to emphasize that this should not be allowed to interfere with the work of *bona fide* epidemiologists. The epidemiologist has not yet found ways of examining the effects of relatively low doses of weak carcinogens, acting singly or in combination with others.

Much valuable knowledge of the role of the environment has come from studies of cancer risks in migrant populations, whose cancer rates have been shown to approach the cancer rates of the population of the adopted country fairly rapidly—sometimes within a generation. There are still a number of migrant populations of different ethnic origin among whom epidemiological research could yield valuable etiological clues.

While there are differences in cancer risk between occupational groups, studies in England and Wales have shown that only 12% of the differences are due to exposures at work. The differences in life-style associated with each of the occupational groups studied contributed much more to the group's cancer risk than did its specific on-the-job exposure. Similar studies need to be undertaken in other countries, since a confirmation of the findings would point to the need for an extension of research into the effects of life-style.

Diet is an intrinsic part of life-style, and there is a growing body of evidence implicating dietary components as factors that alter carcinogenic risk, either increasing or decreasing it. Studies of the effects of high fat diets, of dietary fibre, and of the consumption of fresh green vegetables are being pursued by epidemiologists and, at the same time, by laboratory scientists studying tumour promotion and inhibition.

Another major obstacle that is limiting the development of epidemiological research is the shortage of trained cancer epidemiologists. Few medical school curricula cover the concepts of modern epidemiology and their importance in a sufficiently striking way, and there are few places where the medical services offer career prospects for epidemiologists, even though their contribution to the evaluation and planning of health care delivery is as important as their contribution to research.

Respiratory diseases

During the period under review, communicable diseases of the respiratory system, as a group, were one of the principal causes of morbidity and mortality in many countries.

Data reported to WHO by 88 countries with a total population of about 1200 million[1] show that, in the year 1972 alone, more than 666 000 deaths were related to acute respiratory infections. This represents an average of 6.3% of all deaths reported, although there are considerable differences between continents and between countries, with an overall range of from 3.0% to 13.6%. Pneumonia, both viral and bacterial, accounted for 75.5% of the deaths related to acute respiratory infections.

Mortality rates for acute respiratory infections were highest in infants and, in some countries, exceeded 2000 for every 100 000 liveborn babies. The rates declined in childhood and early adult life, but increased progressively with age in the middle and old age groups. However, acute respiratory infections in infants and children below 15 years of age accounted for 20.3% of the total number of deaths from all causes, against the 4.2% represented by deaths from the same cause in persons belonging to the age group 55 years and over.

Some of the acute respiratory infections leave the patients with sequelae and are known also to exacerbate already existing disease of the respiratory tract; both situations may lead to the development of chronic lung conditions.

As regards chronic respiratory diseases (this group including chronic bronchitis, emphysema, and bronchial asthma) a total of 304 298 deaths was reported from the above-mentioned 88 countries for 1972. This represents an average of 2.9% of all deaths reported by them for that year, the highest mean percentage being reported from Africa (6.3%) and the lowest from Asia (2.0%). Of all deaths from chronic respiratory diseases, 18.4% occurred in infants and children and 81.6% in adults (15 years and over).

Chronic respiratory diseases are responsible also for widespread morbidity and invalidity in several parts of the world, in spite of the fact that some causative or aggravating factors (such as smoking, air pollution, socioeconomic conditions and respiratory infections in children) are already known. Differences in terminology, medical traditions, the use of diagnostic facilities, and the organization of health services seem to be responsible for the apparent contrasts between countries in the reported mortality and morbidity rates.

The investigation of likely factors could well form the basis of further international collaborative studies in the epidemiology and control of respiratory disease in the community. These studies should include a more detailed investigation of mortality, field

---

[1] BULLA, A. & HITZE, K. L. Acute respiratory infections: a review. *Bulletin of the World Health Organization*, **56**: 481–498 (1978).

surveys of morbidity employing standardized measurement techniques, the rationalization of the utilization of medical services, and control measures, including primary and secondary prevention. A number of factors readily suggest themselves for inclusion in such studies, and extension of the statistical investigations would suggest others.

In view of the importance of the health problem posed by respiratory diseases, the World Health Assembly decided that more attention should be given to this group of diseases during the period of its Sixth General Programme of Work (1978–1983).

Human genetics

There has been significant progress in genetics, and most of the accumulated knowledge can be used in the solution of various public health problems. In other words a proper transition from high technology to priority needs at different levels of medical care can now be made on a much broader basis.

(a) Hereditary diseases

About 2500 hereditary diseases, including chromosomal abnormalities, have been described in man. Some of them of course are rare, but more important than the actual numbers it is necessary to know, and keep under control, the percentage of carriers of the harmful genes responsible for the development of hereditary diseases. The problem of detecting carriers is well illustrated by haemophilia.[1]

(i) Haemoglobinopathies and allied disorders

The single most important qualitative haemoglobinopathy is sickle-cell anaemia. The areas in which this abnormality occurs all have, or have had, a high endemic incidence of malaria. Other abnormalities, such as haemoglobin E, haemoglobin C, and glucose-6-phosphate dehydrogenase deficiency, are also associated with malarious areas.

Thus these abnormalities are important public health problems in countries where malaria has been recently eradicated or its eradication is still on the WHO priority list. For example, the incidence of haemoglobin S reaches 20–30% in certain areas of Africa, South America, and South-East Asia, and in some countries it is as much as 40–50%.[2] Some of these abnormalities—for example, glucose-6-phosphate dehydrogenase deficiencies—are capable of inducing drug haemolytic anaemia, favism, and other diseases.

(ii) Chromosomal diseases

A special registry has been established in Texas, USA, to collect data from 28 countries on chromosomal abnormalities (structural variants and anomalies, numerical abnormalities, chromosomal breakage syndromes) and is used by paediatricians, gynaecologists,

---

[1] Methods for the detection of haemophilia carriers: a memorandum. *Bulletin of the World Health Organization*, **55**: 675–702 (1977).

[2] WHO Technical Report Series, No. 509, 1972 (*Treatment of haemoglobinopathies and allied disorders. Report of a WHO Scientific Group*).

geneticists, and others. So far it has produced five publications and listed over 200 000 different chromosomal variants and anomalies in man.

(iii) *Clinical genetics and genetic counselling*

Through further study of a wide variety of clinical pictures of many other genetic disorders, it should be possible to understand the clinical heterogeneity of these conditions and their distribution in the world. This would permit the organization of a proper system for the medical care of patients and for the antenatal detection of dangerous and common hereditary diseases and prevention of the birth of affected infants. Genetic counselling services have now been established in the majority of developed countries and are gradually being started in some developing countries.

(b) *Genetic markers and susceptibility to infectious diseases*

Medical genetics should not concentrate only on the study of diseases that are inherited in a relatively simple way. For example, recent findings show that many diseases of public health importance are partially associated with human genotypes, so that an individual may be genetically predisposed to contracting a given disease. The actual manifestation of the disease (e.g., its severity and duration) is due to the interaction of the predisposing genotype with environmental factors. The study of such genetic predispositions, which have hitherto defied ordinary genetic analysis, has now become possible because of recent advances in many fields of biomedical science.

Thus, even infectious diseases which were previously regarded as being typically due to external factors are in part genetically controlled because relative resistance or susceptibility to them derives in part from the genotype of the host (in this case, man).

The fact that different individuals and different human populations do not run the same risks of infection in areas highly endemic for such diseases as malaria, schistosomiasis, filariasis, trypanosomiasis, leprosy, and leishmaniasis has practical implications for public health and preventive medicine, whose tasks will include giving protection against the above-mentioned diseases by preparing vaccines in the light of the genetic characteristics of individual populations and developing appropriate treatment in relation to the human genotype.

To conclude, up to now most progress has been made in the following branches of human genetics: the study of immunogenetic mechanisms of susceptibility to different infectious and noninfectious diseases; the antenatal diagnosis of X-linked disorders, some inborn errors of metabolism, Down's syndrome, and congenital malformations; and the linkage and mapping of human chromosomes. It is expected that research on these subjects will do much to improve medical care.

Other chronic noncommunicable diseases

Disease control should be based on effective primary and secondary prevention in the community. In practice, this approach involves a combination of various measures— psychosocial, economic, sanitary, hygienic, medical, etc.—to improve the health situation of the population and is a government responsibility.

113

In the past the killing diseases received a great deal of attention, whereas disabling and crippling diseases were relatively neglected—and yet the social and economic burden imposed by the latter is probably greater. Activities to control such diseases as diabetes mellitus, rheumatic diseases, and chronic liver and renal diseases have accordingly been intensified within the past few years.

Current morbidity and mortality data, the enormous increase expected in the world's population, and the anticipated shift in the age structure of populations towards a higher proportion of older people—all these factors suggest that the chronic noncommunicable diseases will become a matter of increasing concern and that complications of these diseases will become more frequent in both developed and developing countries. The problem in the latter might be expected to be more serious since their populations, genetically and otherwise, are less well equipped to resist these diseases.

(a) Diabetes mellitus

In the developed countries, diabetes mellitus is a major public health problem, being among the ten leading causes of death by disease.

Diabetes mortality is the indicator most commonly used to express the importance and distribution of the disease. However, the death rates reflect only part of the problem. Medical certificates are not usually standardized, and diabetes mellitus is not usually mentioned as the basic cause of death, since there are other conditions that are more obvious, although they are often the direct or indirect consequence of diabetes. Moreover, special surveys have showed that 50% of cases of diabetes remain undetected in the developed countries (e.g., the USA), and only 10% of cases are being detected in the developing countries (e.g., Senegal). Real differences exist in morbidity and mortality from diabetes mellitus in different geographical areas, and this is probably related to certain known or unknown factors—perhaps genetic, environmental, nutritional, or psychosocial—in the etiology of the disease. International research and comparative studies might be of great help in discovering these factors and provide a basis for organizing national diabetes control programmes in the community.

(b) Chronic rheumatic diseases

Rheumatic diseases are a serious problem with widespread social and economic consequences in all societies. This varied group of diseases includes at least 100 different conditions, the etiology and pathogenesis of which need further study. Successful control might be achieved through the development of appropriate technology on the basis of scientific research, followed by its application in response to the will of the community to overcome the problem. Perhaps the most fundamental difficulty with regard to rheumatic diseases today is that the problem is insufficiently appreciated and understood.

There are a number of rheumatic conditions whose succesful control is probably feasible, and further efforts to this end should have priority. The primary prevention of rheumatic fever depends on the early and efficient treatment of streptococcal infections and on improved nutrition and living conditions. As the condition is theoretically largely preventable, health education should be able to make an important contribution to its primary prevention. The potential for the primary prevention of most other rheumatic diseases is at present limited. Here, not only is more research required, but the available services for dealing with these diseases need to be rationalized. Effective secondary prevention of rheumatic fever is available in the form of prophylaxis against relapses. Community control programmes are possible and have been initiated. Secondary prevention is possible for some other rheumatic conditions, notably those related to occupation. Effective treatment has opened up new possibilities for the control of gouty arthritis and the infectious arthritides.

The control of chronic diseases at the community level calls for a multidisciplinary approach. It must be realized that their routine long-term management rarely requires continual recourse to the specialist but can be carried out at the primary health care level, provided that expert guidance is available when needed. At the same time further research, particularly at the international level, is needed on preventive measures, early detection in the community, treatment, and rehabilitation.

Oral health

The incidence of oral disease in the world falls into three general categories, according to the latest data on caries prevalence: very low to low in most countries in Africa and parts of South-East Asia and the Pacific, moderate in many countries in the Eastern Mediterranean Region and some countries in Asia, and high to very high in most of the industrialized nations. Superimposed upon the caries problem is that of periodontal disease; broadly speaking, this disease tends to be worse in developing populations, especially in Africa and Asia, and somewhat less so in Europe and the Americas.

In the past, only isolated attempts were made, usually at national level, to consider trends in oral health, the main preoccupation being with disease prevalence, even to the extent of overlooking previous data once a new set of data was available. Thanks to a growing body of information, however, it is now possible at least to identify trends in dental caries.

At one extreme, all countries where prevalence is very low or low—for example, Kenya and Nigeria—are probably experiencing increases in the prevalence and severity of dental caries. In some of these countries, substantial increases in the overall level have been demonstrated; in others, it is clear that increases—some of them rather large—are occurring, but only in urban centres. The vast majority of such populations living in rural areas—for example, in Indonesia—have not as yet been shown to be affected.

The other extreme is provided by countries with high and very high prevalence; this group includes Japan and French Polynesia. Japan has only recently reached this high level, having moved from the lower part of the moderate range well into the high prevalence category in the space of 20 years. French Polynesia, where caries was almost zero at the beginning of the twentieth century, now has one of the highest levels ever recorded among children of 12 years of age. There also appear to be certain countries in this group with a very stable overall prevalence of caries, as for instance Canada and Norway.

Several countries which traditionally have had very high caries levels—Australia, New Zealand, and Switzerland—now tell a different story. Large sections of their populations have been exposed to preventive programmes, including water and salt fluoridation and topical applications of fluoride, as well as regular oral hygiene instruction and health

115

education for 10–15 years and even longer. Some very dramatic decreases in prevalence have been achieved in this way. It is estimated that overall levels are now approaching the moderate range, and some quite large sections of the community are even in the low caries category.

The situation between the two extremes is less easy to classify as it constitutes the crossroads, as it were, of the various trends. Included in this group are countries with increasing prevalence which previously had low levels, the group—already discussed—with decreasing levels, which previously belonged to the high and very high groups, and yet a third group in which prevalences have probably been stable for some time at the moderate level.

It is quite clear from the foregoing that, if planning, programming, and evaluation are to be soundly based, regular inexpensive surveillance activities are essential. The special importance of surveillance in developing countries to ensure that preventive programmes are established before disease levels overwhelm available services is evident.

There is also a strong case for regular surveillance, in developed countries, both to monitor the effectiveness of preventive programmes and to provide data for realistic periodic adjustments in overall dental manpower plans. Only in this way can an appreciable number of countries react in time to the complex interaction of zero or negative population growth, the continuing expansion of educational facilities (especially for the health professions), and the dramatic decreases in disease prevalence already being achieved but often going unrecognized. This situation, coupled with the new and more effective possibilities of prevention that may emerge in the next few years, might cause a manpower surplus that would be extremely wasteful and insupportable even in the richest of economies.

The number of dental schools in the world rose from 320 in 1958 to 371 in 1963 and 478 in 1974, but an analysis of the dental manpower situation shows that in general the number of dentists has increased less rapidly than the population. The population per dentist in the world was 7310 in 1963 and rose to 7566 in 1975. The dentist/population ratio differs widely from country to country, ranging from 1:1140 in Sweden to 1:1 150 000 in Niger. The overall figures for the world, even in 1975, were far from high and the increase in the number of dentists is tending to become less rapid than it was 20 years ago.

The geographical distribution of dentists within countries varies considerably, rural areas almost everywhere having fewer dentists and a much higher population/dentist ratio. Although this is a universal problem, it is particularly serious in developing countries where the proportion of the population living in large cities is low.

Although efforts should and obviously will be made not only to maintain the present number of dentists but to increase it substantially, the figures seem to support the hypothesis that this course alone will not suffice to solve the problem of achieving adequate dental health coverage of the population in very large areas of the world before the end of the century. Hence the very great need to seek alternative, more feasible solutions.

To increase the numbers of professional dental personnel in order to provide an equitable oral health service for all children or all populations is not a realistic approach in the majority of countries, especially the developing ones. The advanced skills of the dental graduate are not required for many routine operative procedures, and it is possible to train dental auxiliary personnel to carry out a range of tasks with high standards of efficiency and correct ethical attitudes. The use of operating and non-operating dental auxiliaries is one of the most effective methods of meeting the ever-increasing demand for dental care. A great deal of attention has been paid to the training of such auxiliaries in South-East Asia, the Americas, and the Western Pacific. The following table shows the numbers of schools for dental auxiliaries in the various WHO Regions.

Region	Number of schools for dental operating auxiliaries	Number of schools for dental non-operating auxiliaries
Africa	6	4
America	171	210
South-East Asia	9	4
Europe	42	186
Eastern Mediterranean	2	6
Western Pacific	91	71

Source: *World directory of schools for dental auxiliaries*, 1973. Geneva, World Health Organization, 1977.

During the last 30 years school dental nurses or dental therapists have been introduced in more than 30 countries and territories. In many of these countries they have been the main clinical personnel for large, well developed school dental services. While training and duties may vary to some extent, this category of auxiliary remains easily recognizable as an offshoot of the New Zealand original. There are definite signs that more, perhaps most, countries will maintain or introduce this type of auxiliary.

It is now recognized that the basic features of any oral health delivery system, from the simplest to the most complex, are preventive services, services on demand, systematic services for specified groups, provision of the manpower needed for these various services, and an in-built monitoring system.

It is also important to recognize that situation analysis will have a very important effect on the content of the preventive programme. At the present stage of knowledge, periodontal disease control programmes can be taken as a constant. Thus, if the prevalence of dental caries is extremely low and stable, the control of periodontal disease through health education and consequent improvement in oral hygiene practices, plus surveillance to detect the first signs of increasing caries, would be the type of response indicated. Where caries prevalence is on the increase or the level is already moderate to high, a preventive goal has to be chosen and pursued in addition to the activities for the control of periodontal disease. Various preventive goals are indicated below.

Caries prevalence	Trend	Preventive goal
Very low to low	stable	none
	increasing	halt increase
Moderate	decreasing	to 2.5–3.0 DMFT[a] or stabilize
	stable	to 2.5–3.0 DMFT[a] or no change
	increasing	to 2.5–3.0 DMFT[a] or halt increase
High to very high	any	to 2.5–3.0 DMFT[a]

[a] Decayed, missing, or filled teeth.

Environmental health

Policies and programmes

A study of the environmental health situation in Member countries during the period under review reveals certain encouraging trends and an improvement over the previous five years. Not only is there greater awareness of the problems involved and the need to solve them, there has also been progress in real terms, though mostly unevenly distributed between different parts of the world and often between more and less privileged parts of the same country. Although virtually all countries show some progress, there is no country without continuing environmental health problems. In the developing countries these are mostly, but not exclusively, due to inadequacy of basic environmental sanitation, while in the more developed countries they are outstandingly the environmental hazards associated with industrialization and urbanization. Many countries face the traditional sanitation problems, which are still to be solved, while the newer environmental hazards to human health are being created.

Often the lack of a positive national environmental health policy is a major constraint on programme planning and implementation. A national policy and general legislation are needed as foundations for action and also to facilitate the establishment of an appropriate infrastructure and the assignment of responsibilities for the execution of programmes. In most Member States, environmental health programmes must operate within limited budgets, even where environmental health is considered as an investment or where the need for action is recognized. This often delays or jeopardizes programme implementation, and may even increase costs over time. A national policy for environmental health should give particular attention to the allocation of additional resources, in keeping with their appropriate utilization and distribution. At present, too large a proportion of scanty environmental health resources goes to already privileged areas. The enhanced primary health care orientation of Member States offers new opportunities for more appropriate environmental health policies.

Many countries have initiated or expanded basic environmental sanitation programmes. Some countries are reviewing their often fragmented and highly varied legislation on environmental problems and enacting overall framework legislation on the environment that is more appropriate for current problems and needs. Many countries are also engaged in reorganizing the ways in which environmental programmes are carried out. There appears to be no consistent pattern, but typically the tasks are divided among a number of ministries, one of which is usually the ministry of health. Sometimes a ministry of the environment or an environmental protection agency is established, with responsibility both for matters of environmental pollution and for some aspects of natural resource management. In almost all cases, however, important programmes relating to the environment are the responsibility of several ministries. Coordination among ministries and among various levels of government is frequently inadequate, and environmental investments are often made without sufficient consideration to their health aspects, the need for qualified manpower, or the inspection of facilities. The absence of adequate coordination and collaboration at the national level is at least partly responsible for the establishment of environmental priorities that tend to ignore health goals. This situation has led many countries to establish, or to consider establishing, high-level coordinating bodies to exercise a broad surveillance of environmental policy.

The objectives of national environmental health programmes and projects may not be achieved when these are not integrated or closely linked with national development plans. It has been observed that programmes for basic environmental sanitation in rural areas have a better chance of acceptance and implementation when pursued as an integral part of total rural development, sponsored and piloted by key multiple agencies and ministries. Likewise, programmes for the health of working populations and the control of environmental pollution and hazards have yielded results more rapidly when made part of overall policies of industrial development.

Community water supply and wastes disposal

A WHO review of the situation regarding community water supply and wastes disposal in 70 developing countries in 1975 showed that progress in the provision of water supply and sanitation had more than kept pace with population growth in the urban and rural sectors.[1] Surveys show that 77% of urban populations have access to a piped water supply, and 75% to reasonable sanitation facilities. The arrears of work to be carried out in the rural areas are also quite apparent: only 22% of this population have an adequate water supply and only 15% have satisfactory sanitation services. Coverage by public urban supplies ranges from 22% of the people served (Bangladesh) to substantially higher levels in such countries as Malaysia (100%), Tunisia (93%), Nepal (85%), India (80%), Pakistan (75%), and Mexico (70%), and close to 100% in Algeria and all other countries in the European Region. For rural supplies, the prevailing range of coverage by community water supply services goes from as low as around 5% (Afghanistan, Ethiopia, Indonesia, Nepal) to as high as 61% in Algeria and 91% in Jamaica. Bangladesh and Turkey are the only countries in which rural service coverage has outpaced urban coverage.

Fig. 14 shows the percentages of populations served in the different WHO Regions with adequate drinking water and excreta disposal systems as of 1975.

The importance of water supply and sanitation, as essential health measures, particularly in respect of rural and "urban fringe" populations, has been underlined by the recommendations of two recent United Nations conferences: United Nations Conference on Human Settlements (HABITAT) (Vancouver, 1976), and the United Nations Water Conference (Mar del Plata, 1977). WHO and the World Bank jointly prepared the plan of action adopted by the latter conference. The recommendations have been adopted in resolutions of the World Health Assembly. At the end of 1977, the United Nations General Assembly endorsed the plan recommended by the United Nations Water Conference, namely the adoption of programmes based on realistic standards for quality and quantity, with a view to providing safe drinking-water and adequate sanitation for all by the year 1990.

Human settlements and housing

Accelerated urbanization is a worldwide phenomenon, occurring most noticeably in developing nations, though at widely different rates. It leads to the unplanned and

---

[1] See *World health statistics report*, **29**: 544–631, 1976.

Fig. 15. Percentage of urban and rural populations of the developing countries with reasonable drinking water supply and excreta disposal systems, 1975[a].

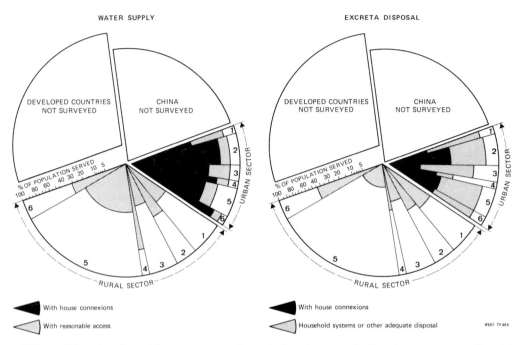

WATER SUPPLY   EXCRETA DISPOSAL

With house connexions   With house connexions

With reasonable access   Household systems or other adequate disposal   WHO 79486

[a] The radial scale adopted for percentages is such that the areas in the charts are proportional to population. The numbers refer to WHO Regions as follows: 1: Africa. 2: Americas. 3: Eastern Mediterranean. 4: Europe (Algeria, Morocco, Turkey, and Malta only). 5: South-East Asia. 6: Western Pacific.

uncontrolled growth of metropolitan agglomerations, particularly in low-income countries. The social problems thus created are associated with a continuous deterioration of the human environment. Industrial pollution, traffic problems, noise, lack of sanitary facilities, and a reduction in the quality of urban air and water resources have become very serious problems in many large cities.

The United Nations General Assembly at its thirty-second session recognized the need for urgent action to improve the quality of life for all people in human settlements. The fact that such action is primarily the responsibility of governments was reaffirmed. The General Assembly also reiterated its view that problems of human settlements constitute a primary field of action in international cooperation, which should be strengthened in order that adequate solutions may be found, based on equity, justice, and solidarity, especially among developing countries.

Great differences are to be expected between human settlements in different parts of the world. A study of mortality in children under 5 years old in 10 countries of the Americas by PAHO showed great differences between developing areas and the more developed areas that had good health and social services and good standards of living. Children were chosen as the group to be studied, since they are the most susceptible to deleterious health conditions. The findings would be applicable to many other parts of the world. Very large differences in child mortality were observed, particularly in the postneonatal period (i.e., between the ages of 1 month and 1 year). The greatest differences were in deaths from communicable diseases, and notably from diarrhoea. Thus, in one area investigated in a Latin American country, deaths from diarrhoea in children under 5 years were approximately 1000 times as great as in a healthy suburban area in Northern America. Measles was also a very important cause of death in the Latin American countries.

Nutritional deficiency was found to be the predominant underlying or associated cause of death, making children more susceptible to the effects of disease. In some areas two-thirds of the deceased children had shown evidence of malnutrition. Malnutrition of the mother was also an important factor, since infants of low birth weight resulted, among whom there was excessive mortality during the first month of life. A similar nutritional situation is to be found in many developing countries.

The provision of piped water and adequate sanitation was shown to be an important health factor. There is a greater likelihood of children dying in houses without these facilities. An inverse relationship existed between the deaths and the educational status of the mother, the latter probably being a reflection of the effects of socioeconomic status. More children died in crowded houses, although socioeconomic and cultural factors may have been largely responsible for this. Mortality was greater in the rural areas studied in Latin America than in the associated urban areas and it was thought that even greater differences would have been found if more isolated rural areas had been investigated.

National statistics indicate that, in many developing countries, a higher than average proportion of adults die during early and middle adult life. Furthermore, health conditions are usually worse in rural than urban areas. This is likely to be the standard pattern in most developing countries, with poor and inadequate water supplies, inadequate sanitary facilities, and poor health care services in the rural areas, often accompanied by higher communicable disease rates. Housing conditions in certain areas may favour the breeding of specific vectors of disease, e.g., the triatomid bug responsible for the spread of Chagas' disease in Middle and South America, mosquitos capable of carrying malaria, or rats capable of carrying plague, typhus, jaundice, and other diseases.

Studies in various regions in recent years suggest that the amount of mental ill health in a community is difficult to quantify. Conditions causing stress are known to affect mental (as well as physical) health. Thus, excessive noise and crowded housing—particularly where members of different families share accommodation—may increase stress. Over-crowded slum areas are frequently associated with serious behavioural difficulties in some members of the community. Life at the top of high-rise tenement buildings may cause stress in mothers because of the difficulty of supervising their children; it may also be associated with a sense of loneliness. Badly planned new housing schemes, by giving inadequate opportunities for social intercourse, may have a deleterious effect on the psychological and social development of the family, more particularly its younger members. New housing schemes, particularly if associated with the compulsory removal of population groups, may cause increased loneliness, especially in old people.

No single approach to the problem of providing adequate health services in human settlements can be successful. To ensure that a population is adequately covered, it is necessary: (1) to ensure that adequate health care facilities are available and that the population is well informed about them and uses them; (2) to ensure that adequate preventive health services exist, in particular environmental services dealing with housing standards, water and food hygiene, and protection from environmental hazards; (3) the proper integration of the health services with other government and administrative services to ensure that health problems are taken into consideration and given due weight when decisions on economic, occupational, and social policies are being made. Community participation is often the only means whereby improvements on the necessary scale may be achieved. In addition, there is a need in most countries for increased participation by health authorities in urban planning.

A significant social indicator of housing conditions is provided by the proportion of dwellings equipped with electricity. Data are available on the situation in the early 1970s in 31 developing countries with a population of almost 500 million, i.e. one-fifth of the total population of the developing countries. A summary of this information is presented below.

Percentage of dwellings with electricity	No. of countries	Population (in millions)
less than 10	1	15
10–24	2	75
25–49	13	195
50–74	7	175
75 and over	8	15

Source: Research data bank of development indicators, Vol. III. Geneva, United Nations Research Institute for Social Development, 1976 (Report No. 76.3).

Urban areas are, on the whole, relatively well equipped, i.e., more than 75% of the dwellings have electricity. However, in rural areas only a little more than 25% of the dwellings are equipped with electricity (in some countries it may be as little as 5%). Data are available for 23 developed countries containing 67% of the total population of such countries. In only two of them are less than 90% of the dwellings equipped with electricity.

The countries for which no information is available fall primarily into one of two categories: those sufficiently developed to have virtually 100% coverage with electricity, and those in which housing standards are extremely poor for the overwhelming majority of the population.

New approaches to environmental problems

Although in recent years governments have become aware of the need to protect, enhance, and preserve the environment, the major issues relating to planning and management in respect of environmental quality have not been adequately dealt with. However, it has been recognized that the traditional *ad hoc* approach of developing countries towards environmental problems through a diversity of programmes and agencies is no longer adequate, if only because of the increasing size and complexity of these problems. The need for a multidisciplinary approach is clear, but progress has been hampered by an inadequate understanding of the problems, by deficiencies in organization and management, and by a shortage of trained personnel. In some countries the necessary changes are already taking place, including more sustained political support, institutional and policy changes at all levels, and the development of action-oriented programmes. These include, among other things, the establishment of systems for environmental monitoring with special reference to the health aspects. The emphasis is on the estimation of human exposure to hazards of high public health significance and the identification of indices of environmental health that may be considered in future programmes.

Control of physical and chemical hazards in the environment

Three trends were continued, if not accelerated, during the 1973–1977 period in many Member States:

(*a*) intensive industrialization,
(*b*) even more rapid urbanization, and
(*c*) increased use of chemicals.

The creation of new industrial centres, particularly in developing countries, usually leads to the establishment of factories with a minimum of control over the discharge of wastes. Narrow and short-run economic considerations frequently dominate broader and longer-term environmental health concerns, which often means that costly control measures need to be taken afterwards. A number of cases in highly as well as marginally industrialized countries have been reported in which accidental spills, continuous liquid waste effluents and air emissions, or the use of chemicals in agriculture caused serious human exposure to toxic chemicals. Severe effects on health were reported, and public awareness of the potential dangers associated with certain industrial processes and products, particularly chemicals, has been growing rapidly throughout the world in recent years. It should also be recognized that not only accidental exposures and acute effects but also the chronic effects of long-term exposure to various chemicals are of concern.

There has been considerable concern about coastal areas in recent years arising from the intensified use being made of them. Industrial complexes, large cities, and congested ports are competing with tourist sites, recreational beaches, and seafood production zones in these areas, with alarming implications for health. Coastal states in such areas as the Mediterranean have initiated joint legislative, scientific, and environmental management action to remedy the situation and protect their marine and human resources.

In the developing countries a substantial effort in waste-water treatment is needed to prevent increasing health hazards from biological contaminants discharged into water bodies. Chemical contamination of water bodies is also increasing. Emphasis must be placed in developing countries on (*a*) planning the use of water resources and (*b*) enacting water pollution legislation at as early a stage as possible in the process of urbanization and industrialization. These measures will make it possible to avoid the acute problems of pollution that have occurred in industrialized and developed countries.

Soil pollution through faeces is a major cause of disease throughout the world. The disposal of solid wastes presents another problem. Garbage dumps provide harbourage for insects and rodents, both of which are vectors for a broad spectrum of diseases.

Protection against exposure to radiation from all sources is an area of continuing public health concern. Although the medical uses of radiation and radioisotopes remain the most important man-made sources of exposure of population to ionizing radiation, and require continuous attention, the increased uses of nuclear energy are becoming an additional source of concern, particularly as new countries are embarking on nuclear power production.

Food safety

Food may be the origin or vehicle of contaminants and agents (biological, chemical, and physical) that can cause human disease. The contamination of food by living organisms is still the primary concern in the majority of Member States, although food safety problems related to chemicals are increasing in both highly industrialized and developing countries. To ensure the safety and wholesomeness of food, a broad range of action at all stages from its growth, production, or manufacture to its final consumption is needed. In most countries there is no single programme addressing itself to all these aspects. Food safety problems vary greatly among countries and from area to area, mainly according to the level of basic hygiene (including water supply) and the diversity of foods eaten (from home-grown fresh foods to mass-produced processed foods). Despite persevering efforts, in many countries the infrastructure to deal with food safety problems is inadequate. Of 27 African countries replying to a questionnaire, 23 indicated that they had legislation for food hygiene and only 9 considered that livestock were slaughtered according to proper hygienic rules. To protect populations at high risk from foodborne diseases, basic sanitation, public education on simple measures of hygiene in the production and preparation of food, adequate food storage, and the proper use of agricultural chemicals and chemical food additives are all essential.

Primary health care and environmental issues

The emphasis now being placed on primary health care offers vast new opportunities in all areas of environmental health. This was borne out by the discussion at the twenty-second session of the UNICEF/WHO Joint Committee on Health Policy in 1979, which reviewed a report on water supply and sanitation components of primary health care based on studies carried out jointly by the two organizations in Bangladesh, Colombia, Ghana, India, Nepal, and the Philippines as well as documents on experience in other countries. There is now a great deal of evidence of the capacity of communities to guarantee locally created and managed water supply and waste disposal schemes, housing improvements, control over food sanitation, etc. In fact, there are few environmental problems, at least in smaller communities, that cannot be substantially dealt with at the local level, provided that the necessary support is obtained from the relevant technicians and administrators and that due attention is paid to the use of locally available and inexpensive technology.

Family health

There is a growing consensus that the family, in its structure and functions, not only influences the health and disease pattern of the individual and the community but is also a logical unit for self-reliance in health care and a channel for the improved delivery of health and other social services. However, the relationship between health and the family is reciprocal, since the health situation in a family influences family organization, functioning, and attitudes as well as affecting the quality of family life.

Health largely depends on the family's social and physical environment, and its life-style and behaviour. The primary health care approach emphasizes the crucial importance of the family in health promotion, and in the prevention, early diagnosis, and care of disease. The bulk of health actions are carried out by individuals and families before they come into contact with any health worker. The mother is usually the family's first health care worker. But women often have no access to information and technology, or to income and education, and have to cope with an overload of work. They therefore need organized support in providing health care to the family and themselves.

In more and more areas of the world today, man-made and natural disasters (including war and other violence), political upheavals, changing patterns of women's work, and migration of men away from rural areas have far-reaching effects on the family's functioning, especially with regard to child-bearing and child-rearing. The supporting mechanisms that the family has provided for its members in the past are eroding because of economic and social pressures far beyond its control, and this is profoundly affecting the health of mothers and children.

In the past decade the tendency towards overdependence of families on professional expertise and costly technology, particularly in child-bearing and child-rearing, has been challenged. Governments are increasingly recognizing that all types of unconventional as well as conventional activities and workers of the health, social, and other systems are needed to support the self-care functions of the family. For example, in many areas traditional birth attendants are increasingly being trained by national health authorities to promote good family health care.

In the 1970s, changing patterns of social and economic development and the possibility of planning the timing and spacing of children have had an important impact on family structures and functioning. The changes influence women's and men's economic and social roles as well as the patterns of child-bearing and child-rearing and hence the health of the family. The changes in traditional family structures in some areas have left many women without adequate alternative support mechanisms—a situation that has implications for women's health as well as the health and health care of the family as a whole.

A breakdown of the extended family system, such as is taking place, for example, in the periurban areas of many developing countries, is a threat to the social and physical well-being of the people, and particularly the children, because of continued high mortality rates and the lack of a functioning system of nuclear families with adequate organized support. This may be illustrated by the following figures: in the least developed countries, where life expectancy at birth is about 40 years, some 40% of people aged 20 years have only one parent left alive and a further 8% have lost both parents, i.e., almost every second 20-year-old is either a full or a partial orphan. At the mortality level of developed countries, where life expectancy at birth is about 70 years, fewer than 2% will be complete orphans and only a further 10% will have lost one parent, i.e., nine out of ten 20-year-olds will have both parents still alive.

In general, the priority health problems of mothers and children and high levels of mortality and morbidity derive to a large extent from the synergistic effects of malnutrition, infection, and uncontrolled fertility, themselves consequences of poor environmental and socioeconomic conditions, including unavailability of health care. It has become increasingly clear that activities and programmes in all developmental sectors, not only the health sector, are essential to improve health, particularly that of mothers and children. Within the health sector, experience in different countries has shown that activities and programmes in family and maternal and child health are more successful when they are closely linked with other essential tasks, such as education on prevailing health problems, nutrition programmes, and communicable disease control activities, including immunization, and when a multidisciplinary integrated approach, ensuring the effective participation of individuals, families and communities, is adopted.

Maternal and child health

Of the total world population, 24% are women of reproductive age and 36% children below 15 years of age. While the proportion of women of reproductive age is about the same in all parts of the world, children under 15 years of age make up 24% of the population in the developed areas and 40% in the developing areas. Thus, while the actual percentage may vary from one country to another, these two groups together make up the majority of the population in almost all parts of the world today. The following world population estimates are for the year 1978.[1]

	World (millions)	Developing areas (millions)	Developed areas (millions)
Women aged 15–49 years	1005	727	278
Children aged 0–4 years	565	472	93
Children aged 5–14 years	957	778	179
Sub-total	2527	1977	550
Total population	4219	3105	1114
Children 0–14 years and women aged 15–49 years as percentage of total population	60%	64%	49%

Exact data on the health status of mothers and children are available in only a few countries, but enough mortality and morbidity estimates are available from most parts of the world to provide a realistic picture of the situation. One drawback of the existing data is that they are mostly expressed as national averages, whereas it is known that considerable differences in health status often exist between different population groups within the same country.

It is also increasingly being questioned whether mortality and morbidity data fully reflect health status, particularly in respect of young children for whom survival rates and incidence rates for specific diseases are not very clear expressions of health. New and positive indicators of health are emerging, such as indices of growth and development, as well as maturation during adolescence. Birth weight is an important example; it reflects both the past and present health status of the mother and is a sensitive guide to the chances of an infant's survival and subsequent health.

---

[1] Based on estimates by the United Nations Population Division.

The inadequacy of data on mortality and morbidity is most serious in precisely those parts of the world where health problems are most widespread and severe, the data on pregnant women and children, especially the newborn, being particularly poor. These limitations should be borne in mind.

(a) Maternal mortality[1] and morbidity

In countries that have well developed health care systems and where the maternal mortality rate is well documented, this rate is of the magnitude of 5–30 per 100 000 live births and is continuously decreasing. In most of the developing countries, for which information is only fragmentary, the situation is worse—and, in some cases, much worse—than in those for which comprehensive statistics on maternal mortality are available. Evidence from special WHO/UNFPA-supported and other studies in a number of developing countries indicates that maternal mortality rates in excess of 500 per 100 000 live births are by no means exceptional. Rates of over 1000 per 100 000 have been reported in parts of Africa. In a survey in rural area in Bangladesh, maternal mortality was found to be 570 per 100 000 live births, the mortality rate for the youngest group of mothers being as high as 1770 per 100 000. Maternal mortality accounted for 57% of deaths of women aged 15–19 years in the area and 43% of deaths of women aged 20–29. In Afghanistan, maternal mortality has been estimated to be around 700 per 100 000 live births. Variations within countries are considerable. In Afghanistan, for example, the urban rete was almost half the figure quoted above, and in Malaysia the highest rate for a district was 18 times the lowest rate.

With growing recognition of the importance of the health of women in the development process, it has become increasingly obvious that the high mortality of women in developing countries in their middle years is a cause for grave concern. Age-specific death rates for women rise sharply at ages 20–30 in many countries, where women often have less chance than men of surviving from 15 to 45 years of age. In a number of countries in Asia, life expectancy at birth is actually lower for women than for men.

Despite the known underrecording, maternal causes are still among the leading causes of death for women in the child-bearing ages. In almost all developing countries deaths from maternal causes are among the 5 leading causes of death for women aged 15–44; in one-third of these countries they come first or second. Because childbearing is spread over a longer period in developing than in developed countries, women in developing countries not only undergo a higher risk per pregnancy but they are at risk over a longer period of their lives. It has been estimated that, in the areas with the highest maternal mortality, i.e., most of Africa and West, South, and East Asia, about half a million women die from maternal causes every year, leaving behind at least one million motherless children. In Latin America, the maternal mortality rates are much lower, but several studies have shown serious underreporting of maternal causes of death; in some countries up to half of such deaths were not reported accurately.

Postpartum haemorrhage, often with anaemia as an underlying or associated cause, and sepsis are the most frequent causes of maternal deaths and are directly related to the

---

[1] The term "maternal mortality" is used here as a convenient way of referring to Section XI of the International Classification of Diseases (ICD), comprising "all deaths ascribed to childbirth and puerperium".

absence or inadequacy of prenatal and delivery care. In addition, hypertensive disorders of pregnancy—toxaemia—are important, not only in the developed countries where they account for 23–25% of all maternal deaths, but probably even more in the developing countries. The epidemiology of toxaemia is not well known, but it appears to be most frequently associated with very young mothers and with maternal depletion and malnutrition in high-parity women. Anaemia and hypertensive disorders of pregnancy, in addition to their effect on maternal mortality, also cause high rates of fetal death and low birth weight. Large numbers of pregnancies, short birth intervals, and pregnancies occurring at the extremes of reproductive age are closely related and carry an increased risk of unfavourable outcome for both mother and child, manifested *inter alia* in higher neonatal and infant mortality rates. In a WHO study in rural India,[1] it was found that both neonatal and infant mortality rates were more than twice as high among infants born less than 2 years after the preceding pregnancy termination (abortion, fetal death, or live birth) than among those born more than 4 years later.

It is now generally recognized that family planning can favourably influence the health, development, and well-being of the family, particularly mothers and children, through (1) avoidance of unwanted pregnancies and the occurrence of wanted births that might otherwise not have taken place; (2) a change in the total number of children born to a mother; (3) achievement of an optimum interval between pregnancies; and (4) changes in the time at which births occur, particularly the first and the last, in relation to the ages of the parents and especially that of the mother.

The role of illegally induced abortions as a cause of maternal deaths is well recognized, but difficult to estimate, even approximately, because of the secrecy surrounding such abortions. In Latin America, where abortion is illegal in most countries, it has been estimated that induced abortion is the cause of between one-fifth and one-half of all maternal deaths.[2]

Reliable data are even more scarce for maternal morbidity than for maternal mortality, but some general observations can be made. Chronic malnutrition and anaemia are closely linked with acute and chronic infections, such as malaria, infectious hepatitis, urinary tract infections, and pulmonary tuberculosis, and cause much suffering. Malaria in particular is very widespread. Pregnant women lose part of their acquired immunity, and malaria attacks are therefore often more severe in pregnancy. Malaria of the placenta increases the risks of abortion and low birth weight.

Anaemia is widespread among women of child-bearing age in both developed and, in particular, developing countries. In the latter the percentage of non-pregnant women with haemoglobin levels indicative of anaemia ranges between 10% and 100%, the range in developed countries being between 4% and 12%.

Almost all chronic diseases, such as hypertension, renal disease, and diabetes, are aggravated by pregnancy. The use of addictive drugs, alcohol consumption, and smoking during pregnancy can lead to intrauterine growth retardation and even malformation. Psychological stress factors are also of increasing concern.

---

[1] OMRAN, A. R. & STANDLEY, C. C. ed. *Family formation patterns and health.* Geneva, World Health Organization, 1976.

[2] Based on data in PUFFER, R. R. & GRIFFITHS, G. W. *Patterns of urban mortality.* Washington, DC, Pan American Health Organization, 1967 (Scientific Publication No. 151).

Involuntary infertility is a condition that causes great personal distress and has important social implications. In most parts of the world, about 2–10% of couples are affected, but in certain areas of Africa the proportion of infertile couples may be as high as 40%. It is thought that the causes of this high prevalance include sexually transmitted disease resulting in tubal obstruction, as well as other sequelae from obstetric conditions.

(b) Infant and childhood mortality

Of the some 122 million infants born each year, roughly 10% will die before reaching their first birthday, and another 4% before their fifth birthday. But the chances of survival are very unevenly distributed in the world. Thus, while the risk of dying before reaching adolescence is about 1 in 40 in developed countries, it is 1 in 4 in Africa as a whole, and even as high as 1 in 2 in some countries. There are vast differences between regions, in particular Africa and South Asia, where life expectancy is below 60 years, and the rest of the world. In some parts of Africa and South Asia, nearly two-thirds of all deaths are of children below 5 years.

The enormous differences between countries in maternal and child mortality rates are shown below:

National maternal and child mortality rates[a]

	Highest levels (1)	Lowest levels (2)	Ratio of (1) to (2)
Perinatal mortality[b]	120	12–15	8–10:1
Infant mortality[b]	200	8–10	20–25:1
Childhood mortality[c]	45	0.4–1	45–75:1
Maternal mortality[d]	1000	5–10	100–200:1

----

[a] WHO estimates based on a variety of sources.
[b] Per 1000 live births.
[c] Per 1000 population.
[d] Per 100 000 live births.

The association between infant mortality and socioeconomic development may be demonstrated by the following data for the mid-1970s:

	Infant mortality per 1000 live births	Daily energy consumption per head (MJ)	GNP per head (US $)
Developed	22	14.2	5200
Less developed	109	9.2	470
of which: least developed	156	8.4	140

Infant mortality in countries with per capita GDP in 1970 of less than US $200 was 12%; in those countries one-third of the world population live. In contrast, in countries with a per capita GDP in 1970 of between US $400 or more but less than US $1000, infant mortality was less than one half (5%).

Differences within countries are also considerable. In Senegal the infant mortality rate was 57 per 1000 live births in Dakar compared with 247 in some rural areas. In Sri Lanka rates in some districts are three times higher than in others. Differences in rates according to social groups exist in all countries. In the Philippines the infant mortality rate in the farming occupational group is 98 per 1000 live births compared with 40 in the professional, administrative, and managerial group. In developed countries the differentials are less pronounced, but still exist; in the neonatal period they are of the order of 1.5, and in the postneonatal period they can be as high as 2.6 (New York State, USA).

Differences in urban and rural infant mortality rates have followed various directions in and between countries. In general, rapid urbanization has been followed by higher infant mortality rates in urban than in rural areas. This occurred in the United Kingdom and other European countries in the nineteenth and twentieth centuries and is apparent at present in the cities of Africa, Asia, and Latin America, where there are serious problems of overcrowding, poor sanitation, pollution, accidents, and unequal distribution of wealth. Where life in cities has become less hazardous for small children in poor families as a result of improved sanitary conditions and the concentration of health services, the infant mortality rate in urban areas has dropped below that in rural areas. Yet, among 22 countries submitting infant mortality data for urban and rural areas to the United Nations and WHO, 8 developed countries now show higher rates for urban areas.

There are indications in many parts of the world that infant and childhood mortality rates are declining. In developed countries the infant mortality rate has fallen by 2–7% a year since 1960, the strongest decline taking place in the countries with the highest initial rates. The most spectacular reduction has taken place in Japan, where the rate fell from 60 per 1000 live births in 1950 to 31 in 1960 and 11 in 1974. A goal of a 40% reduction in infant mortality rates was set in the Ten-Year Health Plan for the Americas (1971–1980). By 1975, of 32 countries of the Region for which data were available, 15 had reduced their rates by 20% or more since 1970. Encouraging as these trends are, they cannot be assumed to extend to all parts of the world.

Regardles of the level of child mortality, the probability of a baby dying is at its peak at the time of birth, including the period immediately before birth, and, except for a minor peak which marks the end of breastfeeding, declines thereafter. Both the probability of dying and the main causes of death change rapidly during the early years of life. The conventional distinction between perinatal (28th week of gestation to 7th day of life), neonatal (first 28 days of life), postneonatal (29th day to one year), and child (1–4 years) mortality is convenient from both the analytical and the programmatic points of view. Of particular importance is the different impact of adverse environmental factors, especially nutrition, on mortality in each of these periods. In countries where infant and child mortality has been reduced, mortality in the age group 1–4 years has fallen first and most rapidly, while perinatal mortality has declined much more slowly.

Perinatal mortality now accounts for about 90% of all fetal and infant mortality in the developed countries with the lowest infant mortality rates, where more deaths occur in the short perinatal period than in the next 20 years of life. The underlying causes of perinatal deaths are linked to those of maternal deaths, i.e., poor health and nutritional status of the mother and complications of pregnancy and childbirth.

Perinatal mortality is also closely associated with low birth weight, defined as a birth weight below 2500 g; this affects mortality in the whole first year of life and probably also for a few years afterwards, and has adverse long-term effects on the development of the child. A WHO study in seven developed countries revealed incidences of low birth weight of between 4% and 11%, yet deaths of babies of low birth weight accounted for between 43% and 74% of all perinatal deaths.[1] An estimated 22 million such babies are born each year, 21 million of them in the developing countries, mostly in the least privileged populations. There are strong indications that these babies contribute to a large proportion of deaths and child morbidity, the risk of mortality being up to 20 times higher for them than for other babies, both in the neonatal period and later.

Approximately two-thirds of all babies of low birth weight born in developed countries are estimated to be pre-term (i.e., less than 37 completed weeks of gestation). In developing countries, on the other hand, three-fourths of all babies of low birth weight are full-term but, significantly, are undernourished and small for their gestational age. Late neonatal and postneonatal deaths (infant deaths after the first week of life) are now uncommon in developed countries. In many developing countries, however, they account for almost two-thirds of all infant mortality. In many areas, tetanus may account for up to 10% of all mortality among newborns, but diarrhoeal diseases, closely followed by respiratory infections, are the leading causes of morbidity and mortality in infancy. Malnutrition, as an underlying cause, is also important; it has been cited as responsible for up to 57% of infant deaths in some countries.[2]

The single most effective measure for the prevention of malnutrition and protection against infection in infancy is breastfeeding. The data suggest that infant mortality rates in developing countries are 5–10 times higher among infants who have not been breastfed or who have been breastfed for less than 6 months. Despite the marked advantages of breastfeeding, its popularity—as shown by the number of women who practise it and how long they go on with it—has declined significantly in many parts of the world.

Historically, the decline has been particularly marked in highly developed countries, but now there is evidence suggesting that the prevalence and duration of breastfeeding may be increasing in these countries. In developing countries where the value of breastfeeding is most marked and where larger proportions of infants are at risk of malnutrition and infection, data gathered by a WHO collaborative study on breastfeeding indicate that in some urban areas relatively large proportions of mothers do not undertake breastfeeding—in the Philippines, for example, 33% of urban upper-income mothers and 15% of urban poor mothers who were interviewed had not breastfed their youngest child. Of those that do undertake it, many wean their infants before the age of 6 months. This appears to be the pattern among urban low-income families as well as upper-income groups. The prevalence and duration of breastfeeding among rural populations in developing countries, however, continue to be high although in some cases nutritional and other health problems in infancy appear to be associated with the late introduction of appropriate and regular supplementary feeding.

Mortality at ages 1–4 years is much lower in all populations than infant mortality. In

---

[1] Main findings of the comparative study of social and biological effects on perinatal mortality. *World health statistics quarterly*, **31**: 74–83 (1978).

[2] PUFFER, R. R. & SERRANO, C. W. *Patterns of mortality in childhood. Report of the Inter-American Investigation of Mortality in Childhood.* Washington, DC, Pan American Health Organization, 1973 (Scientific Publication No. 262).

some areas with exceptionally high mortality levels, the probability of surviving from age 1 to age 5 may, however, be as low as 80%, mainly because of high death rates in the second year of life, when the main underlying causes of infant mortality continue to be important. The infectious diseases of childhood, such as measles, pertussis, and pneumonia, begin to appear in the second half of the first year, or in the second year. When combined with malnutrition, these diseases have high case fatality rates. For example, during the famine in Sahel in Africa, the case fatality for measles was estimated to be up to 50%. In other parts of tropical Africa it is 7–10%, which is still very much higher than in most parts of the world.

(c) Childhood morbidity

For every childhood death there are many episodes of disease and ill-health. Many common childhood diseases and conditions do not usually kill their victims, but may cause serious chronic damage. Some of this is already apparent in childhood (blindness, paralysis), while other sequelae become manifest later in life (chronic heart disease, mental retardation).

In the developed world accidents are the leading cause of death among children aged 1–4 years and are also responsible for a substantial amount of disability in childhood. In the USA, for example, about 300 000 children are hospitalized annually because of head injury and about 20 000 of these will suffer from some degree of permanent brain damage.[1] There is every reason to believe that accidents among children are frequent also in the developing countries, especially burns and traumas from home accidents and, to an increasing degree, traffic accidents.

Behavioural disturbance is another child health problem increasingly recognized as important in most countries. In some countries children abandoned by their families present severe social and health problems; for example, there are estimated to be two million such children in Brazil and 1.5 million in India.

Malnutrition is the most widespread condition affecting the health of the world's children, particularly those in the developing countries. Some 100 million children under 5 years of age are suffering from protein-energy malnutrition—more than 10 million of them having the severe form, which is usually fatal if left untreated. The prevalence is highest in Africa, where in some areas up to 23% of children aged under 5 years are suffering from severe, and up to 65% from moderate, protein-energy malnutrition.

Other nutritional deficiencies include insufficiencies of vitamins A and D. The extent of blindness in children primarily due to vitamin A deficiency is tragic. In spite of the abundance of sunshine, which promotes the synthesis of vitamin D in the body, children in parts of Africa and Asia suffer from rickets mainly because of traditional practices in child-rearing. This problem can also be found in migrant populations in the industrialized countries.

---

[1] FALKNER, F. ed. *Prevention in childhood of specific adult health problems.* Geneva, World Health Organization, 1980 (in press).

(d) Health in adolescence

Overall mortality is relatively low in adolescence, compared with other phases of life, in both developing and developed countries. Mortality rates in adolescence are generally higher for males than for females. Secular trends may be noted for some causes such as accidents, suicides, and homicides, all of which are increasing,[1] with the result that the death rates for males aged 15–19 years have risen in a number of developed countries. The most recent data available indicate, however, a levelling-off of this increase or even a slight decrease, but the levels are mostly still above the level of 1955–1959. Of particular importance is the increase in mortality from accidents, which constitute the main cause of death in adolescents in developed countries and also play a dominant role in many developing countries. In developed countries they account for between 50% and 75% of all deaths in adolescence.

Next to accidents, the most important causes of death in adolescence are suicide and malignant disease, including severe blood disorders in the more developed regions, and gastrointestinal and respiratory infections, including tuberculosis, in other areas. A disturbing trend is the recent increase in suicide rates for adolescents and in the abuse of alcohol and other addictive drugs. In several countries suicide is the second cause in the age group 15–19 years, but the recording of data on this cause varies greatly from country to country. This reflects both the inadequacy of the reporting system and the sensitivity about suicidal behaviour that exists in many cultures, making camouflage in reporting common.

For reasons that differ from country to country, and culture to culture, there is widespread experimentation by adolescents with alcohol and other drugs as well as tobacco. In many countries, about half the adolescents indulge in such exploratory behaviour. As for smoking, there have been some encouraging signs of a decline in recent years. In the USA, for example, 34% of the boys and 35% of the girls in the 13–19 year age group had given up smoking.[2]

The sexual behaviour of adolescents is rapidly changing in many parts of the world, the trend being towards more and earlier sexual activity. In most industrialized countries and in many areas of Africa, the incidence of sexually transmitted disease among adolescents is more than twice as high as it is among those aged 20–29 years. A striking increase in the incidence of sexually transmitted diseases, especially gonorrhoea, has been observed since 1960. This has been confirmed in most of the countries that provide data. In some countries the reported incidence for persons below 17 years of age doubled for boys and tripled for girls between 1966 and 1977. The age group 16–17 years showed a fifty- to eighty-fold increase over the age group below 15 years, indicating the start of sexual activity by a large group of high-risk adolescents at that point.

Information on the frequency of teenage pregnancies in developing countries is limited. However, where the minimum legal age at marriage is low, the first pregnancy can be expected to occur during the mid-teens and repeated pregnancies are likely to follow before the age of 20 years. In some countries 50% of first births occur to mothers aged

---

[1] WHO Technical Report Series, No. 609, 1977 (Health needs of adolescents. Report of a WHO Expert Committee).

[2] WHO Technical Report Series, No. 636, 1979 (Controlling the smoking epidemic. Report of the WHO Expert Committee on Smoking Control).

less than 20 years, as do 25% of second births, and 10% of third births. This is illustrated by the following data from the Americas:

	Proportion of births to mothers under 20 years of age		
	First births (%)	Second births (%)	Third births (%)
Barbados (1973)	51	29	12
Costa Rica (1974)	46	25	10
Venezuela (1974)	40	21	9

Source: *Demographic yearbook 1975* New York, United Nations, 1976.

Early teenage pregnancies pose special health risks not only for the mother but also for the child. Evidence clearly shows that maternal mortality rates are considerably higher for younger women and that teenage mothers also run a higher risk of losing their babies in infancy.

In many developing countries, complications of pregnancy, childbirth and the puerperium are among the main causes of deaths among females aged 15–19 years. The death rates from causes related to abortion and delivery are particularly high in girls below 18 years of age.[1]

Trends in maternal and child health care

Maternal and child care was traditionally designed and provided in the form of vertical programmes with "standard" technical content, based on models from a few developed countries. These models were geared to the provision of continuous supervision and preventive care for mothers and children in affluent societies where institutional and other basic needs were satisfied, and where coverage by other health programmes was practically universal. Applied in different socioeconomic situations, such vertical programmes have been unable to provide more than minimal coverage, because of their cost, and they have scarcely been of a kind to solve the priority problems of the majority of mothers and children.

The emergence and application of the primary health care approach is now changing the organization and management of maternal and child health care in an increasing number of countries. Separate organizational structures and standard technical content are giving way to local or country-specific strategies based on self-care and organized community participation, with the primary health care—or community health—worker providing maternal and child health care in an integrated manner and as a major and essential element of primary health care. The intermediate and higher levels of referral provide advice, guidance, logistics, and continuous training to the village health worker, as well as care for problem cases that cannot be dealt with at the primary level.[2] Specialized maternal and child health units are increasingly being fully integrated with the rest of the health care system and assigned tasks in support of the first-level workers.

---

[1] WHO Technical Report Series No. 609, 1977 (*Health needs of adolescents.* Report of a WHO Expert Committee).

[2] WHO Technical Report Series No. 600, 1976 (*New trends and approaches in the delivery of maternal and child care in health services.* Sixth report of the WHO Expert Committee on Maternal and Child Health).

The health of mothers and children is affected by the environment, in particular the immediate family environment. Maternal and child health care is therefore increasingly seen as consisting of total care of mother and child in the context of family health as a whole, rather than being centred on individual health problems. There is a growing consensus that not only do family structures and functions influence the health and disease patterns of the individual, the family, and the community, but that the family is also a natural context for self-reliance in health care and one in which health and other social services can be provided more effectively.

In the developed countries, new problems and new knowledge are emerging rapidly, stimulating rethinking of the approaches to maternal and child health care. As the perinatal and infant mortality rates in the developed countries fall, there is increasing emphasis on morbidity and on the quality of care for children. Chronic diseases in childhood and adolescence are also receiving increasing attention, including specific measures of support to the families concerned. More and more stress is being laid on appropriate education and information, on family care and self-care, and the organized health care systems are reoriented to provide support for these activities. In some developed countries, for example, an increasing number of deliveries are taking place at home and maternity routines are changing, because the existing organization of hospital delivery care does not always satisfy the psychosocial needs of the mothers and their families.

In all countries increasing dependence on costly and complicated medical equipment and overdependence on drugs are also being questioned, and more appropriate technologies are being developed in consequence.

(a) Organization of care

The recognition of the importance of the home and the community as the first level of care is leading to changes in the organization of maternal and child health care, with greater emphasis on the support and care provided by primary health care workers. It is estimated that nearly 80% of the tasks of these workers are related to the health care of mothers and children. Depending upon the overall structure of a national health care system, the intermediate levels of maternal and child health care provide support for the peripheral levels and the necessary referral facilities for problems that cannot be dealt with at the earlier levels. Maternity homes with facilities for hospitalization function at the district level for referral and services, such as Caesarian section, neonatal care, and laboratory diagnosis. Paediatric and obstetric outpatient facilities or hospital beds exist in all countries, usually at the central and district levels. At the central level nearly all countries have established maternal and child health units within the ministries of health or other, related ministries, to provide guidance in technical policy and planning with regard to training and service.

Evaluation of a number of maternal and child health care programmes has shown that many specific measures and interventions are rigidly repeated everywhere irrespective of their relevance to actual local needs, resulting in the inefficient use of already scanty resources. This is particularly true of prenatal care.

The technical content of maternal and child health care programmes is accordingly changing in order to respond to problems that, like the possible solutions, vary from one

135

community to another. The broad areas of care do of course continue to be related to the particular biological needs of mothers and children and include: care during pregnancy and childbirth; promotion of breastfeeding and appropriate nutrition of infants and young children; supervision of growth and development, and prevention of infections, including immunization; the prevention and management of infant and childhood diarrhoea, including oral rehydration; family planning, including prevention and treatment of infertility; education in health within the family in support of family self-reliance.

Programmes based on visiting schedules and routine technical tasks have been particularly resistant to the adoption of a more problem-oriented approach. A systematic approach to the formulation of national maternal and child health care projects, based on knowledge of local epidemiological and sociocultural situations, has been developed by WHO in collaboration with Member States and found to be of practical value in effecting changes in technology.[1]

The former tendency in many countries to split up maternal and child health care among separate clinics for antenatal care, "under one" clinics, and services for postnatal care, health education, and family planning is rapidly changing. The primary health care approach which is becoming more and more widespread is accelerating the move away from this piecemeal approach, which most research studies on the subject have shown to be both inefficient and ineffective. In the past many countries put particular emphasis on the provision of family planning as a separate, vertical activity. In the light of experience during the last decade, however, the delivery of family planning care and advice now tends to be integrated into the activities and programmes of the health section and other relevant sectors at various levels. This integrated approach also reflects an increased recognition of various interrelationships between fertility regulation and maternal and child health with a bearing on services and training.

The linking together of various components of maternal and child health care, including family planning, has been shown to be efficient, effective, and advantageous in many instances. The integration of family planning in the maternal and child health and general health services in the last decade has taken various forms. Where the national policy of the country favours integrated delivery of family planning care, the degree and type of integration vary extensively. In some instances integration has only affected the planning or administrative levels. In many others, efforts are made to provide integration at the local level, sometimes at the level of the health worker or health centre.

The integrated, comprehensive approach to maternal and child health care implies that every contact of mothers or children with the health care system is seen as an opportunity to deal with the health probems of all the members of the family, and to view each individual's problems and needs in the context of the family and community.

One of the main conclusions of the UNICEF/WHO study on alternative approaches to meeting basic health needs in developing countries[2] was that integration of components of health services yielded the best results. A feature of the integrated system was the use of

---

[1] BAINBRIDGE, J. & SAPIRIE, S.: *Health project management.* Geneva, World Health Organization, 1975 (Offset Publications, No. 12).

[2] DJUKANOVIC, V. & MACH, E. P. *Alternative approaches to meeting basic health needs in developing countries. A joint UNICEF/WHO study.* Geneva, World Health Organization, 1975.

field workers, who carried out maternal and child health care as part of their overall primary health care functions and who served as a link between the village families and other levels of the health services.

A new and promising means of improving the coverage and efficiency of maternal and child health care and family planning is the "risk approach". The detection of persons and groups at special risk has been used in the past to provide more care for individuals in particular need of it. The new approach provides care for the community, as well as the individual, through a flexible and more rational distribution of existing resources according to levels of risk so that some care will be provided for all, and more skilled care for those at greater risk.

(b) Manpower and training

Shortage, poor utilization, and maldistribution of manpower, together with inadequate and often irrelevant training, are particularly acute problems in maternal and child health care.

The special category of "maternal and child health worker" at the primary level is gradually being phased out. A wide range of workers are now considered necessary for maternal and child health care. They include primary health care workers, crèche staff, extension workers, members of women's organizations, schoolteachers, and traditional birth attendants. However, in most instances training in maternal and child health has mainly been confined to health workers.

Much of the maternal and child health training of health workers before the 1970s was based on curricula devised in academic surroundings and was not geared to the solution of the major health problems of those at the social periphery. Nowadays it is considered more effective to develop the curriculum from the community level. Such an approach is being used, for example, in Sudan in one programme where teachers of health visitors, village midwives, and community health workers are being trained in the village context and are themselves participating in the planning of community health programmes.

In developing countries the training of health professionals in maternal and child health is often based on foreign models; many of the paediatricians and obstetricians, professional midwives, and maternal and child health managers were trained abroad in university centres in developed countries. The trend is now away from training in foreign countries towards training in national institutions and/or regional centres.

(c) Coverage and utilization of services

In recent years increasing concern has been expressed about the fact that the health needs of populations are not being met, despite the efforts made in many developing countries to strengthen the health services. In most countries the bulk of resources are still used for urban specialist and hospital care. In a large Asian country, for example, only 32% of the rural population lived within a two-mile (3 km) radius of any kind of health facility at the end of 1975, while the corresponding percentage for the urban population was 98%.

However, in some instances existing maternal and child health facilities are underutilized, probably because of their poor adaptation to the needs and life-styles of the community.

Some of the reasons for the underutilization of services are specific to material and child health as they relate directly to the lives of women, who are the main "users". The excessive burden of work in women's lives has already been referred to in a general way: in many areas, women spend the day in agricultural work, in fetching water, in preparing meals, and at the market and thus might not have the time or energy to make use of the services. Also, in some societies, women prefer to consult or be examined by female health workers, and these are often not available.

To be meaningful, data on coverage in maternal and child health care would have to be based on more than a count of health facilities and health staff per person. They would have to show how the whole series of promotive, preventive, curative, and rehabilitative activities are made available to, perceived by, and utilized by those in need. Not surprisingly, data of this kind, in particular on underprivileged population groups, are practically non-existent. There are however service statistics for several components of maternal and child health care that give some indication of "coverage":

Care during pregnancy and childbirth. Care during pregnancy and childbirth exists in different forms; special clinics and outpatient and other services may be involved. The degree of coverage varies greatly both between and within countries. In the Americas the proportion of pregnant women receiving antenatal care ranges from 14% (Uruguay) to 98% (Trinidad). On the whole, the proportion receiving care has been increasing: from 12% in 1969 to 21% in 1973 in Ecuador, from 29% in 1972 to 35% in 1976 in El Salvador, for example.[1] In Botswana the proportion of women receiving antenatal care increased from 40% in 1973 to 70% in 1977.[2] Frequently antenatal care is available but not utilized. Studies in India show that in a rural area with a clinic and in urban Delhi, 69% and 64% of mothers, respectively, did not attend any maternal and child health centre.

Figures for births attended by trained personnel in developing countries show a wide range among regions: in Africa, the figures range from 6% to 67%; in Asia from 3% to 95%; in Latin America from 12% to 97%. In most countries there are vast urban/rural differences. In Korea, for example, 49% of births in urban areas are attended by a physician or midwife, whereas in rural areas only 6% of births are so attended. In Uganda the percentage of institutional deliveries varies by district from 5% to 66%. Although the proportion of deliveries attended by trained personnel is rising steadily in many countries, it appears from a review of the most recent information that in some parts of the world at least 50%, and in some instances as many as 85%, of births are assisted by untrained traditional birth attendants or relatives. In a rural area in Nigeria, 2% of deliveries were attended by a physician or took place in hospital, 52% were attended by a native practitioner, 40% by a family member and 6% of the babies were delivered by the woman herself. In the Philippines 41% of deliveries are attended by traditional birth attendants. Although in the past these attendants were not officially recognized by health authorities in many countries and thus received no support, more and more countries are now paying

---

[1] *Health conditions in the Americas* 1973–1976, Washington, DC, Pan American Health Organization, 1978.
[2] *World health*, February–March 1979.

attention to their training and utilization, and providing support, supervision, and referral for special cases to the organized health care system.

Family planning. In recent years there has been a marked improvement in fertility control methods and their application. New types of intrauterine device, various steroidal preparations, new approaches to female sterilization, and easier, safer methods of pregnancy termination are now an important part of maternal and child health and family planning services and appropriate training programmes are necessary.

In rural areas, new approaches are being tested in order to extend coverage and improve the quality of maternal and child health and family planning programmes. Some of these are large-scale programmes, others are local adaptations. The common aim is to bring maternal and child health and family planning services virtually to the doorstep of every household. How to do this will be a major concern of health authorities over the next 10–20 years.

New ways are being explored of identifying those who need assistance in the field of family planning and would like to benefit from the services provided in this connexion by local health personnel and traditional community health practitioners.

In some countries, maternal and child health programmes are extending their scope to include family life education in schools, education programmes for adolescents, premarital counselling, and the participation of husbands in educational activities. Many programmes seek to involve community groups such as women's clubs, rural development societies, and agricultural cooperatives in educational and motivational action.

According to a recent worldwide survey, the total percentage of sexually active women of reproductive age practising family planning nearly doubled in some regions during the first half of the 1970s, and it was estimated that, in 1976, 34% of sexually active couples of reproductive age throughout the world[1] were using some form of contraceptive method regularly. A comparison of rates of use of contraceptive methods by persons attending health care services in 1971 and 1976 indicates a significant increase over the five-year period. Among couples practising family planning, the percentages of those using oral contraceptives or intrauterine devices and of persons undergoing sterilization increased. However, there are wide differences within and between countries; for example, an estimated 53% of sexually active women of reproductive age practised family planning in the Western Pacific Region, whereas in West Africa the figure was only 3%. A series of fertility surveys in all parts of the world showed a large proportion of women who wanted no more children, yet did not practise contraception. Inadequate contraceptive information and services were seen as among the main reasons for failure to meet the national population growth targets set by some countries with high fertility levels and large populations.

About two-thirds of the people of the world, mostly in Asia, North America, and Europe, live in countries where there are liberal abortion laws and policies. The remainder lives in countries—mainly in Africa and South and Middle America, though there are also a few in Europe—where abortion is either illegal or permitted only to protect a woman's life or health. Whatever the legal position, induced abortion is widely practised

---

[1] The survey did not include China and the USSR.

in most parts of the world; in fact, it is estimated that in the mid-1970s it accounted for about one pregnancy termination for every three live births, approximately half the abortions being performed clandestinely. Illegal abortions performed under unhygienic conditions and with unsafe techniques are a major cause of maternal death and disability and of secondary infertility.

The problem of infertility has received increasing attention in many countries; in most of the developing world, however, fertility regulation has remained a specialized service reserved for a privileged few.

Infant and child care. In developing countries, national data are even more difficult to obtain for infant and child services than for other components of maternal and child health care. The content of such services varies, but in general they include continuous supervision of the growth and development of the child; prevention and management of common infections and specific childhood diseases; and promotion of good nutrition. Data from Latin American countries show rates for the attendance of infants at child health centres ranging from 23% (Colombia) to 66% (El Salvador). Figures for specific activities such as immunization also give some indication of coverage. It is estimated that less than 10% of the children born each year are immunized against the six common childhood diseases: pertussis, tetanus, diphtheria, measles, tuberculosis, and poliomyelitis. One may assume that these 10% at least also receive appropriate preventive health care in other respects. But in spite of a growing realization of the importance of preventive care, the great majority of the world's children come into contact with the health services only when they need curative care, if indeed they come into contact with them at all.

Family life education. While mothering and fathering are known to be powerful influences on the development of the young child, adequate counselling on the subject is provided only rarely to mothers during pregnancy and even less often to fathers. Moreover, the health services pay little attention to educating the public on ways and means of improving the health of mothers and children although the urgent need for such education is commonly admitted. This is mainly due to pressure of time, inadequate preparation of health workers, and lack of suitable educational materials.

(d) Other relevant services and legislation

Day care of children. The child has various physical, intellectual, emotional, and social needs that, for healthy development, must be met in an integrated way. The role of day-care services is to provide for these needs in coordination with the family, enhancing family functioning and improving parent-child interactions.

There is an increasing tendency in many countries for both parents to work away from the home, which means that the care of the dependent child becomes a task for the community, acting through professional or semi-professional groups that gradually take over roles previously played by mothers, relatives, or neighbours.

The pattern of women's participation in paid employment in some developed countries has been changing rapidly over the last 15–20 years. An increasing number of women in these countries now stay at work through the child-bearing and child-rearing years.

In 1977, 12 million children in the USSR attended day-care institutions such as nurseries, kindergartens, Pioneer camps, and children's homes. Other countries in Europe have developed day-care facilities along similar lines. Recent figures show that the percentage of children aged 3–5 years attending day-care institutions in different European countries ranges from about 27% to 90%. The proportion of younger children being provided with such care is lower, i.e., from about 7% to 25%.

In some developing countries, such as Cuba and Viet Nam, well organized day-care facilities are available for large numbers of children of pre-school age. In other developing countries there are isolated undertakings in the private sector; however, they mainly benefit the richer classes. Nevertheless, in Africa there are some examples of community-organized group care of children, involving women's groups or political organizations, in newly developed urban areas and in agricultural areas. Depending upon the sociocultural setting, other approaches are being developed. They include organized systems of day care in factories or industrial facilities, neighbourhood centres, cooperative self-help women's groups, and family-based day-care facilities in which older members of the family and neighbours take part.

School health. In the past the emphasis was on routine health examinations of school-children, which in many instances did not make any significant contribution to the improvement of their health. School health now increasingly concentrates on motivating children to develop healthy habits. Schoolchildren also learn about the health problems of their community as a whole and carry out selected health activities for themselves as well as for other children and their families. Schools can also effectively carry out specific activities such as updating immunization, nutrition education, accident prevention, and screening for hearing and eyesight problems. The training of schoolteachers and other school employees to give health guidance is being increasingly emphasized.

In areas where school attendance is low and where the social environment is poor, the health needs of children of school age who do not attend school are likely to be more acute than those of children at school, and it is estimated that by 1985 the number of children who receive no formal schooling whatsoever will have increased considerably.

Health care of adolescents. Adolescents in most of the world are given health care through the ordinary health services and sometimes through special services such as school health services. Special services for adolescents have been developed in some urban centres in industrialized countries; they are usually provided through nongovernmental or voluntary systems of care, but their coverage is very limited, as they are geared mainly to special problems such as drug addiction, juvenile delinquency, and teenage pregnancy.

Social legislation. During the past decade many countries, both developed and developing, have enacted legislation that upholds the rights of individuals with respect to the availability of necessary services. International labour conventions governing maternity leave, flexible working hours to permit mothers to breastfeed their children, and the provision of day-care facilities for young children have now been implemented in almost all developed countries and in some developing ones. For example, recent social legislation enables mothers in outside employment to stay at home with full or partial pay for a year or more in order to care for a child. Legislation in one country provides for the mother or father to stay at home for the first 8 months of the child's life. Furthermore, legal developments since 1967 reflect a change in attitudes towards abortion and family planning. In an increasing number of countries legislation now focuses on the rights of women, as well as the health conditions and social welfare of women and their families, as a basis for the provision of family planning services and the lawful termination of pregnancy.

Nutrition

Malnutrition continues to be one of the leading causes of illness and death among young children in most developing countries. Among those who survive, a background of poor nutrition contributes to chronic debility and to impaired functional performance, both intellectual and physical. Recently, and especially since the World Food Conference of the United Nations in 1974, there has been considerable interest in problems of nalnutrition. Contrary to earlier expectations, the extent of the problem appears to be increasing in spite of a large number of measures taken by different sectors of the government that are directly or indirectly involved in ending malnutrition. The need for a new strategy to combat malnutrition has thus emerged.

Malnutrition is not merely a health problem, and the need for a multisectoral approach to it is obvious. The recent emphasis on national food and nutrition strategy within the framework of national development plans is a step in the right direction. At the national level, the roles of different sectors in reducing malnutrition will have to be clearly defined in the broader context of overall development planning and policy formulation. The national food and nutrition strategies now being adopted in different countries have several distinct components. Not only should they improve the pattern of income distribution and agricultural productivity, but, at the same time, they will include a large number of measures relating to food conservation, processing, marketing, pricing, and distribution. Equally important are environmental measures that will reduce the level of the intestinal infections and infestations that at present impede the normal absorption of food by many people in developing countries.

Extent and nature of problem

To define the extent and nature of the malnutrition problem on a worldwide scale is a difficult task for a number of reasons, the most important being the lack of reliable data from various parts of the world.

On the basis of the data available, malnutrition in the world can be seen to fall into two broad categories:

(*a*) malnutrition of underprivileged populations, common in the developing world;
(*b*) malnutrition of "affluence", common in industrialized countries, as well as in the upper socioeconomic strata of the developing countries.

In most developing countries, undernutrition affects all age-groups, especially children under 5 years of age. Protein-energy malnutrition, of which the two extreme forms are kwashiorkor and marasmus, is the most predominant form of undernutrition, greatly contributing to the high mortality and morbidity rates in the above age group in most developing countries. An estimate made during the World Food Conference in 1974 put the figure for the world's undernourished population at not less than 400 million, a great majority of whom would be young children. The condition is not only a killer of children, but can produce severe impairment of physical and mental functions in those who survive. This situation prevails throughout the developing world, and there is no evidence to indicate that it has improved in recent years.

Specific nutritional deficiencies of considerable public health importance continue to be alarming problems in a large number of developing countries and, of these, three have attracted attention, not only as health problems, but also because they have grave socioeconomic implications—vitamin A deficiency and xerophthalmia, endemic goitre and cretinism, and nutritional anaemia. Vitamin A deficiency, leading to blindness in severe cases, is a grave problem in many countries in Africa, Eastern South Asia, the Middle East, and Latin America. Each year, about 100 000 children under 5 years of age become blind in these parts of the world.[1] In India, alone, about 12 000 children become blind every year. The condition prevails with equal severity in several other countries in the same region, such as Indonesia and Bangladesh.

Endemic goitre and cretinism caused by iodine deficiency and associated with mental retardation have grave health and socioeconomic implications in various African, Asian, and Latin American countries. In certain mountainous areas, e.g., in parts of Nepal, the incidence of goitre is as high as 95–100% of the population. Cretinism in the same country affects as many as 10% of the child population in certain areas. Nutritional anaemia, caused by iron deficiency, folate deficiency, or both, affects pregnant and lactating women and young children, not only in the developing world but to a lesser extent in the industrialized countries as well.

"Malnutrition of affluence" i.e., disorders due to overnutrition, is now one of the major health, social, and economic problems of the industrialized countries, being found especially in Western Europe and the USA. The main manifestations are obesity, cardiovascular diseases, diabetes mellitus, and dental caries.

The task of the health sector

There has been growing awareness in the health sectors of national governments in recent years that direct health action cannot remove or reduce the basic cause of malnutrition, namely, socioeconomic deprivation. However, the immediate causes, which are mostly manifestations of poverty, can be effectively rectified by well designed measures on the part of the health care system. For example, infections and parasitic infestations, unregulated fertility, and inadequate environmental sanitation are poverty-related factors that generate malnutrition and that can be rectified to a large extent by

---

[1] WHO Technical Report Series No. 590, 1976 (*Vitamin A deficiency and xerophthalmia*. Report of a Joint WHO/USAID Meeting).

interventions on the part of the health sector. It is now rightly recognized that protein-energy malnutrition, the predominant nutritional problem in most developing countries, is not an independent phenomenon. It is precipitated by diarrhoeal and other infectious diseases and births at too close intervals; thus oral rehydration, measures for birth-spacing, and immunization are recognized as being conducive to sound nutrition. Direct nutrition action, such as nutrition education, nutrition rehabilitation, and prophylaxis against specific nutrition deficiencies, is increasingly being combined with the indirect action just mentioned. In most developing countries, the systems of integrated health care now being developed could go a long way in combating malnutrition, but, owing to the grossly inadequate coverage of the population, they are unlikely to make a significant impact on the problem. The solution lies in the primary health care approach. Since malnutrition is a major health problem in most developing countries, realistic and effective nutrition and nutrition-related activities are recognized as cornerstones of primary health care. Such activities are accordingly being vigorously promoted in various developing countries, together with appropriate training programmes for community health workers.

The strategies for combating specific deficiencies are being developed, revised, and refined in order to overcome the logistic and operational problems encountered in the past. Prophylaxis against vitamin A deficiency through the administration of massive doses of vitamin A, now in operation at the national level in various countries, is being carefully studied for its effectiveness and feasibility. The fortification of foods with vitamin A and iron is being tried out in several countries, and further technological improvements are being made with a view to developing national programmes based on this measure.

Health education

Health cannot be imposed on communities nor is it something that can be provided for people. What can be provided is health care. But that is only one link in the chain. It is the people themselves who decide whether to utilize the services or not. It is they who decide whether to collaborate effectively in health matters, to take an active part in the promotion and maintenance of their own health and the health of their community or leave the matter to chance. The challenge of health for all by the year 2000 is that health has to be attained and cannot be imposed. This requires commitment, and commitment requires adequate education. The challenge of primary health care has therefore brought to light the need for more dynamic health education, based not on teaching people to utilize available resources as passive receivers, but on the fact that individuals, regardless of their level of education, are capable of making suitable decisions in respect of their own health, when properly informed and motivated.

This new trend emphasizes not only the prevention and care of disease, but also the promotion of health and, in particular, the crucial role of the individual in taking care of his own health. Much attention has been given in recent years to the demystification of treatment. The number of books, articles, and pamphlets dealing with self-care is rapidly multiplying in many countries, and the public is becoming increasingly aware of the basic requirements for the care of a number of diseases, ranging from gastroenteritis to essential hypertension.

Through involvement and participation in health activities, as individuals, as families, or in groups and communities, people come to identify with and feel responsible for such activities, so that they cease to be passive receivers and become individuals interacting with the health care system in full awareness of the decisions they have to take. Participation thus means a process of involvement in thinking, decision-making, and acting. For those who plan health education activities, the encouragement of active participation requires insight into the community's culture, habits, and values, as well as needs and constraints. Thus, although it may take some of its premises from the field of teaching, health education today goes far beyond the actual provision of knowledge and seeks to create an atmosphere in which individuals, families, and communities consider health a valued asset. This can be achieved by systematic, well planned activities within the context of health promotion. A health service with no educational component cannot be considered a comprehensive one. Although governments are aware of the contributions that should be made by health education specialists in planning, guiding, and evaluating educational activities, they nevertheless believe—and rightly so—that health education activities must be part of the work of every health worker as well as of every community or socioeconomic development project. Examples of such approaches are seen in the Philippines and the Sudan, and in a number of Latin American countries. For example, by the end of 1977 a health coverage of more than 90% of the scattered rural population in Costa Rica had been achieved through the efforts of 244 communities; this community action was encouraged by health staff, who provided liaison with the various governmental and private agencies involved in the programme. This type of thinking has resulted in the incorporation of health education and effective educational approaches in the programmes of training of all health workers—physicians, nurses, sanitary engineers, and others.

Increased attention has been given to informal education in recent years. Whereas health education previously took place in schools, during mass campaigns, in adult literacy classes, etc., today, while efforts in settings like these are maintained, they are reinforced by informal education carried out between individuals, in the family, the community, and by the health workers.

While there have been a number of successes in health education, as reflected in reduced infant mortality, increased immunization coverage, or better nutrition, there have also been failures for various reasons. Health education is often used as a last resort, and educational activities have been based on false premises. It is essential therefore not to proceed on assumptions, but to verify them by community-based applied research. The search for effective ways of bringing about and maintaining changes in behaviour may require research into such factors as, for example, the particular role of established leaders as opinion-formers or innovators, the functions of volunteers in health promotion, and the role of the school in encouraging health behaviour. It should be noted that health education does not operate in a vacuum and will not be successful if people are encouraged to adopt practices for which facilities either do not exist or cannot be prepared. Health education does not replace other services, neither do other services replace health education. For this reason it has to be part of the very fabric of the health services.

145

While health education was already regarded as a means of changing behaviour, the new approach also encourages the maintenance of good health once the change has occurred. Some habits, such as breastfeeding, should be maintained and not changed.

The team approach in health development, with the "consumer" as an accepted team member, requires a type of health education in which the individual, the family, and the community become partners rather than mere recipients. The new challenge then, is that of education for partnership.

Health of the working population

The world's countries are at different stages of development. Some are developed, some are rapidly developing, and the rest are developing at a slower pace. Some countries are mainly agricultural, others are in the throes of rapid industrialization. Workers in agriculture, manufacturing, mining, and building constitute the main bread-winning adult groups. Hence, the specific health risks associated with these types of employment must be added to the general problems of endemic disease and malnutrition that are especially prevalent in developing areas.

Health effects of working conditions

(a) *Extent of the problem*

Statistics on workers' health problems are limited, and the available data suffer from inconsistencies due to the lack of a uniform reporting system. Data on occupational diseases may be misleading, reflecting the standard of the national occupational health services rather than disease incidence or prevalence. Occupational health services are often separated from national health services and reporting may involve complicated legal procedures—two factors that may also affect the completeness of the data.

There is satisfactory evidence, however, that occupational health problems are of some magnitude in developing countries, and that measures for their control are urgently needed. In the industrialized countries they are many and varied, and a great deal is spent annually on compensation for occupational disability, premature retirement, and occupational mortality.

Field investigations in different sectors of industry have shown that a wide variety of occupational diseases are prevalent among workers, sometimes highly so. Respiratory diseases from the inhalation of organic and vegetable dust are common. Fibrotic pneumoconioses caused by mineral dusts are widely reported. Poisoning by pesticides in the course of their manufacture, formulation, and use in agriculture sometimes affects large numbers of workers. Poisoning by chemicals and metals (particularly lead), occupational dermatoses, and noise-induced deafness are also reported.

Occupational accidents differ from occupational diseases in that they are more obvious, undisputed, and acute. They are the major cause of death and disability due to occupational hazards. In terms of loss of working days and payment of compensation, they constitute a heavy burden in many countries.

146

Statistical returns from different countries show clearly that the rates for occupational diseases and accidents are still soaring despite efforts to reduce them. For example, in the Philippines in 1975, there were 2444 work injuries, with 24 deaths. Of these injuries 136 occurred in agriculture, 666 in mining (20 deaths), and 185 in building (1 death), with cases of disability numbering 136, 448, and 183 respectively. In Bolivia in 1974, 5432 occupational accidents were reported in mining in one year. Some US $ 6 000 000 were paid out in compensation.

Some other examples of the toll taken by occupational accidents may be mentioned: France in 1974 recorded a total of 1 154 371 accidents (2117 deaths); the Federal Republic of Germany in 1974 recorded a total of 1 989 315 accidents (3644 deaths); the United Kingdom in 1975 recorded 343 140 accidents (427 deaths); Malaysia in 1973 reported 12 743 accidents (370 deaths) with compensation payments of M $ 12 355 367; Saudi Arabia in 1974 recorded 1088 accidents (29 deaths) with compensation payments of 1 121 870 riyals.

Occupational diseases have more or less the same profile, as the following examples show: in the United Kingdom in 1975 there were 1137 cases of pneumoconiosis (including byssinosis). In Australia, Poland, and Spain the number of new cases of pneumoconiosis for the year 1974 were 2448, 1008, and 1656 respectively. Cases of noise-induced hearing loss in Australia, Finland, Poland, and the Republic of Korea for the year 1974 were 1568, 998, 1447, and 1332 respectively, excluding cases discovered in surveys.

Occupational mortality studies are another source of information. In an increasing number of developed countries, population censuses are used as points of departure for detailed investigations into occupational differentials in mortality; relevant information for less developed countries is still very scarce. In developed countries the risk of premature death is consistently high among miners, transport workers, labourers, and unskilled workers. It must however be emphasized that hazards in the working environment are not the only factors involved.

(b) Occupational health problems of special working groups

(i) Workers in agriculture

Throughout the world and particularly in the developing countries, the majority of the work force is engaged in agriculture. Agricultural workers have a great many health problems, some of which are the result of work hazards. These facts are often forgotten because of the widespread misconception that occupational health is concerned mainly with industry and industrialized countries and because of the lack of adequate information about health problems in agriculture.

Several studies carried out by occupational health institutions in different parts of the world show that the main health hazards relating to work in agriculture include: zoonotic diseases, pesticide poisoning, accidents, and respiratory diseases due to organic and vegetable dusts. The extent of the occupational occurrence of zoonotic diseases in most parts of the world is unknown; some studies suggest that they are frequent and others that they are on the decline.

The number of agricultural chemicals now in use is very large, and new ones are constantly being discovered and used. The main problems seem to arise from poisoning

147

by the more toxic organophosphorus compounds. Even in highly industrialized countries, this form of poisoning is underreported since the early symptoms are mild and short-lived and frequently pass unnoticed. Developing countries, from which reports on the subject are very scanty, are currently increasing their use of agricultural chemicals in connexion with their development plans which aim at increased agricultural yields. The shortage of information may be illustrated by the fact that, in 1973, the Director-General of WHO requested all countries in a position to do so to notify the Organization of the number of accidental poisonings in 1974. By October 1975, returns had been received from only 6 countries, 5 of them in Europe.

In some countries field surveys among spraymen exposed to agricultural chemicals revealed an average prevalence of symptoms of poisoning in up to 40% of them during a spraying period.

With the increasing use of agricultural machinery occupational injuries are becoming more frequent in developing countries, and in some industrialized countries the occupational accident rate for agriculture now ranks third, after those for mining and building. The estimates of the National Safety Council of the USA for 1971 indicated that, although farm workers comprised only about 4.4% of the work force in the USA, about 16% of total occupational deaths and 9% of all occupational injuries occurred in this group. The rapid spread of mechanization in the agriculture of the industrialized countries and many developing countries has had the beneficial effect of reducing human effort and increasing yield, but has brought with it hazards that up to now seemed peculiar to industry.

Because of the large number of workers employed in agriculture and in the processing of agricultural products, exposure to vegetable and other organic dusts is widespread. Several occupational diseases due to such exposure have been described, and some are included in the statutory lists of notifiable diseases in certain countries, e.g., byssinosis, farmers' lung, bagassosis, and occupational asthma. Many dusts and their health effects have not been systematically investigated. Exposure to dusts of grain, rice, cocoa, coconut fibres, tea, kapok, tobacco, and wood is common in the countries where these products are grown. There is evidence that obstructive respiratory disease and asthma may be caused by exposure to some of these dusts.

Respiratory disability has been observed among young villagers exposed since childhood to flax dusts at home. Investigations in almost all countries producing and processing textile materials made of cotton, flax, or soft hemp have revealed a significantly high rate of byssinosis. In some instances, byssinosis has affected most of the workers exposed (up to 90%) and, in others, depending on the dust concentration and duration of exposure, a prevalence of from 20% to 40% has frequently been observed, and permanent pulmonary disability has been found in up to 20% of the workers affected.

(ii) *Workers in small industries*

The small industries and mines (less than 100 workers) have been estimated to employ almost 70% of the world's work force in manufacturing, mining, and related trades (with a range of 45–95% in different countries). In spite of their large number and their importance to the national economy of the countries concerned, the general working conditions have tended to depend on the attitude of the employers or owners. Some regard the workers as members of their own households. Indeed, an appreciable sector of small industries are operated in the owners' own houses or backyards.

The problems of small industries are not restricted to developing countries, but may also be serious in some highly industrialized countries. The health hazards encountered in these industries are in almost all cases much more serious than those in large establishments engaged in similar industrial activity.

In small industries, health problems, including occupational diseases, sometimes take on epidemic proportions. Lead poisoning and absorption were found to affect almost all workers in one small battery factory in Lima, Peru, in 1973; in another, 23% of the workers were affected. In 1974 a survey in Guinea showed a considerable proportion of lead absorption among exposed workers.

In stone-crushing plants in Singapore, 181 cases of established silicosis were reported in 1973 and an additional 22 cases in 1974, all eligible for compensation. Byssinosis and obstructive lung diseases were found to be prevalent among 26% of workers employed in small ginning plants in the Sudan. Cases of asbestosis were observed in field studies in Singapore and Colombia in 1973 and 1974.

Poisoning by solvents also occurs in many small factories. In Singapore, 13 cases of toxic jaundice resulting from exposure to hepatotoxic chemicals in small plants were reported in 1974. The situation is similar in the Republic of Korea, where 226 cases of symptoms caused by hydrocarbons were found in small factories in 1973 (corresponding to 5.7% of the workers), compared with 44 cases (1.2%) among workers in large factories.

Occupational injuries are also common in small industries because of lack of training on the job, poor housekeeping, deficient handling methods, and bad layout of machinery. A study in the Republic of Korea showed an average frequency rate of 185.4 per 100 000 man-hours in small workplaces compared with 35.6 in larger ones.

Small industries usually hire workers indiscriminately from many vulnerable groups, including the very young, the old, and the partially handicapped. The lack of the social amenities required to facilitate the employment of women imposes a strain on working mothers as regards the care of their children.

The problems of small industries have not been ignored. Developing countries have started to extend regular health services to workers in small plants and some (e.g., the Republic of Korea, Sudan, and Thailand) have established occupational health centres for these industries. In France, an interenterprise health service is provided by statute, with regional and rural centres of occupational medicine. In Scandinavian centres, cooperative schemes among employers, unions, and government provide regular health services for small workplaces.

(iii) Migrant workers

The migrant worker is typically a young person in the prime of life, physically fit, enterprising and highly motivated, and yet he is vulnerable. He has various characteristics that limit his ability to adapt to the environment in which he must live and work. In many instances, he has to face a wide variety of new conditions, including climate, eating habits, social customs, cost of living, housing conditions, and type and rhythm of work. He is handicapped in dealing with them because of his inexperience of urban life and his inadequate knowledge or complete ignorance of the language of the country. His cultural background, customs, and traditions often create a barrier to his integration into the host country. Such factors have an important influence on migrant workers' behaviour and can predispose them to ill-health.

The social isolation, loneliness, and stress resulting from this complex of factors may lead to depression, nervous breakdown, and psychosomatic disorders, possibly to suicide, and, indirectly, to alcoholism and venereal diseases.

The new environment in which the migrant finds himself is potentially hostile in several ways. Jobs taken by migrants are generally the least attractive and most poorly paid. Many work in mines, quarries, agriculture, forestry, building and various industries, most of which carry specific disease and accident risks against which no particular preventive measures may have been taken.

(iv) *Other vulnerable groups*

The extent of the occupational health problems of vulnerable groups of workers such as the young, the old, and the handicapped has yet to be fully investigated. Statistics on them are on the whole lacking, particularly in developing countries. These groups are mostly employed in agriculture and small-scale industries, or self-employed. Malnutrition and other diseases, as well as indiscriminate employment without a preliminary medical examination, make them particularly vulnerable to toxic hazards, industrial accidents, and other occupational risks. The health of working women is also an area of special concern.

(c) *Identification and control of psychosocial factors at work*

The continuous interaction between man and his physical and psychological working environment may influence his health either positively or negatively, and the production process itself is influenced by the worker's state of physical and mental wellbeing. The fact that work, when it is a well-adjusted and productive activity, can do much to promote health is not yet sufficiently appreciated. WHO has an important role to play in drawing up a programme of action in this field; present knowledge of work physiology and ergonomics needs to be further developed and applied for the benefit of workers.

In the developing countries work is becoming increasingly mechanized. A number of working processes have been developed that treat people simply as tools in the production system, with little regard to their needs and aspirations or to the wide variety of risks that threaten workers' health and lives. The lessons learned during the process of industrialization elsewhere should now be borne in mind in planning for health and economic development in the developing countries.

Psychosocial factors in the working environment influence workers' health in a number of ways. Negative influences can result from inappropriate organization of work, automation, poor working relations, job tenure policies, the degree of responsibility, repetitiveness, speed, alternating shifts, overwork, and underwork. There is increasing evidence of the role of work stress in causing overt disturbances such as the excessive use of alcohol or drugs, psychophysiological symptoms, and heightened susceptibility to physical illness. At the same time, it appears that much larger numbers of people are suffering from dissatisfaction in their work, fatigue, and low motivation. Extensive research is needed in these areas, which so far have received only limited attention. Yet effective preventive measures could be taken through occupational health work at the plant level. The health services at this level are in a good position to identify causes of disturbance at an early stage, in collaboration with the management. Once the causative factors have been identified, preventive measures can be introduced and a considerable amount of ill health can be avoided. Adverse psychosocial factors in the place of employment are more susceptible to control than those in the general environment, which are more complex and less easily identifiable. There is an urgent need to develop an international programme of action in this field.

(d) Occupational health services

In the five years under review several countries revised their occupational health systems and some have established new ones. While occupational health programmes are still at an early stage in many less developed countries, awareness is growing among the health authorities of these countries of the urgent need to devise ways and means for the effective delivery of health care to working populations. Occupational health services in some countries come under the jurisdiction of the health authorities or the labour authorities, or partly under labour and partly under health.

(e) Epidemiological studies

Occupational institutes in several countries have carried out epidemiological studies of some of the outstanding health problems of workers. However, systematic data on occupational health problems are limited, particularly in less developed countries. This is mainly due to the weakness of occupational health units at places of work and the widespread shortage of trained occupational health personnel, as well as epidemiologists and statisticians. From the standpoint of assessing needs and identifying priorities, information on occupational health problems is fundamental to the development of an adequate health programme. Unfortunately, in many countries the development of an epidemiological information base is still at a rather rudimentary stage, though potentially suitable information is often not screened for its relevance to occupational health.

The greatest problem in this area is that the majority of working people, particularly in developing countries, are still outside the immediate range of occupational health care. The obstacles to the proper delivery of such care might be eliminated if an adequate information system on the nature and extent of workers' health problems was organized, coordination between different national bodies concerned with workers' health established, a suitable legal framework drawn up, and the shortage of occupational health personnel overcome through proper training strategies geared to the needs of countries.

Social and economic effects of health conditions of the working population

The attention now being paid to the potential contribution of health programmes to socioeconomic development is a reflection of the increasing awareness among health policy makers and administrators of the strategic importance of the health sector in national planning. The World Population Plan of Action, adopted by the World Population Conference in 1974, stipulates that particularly vigorous efforts should be made to achieve an improvement in the poor health and nutritional conditions that adversely affect people of working age and their productivity and thus undermine efforts for development.

151

Evidence is now accumulating that:

(a) disease control (or eradication) programmes, such as those against malaria and yellow fever, open up for settlement previously uninhabitable areas with a great potential for agricultural development;

(b) the improvement of health conditions raises workers' morale and productivity;

(c) the number of working days lost through disease may be significantly reduced; and

(d) an improvement in health status can lead to a change in behavioural patterns and attitudes conducive to economic development, reflected *inter alia* in an increase in the number of persons engaged in "growth-contributing activities" in absolute as well as relative terms.

Many of the "macrolevel" effects of changes in the health status of the population in general, and the working population in particular, are still essentially unknown territory. Progress is being hampered by difficulties in the measurement of quantitative (and quantifiable) effects and their differentiation from qualitative ones. To some extent, it can be argued that every change in quantity implies or induces a change in quality.

Above all, it is the malnourished, disease-stricken members of the working population that will encounter difficulties in finding employment. It has been estimated that in 1975 in developing countries there were about 285 million persons either unemployed or underemployed out of a total working population of 700 million[1] (i.e., 40%). This estimate indicates the extent of the obstacles facing individuals caught up in the vicious circle of poverty and poor health. It also shows the magnitude of the challenging task of making full use of available labour resources and allowing the poor to meet their basic needs (of which health is one).

A further example of the importance of improving the health status of the working population is provided by the effects of declining mortality on the labour force. The productive age is usually considered as the 50 years between age 15 and age 65. At a level of life expectancy at birth of 40 years, which is the average for the group of the 29 least developed countries (in which 245 million people, i.e., roughly 10% of the total population of the developing world, live), the years of productive life amount to 38 out of the potential maximum of 50 years, i.e., the productive lifetime is, on an average, reduced by about one quarter. At a life expectancy at birth of 55 years (roughly the average for the group of less developed countries), the expected productive lifetime is 43 years, i.e., still some 15% less than the maximum. In contrast, in the developed countries with a life expectancy at birth of 70 or more years, the average working lifetime is 48 years, i.e., the loss amounts to only 5% of the maximum. It should also be borne in mind that in several less developed countries life expectancy at birth is below 40 years, which implies that an average of as much as 15 years of the working lifetime, or one-third of the potential maximum, may be lost through death.

Thus, a decline in mortality leads to a dramatic increase in active as well as total life expectancy. This should make a nation's investment in education and social planning more

---

[1] These estimates exclude China and other Asian countries with a centrally planned economy.

effective, besides preserving valuable skills and experience. It should also make it more rewarding to train people more intensively and should increase man-years at work. Advances could be made in technology and science, and productivity and output could be greatly increased.[1] Reduction of mortality at the working age—combined with a determined effort to reduce morbidity—is thus a key factor in national development strategies. However, a firmer basis for the more vigorous health policies required must be provided through more complete health statistics and comprehensive and intensive research.

Mental health

Several of the seemingly contradictory tendencies that characterized mental health sciences and their application in the past two decades have found their resolution in the last few years. Though institutional treatment still remains necessary for selected conditions at a certain stage of their development, community-oriented services now have universal support. Care for the mentally and neurologically ill and for those suffering from psychosocial disorders such as drug dependence is being increasingly often provided through the general health services, although the further development of the specialized disciplines involved—such as neurology, psychiatry, and the behavioural sciences—is still needed since they have to continue producing the necessary technology. The need to apply mental health knowledge in various social pursuits—from welfare services to better urban planning—is now recognized, while the exaggerated aspiration of psychiatry to deal single-handed with all phenomena—from poverty to war—has abated. Close collaboration between the social sectors is gradually becoming a basic principle of mental health care provision, but without the earlier tendency towards the domination of the activities of such sectors by medical professionals and behavioural scientists. Though centralization of resources for research remains necessary, decentralization of responsibility for service organization and provision has become an obvious—though not yet generally accepted—principle for action. The fight between "classical" psychiatry and "antipsychiatry" is losing vigour and at the same time there is wider acceptance of the need for more humane care and greater respect for patients' needs and rights.

Arguments about the relative priority of research and service have also found their resolution in the recognition that there are effective, economically and socially acceptable techniques of treatment and prevention that need wider application, while at the same time more research needs to be done in certain areas.

Finally—and perhaps most significantly—the arguments about the applicability of modern psychiatric concepts to other parts of the world are also losing their topicality, because a significant number of scientists and thinkers have emerged in the developing countries and have skilfully adapted many of the positive achievements and methods of the mental health sciences and produced new knowledge needed for improving care.

---

[1] It is true that a lowering of mortality leads—other things being equal—to an increase in the growth rates of the population and the labour force as well as in the average inactive life span. However, the upward trend in the population and the labour force begins only gradually, generally leaving governments enough time to initiate measures for stimulating productivity and expanding production. The net effect of an increase in the inactive life span can be determined only in relation to the general social and economic conditions and requirements of a given country. For a more detailed discussion see, e.g., HAUSER, J.: The effects of declining mortality on the labour force. *World health statistics quarterly* (in preparation).

While these conceptual clarifications and the growing unanimity about objectives and methods represent an enormous step forward, there are a number of serious constraints to further development. Some are common to health care in general, such as the lack of resources and the scarcity of trained personnel; others are specific to the mental health field and stand as formidable obstacles on the road to progress. Among them are: the stigma attached to mentally ill individuals, their families, and the members of health professions dealing with them; difficult ethical issues specific to the treatment of the mentally disturbed; traditional professional attitudes that block—among other things—better information of the public about the extent and nature of the mental health problems and the availability of solutions to them.

This section gives a summary review of the present state of knowledge about the extent and nature of mental health problems of major public health importance, followed by an account of recent advances in mental health care (including trends in the organization of services and control and treatment measures) and of legislative implications and action at both national and international levels.

Extent and nature of the problem

At the Thirty-first World Health Assembly, Member States of WHO defined the scope of mental health action as including: the promotion of mental health as exemplified in measures to ensure the optimal psychosocial development of the child; the prevention and control of mental and neurological disorders and of psychosocial problems such as drug dependence, alcohol-related problems, and psychological components of physical disease; and the consideration of psychosocial factors in health and health care, for example, those that affect the acceptance of major public health initiatives, community participation, and motivation of health workers.[1]

Mental disorders

Mental disorders form a significant proportion of overall morbidity and are a major source of chronic disability as well as a burden on the health services and the community. Variations in the incidence and prevalence of mental disorders in different parts of the world, or among groups of the same population, may reflect demographic differences or differences in the distribution of various etiological, pathogenetic, and pathoplastic factors. In general, however, these variations do not appear to be large, and it could be said that in most countries approximately 10% of the population suffer from severe and chronic incapacitating psychotic or dementia-producing disorders while another 10% have non-psychotic mental disorders (including mental retardation, neurotic illnesses, and various behaviour disorders) that interfere with normal functioning. These figures do not cover the frequent psychological and social dysfunctions accompanying physical disease.

Of the severe mental disorders, schizophrenia and organic brain syndromes at present account for the largest proportion of patients in institutional care with chronic disability.

_____
[1] WHO Official Records, No. 248, 1978, pp. 358–364.

Incidence rates for schizophrenia rarely exceed 0.5 per 1000 and are much the same for men as for women. Owing to the chronic nature of the disorder, the prevalence is high (about 9–10 per 1000) and can be expected to increase faster than the rate of population growth in some parts of the world, even if the incidence rates remain constant. A more rapid increase in the prevalence of schizophrenia can be expected, particularly in developing countries where the proportion of people surviving into and through the specific risk age (15–54 years) for this condition is rapidly growing. The longer survival of individuals affected by schizophrenia is also more likely because of increasing life expectancy in most countries.

Depression, neurotic illnesses, and psychological dysfunction associated with physical disease may occur at almost any age, and the cumulative risk of developing at least one episode of one of these disorders, assuming survival up to the age of 60, has been estimated at 43% for men and 73% for women.

Mental disorders are associated with high mortality from a variety of causes, which suggests that they can be considered a serious health risk in more ways than one. The social burden and the amount of disability resulting from mental disorders are more difficult to measure, but there can be little doubt that from the point of view of adverse social consequences mental disorders rank very high among health problems. In a study that aimed at quantifying the "burden" constituted by different categories of potentially disabling conditions and developing an index that would take into account such factors as the amount of hospitalization, the load on outpatient and general practitioner services, and sickness benefit days, mental disorders emerged as the largest single contributor to the burden of disability on the community.

Although there have been major advances in methods of epidemiological research—e.g., the refinement of assessment and diagnostic tools, and the adoption of standardized classifications—substantial gaps remain in the epidemiology of mental disorders.

Similarly, biological research has resulted in significant new findings, but their application in prevention and treatment programmes is still awaited. Modern genetic studies have, for example, shown that the inheritance patterns of mental disorders such as schizophrenia do not correspond to simple Mendelian distribution: more studies are, however, necessary to disentangle the relative contributions of genetic factors and of environmental influences. The study of neurophysiological parameters as biological markers of inheritance in the course of endogenous psychosis is one promising approach. Neurophysiological and pathophysiological research into different behavioural reactions has demonstrated the potentialities of the study of experimental models as an analogue of the pathology of the human central nervous system. Here, the neurophysiological analysis of the effects of the wider spectrum of psychopharmacological compounds is of particular interest. Noticeable progress has also been achieved in research on physiologically active compounds with neurotropic action. The discovery that a number of low molecular compounds of a peptide nature have a certain influence on human and animal behaviour has led to a series of studies aimed at uncovering their role in the pathogenesis of schizophrenia, drug dependence, and pain. It is difficult to overestimate the importance of the discovery of receptors with a high affinity to psychotropic compounds (e.g., the diazepine receptors), which was one of the results of concentrated neurochemical research. This discovery has widened the scope of research to find specific receptors with different functional activities.

During the last few years biological research in psychiatry has concentrated on the prediction of the clinical effects of psychotropic drugs. However, it is at present impossible to determine pharmacokinetic parameters for application as predictors in therapeutic practice. Contradictory data concerning the relationships between the plasma level of psychotropic drugs and therapeutic response need further investigation. The understanding of mechanisms of individual sensitivity and of sensitivity of different populations to psychotropic drugs has become a very important issue. The investigation of antigens of neurotissue has led to the discovery of 17 neurospecific proteins. The physiological role of the majority of these proteins is not well defined but it can be accepted that these antigens, under certain conditions, could be involved in immunopathological processes in different forms of neuropsychiatric pathology. The involvement of some neurospecific antigens in immune processes in the course of such diseases as multiple sclerosis, lateral amyotrophic sclerosis, and schizophrenia has been demonstrated.

(a) The elderly

The prevalence of the organic brain syndromes and particularly the dementia-producing illnesses of old age is also increasing dramatically. The rates for senile and arteriosclerotic dementia in the age group 70–80 have trebled in many developed countries over the last two decades; these conditions now affect on the average 10–15% of all people aged 65 and over, and over 20% of those above the age of 80. With the increase in average life expectancy, the prevalence of dementia and allied conditions can be expected to rise also in many developing countries.

(b) Children

At the other end of the life span, surveys of general populations show that the prevalence of persistent and socially handicapping mental health problems among children aged 3–15 years in developed countries ranges from 5 to 15%.[1] More limited data from developing countries suggest a roughly similar rate. For example, in a recent WHO collaborative study in three developing countries, it was found that the rate of psychiatric disorders in children attending general health clinics in a densely populated urban area was as high as 29%, and in two rural areas the rates were over 11% and 20%. These disorders do not include common emotional or behavioural difficulties (e.g., fears, or disturbances in sleep or in eating patterns) of a transient nature, which the majority of children experience at some time or other during their development.

Relatively little is known about the prevalence of mental health problems in children under 3 years of age, but there is evidence that emotional disorders and developmental delays do occur in very young children. In many cases the problems in this age group have to do with parent-child interaction rather than the behaviour of the child.

Psychotic disorders are far less prevalent in childhood than they are later in life. Autism occurs in 3 or 4 children out of every 10 000, and functional psychoses such as schizophrenia or manic-depressive disorder are quite rare before adolescence.

---

[1] WHO Technical Report Series, No. 613, 1977 (*Child mental and psychosocial development.* Report of a WHO Expert Committee).

Particularly in developing countries rapid social changes such as urbanization, industrialization, altered family structure, compulsory schooling, etc. have often led to the disruption of social support systems, thus probably facilitating the occurrence of mental health and psychosocial problems in children and adolescents, e.g., abuse of drugs, juvenile delinquency, and behavioural problems.

Mental retardation

Five to ten children in every 1000 are affected by severe mental retardation. The rates in many developing countries may be higher because of widespread infectious and parasitic diseases that may affect the brain. A study in a developing country established that at least 40% of all cases of mental retardation were potentially preventable and that 20% were caused by bacterial meningitis in infancy or early childhood.

Further advances in the last five years in research on chromosome aberrations and congenital errors of metabolism have led to a better understanding of the manifold and complex causes of mental retardation, but it is now widely appreciated that general public health measures, such as immunization, improved perinatal care, adequate nutrition, and protection against chemical and other physical hazards are the most important means of prevention. The value of genetic counselling has been improved by recent research, and it can be applied preventively. As regards prevalence, however, it is unlikely that a decline in the prevalence of such organic affections of the brain would quickly follow improvements in obstetric, neonatal, and child care, because, at least initially, the effects of prevention would be offset by the increased chance of survival for those already affected.

Neurological disorders

Neurological disorders are a major cause of death and of long-term disability in all age groups in all parts of the world.[1] Epilepsy and convulsive disorders, neurological involvement in cerebrovascular pathology, infections (bacterial and viral) and parasitic infestation of the nervous system, motor system abnormalities, and nervous system disorders due to malnutrition are of major public health concern.

Thus, for example, more than 15 million persons suffer from leprosy, which in most cases affects the nervous system, and in many countries in the Third World tetanus is one of the commonest causes of death. Disorders of the nervous system caused by bacterial diseases (e.g., the meningitides), parasitic diseases (e.g., cysticercosis), and viral infections (e.g., poliomyelitis) afflict millions of people every year in Africa, Asia, and Latin America. Epilepsy also appears to have a much higher prevalence in developing than in developed countries. Neurotoxins are responsible for a further increase of neurological disorder in many developing countries. Studies of local diseases such as kuru—a toxic neuropathy associated with a cassava diet—and juvenile motor-neuron disease have yielded some results that have implications for a variety of disciplines outside neurology. Malnutrition affects millions of children in the developing countries, and it remains

---

[1] WHO Technical Report Series, No. 629, 1978 (*The application of advances in neurosciences for the control of neurological disorders.* Report of a WHO Study Group).

uncertain whether the sequelae of protein-energy malnutrition in childhood are permanent or not. Cerebrovascular diseases seem to be on the increase in some of the developing countries where they apparently affect younger age groups.

Research into the molecular aspects of synaptic transmission has been largely facilitated by the discovery of sodium channels in the excitable membrane by the use of drugs or toxins. Interneuronal communication has been positively clarified by the characterization of transmitter molecules that neurons secrete, and by the study of the temporal and spatial domains in which cells regulate each other and the intercellular conditions imposed by the signals. The identification of specific receptors at neuronal membrane level and of their binding kinetics made it possible to design experiments which have indicated abnormal receptor function in encephalomyelitis and multiple sclerosis. Myasthenia gravis is today regarded as a neuroimmunological disease.

Alcohol-related problems

Over the last few years there has been a move in many parts of the world toward the consideration not only of alcoholism[1] but also of the much broader area of alcohol-related problems. These include the physical, mental, and social problems of the individual drinker and also the consequences of excessive drinking for the family and the community as a whole.

There has also been much emphasis in recent years on the detrimental consequences, both social and physical, of the rapid increase in the average per capita consumption of alcoholic beverages. The prevalence of cirrhosis of the liver has risen in such a way as to suggest a direct link with rises in alcohol consumption. In the age group 25–64 years, cirrhosis of the liver now ranks among the five leading causes of deaths. Mortality from cirrhosis of the liver showed an increase of epidemic proportions during the period 1950–1971, mainly affecting males. This trend continued during 1974–1976 for several countries, but at the same time the figures for females showed a decrease in some countries (see Table 13).

Mortality from cirrhosis of the liver is positively correlated with alcohol consumption, expressed in litres of absolute alcohol per capita and per year. While the relationship between alcohol consumption and other physical disorders is less clear it is estimated that, for males, a daily intake of 80–100 g ethanol threatens serious liver damage, while levels in excess of 150 g present an even greater risk. The risk levels for females appear to be lower. Other research has shown that the relative risk of cancer of the oesophagus (adjusted for tobacco use) rises from 1.0 for a daily ethanol consumption of 0–20 g to 18.3 for a consumption of 101 g and over.

A recent review of the evidence for a hereditary factor in alcoholism indicated that the findings from twin studies are inconsistent, though there may be genetic control over the metabolism of alcohol. Studies attempting to replicate findings of an association between a genetic marker (blood groups, genetically determined proteins, finger-ridge count, etc.)

---

[1] The term "alcoholism" has been replaced in the Ninth Revision of the International Classification of Diseases by "alcohol dependence syndrome".

[2] MASSÉ, L. JUILLAN, J. M. & CHISLOUP, A. Trends in mortality from cirrhosis of the liver, 1950–1971. *World health statistics report*, **29**: 40–67 (1976).

Table 15. Mortality from cirrhosis of the liver[1] per 100 000 population, and alcohol consumption in absolute alcohol in litres *per capita* and per year[2]

Country or area	Year	Mortality		Alcohol consumption in absolute alcohol, 1972 (litres per capita)
		Males	Females	
France	1974	47.6	18.6	16.8
Italy	1974	46.4	18.1	13.6
Austria	1976	46.5	16.8	12.4
Portugal	1975	51.0	19.9	11.7
Spain	1974	31.2	14.2	11.4
Federal Republic of Germany	1975	39.5	17.4	11.0
Switzerland	1976	19.8	6.1	10.8
Hungary	1976	25.3	13.4	9.5
Belgium	1975	17.4	10.6	9.3
Czechoslovakia	1974	25.2	10.6	8.6
Australia	1975	11.7	4.2	8.5
New Zealand	1975	8.4	4.0	8.2
Denmark	1976	13.6	7.6	7.7
Yugoslavia	1975	18.6	7.7	7.7
Canada	1974	16.0	7.3	7.6
USA	1975	20.1	9.9	6.8
German Democratic Republic	1976	17.1	9.5	6.8
Chile	1975	37.4	15.1	6.4
Netherlands	1976	6.3	3.3	6.4
Bulgaria	1976	11.0	5.2	6.1
Poland	1975	13.2	7.3	6.0
Sweden	1976	17.5	8.3	5.8
Japan	1976	20.5	7.2	5.5
Greece	1975	18.7	8.4	5.4
Finland	1974	8.3	2.8	5.1
Uruguay	1975	14.7	4.2	4.6
Norway	1975	6.3	3.6	3.8
Romania	1976	27.7	16.3	3.8
Venezuela	1975	9.7	3.6	2.1
Hong Kong	1976	13.5	3.5	1.8
Israel	1975	7.8	4.7	1.7

[1] *World health statistics annual, 1977. Vol. I. Vital Statistics and causes of death.* Geneva, World Health Organization, 1977; *World health statistics annual, 1978. Vol. 1. Vital statistics and causes of death.* Geneva, World Health Organization, 1978.

[2] Finnish Foundation for Alcohol Studies and WHO European Office (1977), *International statistics on alcoholic beverages: production, trade and consumption 1950–1972,* Helsinki, (Finnish Foundation for Alcohol Studies, Vol. 27).

have given contradictary results except for colour blindness, which, however, seems to be reversible and may be caused by malnutrition or toxic effects. Adoption studies have indicated that children of alcoholics, especially sons, are particularly vulnerable to alcoholism, whether raised by their parents or by non-alcoholic foster parents. In such instances it would appear that genetic and environmental factors combine to produce what has come to be termed "familial alcoholism". Another investigator has pointed out that genetic factors may be implicated in the complications of alcoholism such as liver damage and especially its progression to cirrhosis.

Evidence amassed from a large number of countries indicates that the consumption of alcohol is increasing in all countries, almost without exception. It is interesting to note that countries undergoing rapid socioeconomic development may be particularly vulnerable to problems related to alcohol. As a result of the application of industrial techniques to liquor production and the activities of multinational companies, traditional methods of brewing or distilling have been supplanted and there has been a vast increase in supply. Rapid sociocultural and economic change has in some areas also led to massive increases in the availability of alcoholic beverages, often with unhappy results.

The relationship of ethnic status to alcohol consumption and its consequent problems has been known for some time. What has become apparent in recent times is that, as traditional patterns of consumption come under the influence of alien factors, whether as a result of migration, tourism, or a deliberate policy of assimilation, consumption levels frequently rise. Periods of cultural transition in general appear to be marked by increased consumption of alcohol.

Rapid development brings about sociocultural changes that loosen old forms of informal control on the individual. In many developing countries individuals are subjected to new demands and stresses at a time when old forms of family and community support are diminishing. Drinking often becomes a symbol of prestige and success, as well as being a ready tranquillizer. Young people, alienated from traditional values, are often at particular risk, and increasing concern has been expressed about the relationship of drinking to delinquency, road traffic accidents, and other problems. Similarly, alcohol-related problems in women are receiving more attention because of the consequences for the welfare of family members and the possible danger to the unborn and to child development.

Some countries consider the principal alcohol problems to be those relating to traffic accidents. Although there has been a declining trend in fatality rates from traffic accidents in industrialized countries since 1973, the rates are still increasing in countries undergoing rapid industrialization.

Excessive drinking also has a special impact in communities where nutritional standards are at best marginal. This is apparent not only in terms of physical damage, but also in the frequency with which organic psychoses are precipitated in such circumstances.

While no startling advances have been made in recent years in the treatment of persons with the alcohol dependence syndrome, encouraging results have been reported from the development of occupationally linked rehabilitation programmes, and at least one study has indicated that a single counselling session was as effective as several months of inpatient and outpatient treatment.[1] In view of the high cost of treatment, in terms of manpower and services, and the often poor return, increasing attention is being paid to possibilities of prevention. The two main preventive strategies considered have been (a) measures for the reduction of average per capita consumption and thus of alcohol-related problems and (b) the sociocultural approach, based on the integration of alcohol use into social and family activities and the encouragement of moderation. An educational approach has been seen by some as offering the main hope of prevention; others believe that social change is the best strategy. There has, however, been a tendency recently to consider these approaches and strategies as complementary to one another.

Drug dependence problems

While sound statistical data on national trends in drug abuse are available for only a few countries, information collected annually by the United Nations Commission on Narcotic Drugs provides a basis for examining international trends. In the light of this information and other data available to WHO, some observations on major regional trends can be

---

[1] EDWARDS, G. ET AL. *Alcohol-related disabilities.* Geneva, World Health Organization, 1977 (Offset Publications, No. 32).

made. Recent reports suggest that the extent of drug abuse has remained stable in Eastern European countries, where the problem is a relatively minor one. The extent of drug abuse in African countries is unknown in most cases, but a number of them have expressed concern about the use of cannabis and psychotropic drugs. In some countries in the Middle East the use of opium, cannabis, and khat has long been widespread. The extent of heroin abuse in North America continues to be serious, but appears to have declined somewhat after its dramatic increase during the previous decade. On the other hand, the abuse of phencyclidine, cocaine, cannabis, barbiturates, and tranquillizers appears to be increasing in North America. In several Middle and South American countries the abuse of volatile solvents by children has given rise to concern. In certain countries in the South-East Asia and Western Pacific Regions, the serious and long-standing problem of opium dependence continues. There has been an increasing tendency towards multiple drug abuse in the South-East Asia Region, and the use of synthetic narcotics and methaqualone is spreading in the Western Pacific Region.

Four other trends are of regional or worldwide concern. The first is the increased spread of heroin use among urban youth in a number of South-East Asian and Western Pacific countries in close proximity to the opium-producing region commonly referred to as the "Golden Triangle". A second alarming trend has developed in the region of the coca-producing countries in South America where the smoking of "coca paste" has spread rapidly among young people in the towns. Coca paste (cocaine sulfate) is an intermediary product in the illicit conversion of coca leaf to cocaine hydrochloride and was not previously abused. Beginning in 1975, however, an increasing number of users have been seeking admission to psychiatric hospitals because of various adverse effects. The third disturbing trend exists in Western Europe where illicit drug traffic patterns have recently changed, the result being a rapidly shifting, mixed pattern of drug abuse with a relatively stable situation in some countries, but with dependence on heroin and other drugs of abuse spreading in some countries of Central and Southern Europe where it had not been a problem before. Finally, there is a general impression that abuse of psychotropic drugs is increasing throughout the world in association with their increased availability on both licit and illicit markets.

The tendency for patterns of drug use to shift within countries or regions is not peculiar to the period under review. A recent study of earlier experience revealed that, in a number of countries where opium use was suddenly suppressed, the drug-dependent population merely shifted their patterns of drug use, often to heroin with all the problems it creates.

Despite the general increase in the number and types of treatment services, both voluntary and involuntary, there have been too few studies of the effectiveness of current treatments outside Northern America. Of the few systematic studies completed, one showed, for example, that intravenous heroin was superior to oral methadone for maintenance, since patients remained longer in treatment and there were fewer criminal convictions among them. Oral methadone had better results in producing total abstinence from drug use and those who remained in treatment were on lower doses of opiates.

The relative effectiveness of methadone and methadol (levo-alpha acetyl methadol) has also been compared. The results to date support the view that methadol is as effective and safe as methadone, and it has the advantage of 3 days' duration of action. Naltrexone, a promising narcotic-blocking agent, is also being tested in a series of clinical trials in the

USA. The results suggest that it can be safely used by healthy male heroin addicts but there are sometimes gastrointestinal side effects. Because the blocking agent can be stopped at any time and the full euphoric effects of opiates can again be experienced after several days, it is useful only for highly motivated patients.

Measures of social rehabilitation are also being applied in a number of countries but the results of systematic evaluation studies are not available. Other treatment evaluation studies and clinical trials are now being carried out in a number of developing countries in collaboration with WHO. These include studies of indigenous treatment methods and a study to determine the impact of primary health care on the incidence and prevalence of opium use in rural areas.

Psychosocial factors

In recent years, approaches based on epidemiology and the social sciences have increasingly been applied in investigations of the psychosocial factors affecting health or individual and collective wellbeing.

Instead of an "either/or"—biological or social-environmental—strategy in the study of mental illness, a "medicosocial" paradigm of mental illness has been increasingly accepted, and more emphasis is now being placed on multifactorial approaches aimed at determining the conditions under which one or another group of factors produces specific manifestations of disease and responds to specific treatment regimens. Although such investigations present considerable methodological difficulties at the moment, they will gain in importance as accelerated social change affects increasingly large proportions of the population in different parts of the world. Conventional indicators of mental morbidity are of limited value in assessing the psychosocial problems affecting populations, and no alternative means of measurement has yet been fully developed and validated. In spite of these limitations, it is possible to consider tentatively a number of factors that to a varying extent may reflect community characteristics such as levels of stress, social cohesion, and availability of social support systems. These include, for example, suicide rates, the social characteristics of the aging process, and the integration of the aged in the community, the spread of alcohol and drug abuse and the community's way of dealing with it, the prevalence of institutionalism and the proportion of "non-dischargeable" mental patients, the average per capita consumption of psychotropic drugs, and trends in crime and juvenile delinquency. Although there is some evidence from social research of a correlation between several of the above-mentioned factors in certain communities, very little is known at present about the distribution and trends of such variables in different cultures and social systems.

One dramatic example of a consistent deterioration in indicators of psychosocial well-being for the majority of a population over a period of decades is provided by the situation created by racial discrimination and apartheid in South Africa,[1] where industrialization and the accumulation of wealth by a small ruling minority have been achieved at a tremendous social cost, including the economic exploitation and political oppression of the majority.

---

[1] See JABLENSKY, A. Racism, apartheid and mental health. *World Health*, December 1977, pp. 17–21.

Processes of rapid social change may have certain negative side effects unless specific measures are taken by planners and political leaders to avert or minimize the negative side of social change and maximize its positive impact.

Migration, across or within national borders, for example, may result in social and cultural uprooting, if conditions favouring adjustment are not created. Similar considerations apply to rapid urbanization, overcrowding, deterioration of the physical environment, and other social, economic, and ecological processes that may lead to "marginalization" of certain social or population groups, such as the aged and those suffering from chronic diseases or disabilities, and to a breakdown of traditional social support systems without adequate replacement.

There is however no reason to accept such problems as being an unavoidable concomitant of development, and the study of variations in their incidence between groups of countries which have adopted different strategies of socioeconomic development could become an important source of information for health and social planners throughout the world.

Other psychosocial factors relating to health are reviewed in Chapter 2, pages 28–33.

Mental health care

(a) Control and treatment measures

Although some new drugs have been synthesized within existing psychotropic classes, there have been no major developments in the use of certain compounds for the treatment of the main mental disorders. Affective psychoses show a relatively fair response to tricyclic antidepressants; mania requires treatment with a neuroleptic drug and lithium salts; and schizophrenic-type psychosis responds positively to neuroleptics and to so-called "long-acting neuroleptics".

In addition to the use of psychotropic drugs in the treatment of mental disorders, there has been a more critical approach, based on carefully conducted therapeutic trials, to other physical treatments. Insulin coma therapy is now used on a very limited scale for the treatment of schizophrenic-type psychosis. In some countries modified electroconvulsive therapy remains an important part of the treatment of certain severe forms of psychotic illness (e.g., severe depression).

The development of computerized axial tomography (CAT) now permits the accurate diagnosis of several conditions, notably epilepsies, cerebrovascular disorders, tumours, and trauma. In addition, the positron emission scanner has permitted a detailed *in vivo* study of cerebral metabolism and of the way drugs act on it. Correlation studies, in which the results of CAT examinations are being compared with those of clinical investigations, promise to lead to important improvements in the diagnosis and treatment of neurological disorders. However, the new techniques have raised difficulties for health planners because of the high capital costs of the necessary equipment and the continuing costs of operation and servicing. There is however no doubt about their diagnostic efficacy or about the value of their contribution to neurological research.

Further advances have also been made in non-physical methods of treatment for mental disorders. Briefer forms of psychotherapy are now widely used not only by psychiatrists but by general practitioners, nurses, and social workers. Group psychotherapy is also more widely used. In the case of severe psychoses, particularly schizophrenia, various forms of social therapy are more frequently used, in conjunction with antipsychotic drugs. Other examples of recent research include work by various investigators on the relationship between life events and the onset of severe mental disorders; an investigation of the effects of family emotional environment on psychotic relapse; and a major WHO study that has shown that schizophrenic disorders do not invariably result in chronic mental deterioration and disability and that the tendency toward clinical and social recovery may be more pronounced in the less industrialized societies.[1]

Another aspect of the psychosocial approach can be seen in recent developments in behaviour modification techniques, which have been particularly widely applied in the education of the mentally handicapped and have been shown to increase both social and industrial skills. They have also been tried in the treatment of various neurotic disorders, particularly those having clear behavioural manifestations, such as phobias and compulsions, and have been found efficacious in combination with other forms of therapy. Of particular note is the recent attempt to apply behaviour modification techniques to a wide variety of somatic complaints, including headaches, high blood pressure, and obesity.

The fact that many institutional environments have been shown to maintain maladjusted behaviour, or at the very least to fail to reinforce well adjusted behaviour, has given rise to a number of programmes involving the award of tokens to encourage and maintain more social behaviour among long-term patients in institutions.

Of particular interest, because it suggests that the application of behaviour modification techniques need not be the prerogative of psychologists, is evidence suggesting that parents, spouses, and nurses can learn these techniques and apply them efficaciously, being in any case the principal source of support in the lives of those under treatment. This development is only one manifestation of the all-pervading tendency toward increasing "self help" in the field of psychological disorders—a tendency that is partly due to the discovery that therapeutic expertise can no longer be regarded as the exclusive province of professional therapists.

Another important development in recent years has been the growing attention paid by behavioural scientists and international health planners to those medical and professional attitudes and actions that can make health measures inacceptable to the population, particularly in the developing world—for example, the tendency of professional health workers to emphasize the kind of health problem they feel to be important, rather than the actual needs of the indigenous population, and the tendency for service agencies to pay greater attention to the comfort and morale of their resident staff (e.g., in terms of working hours, location of facilities, etc.) than to the corresponding requirements of local recipients of health care.

Another significant area of investigation is that of doctor-patient communication or, to use a more general term, "audience research". It has become increasingly apparent that the failure of patients to do what their doctors suggest or to respond positively to health education campaigns reflects, in part, the failure of recipients of health care to understand the message conveyed to them or, if they understand it, to be persuaded by it. The idea

---

[1] *Schizophrenia: a multinational study.* Geneva, World Health Organization, 1975 (Public Health Papers, No. 63).

that attitudes (and hence behaviour) could be changed merely by providing information has been shown to be simple-minded, while the interactions involving the communicator, the communication, and the audience have been shown to be much more complex than was previously supposed.

(b) Organization of services

Large mental hospitals were the principal feature of the mental health services in almost every country until early in the 1960s. Many of these hospitals were built in the nineteenth century as asylums, remote from centres of population; conditions in them were poor, with overcrowding and inadequate physical facilities. In many countries psychiatric beds made up about half the total hospital bed capacity, but the turnover was very slow. The resident mental hospital population reached its peak in the mid-1950s in many of the industrialized countries and has steadily declined since then (although the rate of decline has slowed down in recent years). Mental hospitals remain an important part of mental health services, but their function has been supplemented, and to some extent replaced, by a range of other services. Thus, for example, in areas where a variety of services are available, people who need to be admitted to psychiatric hospitals form only a small proportion of the total number of people suffering from mental health problems. In one study it was indicated that only 1.9 new cases of mental disorder per 1000 population need to be admitted to a psychiatric hospital each year and that the duration of hospitalization for one-third of them is less than 2 weeks, while 4.4 per 1000 population are treated in psychiatric outpatient services and 81 per 1000 population receive treatment from general practitioners for recognized mental disorders.

Community mental health centres staffed by multidisciplinary teams and offering a range of diagnostic, treatment, counselling, and aftercare services have been introduced in some countries. The professional roles of psychologists, social workers, and nurses in mental health care have grown considerably. In many countries, outpatient clinics have been developed in close association with general health facilities, and the role of mental health in primary health care has been emphasized.[1]

Psychiatric units in general hospitals have been established in many countries, and in some areas they now have responsibility for the provision of all inpatient psychiatric care. Day-patient facilities have expanded rapidly in some countries. All these changes have been accompanied by a steady improvement in public attitudes toward the mentally ill. Prejudices still exist, but public recognition of the frequency of minor forms of mental disorder and of the improved prognosis in most forms of mental illness has facilitated community-based programmes and integration of services.

On the other hand, differentiation within mental health services has grown strikingly since 1955 in those countries with the available manpower and resources. Separate clinics and units for children, adolescents, patients with alcohol problems, and psychogeriatric patients exist in certain countries, while separate care for mentally deranged criminal offenders is provided in most countries.

In the developing countries there has over the past decade been a thorough reassessment of mental health needs and the way in which the relevant services should be

---

[1] MAY, A. R. Mental health services in Europe. Geneva, World Health Organization, 1976 (Offset Publications, No. 23).

organized. Scanty resources have forced governments and public health authorities to put increasing emphasis on health planning and on the development of more reliable basic data reflecting the needs of their populations. Planning for services to deal with mental health problems has, however, become something of a vicious circle, i.e., problems are not recognized or diagnosed (or the patient is ostracized and not brought to the attention of the official services), hence there is no information on their extent to justify the need for services, and this in turn perpetuates the myth that there are no mental health problems and therefore no mental health services have to be planned. In addition, there have, until recently, been no simple statistical methods for the collection and interpretation of mental health data. Increasingly, however, such methods are being developed for use at the primary health care level and within general health and related services.

It is now clear that the frequency of seriously incapacitating mental disorders is at least as high in the developing as in the developed countries. It is also clear that the mental hospitals established during the colonial era in many developing countries and used primarily as instruments of social control are particularly unsuited to the rural-agrarian societies of the Third World. In a paper on the state of psychiatry in Africa at the end of the colonial era, it is pointed out that there were "only a few prison-like facilities, completely insufficient to meet the demand, which in most cases is not for care but for custody, i.e. removal of the individual from his family and the community".[1] For millions of people the only source of help in the event of mental disorder has been, and remains, some form of traditional health care. Such care can undoubtedly be effective and helpful, but malpractice and mistreatment also occur.[2]

The key question for the developing countries is therefore: how can mental health care be made available to widely dispersed rural populations, given that resources are seriously limited? During the last few years, the answer increasingly endorsed is: through the decentralization of mental health services, their integration into general health services, and the provision of "basic mental health care" by primary health workers with the involvement of the community and a variety of non-medical community agents such as traditional healers, teachers, and religious leaders.[3] Initiatives of this kind have already been taken in many developing countries including Colombia, India, the Philippines, Senegal and Sudan.

There has thus been a major shift in policy on mental health care in many developing countries away from institutional forms of care and towards the integration of mental health services with the general health services and community involvement. The new policy has been reinforced by the development of the primary health care concept and the recommendations of the International Conference on Primary Health Care held at Alma-Ata. The treatment of priority mental disorders is now seen as an essential component of primary health care, and the promotion of mental health within the community is an ingredient of the primary health care approach. At present many people

[1] COLLOMB, H. Public health and psychiatry in Africa. In: *Biomedical lectures.* Brazzaville, WHO Regional Office for Africa, 1972 (AFRO Technical Papers, No. 4).

[2] ASUNI, T. Existing concepts of mental illness in different cultures and traditional forms of treatment. In: Baasher, T. A. et al., ed. *Mental health services in developing countries.* Geneva, World Health Organization, 1975 (Offset Publications, No. 22).

[3] WHO Technical Report Series, No. 564, 1975 (*Organization of mental health services in developing countries.* Sixteenth report of the WHO Expert Committee on Mental Health).

with serious mental disorders are still kept in prisons or police stations, or become vagrants. Treatment within the community by primary health workers is now a realistic alternative. In some countries this has been backed up by the creation of "psychiatric villages" where brief periods of intensive treatment can be given in a setting that is familiar to patients from rural areas and that does not inspire the alienation they would feel in a mental hospital. Other developing countries are stressing the creation of small psychiatric units, staffed by non-specialists, in general hospitals.

(c) Legal basis of mental health care

The changes in the pattern of mental health services, outlined above, have far-reaching legal implications. Until now, they have been reflected in new legislation only to a limited extent. In many countries the existing law conflicts with current programme objectives. Legal provisions should take account of the shift of the centre of gravity of mental health services from the mental hospital to other less centralized facilities; of the widening involvement of non-specialists, including auxiliary health workers, in mental health care; of the multidisciplinary team approach; of the range of treatments now available and the need for their proper control; and of changing public attitudes to the mentally ill and their acceptance in the community.[1] Some interesting developments have taken place in mental health legislation in Algeria (1975), Senegal (1975), Swaziland (1978), and Trinidad and Tobago (1975), and in sections of public health laws dealing with mental health in Costa Rica (1973) and Sudan (1975). These changes have tended to increase the availability and accessibility of mental health care by simplifying legal procedures for admission to mental hospital and by allowing (or even encouraging) community care and treatment in general hospitals. There are, however, a number of countries that still have out-of-date legislation, in many cases introduced during the colonial era and never modified.

It is generally recognized that, to be effective, action regarding the control of both narcotic and psychotropic substances must be international. The 1948 Protocol of Lake Success, New York, created a mechanism whereby new products, designated by WHO, automatically came under international control, and thus the role of WHO in the evaluation of drugs was established. The Single Convention on Narcotic Drugs, 1961, simplified and unified earlier treaties and continued to assign to WHO the role of evaluation of drugs was established. The Single Convention on Narcotic Drugs, 1961, Narcotic Drugs, a 30-member body of the United Nations Economic and Social Council. With the increase in the use and abuse of psychotropic drugs, a plenipotentiary conference of the United Nations formulated a Convention on Psychotropic Substances in 1971. After ratification by 40 countries, this Convention came into force in 1976. It requires WHO to recommend to the United Nations Commission on Narcotic Drugs whether a psychotropic substance is to be controlled nationally or internationally, and how. Under this Convention, 32 substances have been placed under four schedules. Schedule I contains general hallucinogens, subject to control measures stricter than those for narcotics; substances in Schedule II are mainly amphetamines and similar stimulants; Schedule III contains mainly shorter-acting barbiturates and similar depressants of the central nervous system: Schedule IV contains mainly longer-acting barbiturates, similar

---

[1] CURRAN, W. J. & HARDING, T. W. The law and mental health: harmonizing objectives. Geneva, World Health Organization, 1978.

central nervous system depressants, and minor tranquillizers. The basis for recommending the control of psychotropic substances is their dependence liability, abuse potential, and actual abuse leading to public health and social problems, on the one hand, and their therapeutic usefulness on the other.

The 1971 Convention also has articles relating to record-keeping, control of prescriptions, and the abuse of psychotropic substances, in respect of which Article 20 requires parties to take certain practical measures. These include the early identification, treatment, education, aftercare, rehabilitation, and social integration of persons dependent on such substances.

Prophylactic, therapeutic and diagnostic substances

Drug policies

While medicinal products alone are not sufficient to provide adequate health care, they do play an important role in protecting, maintaining, and restoring people's health. In spite of the general recognition that medicinal products should be viewed as essential tools for health care and for the improvement of the quality of life, it is not uncommon to find that drug policies are mainly directed towards industrial and trade development, and sometimes contradictory policies exist independently and are implemented in different sectors of the administration.

To meet the health needs and demands of the population, medicinal products are supplied through a countrywide system of established institutions involved in various activities such as the procurement, production, and control of drugs and vaccines, research and development, distribution to health services and to the public, monitoring of marketed products, etc. The term "pharmaceutical supply system" is used to describe these activities, which form a more or less coherent system related partly to the health care system and partly to the industrial, trade, and financial sectors.

Pharmaceutical supply systems have evolved to some degree in all countries, from the less developed countries, where only some components are present, to the industrialized countries, where all components are present, although not always coordinated to form a coherent system. Because of conflicting goals and needs that must be met, and because of the changing interplay of political, economic, and social pressures, the pharmaceutical supply system undergoes continuing change in every country. The pressures are often conflicting because of the diverse interests of the groups involved: government, commercial enterprises, the medical profession, the scientific and academic community, etc.

Drug supply systems

Depending on a country's constitutional, organizational, and administrative structures, form of government, and level of socioeconomic development, its pharmaceutical supply system may be part of the State system, or of another public sector organization, or may belong to the private sector or be partly in the public sector and partly in the private sector. All the components of the system may be under the authority of the health ministry, or some components may be under its authority whilst others may be under the authority of different sectors of the government such as the industrial, trade, and financial sectors. In countries where the pharmaceutical supply system is in the private sector, more or less stringent regulatory control mechanisms exist because medicinal products have an important impact on the health of the people and on the national economy. In other words, balanced drug policies require an integration of health and social policies with industrial and technological components.

The aim of developing clearly formulated national drug policies is to make the pharmaceutical supply system more efficient by improving cooperation and coordination between its different components and the different sectors involved (e.g., health, trade, industrial production, and finance). As the main objective of national drug policies should be to make the most effective and safe medicinal products of established quality accessible, at reasonable cost, to all people, there is a need to plan and review the pharmaceutical supply system as a whole in the light of this objective.

Drug selection, procurement, and utilization

Especially in developing countries where programmes are being implemented to extend health care coverage to all people, pharmaceutical supply has become a crucial issue. National drug policies often focus on the essential drugs and vaccines that are indispensable for the health care of large segments of the population rather than on the demands of the privileged minority who have access to sophisticated medical care in urban areas. In the countries referred to, there is a tendency to develop drug policies that aim at self-reliance through:

— procurement of drugs from a variety of sources by central or regional agencies;

— establishment of government-owned production facilities and, where appropriate, encouragement of private drug manufacture;

— limitation of the range of available medicinal products and selection of essential drugs to meet the health needs of the majority of the population;

— development of a national quality control system linked with procurement and local production;

— improved utilization of locally available natural resources, particularly mecidinal plants, in health care and in local pharmaceutical production;

— establishment of national or regional drug distribution networks parallel to the health services networks.

In countries that have reached a certain stage of development, an important aspect of national drug policy is the building up of a strong domestic pharmaceutical industry. Such an industry is an important asset because it constitutes a vital component of the health care system, is a source of tax revenue and of foreign exchange and savings, has a strategic value in the supply of vitally needed pharmaceuticals, and is a stimulus to research in the medical, biological, chemical, and industrial fields.

Another aspect of drug policy is closely linked with social security and health insurance schemes that provide medicinal products free of charge to the whole population, or to particular segments of the population. In many countries, it is felt that the availability of free medicinal products, combined with commercial pressures, may lead to overconsumption or to wastage through poor patient compliance with prescriptions. As pharmaceutical expenditure is increasing, means are being sought of achieving a better utilization of resources through cost-sharing schemes, restricted lists of reimbursable medicinal products, and price controls.

There are important differences in the types of medicinal product primarily required for health care in developed and in developing countries. For example, in developed countries, where there is a sufficient supply of medicinal products to meet the basic health needs of the whole population, the demand is increasing for certain products used for chronic diseases of the adult or aged population or for mental illness (often linked with living conditions in industrialized societies). The same demands can be found in many urban areas in developing countries, but the implementation of primary health care programmes in larger segments of the population and the control of the major communicable diseases require a range of medicinal products that is not currently used in the developed countries, e.g., products against malaria and other parasitic diseases prevailing in tropical areas.

Although the formulation of national drug policies is clearly a matter of national sovereignty to be decided by the authorities in each country, in consultation with the relevant professional organizations, such policies are, to an increasing extent, influenced also by international policies, particularly those of the transnational pharmaceutical corporations. This is due to the fact that international trade in raw materials and finished pharmaceutical products is continually increasing and very few countries can be entirely self-sufficient in pharmaceutical supply. Furthermore, national policies are often influenced by information in medical journals and in the press which stimulates the demands of physicians and consumers for certain products that are promoted on international markets by transnational corporations.

The formulation of national drug policies is particularly important to enable developing countries to make progress in the pharmaceutical sector and to develop technical and economic cooperation in this sector among themselves or with industrialized countries.

Owing to the complexity of the pharmaceutical supply system, and its bearing on national interests, there is as yet insufficient agreement among countries about the formulation of comprehensive international policies on medicinal products, although some progress has been made in groups of countries, such as the European Economic Community, in harmonizing national drug policies and drug legislation.

Quality and safety control

Ensuring the quality of the drugs marketed in each country is the responsibility of a national health administration. In many countries, including the most highly industrialized ones, special drug control agencies have been created as a part of the health administration.

A fully established system for ensuring drug quality encompasses the following areas: quality control in the process of drug manufacture, quality control of imported pharmaceuticals, and surveillance over drug distribution to ensure that inappropriate storage and shipping do not impair the initial quality of drugs before they reach the patient. The drug control agency performs its surveillance duties through inspection and laboratory testing of drug samples.

It has now been generally accepted that the quality control of drugs has to be "built-in" during the manufacturing process. In 1975, to facilitate a uniform approach to ensuring quality in the process of drug production, the Twenty-eighth World Health Assembly recommended a set of "Good Practices in the Manufacture and Quality Control of Drugs".[1] A number of countries, many of them large producers of pharmaceuticals, have adopted the recommended practices in their pharmaceutical legislation, either without any modification or in a form adapted to suit local conditions.

A number of developing countries are heavily dependent on drugs produced abroad. In such cases, national health administrations often have to rely on quality certificates issued by the manufacturers. To assist countries in this position, the WHO Certification Scheme on the Quality of Pharmaceutical Products moving in International Commerce was introduced by the Twenty-eighth World Health Assembly. By the end of 1978, 38 countries, some of them major exporters of pharmaceuticals, had agreed to participate in the Certification Scheme.

Drug control laboratories exist in a number of countries, usually as part of the national drug control authority. They carry out the tests and assays needed to establish whether pharmaceutical products conform to given specifications.

Quality specifications for drugs should consist of a set of properly selected standards associated with methods of analysis that will permit the assessment of the integrity of drugs and of their basic components.[2] Quality specifications of a public nature are usually given in pharmacopoeias, which include the general methodology for testing, monographs on pharmaceutical raw materials, and in many cases monographs on the most widely used dosage forms. National pharmacopoeias have been issued by a number of countries, and many of them are kept up to date by periodic revision. Pharmacopoeias may also be issued jointly by a group of countries, and the *European Pharmacopoeia* and the *Compendium Medicamentorum* are recent examples. The *International Pharmacopoeia* is issued by WHO. Volume 1 of its third edition has recently been published.[3]

One important drug policy issue concerns the evaluation of the risk/benefit ratio of new drugs to be introduced on the market. Regulatory demands for the introduction of new medicinal products are becoming stricter in many countries, and the question has been raised whether, in some respects, they are becoming too stringent, thus leading to excessive delay in the introduction of some new compounds and, in the longer term, to curtailment of drug research and development.

On the other hand, the assessment of the long-term safety of new compounds still presents intractable difficulties, since the occasional fallibility of animal models as indicators of hazards to man and the difficulty of identifying infrequent and delayed adverse reactions to drugs already in widespread use are problems that resist routine investigational approaches.

Because of the rapid evolution of drug epidemiology, many drug regulatory authorities are now being asked to review all drugs currently available within their jurisdiction. Thus the safety and efficacy of many established drugs are now subject to re-examination. As a result, the terms under which many of these drugs are registered in various countries have

---

[1] WHO Official Records, No. 226, 1975, Annex 12.
[2] WHO Technical Report Series. No. 614, 1977 (Twenty-sixth report of the WHO Expert Committee on Specifications for Pharmaceutical Preparations).
[3] *The International Pharmacopoeia*, 3rd ed., Vol. 1. *General methods of analysis*, Geneva, World Health Organization, 1979.

been modified and others have been withdrawn from use. Different national authorities have, however, sometimes taken divergent action over identical drugs, either as a result of disparate assessments of the available evidence, or because of varying risk/benefit considerations arising from differences in disease patterns. Such instances underline the need for the rapid and efficient transfer between national drug regulatory authorities in both the developed and the developing world of the technical information justifying certain important decisions.

Drug policies and management

In 1975, the Twenty-eighth World Health Assembly considered a comprehensive report of the Director-General[1] which reviewed the main components of drug policies, involving not only the health sector but also the industrial, trade, and financial sectors, outlined problems in developed and developing countries, and emphasized the need for adequate policies to meet the needs of developing countries where large segments of the population do not have access to the drugs and vaccines that are most essential to effective health care. The Assembly stressed the need to develop drug policies linking drug research, production, and distribution with the real health needs, and requested the Director-General *inter alia* to advise countries on the selection and procurement, at reasonable cost, of essential drugs of established quality corresponding to their national health needs.

The WHO Executive Board at its sixty-first session in January 1978, having reviewed the Report of the Expert Committee on the Selection of Essential Drugs[2] and a progress report on drug policies and management by the Director-General, called for urgent international action to strengthen the national capabilities of the developing countries in the selection and proper use of essential drugs to meet their real health needs, and in the local production and quality control, wherever feasible, of such drugs. The Board requested the Director-General to maintain a dialogue with the pharmaceutical industry in order to assure its collaboration in meeting the health needs of large underserved segments of the world's population, and to appeal to governments and the pharmaceutical industry to participate in WHO's action programme on essential drugs.

Since 1977 in almost all WHO regions, drug policy and management have been discussed by regional committees and by working and study groups with the full participation of Member countries. Emphasis has been placed on national drug policies and technical cooperation, especially among developing countries.

Within their terms of reference, other United Nations bodies, notably UNICEF, have developed activities relating to medicinal products. A joint programme on economic and technical cooperation among developing countries in the pharmaceutical sector has been initiated by UNCTAD, UNDP, UNIDO, and WHO with the Ministry of Foreign Affairs of Guyana as executing agency.

Problems relating to medicinal products were discussed in 1976 at the Fifth Conference of Heads of States of Governments of Non-Aligned Countries in Colombo and at the Conference on Economic Cooperation among Developing Countries in Mexico City.

---

[1] WHO Official Records, No. 226, 1975, Annex 13, pp. 96–110.
[2] WHO Technical Report Series, No. 615, 1977 (*The selection of essential drugs.* Report of a WHO Expert Committee).

Biologicals

As far as vaccines are concerned, the greatest emphasis must be placed on quality control, and this involves responsibilities at the global, regional, and national levels. Infectious diseases will not be contained unless steps are taken to ensure (*a*) that vaccines of adequate potency are being used; (*b*) that they reach at least 80–90% of the target population; and (*c*) that the child population is responding satisfactorily. Similar criteria apply to drugs because they too must be available in adequate quantities to correct the abnormal body functions for which they are administered.

A good quality control facility can (*a*) check on the quality of drugs and vaccines produced locally and imported; (*b*) check on storage facilities to see that potency is ensured throughout the shelf life; and (*c*) measure the immune status of a community for any infectious disease and thus predict which vaccines are required.

Such a facility is of invaluable assistance to a health authority and is one of the most cost-effective investments in a health budget. Both drugs and vaccines will be used indefinitely, and the establishment of quality control is thus a lasting commitment.

WHO has formulated requirements for the production and control of all vaccines used against childhood diseases, and requirements are also available for good manufacturing practices. In addition, manuals giving technical guidance on every detail of the production of diphtheria, pertussis, and tetanus vaccines have been prepared.[1]

WHO has established International Standards and Reference Preparations for some 200 biological substances, and there is also a list of International Chemical Reference Substances for Pharmaceuticals for use when the active principle of a product can be determined by chemical analysis.[2]

The technology is there for the developing countries to adopt in their efforts towards greater self-reliance. The main constraint is lack of trained personnel. Through a joint UNDP/WHO project money and resources are available to provide training in quality control for specific scientists selected by governments and give them the physical, technical, and financial support they need in order to exercise effective control over biologicals in the developing world.

Accident prevention and control

The importance of accidents, poisonings and violence as health hazards is perhaps not sufficiently recognized. Prevalent in developed and developing countries alike, they can be considered as constituting a veritable pandemic. Views on this subject are often not exempt from a certain fatalism, an acceptance of accidents as unavoidable hazards of our technological civilization.

To gain some idea of the public health problems created by accidents, it would be neccessary to have adequate statistical information on at least morbidity, disability, and mortality due to accidents. At the international level, unfortunately, readily accessible

---

[1] Available from Chief, Biologicals, World Health Organization, 1217 Geneva 27, Switzerland.

[2] *Biological substances: International standards, reference preparations, and reference reagents, 1979.* Geneva, World Health Organization.

information is confined to mortality data compiled by WHO (covering 75 countries, or 30% of the world's population), data on injury and deaths from road traffic accidents only, compiled by ECE (27 European countries, or 18% of the world's populations) and data on fatal industrial accidents compiled by ILO (40 countries, or 40% of the world's population).

Mortality

Statistical data on 58 countries for the latest year for which information is available: 1973, 1974, 1975, or 1976) show a total of 705 678 deaths from accidents, poisonings and violence[1] for a population of 1 104 855 000, or a death rate of 64 per 100 000 population.

The mortality rates vary considerably between countries. This can be seen from the following table based on the mid-year accident mortality rates in 45 countries for the period 1970–1974:

Accident death rate per 100 000	Number of countries with corresponding death rate		
	Both sexes	Males	Females
0–19	2	—	13
20–29	2	2	10
30–39	12	2	15
40–49	11	3	4
50–59	13	14	2
60–69	2	6	1
70–79	3	11	—
80–89	—	3	—
90–99	—	3	—
100+	—	1	—

There are also very important differences between the accident mortality rates for males (more dispersed) and those for females (more concentrated). The data show that 38 of the 45 countries have a rate for females ranging from 0 to 39 per 100 000, while that for males in 41 countries out of the 45 varies between 40 and 100 and over per 100 000.

The proportion of deaths by accidents to all deaths varies over a wide range for males, but is more concentrated for females, as is illustrated by the following table for 48 selected countries:

Accident deaths in proportion to all deaths	Number of countries with corresponding percentage		
	Both sexes	Males	Females
0–4.9%	7	3	25
5–9.9%	35	31	23
10–14.9%	6	11	—
15+%	—	3	—

In the developed countries, mortality from accidents generally takes third place after cardiovascular diseases and neoplasms. In the age groups from 1 to 44 years, which have

---

[1] Categories E800–E999, International Classification of Diseases (1965 revision).

relatively low general mortality rates, accidents occupy the first place. For example, in the USA, in 1975, for both sexes, 79.5% of all deaths in the age group 15–24 years were due to accidents, as were 65.4% in the age group 25–34 years, 62.0% in the age group 5–14 years, and 47.4% in the age group 1–4 years.[1] The situation is similar in other developed countries.

In a recent study[2] covering the age group 1–14 years, it was pointed out that for the 50 countries studied, the average accident mortality in the age group 1–4 years was 32.7 per 100 000 for boys, and 22.8 for girls, dropping to 23.1 for boys and to 10.9 for girls in the age group 5–14 years.

The importance of this mortality can be judged by the proportion of total mortality it represents. In the developing countries this proportion is often less than 10%, while in the highly industralized countries it is over 40% for boys and 30% for girls. An intermediate position is held by those developing countries where industrialization is progressing and where total mortality has already been reduced. Industrial countries that have succeeded in considerably reducing not only the general mortality rates but also the accident mortality rates bear out the contention that accidents can be reduced in all countries.

In many countries motor vehicle accidents rank first among all fatal accidents; they account for 40% (unweighted average) of all fatal accidents to both sexes (all ages) in the 50 countries studied. Northern America, Europe, and Oceania have above-average median values, and Asia and South America have below-average median values. While there are no big differences between age groups in the average values, the differences between the values for boys and those for girls are considerable.

In many countries accidental drowning takes second place among fatal accidents; in the age group 1–14 years, it accounts for 23% and 17% of all fatal accidents among boys and girls respectively.

A comparison of mid-year death rates for 31 countries in 1960–1964 and 1970–1974 shows an overall trend towards an increase in mortality from accidents. For example, in 18 countries there was an increase and in 5 countries there was a decrease, both for males and females; in 4 countries there was an increase for males but a decrease for females; in 4 other countries, on the contrary, there was a decrease for males and an increase for females.

The mortality from different kinds of accidents, classified according to the International Classification of Diseases (1965 revision), varies considerably but in the developed countries the most important groups rank as follows:

AE 138	Motor vehicle accidents
AE 147	Suicide and self-inflicted injury
AE 141	Accidental falls
AE 146	All other accidents
AE 145	Accidents mainly of industrial type
AE 143	Accidental drowning and submersion
AE 140	Accidental poisoning
AE 142	Accidents caused by fires, etc.

[1] WORLD HEALTH ORGANIZATION. *World health statistics annual, 1978. Vol. 1: Vital statistics and causes of death.* Geneva, 1978, Annex III, Table 2.

[2] MARCUSSON, H. & OEMISCH, W. Accident mortality in childhood in selected countries of different continents, 1950–1971. *World health statistics report,* **30**: 57–92 (1977).

Suicide. According to WHO statistics (figures for the latest available years), in 54 countries in 5 continents that report suicide (AE 147) as well as motor vehicle accidents (AE 138), 120 000 people are killed by suicide and 173 000 by motor vehicle accidents each year. Assuming 30% underreporting for suicide, it can be safely stated that the mortality from suicide is on the same scale as that from motor vehicle accidents.

Attempted suicide—including "epidemics" of self-poisoning by young adults, a problem that confronts all developed countries and places an increasing burden on primary health care, general hospitals, and specialized psychiatric services—has been estimated to be 10 times as frequent as suicide, so that there are probably close to a million cases each year in the European Region alone.

An analysis by age and sex of the suicide statistics available for the period 1972–1974 as compared with those for 1961–1963, reveals that the increase in suicide mortality of over 30% in Denmark, Hungary, Ireland, the Netherlands, and Poland and the lesser increase in nearly all other reporting countries are due to rising suicide rates among women of all age groups and also among men, the increase being particularly spectacular among young men. England and Wales and Greece are the only countries where there were substantial declines in the suicide rate over the same period i.e., 33% and 21% respectively. This decline can be largely attributed to decreased incidence in males, mainly in the older age groups, and in older females in the United Kingdom and younger females in Greece.

A comparative epidemiological study, undertaken by the WHO Regional Office for Europe, shows that rapid changes in the social and economic conditions in a country have a strong influence on the national suicide rate and that improvements in primary health care may contribute to a lowering of the suicide mortality level.

Morbidity

Hospital statistics on admissions and discharges are one source of morbidity data on accidents, though representing only the "tip of the iceberg". Despite their incompleteness and inherent weaknesses due to their lack of representativeness, hospital statistics from a few selected countries may perhaps help to give a general idea of morbidity from accidents.

It has been estimated that in England and Wales in 1975, 311 667 males (15.5% of discharged male patients) and 247 384 females (8.5% of discharged female patients) were hospitalized as a consequence of accidents.[1] This represents a rate of 1301 per 100 000 males and 980 per 100 000 females. There is one death from an accident for every 26–27 patients hospitalized because of accidents.

In the Netherlands, in 1975, 62 281 males (or 9.6% of discharged male patients) and 43 157 females (or 5.5% of discharged female patients) were hospitalized because of

In the Netherlands, in 1975, 62 281 males (or 9.6% of discharged male patients) and 43 157 females (or 5.5% of discharged female patients) were hospitalized because of

In France, according to incomplete data for 1974 covering only 302 public hospitals, 239 558 males (21.3% of discharged male patients) and 133 673 females (14.6% of discharged female patients) were admitted to hospital because of accidents, which

---

[1] Categories N800–N999, International Classification of Diseases (1965 revision).

constituted the leading cause of hospitalization in the hospital concerned. The rate per 100 000 was 913.7 for males and 500.3 for females. Unfortunately, out of the total of 3 279 476 patients admitted to private hospitals in France in 1974, the number admitted because of accidents is unknown.

In Greece in 1975, out of a total of 977 274 patients discharged (both sexes), 102 113, or 10.4%, had been admitted because of accidents. This represents a rate of 1128.7 per 100 000 population. For every death due to an accident, 24 patients were discharged from hospital.

In New Zealand, in 1971, 255 409 patients were discharged from the public hospitals, of whom 45 429, or 17.8%, were there because of accidents. A breakdown by age groups, with rates per 100 000 population is given in the following table:

				Age group (years)			
	Total	0–4	5–14	15–24	25–44	45–64	65+
Proportion of discharged patients admitted because of accidents as a percentage of all patients discharged	17.8%	18.1%	25.5%	31.3%	16.2%	10.5%	9.9%
Discharged accident patients per 100 000 population	1585.0	1907.5	1408.6	2631.8	1224.2	1020.0	1874.4

The statistical data published by ECE on the number of road traffic accidents and the number of persons killed and injured show an upward trend until 1972, followed by a decline that is probably due to the application of certain preventive measures, such as speed limits and compulsory wearing of seat belts.

It must be pointed out that the case fatality rates for road traffic accidents are 60%–70% higher in Europe than in the USA (see Table 16).

Table 16. Road traffic accidents, killed and injured persons, Europe and USA

	1965	1970	1972	1973	1974	1975	1976
Accidents							
Europe	1 460 000	1 605 632	1 686 000	1 630 000	1 540 000*	1 531 000*	1 563 000*
USA	1 190 000	1 350 000	...	1 348 100	1 240 200	1 239 000	...
No. killed							
Europe	73 700	91 200	97 700	92 300*	84 300*	86 600*	86.600*
USA	49 163	56 800	56 600	55 800	46 200	46 550	45 422
No. injured							
Europe	1 851 000	2 176 000	2 280 000	2 210 600*	2 048 300*	2 053 500*	2 087 000*
USA	1 800 000	2 000 000	2 100 000	2 000 000	1 800 000	1 800 000	1 800 000
No. of injured for each person killed							
Europe	25.1	23.9	23.3	24.0	24.3	23.7	24.1
USA	36.6	35.2	37.1	35.8	39.0	38.7	39.6
Case fatality rate (%)							
Europe	3.8	4.0	4.3	4.2	4.1	4.2	4.1
USA	2.7	2.8	2.6	2.8	2.6	2.6	2.5

*Estimates

In conclusion, it can be said that accidents are one of the most important causes of mortality and morbidity, since they are the cause of approximately 10% of all deaths in developed countries; the proportion of the total population admitted to hospitals because of accidents, is between 0.5% and 1% each year, but accident victims certainly represent more than 1% of the population.

In general, the accident mortality rate for males is at least twice as high as the rate for females, but in some age groups the sex ratio is more pronounced: 1 to 3 or even 4.

Over the last ten years, there has been a marked tendency towards an increase in mortality from accidents, especially in certain age groups, among males, and from specific groups of accidents, for example, motor vehicle accidents (AE 138).

In some countries and for different groups of accidents, there are new and encouraging signs of a stabilization of, or decline in, mortality, probably as a result of the development and application of new preventive measures, legislation, and environmental and behavioural research.

Disasters and natural catastrophes

This is the first time that a section on disasters and natural catastrophes has been included in a world health situation report. Disasters are certainly not a new health hazard, and indeed WHO has been concerned with disaster-related problems from its very inception. Only recently, however, has the total management of disasters begun to attract serious attention and has become a subject for study both at universities and by the public health authorities. WHO is increasingly involved not only in disaster relief, but also in disaster preparedness and prevention, and in the rehabilitation of disaster victims.

Extent of the problem

Disasters are not rare occurrences; they are real threats that often hit with seasonal regularity, destroying laboriously constructed health services and facilities. WHO's activities extend to the health aspects of all disasters, whether natural, technological, due to strife, or the result of epidemics. The Organization is responsible for the health aspects of all emergency relief operations requested by Member States or executed by any United Nations agency.

Because of the wide-ranging variety of disasters, their often overwhelming extent, their sudden nature, and their relatively recent inclusion in academic and health programmes, statistics on them are incomplete, sometimes misleading, at times impossible to obtain, and often non-existent. The response of the health sector to emergencies has been further impeded by such factors as the lack of statistics on past disasters, the relationship between the type of disaster and the resulting health problems, populations at risk, the availability of human resources, etc. Further studies are therefore urgently needed.

WHO's work in disasters

The objectives of WHO's emergency relief operations are to plan for and provide an adequate and appropriate response to emergency situations resulting from disasters due to natural and other causes.

Besides the provision of relief in the form of urgently needed drugs, vaccines, and other medical supplies, which continues to be an essential part of the WHO programme, there is increasing technical cooperation with disaster-prone countries with a view to greater national preparedness, preventive measures, and more effective control of emergency situations. In this connexion the Organization is also becoming involved in activities relating to the public health management of emergencies, research on the epidemiology and statistics of disasters, studies of populations at risk, the assessment of needs and priorities in the event of mass casualties, and patterns of disease and their control after catastrophes. WHO has made arrangements to train WHO fellows from disaster-prone countries in disaster management. The aim is to have key persons in countries or regions at risk who can promote organizational and operational knowledge of how to deal with emergencies.

Because of the paucity of statistical data, a valid systematic tabulation of the various health-related components of disasters cannot be given as yet. WHO's activities included the compilation of country fact sheets, statistics for disaster preparedness, and manuals and simple guides for various types of emergency. A worldwide network of disaster specialists is being established to complement the WHO Disaster Task Force. Meetings and training courses for disaster personnel from developing countries are being organized and the health component of seminars run by UNDRO and other agencies is being strengthened.

Often a disaster destroys a country's painstakingly established health organization at one stroke. A logical component of disaster work is, therefore, rehabilitation, and it is WHO's task in the post-emergency period to work out, as necessary, a medium-term country health programme with the stricken country on the basis of primary health care.

Natural disasters respect no boundaries and often involve several countries. Besides technical cooperation with countries, collaboration among countries is vital and is promoted by WHO.

WHO speedily mobilized considerable sums for emergencies. The regular budget funds allocated to the programme are minimal but there are some unprogrammed sources of funding, such as the Director-General's and Regional Directors' Development Programmes, the Special Account for Disasters and Natural Catastrophes, the Executive Board Special Fund for particular emergencies, and the fund for assistance in epidemics. However, the bulk of assistance is based on extrabudgetary funds, from sources such as UNDP; indeed, the raising of considerable extrabudgetary funds for emergency work from bilateral, multilateral, and nongovernmental sources is an essential feature of the WHO programme. Activities are carried out in collaboration with UNDRO, UNHCR, UNDP, UNICEF, the International Committee of the Red Cross, the League of Red Cross Societies, the European Economic Community, and other international bodies. However, an effort is being made to increase the budgetary component of emergency operations and thus WHO's efficiency in dealing with such aspects of disaster work as preparedness, prevention, mitigation, relief, and rehabilitation.

Health resources

Health manpower

Action by individual governments in the area of health manpower development seems to have followed one or another of the following general patterns during the past two decades. Some adopted what appeared to be appropriate health manpower policies, but failed to apply appropriate technology in their implementation. A number formulated plans for health, health manpower, and education of health workers, but failed to implement them for political, technical, administrative, or economic reasons. Others not only made plans but also implemented them—of these countries, some appear to have achieved success in the resolution of certain problems, while others have discovered that their plans were irrelevant and, if anything, aggravated existing problems. Still other countries tended to apply treatment only to the symptoms of problems and then only on an *ad hoc* basis. Some of the basic problems are identified below.

(*a*) *Current problems.* Jointly with Member States, WHO has identified a number of manpower problems at country level. These form the subject of the Medium-Term Programme for Health Manpower Development (1978–1983), approved by the Thirty-first World Health Assembly in 1978. It should be noted that most of the problems to which the programme is addressed have been recognized for two or more decades. What is new is not so much that the problems have changed as the fact that they are being propounded with increasing frequency and vigour in the literature and elsewhere. It should also be noted that the intensity of individual problems varies with time both within and between countries.

A close look at a list of health manpower problems (cited in detail elsewhere[1]) reveals that many of them derive from more fundamental problems in the socioeconomic system. The most basic problem, of course, and one that transcends the health system, is the low level of social and economic development in a large number of countries, as compared with that in a few highly developed countries, and the broadening gap between the rich and the poor in the developing world. Considering the low economic base from which many countries initiate development activities, a major problem in these countries is the gross imbalance in the allocation of resources for the different sectors of the economy. In developing countries, an average of only 2–3% of national expenditure goes on health. This average has remained constant over the past ten years. The amount spent on health has often been insignificant in relation to that spent on, for example, education and defence. In developed countries, the average spent on health has been 5–6%.

Given the labour-intensive nature of the health industry, manpower consumes between 60% and 80% of the health budget in many countries. As a result, little is left for the infrastructure and non-labour inputs needed for health manpower to achieve optimum productivity. Within the constraints of a limited budget, it might be possible to decrease the proportion spent on health manpower by decreasing the emphasis on those health workers who are costly to train and maintain, and increasing the emphasis on the less costly categories. An alternative, of course, would be to increase the total budget for health.

Apart from the limited funds allocated to it, the main basic problem in the health sector is the frequent lack of coherently formulated and implemented policies and plans for health development, and notably of a realistic approach to health manpower development based on requirements for health services. This problem is due to a number of factors, such as the lack of appropriate planning as a continuous process and the lack of a well organized information system.

---

[1] Health manpower development. Report of the Director-General to the Twenty-ninth World Health Assembly (unpublished WHO document A29/15), pages 17–20.

180

Stemming from or symptomatic of this basic problem are: shortages of appropriately trained teachers and supervisors, appropriate teaching and learning materials, and facilities for training; inappropriate curricula and standards for recruitment to training and employment; a lack of security of tenure and of career-development schemes, including a lack of the continuing education needed to increase work productivity and job satisfaction and to facilitate the vertical and horizontal mobility of health workers; a lack of schemes for the appropriate distribution of health workers geographically, institutionally, and by occupation; and a lack of clear definitions of the functions and tasks of health team members.

All these deficiencies combine to create shortages of certain categories of health personnel having the knowledge, skills, and attitudes neeedeed to perform the work to be done where and when it is needed, together with occasional surpluses of other categories.

There are striking inequalities in the availability of basic health manpower in the world. For each 100 000 inhabitants there are almost 1000 health workers[1] in the developed countries, and a little more than 200 in the developing countries. The situation is summarized in Tables 17 and 18.

Table 17. Distribution of countries (or areas) and population, according to density of aggregate of certain health occupations c. 1975[a]

Density (rate per 100 000 population)	World			Less developed countries		
	Number of countries or areas	Population (thousands)	%	Number of countries or areas	Population (thousands)	%
Less than 50	26	374 172	9	26	374 172	13
50–99	22	786 402	20	22	786 402	28
100–249	59	717 692	18	59	717 692	25
250–499	44	1 184 943	30	36	974 897	34
500–749	23	345 640	9	9	1 478	0
750 plus	19	543 346	14	3	1 755	0
Total	193	3 952 295	100	155	2 856 396	100

[a] "Aggregate of certain health occupations" refers here to data on the following categories:
Physicians
Medical assistants
Multipurpose health auxiliaries (barefoot doctors, village health auxiliaries, etc.)
Professional midwives, assistant midwives, traditional birth attendants
Professional nurses, assistant nurses
Traditional medical practitioners

---

[1] The term "health workers" covers the following categories:

Physicians
Medical assistants
Multipurpose health auxiliaries
Dentists
Operating dental auxiliaries and dental hygienists
Dental technicians
Pharmacists
Nurses and midwives
Assistant nurses and assistant midwives

Medical laboratory technicians
Medical laboratory assistant
technicians
Medical radiological technicians
Medical radiological assistant
technicians
Sanitarians and assistant sanitarians
Traditional medical practitioners

181

Table 18. Distribution of countries (or areas) and population, according to density of aggregate of certain dental health occupations c. 1975[a]

Density (rate per 100 000 population)	World			Less developed countries		
	Number of countries or areas	Population (thousand)	%	Number of countries or areas	Population (thousand)	%
Less than 1	38	395 331	13	38	395 331	21
1–4	33	959 340	32	33	959 340	50
5–9	20	116 204	4	20	116 204	6
10–24	42	330 925	11	37	284 075	15
25–49	27	293 049	10	15	139 288	7
50 and more	28	862 652	29	7	24 111	1
Total	188	2 957 501	100	150	1 918 349	100

[a] "Aggregate of certain dental health occupations" refers here to data on the following categories:
Dentists (dental surgeons, stomatologists)
Operating dental auxiliaries (school dental nurses, dental therapists etc.) and dental hygienists
Dental laboratory technicians (dental mechanics)

It may be noted that traditional medical practitioners are reported only from 13 developing countries in which 60% of the population of the developing world live. Despite the limitations inherent in the information and the need to exercise caution in interpreting it, the figures are sufficiently accurate to underline the tremendous challenge of providing basic health care for the majority of the world's population.

A close look at the list of manpower problems, as identified jointly by WHO and Member States, reveals that only a few are basic or root problems and that the remainder are symptomatic in that they derive from more fundamental problems existing elsewhere in the health system within which manpower operates. Among the most basic problems is one that transcends the health system, namely the low level of social and economic development.

For the same population there are in the developed countries 6 times as many physicians (or 3–5 times, if traditional medical practitioners are included), 5 times as many pharmacists, and 12 times as many nurses and midwives as there are in the developing countries. One important conclusion to be drawn from the data is that the gap between developed and developing countries seems to be at least as large in the case of middle or lower level personnel as in that of university-level professionals. However, it should be borne in mind that an absence of adequate registration procedures with regard to middle and lower level personnel may, to a certain extent, create a misleading impression. The world health manpower structure repeats the top-heavy distribution found in many national health manpower systems which, particularly in some developed countries, may be dysfunctional as regards their own health needs and resources.

Over the past decade there has been a general tendency for an increase in personnel density in the majority of health occupations. However, in 26 countries in which about 200 million people (5% of the world's population) live, physician density has actually declined. It is extremely perturbing to note that in a number of developing countries the ratio of members of other health occupations e.g., medical assistants—to the population has likewise declined. There is little evidence to suggest that any significant progress has been made towards, a reduction of inter-disparities between countries. A more rapid growth in the number of middle- and lower-level personnel than in the number of higher-level personnel can be noted in many developing countries, whereas in many developed countries the opposite tendency, particularly for midwives and nurses and their auxiliaries, may be seen. This tendency is illustrated in the Annex, Table 9 and Fig. 7.

There are a striking inequalities in the distribution of health manpower within many countries, notably between urban and rural areas. In some developing countries, for instance, physician density is at least five times greater in urban areas than in rural areas. In India, for instance, about one-fifth of the population and up to four-fifths of the physicians, are in urban areas, and there has been no change in this situation during the past decade. In some countries of Africa, between 50% and 75% of physicians are in the capital where less than one-tenth of the population resides.

Out of 11 developing countries on which data are available, four show an improvement in the distribution of physicians in recent years and six a deterioration, while in one it remained unchanged.

However, it is important to note that disparities within countries in availability of health manpower are not limited to developing countries but are also a serious problem in the developed world.

Various solutions have been put forward for the problems just discussed. Like the problems themselves, the proposed solutions are being propounded in various media with increasing frequency and vigour, although evidence of their implementation is relatively rare. This does not mean, however, that countries are making no effort to put them into practice. What is not known is the extent to which the isolated efforts that have been reported reflect significant world trends. On the assumption that they do reflect them, the examples cited below may be considered as indicating trends with respect to the health manpower system as a whole and, in turn, with respect to each of the three components of this system, i.e., planning, production, and management.

(b) The health manpower system

The health manpower system comprises all the interacting policies, structures, and mechanisms related to the processes of planning, producing, and using health manpower. Over the years there has been an increasing realization that, in many societies, not only have the components of this system been functioning largely independently of each other, but also the system as a whole has been functioning independently of other systems in the health sector, particularly that concerned with health service delivery. The result has been that the total health benefit gained has been far below the level desired and needed.

This realization has led to the conceptualization and promotion of an approach (described in a WHO study),[1] which, if implemented, would bring health manpower development policies, plans, and action more into line with those relating to health service development. A few countries (e.g., Hungary, Poland, and the USSR) have completely

---

[1] FÜLÖP, T. New approaches to a permanent problem: the integrated development of health services and health manpower. WHO Chronicle. **30**: 433–441 (1976).

integrated these two components of the health system into a single and comprehensive system at the top level of government. In other countries, the steps taken to implement the notion of coordination between these two components vary in nature. In some, efforts have culminated in coordination mechanisms at the top level of government. In the Americas, for example, 12 countries have established health manpower offices or units within their ministries of health. Among them, Colombia has established, in addition, an interministerial coordinating committee. In Canada, coordinating mechanisms have been developed at provincial level, and coordination of these collectively is effected through a federal committee which includes representatives of the health services and the education services respectively. In the United Kingdom, coordination between the universities and the National Health Service has been achieved through mechanisms operating at both national and peripheral levels.

In other countries, some practical steps have been taken with respect to a particular geographical area or a particular type of education. For example, in Israel, the University Centre for Health Sciences, Ben Gurion University of the Negev, participates in the planning and implementation of all levels of health services for the entire region of the Negev.[1] Some progress has been made towards the creation of a department of community health in the University of Sierra Leone. This department is expected to act as a key resource in the development of a programme for the basic and continuing education and training of medical assistants and to have research facilities for identifying priorities and goals in health care delivery and designing strategies for achieving them. In the Province of Fars, Iran, some progress has been made in the development of a strategy for medical education ("schools without walls") based on community needs and using community hospitals and other peripheral health service institutions as sites for the training of students who have been selected primarily because of their desire to work in the community.

Two noteworthy efforts at an international level to promote the concept of an integrated or coordinated approach to health service and health manpower development are: the Ministerial consultation on the subject (Teheran, 1978), which brought together, from 19 countries of the Eastern Mediterranean Region, nearly 100 persons at high levels of authority in the fields of health and education;[2] and the forthcoming World Conference on Education and Health Care, in preparation for which the World Federation for Medical Education, with WHO collaboration, is conducting a series of regional seminars and workshops.

(c) Health manpower planning

A health manpower plan should consist of a coherent set of practical proposals for the production, use, and motivation of health manpower, the aim being to ensure an adequate

---

[1] SEGALL, A. ET AL. University Centre for Health Sciences: Ben Gurion University of the Negev, Beersheva, Israel: an interim perspective. In: Katz, F. M. & Fülop, T. ed. Personnel for health care: case studies of educational programmes. Geneva, World Health Organization, 1978 (Public Health Papers, No. 70), pp. 111–132.

[2] An integrated approach to health services and manpower development. Ministerial Consultation, Teheran, 26 February–2 March 1978. Alexandria, WHO Regional Office for the Eastern Mediterranean, 1979 (WHO/EMRO Technical Publication, No. 1)

supply of appropriately trained manpower to provide health services to those in need, where and when the need is perceived.

The record of national accomplishments in the field of health manpower planning has been very modest; this appears to be due to a lack of adequate management. Further reflection leads to the conclusion that planning efforts will remain unrealistic and therefore ineffective as long as they fail to take into account social, economic, and political constraints, as long as they remain detached from other processes, particularly the planning of health services and of education generally, and as long as health manpower production capacity and health manpower management capability are ignored.

There is disillusionment with planning methods that call for isolated, sophisticated, and costly studies in which more data are generally collected than can be meaningfully used and certain essential data are omitted either because data-gathering is badly organized or because the national information system is incapable of generating the data needed. Such studies have seldom resulted in the formulation and implementation of a plan. For this reason, encouragement is being given to the development of methods in which information requirements are strictly tailored to what is essential for planning purposes and to the financial and technical capacity of national information systems to gather such information. In this context, particular interest is being shown in the development and application of simplified techniques for gauging manpower requirements in situations where the information base is weak and the need to resolve an existing public health problem is so urgent that a plan is needed within a relatively short time, i.e., it cannot await large-scale surveys conducted over extended periods of time. Such a methodology (referred to as crash planning) is being field-tested, with WHO collaboration, in Colombia.

In recent years, in connexion with long-term planning, great interest has been shown in the development of techniques for forecasting health manpower requirements on the basis of assumptions about the future political, economical, and epidemiological situation of a society (as opposed to reliance solely on knowledge of current and past situations). Also, given the greater awareness of the fact that health care delivery and manpower requirements are influenced by a multitude of factors—the weightiest being political and economic factors that are constantly shifting and difficult to control—greater attention is being paid to the need for experts from a variety of disciplines to advise on the health manpower planning process. Along with this goes a growing awareness that planning needs to be considered not as a static, inflexible, and authoritarian process, but as a dynamic one whereby goals, objectives, and even the basic assumptions and concepts underlying the plan change as planners uncover new information through a process of monitoring and evaluation.

From the statistical standpoint, planning efforts are complicated by the growing proliferation of categories of health workers and the fact that, while each category bears its own job title, there may be workers with similar responsibilities but different levels of training in the same category or, under different titles, in different categories. This problem is compounded by the fact that personnel often switch from one level of responsibility to another, regardless of their level of training. As a result statistics on health manpower resources are generally unreliable, techniques are accordingly needed for validating the manpower data gathered for planning purposes. From the international point of view, the problem of reporting on health manpower is further complicated by the fact that, on the one hand, job titles attached to personnel having similar responsibilities may differ from country to country, and, on the other, the same title is sometimes given in different countries to personnel having quite different responsibilities. An international effort to devise criteria for standardizing the classification of health occupations is currently under way.

Concern about the growing cost of health manpower education and whether it is attended by a commensurate improvement in the level of health is gaining momentum. It has already been mentioned that an estimated 60–80% of any given health budget is spent on health manpower. Using an imaginary country not untypical of many in Africa or Asia, it has recently been demonstrated that payments to health personnel could consume nearly 60% of funds for health services.[1] Of this proportion, nearly half would be devoted to the payment of physicians and dentists, a fifth to nurses, and the remainder to auxiliary health workers, practitioners of traditional medicine, and others. Excluded from this hypothetical example is the cost of education, about which these authors make assumptions leading to the conclusion that the cost of medical education per student in many developing countries is closer to the equivalent of US $ 60 000 than to the US $ 10 000 generally estimated, while that of training a medical auxiliary is closer to US $ 8000 than to the previously estimated US $ 4000. This suggests that about 8 medical auxiliaries could be trained for the cost training one physician. When such costs are added to that of paying the physician's salary, the question arises whether the physician's contribution to health justifies the higher training costs and the higher salary. In planning generally, and no less so in the planning of health manpower, choices have to be made between alternatives for the development and use of resources, the basic consideration being what is referred to as "opportunity cost". In relation to health manpower, the assessment of opportunity cost is essentially the assessment of which combination of health manpower would most economically lead to the achievement of a specified health target, consideration being given to the number of personnel of a certain category that could be trained and used efficiently and effectively for the amount of money needed to train and use efficiently and effectively one member of another category.

In relation to health manpower planning generally, WHO's Medium-Term Programme for Health Manpower Development (1978–1983) mentions numerous activities of varying kinds that have been planned or are under way in a number of countries. Among these are activities focusing on: the development of manpower planning methodology; the analysis of manpower policies and the preparation of guidelines for the formulation of health manpower policies; the development of information systems for the monitoring of manpower requirements; the analysis of tasks to be performed by defined categories of health workers; and the development of programmes for the training of national health manpower planners and country health programmers.

(d) Health manpower education

The process of health manpower education involves all the activities and resources concerned with the planning, implementation, and evaluation of basic and postbasic education and training programmes for all categories of health worker. The function of

---

[1] ABEL-SMITH, B. & LEISERSON, A. *Poverty, development and health.* Geneva, World Health Organization, 1978 (Public Health Papers, No. 69).

Table 19. Number of medical schools existing in specified years

Year	Total No.	Developed countries		Developing countries	
		No.	(%)	No.	(%)
1955	631	377	(60)	254	(40)
1960	715	388	(54)	327	(46)
1970	961	472	(49)	489	(51)
1975	1124	516	(46)	608	(54)

the health manpower production process is to educate and train people for health work in accordance with the specifications of the health manpower plan concerning the quantity and quality of health workers required to meet the priority health needs of all segments of a society. Because of the absence of coordination already mentioned, the educational process has failed to meet the stipulations of manpower plans. A significant trend over the past 20 years, particularly in the developing world, has been the overproduction of physicians relative to the effective economic demand for medical services. This over-production, which has been reflected in the migration of a number of physicians, was primarily the result of the increasing demand for medical education. This demand, which was in many cases unrelated to local employment opportunities, was part of the overall demand for higher education as an important means of raising social status. In response to the demand for medical education, many developing countries created new medical schools and expanded the capacity of existing ones.

Tables 17 and 18 show the changes, over the 21-year period 1955–1975 in the number of medical schools in the world, in the proportion of such schools existing in developed and developing countries respectively, and in their number in each group of countries with the corresponding rates of growth.

In relation to the total number of medical schools existing each year, the proportion in the developed world gradually declined while that in the developing world increased. By 1970, the number of schools in the developing world surpassed the number in the developed world. During the 20 years (1955–1975), nearly 500 new medical schools were established throughout the world, representing an overall growth rate of 78%. In the developing world, among countries where increases were high in both absolute numbers and rate of growth during the same period were: Brazil (53 new schools or a growth rate of 230%); China (59 new schools or 210% growth); Mexico (34 new schools or

Table 20. Increase in numbers of medical schools during specified periods

Period	Total increase		Developed countries		Developing countries	
	No.	(%)	No.	(%)	No.	(%)
1955–60	84	(13)	11	(3)	73	(29)
1960–70	246	(34)	84	(22)	162	(50)
1970–75	163	(17)	44	(9)	119	(24)
1955–75	493	(78)	139	(37)	354	(139)

188% growth); India (62 new schools or 141% growth); and Colombia (7 new schools or 100% growth). By comparison, the growth rates in a few developed countries were: Spain (11 new schools or 110% growth); Japan (23 new schools or 50% growth); USA (38 new schools or 45% growth); and USSR (18 new schools or 26% growth). It should also be noted that, of the 119 new schools created in the developing world during the five-year period 1970–1975, 31 or 26% were in countries that had no medical school prior to 1970.

While new medical schools were being created in a number of developing countries, the admission policies of many existing schools were liberalized, the result being excessively large classes and the risk of a deterioration in the quality of the education provided. In Latin America the phenomenon of liberalization was so striking that it became labelled as *"masificación de la educación médica"* Several countries in other parts of the world are experiencing the same phenomenon, e.g., Egypt, Italy, and Spain. In sum, the large output of medical schools, combined with the reluctance of physicians to work in rural areas, has created in many countries a situation in which a plethora of physicians in certain areas coexists with a crying need for their services in other areas of the same country.

Within the past few years an intensified effort seems to have been made in some countries, developing and developed alike, to train auxiliaries of various categories as a means of extending health services to deprived populations with an emphasis on activities for the promotion of health.

During the present decade the traditional education of health workers has been consistently charged with failure to serve the needs of society, lack of response to the concerns of the individual and the community, and wrong priorities in curricula.

For many years the traditional methods of educating health workers were consistently criticized for failure to consider the needs of society as a whole or of individuals as human beings requiring understanding and care. This has led to a greater interest in ways and means of improving the relevance of education to both national health needs and job requirements, as defined in a well designed health system. With respect to educational strategy and technology, the literature, including WHO documents and publications, is replete with theories, concepts, guidelines, bibliographies, recommendations, and the like on ways of making the education of health workers more relevant. Among these are: the grouping of curricular content in a way that cuts across traditional disciplines; the multidisciplinary (health team) approach to education and training; the inclusion in curricula of aspects of the social and behavioural sciences as a foundation for participation in comprehensive community health as opposed to curative medicine for the individual; interspersion of theoretical with practical training; student-oriented rather than teacher-oriented instruction; learning on the job; learning by doing; self-instruction; problem-oriented instruction; the modularization of curricula; the flow-chart system for enhancing skills and facilitating decision-making in patient management by intermediate-level health staff and peripheral health workers, such as traditional birth attendants and primary health care workers; packaged instruction; teaching and learning by task-oriented behavioural objectives;[1] individual and small-group learning systems; and the evaluation of student performance and of the whole teaching and learning process.

---

[1] GUILBERT, J. J. *Educational handbook for health personnel.* Geneva World Health Organization, 1977 (WHO Offset Publications, No. 35).

The extent to which one or more of these concepts (or the practical materials developed by WHO and others in connexion with some of them) are being tested by governments is not generally known. Only a few examples can be cited. In the WHO Regions of Africa, the Americas, South-East Asia, and the Eastern Mediterranean, surveys are being conducted of national needs and resources with respect to teaching and learning materials. In the Americas, an intensive effort has been made to develop medical and nursing textbooks, and plans are under way to extend the textbook programme to all categories of health worker, auxiliary as well as professional. In the Eastern Mediterranean Region, a centre for the design, testing, and production of learning materials in Arabic has been established in Cairo. In the Philippines, beginning in 1977, over 5000 health personnel, mainly midwives and public health nurses, have been prepared through the modular approach to teaching and learning. Experiments with multidisciplinary programmes providing experience relevant to work in a health team have been undertaken in some countries, e.g., Algeria and the United Republic of Cameroon. In the developing countries of the European Region, there has been intensive training of multidisciplinary teams of health and social workers in family health and family planning.

Task analysis, as a guide to the specification of skill requirements and thus of learning objectives, appears to be attracting attention in some countries. In India, for example, a detailed training programme for family planning personnel has been developed and implemented on the basis of task analysis. In Cuba, the Ministry of Health's Department of Medical Education has defined, with respect to general medical practitioners, specialists in paediatrics, and specialists in rehabilitation respectively, broad functions in the areas of administration, teaching, research, and clinical practice. On the basis of these, the objectives of teaching institutions have been specified. At the WHO Regional Teacher-Training Centre for South-East Asia in Peradeniya, Sri Lanka, the tasks of general practitioners in that country have been defined as a basis for modifying curricula. In the USA, the University of California's Department of Research in Medical Education has conducted a national survey of activities and practice characteristics of generalists, medical specialists, and surgical specialists of different types. The detailed data from this survey form a solid information base on which to plan undergraduate and continuing medical education.

All these activities aim at enhancing the relevance of education and training to national needs. Other action to this end can also be cited, notably the evaluation of education programmes and changes in their content and in the teaching and learning processes to give greater prominence to community health and primary health care. In the Americas, for example, nursing education programmes in at least 19 countries have been evaluated and the curricula revised to place greater emphasis on primary health care. The nursing profession has played a pioneering role in the development of methodology for the evaluation of education programmes in the health field.[1]

The dearth of teachers at national level for the various health professions has led to a greater emphasis on the development of national self-reliance in the preparation of teachers to plan, implement, and evaluate education programmes. Between 1969 and 1975, 8 regional teacher-training centres were established in 5 WHO regions, as were

---

[1] ALLEN, M. *Evaluation of educational programmes in nursing.* Geneva, World Health Organization, 1977.

189

several national centres, e.g., in India, the Philippines, the Republic of Korea, and several Latin American countries. Other national centres are at an advanced stage of planning. To date, the regional centres have concentrated mainly on the training of teachers of medicine, but a move is being made to have them undertake multiprofessional teaching and training activities. In Africa, three centres (two for French speakers and one for English speakers) have been set up exclusively for the training of teachers of nursing. Most postbasic nursing education programmes throughout the world have a teacher-training component. Also in Africa, particular attention is being paid to the training of teachers of auxiliaries. Experiments with the use of new teaching methods in this regard have been carried out in Kenya and the United Republic of Tanzania. In the Eastern Mediterranean Region, several medical schools in Egypt, Pakistan, and the Sudan have established units for the planning and conduct of teacher training.

(e) Health manpower management

Health manpower management covers all matters relating to the employment, use, and motivation of all categories of health worker, and it largely determines the productivity of, and thus coverage by, the health system, as well as its capacity to retain staff. The major symptoms of inadequate health manpower management are: uneconomical utilization and therefore inadequate productivity of health staff; imbalances in the overall composition of the health labour force; and inequities in the distribution of health manpower among health service establishments from the geographical standpoint and in terms of functions and occupations. To a large extent, the symptoms of improper management stem from improper planning.

The manpower density calculated on the basis of an analysis of 14 health occupations seems to suggest a certain composition of the basic health team or at least a profile—admittedly incomplete—of the health labour force in developed and developing countries respectively.[1] The available statistical data indicate that, in the developed countries, for every 100 physicians there are, on the average, 294 health workers including medical assistants, midwives, nurses, assistant midwives, assistant nurses, traditional medical practitioners and multipurpose health auxiliaries. The average rises to 489 such health workers per 100 physicians in the developing countries, i.e., about two-thirds more such workers per physician than in the developed world (see Appendix, Table 9).

If it is assumed that physicians cannot function productively without a considerable input from other health workers, the question arises as to what input from how many other workers is necessary to make the physician optimally productive. In general, the answer could be: "The more the better". However, such an answer implies that, in decisions to produce additional physicians, consideration will have to be given not only to the cost of training those physicians, but to the additional cost involved in making them productive, which is several times higher. In countries where cost containment is an imperative—and this is the case in most countries, including some of the richest—consideration will have to be given to intensifying the production of those categories of worker upon whose labour the productivity of the physician largely depends and whose

---

[1] Bui Dang Ha Doan. Statistical analysis of the world health manpower situation circa 1975. *World health statistics quarterly* (in press).

training and utilization are much less costly than those of physicians. Account must also be taken of the fact that, for primary health care on an extensive scale, the amount of other health workers needed will be far greater than that existing today in most countries except China.

To continue with the theme of the productivity of health manpower, several time-and-motion studies of the activities of certain categories of health personnel have been carried out. Efforts in this regard were largely pioneered by the nursing profession, beginning in the early 1950s. Such studies have dealt with: nursing activities in Israel; nursing and midwifery personnel in certain states of India; peripheral health workers in Sri Lanka; and hospital nurses in Switzerland and Thailand. To what extent the findings of these studies have been used to effect changes in productivity levels is not known.

Steps are being taken in a few countries to offer and guarantee better means for both horizontal and vertical career development and mobility in order to increase productivity and job satisfaction. One of the main problems encountered, however, is an excessive emphasis on paper qualifications and a lack of flexibility in the validation of different periods of previous education and experience, even though a number of occupational categories share much of the same grounding of knowledge.

This inflexibility is largely due to the excessive stratification of professional roles and the protection of these roles through accreditation of training and rigid licensing requirements that are often arbitrary and unnecessarily demanding for the duties involved. Nevertheless, the situation is improving considerably, particularly with respect to nursing and midwifery personnel. In the developing world especially, a process of task delegation or substitution appears to occur in the sense that, given two professions that are linked by a complement of function, the one at a lower level grows at a more rapid rate than the other.[1] Thus, for example, the figures for professional nurses and midwives have grown at a greater rate than those for physicians: likewise, the rate for auxiliary nursing and midwifery personnel has been greater than that for professional nurses and midwives. This phenomenon appears to be primarily the result of the promotion of personnel from lower to higher levels. This, in turn, may be due to governmental measures favouring the accession of certain personnel to higher levels of responsibility and social prestige. It may also be the result of a greater emphasis on continuing education and adult education and of the career-development policies of certain institutions.

With a few notable exceptions, continuing education as a means of improving the competence and thus the productivity and job satisfaction of health personnel does not appear to have been institutionalized and has more frequently taken the form of sporadic seminars, workshops, short courses on special subjects, self-instruction, and on-the-job training, which do not lead to progressive and incremental learning and which do not represent a systematic approach towards professional growth and career development. With respect to graduate or postbasic education, there appears to be a trend toward greater self-sufficiency in the developing world. Between the years 1970 and 1977, for example, there was a considerable increase in the proportion of WHO fellowships granted for study in the home regions of the fellows. The following table shows the percentage

---

[1] BUI DANG HA DOAN. Statistical analysis of the world health manpower situation circa 1975. *World health statistics quarterly* (in press).

differences in the proportion studying in their home region:

WHO Region	1970	1977	Difference
Africa	50%	66%	+16%
Americas	88%	91%	+3%
South-East Asia	16%	30%	+14%
Europe	90%	91%	+1%
Eastern Mediterranean	28%	31%	+3%
Western Pacific	48%	64%	+16%

With greater international concern about the role of women in health and development, more interest is now being taken in the relative numbers of men and women in the health occupations. It has been shown[1] that in certain countries an increasing number of women are entering health occupations traditionally regarded as the province of men, e.g., medicine, pharmacy, and dentistry. There is, however, too little scientifically based knowledge about factors that facilitate or deter the entry of women into the health occupations in particular countries, beyond the general assumption that they have to do with the political, socioeconomic, and cultural patterns of individual societies and particularly with cultural attitudes regarding the role of women generally in such societies. Evidence of the increasing interest in the utilization of female as well as male workers in various health occupations is the growing concern about the possibility that women may not have as long a professional life as men because of family commitments. More research is needed, however, to find out how far this is so and, if necessary, to devise measures that will ensure a longer professional life for women.

A problem that continues to plague almost all countries—developed and developing alike—is the inequitable geographical distribution of health manpower. Many countries have tried to deal with this problem by offering material incentives and career prospects of various sorts to attract health manpower, particularly physicians, to deprived areas. This approach appears to have met with little success, partly because of the very nature of deprived areas and partly because the education of the health personnel concerned had not prepared them technically or intellectually to work in such areas. The result has been an excessive concentration of health personnel, particularly professional staff, in the urban areas and the subsequent migration of many of them to other countries.

The international displacement of skilled manpower and the implications of this undesirable development for social equity within and between nations have been constantly debated in the governing bodies of WHO and are a source of mounting political concern. During the past debate, Member States of WHO have expressed themselves forcefully on the subject, which has also given rise to a great deal of written comment and to numerous resolutions by organizations of the United Nations system. In 1972, in response to a resolution of the Twenty-fifth World Health Assembly, the WHO Secretariat conducted a multinational study on the international migration of physicians and nurses which was completed in 1977. The report on this study shows that in about 1972 there were at least 140 000 physicians in countries other than those of which they were

---

[1] BUI DANG HA DOAN. Statistical analysis of the world health manpower situation circa 1975. *World health statistics quarterly* (in press).

nationals or in which they were born or trained or both.[1] These comprised about 6% of the world's physicians at that time, exceeding the total output of the world's medical schools in 1970 (excluding those in China). Over three-quarters of these physicians were found in only three countries: the USA (with about 68 000 in 1972), the United Kingdom (21 000 in 1970), and Canada (9000 in 1971). The Federal Republic of Germany (6000 in 1971) and Australia (4000 in 1972) were also important recipient countries.

The report shows that many countries were losing physicians through migration because the countries concerned could not afford to employ as many as they had trained. It also shows that, for each country that had a certain level of gross domestic product per capita, there appeared to be a certain level of physician density (i.e., physicians per unit of population) that it could afford to maintain. Countries where the level of physician density was higher than the average for countries having the equivalent level of gross domestic product experienced an outflow of physicians, and *vice versa*. Thus, for example, at one end of the development scale, the United Republic of Cameroon, with a lower level of physician density than the average for countries having an equivalent level of gross domestic product, experienced a net inflow of physicians, while India, with a higher than average level of density, experienced a net outflow. The relationship seemed to hold good for developed countries as well. Thus, the United Kingdom, with a lower than average level of physician density, experienced a net inflow, while Austria, with a higher than average level, experienced a net outflow. Quite significant in relation to what might be called the "sustainable level" of physician density is the case of Iran, which for several years experienced a net outflow, but in recent years has experienced both a sharp rise in gross domestic product and a considerable inflow of physicians (some of them returned nationals, and others foreign physicians). The impact of the international migration of physicians and nurses on the situation in both donor and recipient countries is presented graphically in Fig. 16 and Fig. 17.

While the intercountry flow of physicians and nurses has increased during the past decade, its volume and direction are now changing. As a result of recent regulations in the key recipient countries, the flow from developing to developed countries is likely to decline. At the same time, major donor countries are beginning to take measures to increase the capacity of their respective health systems to retain trained personnel and use them properly. These measures include the adoption of an incentive policy and the improvement of career prospects. The extent to which they will be effective cannot yet be assessed.

The lack of realistic planning and management in respect of health manpower development in almost all countries is partly—and perhaps largely—due to a lack of realism on the part of the managers and educators concerned. The increasing realization of this fact led the Thirty-first World Health Assembly to adopt a resolution which stresses "the need for a unified managerial process for national health development, incorporating country health programming, national health programme budgeting and health programme evaluation, as well as adequate information support". It also urges Member States themselves

---

[1] MEJÍA, A., PIZURKI, H. & ROYSTON, E. *Physician and nurse migration: analysis and policy implications. Report of a WHO study.* Geneva, World Health Organization, 1979.

Fig. 16. Effect of migration on physician density (18 donor countries)

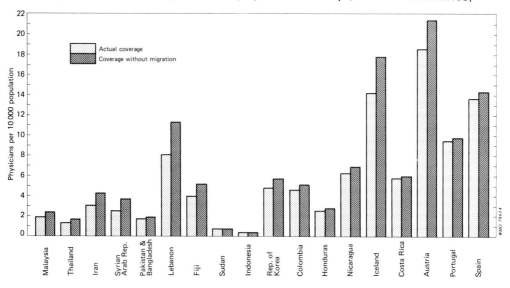

Fig. 17. Effect of migration on physician density (18 recipient countries)

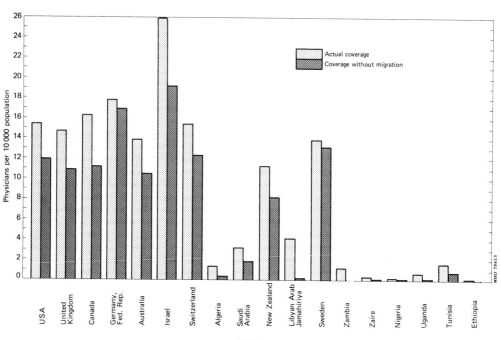

"to provide appropriate training for all workers in managerial processes and continued education in this field", and it requests the Director-General "to foster appropriate training in health management, particularly through learning-by-doing". However, to be effective, it will be more necessary than in the past to link health manpower strategies to overall development policies, particularly in the areas of education and manpower.

Facilities

Building accounts for by far the greatest part of the development budget of any Ministry of Health. This is not surprising since so much of all health service activities are carried out within specialized buildings of one sort or another. Although there is general agreement that health services should be brought to the population to a much greater extent, particularly in the form of preventive and promotive health care, a very substantial part of all services will continue to be delivered from within the confines of health service facilities. Most developing countries have three basic levels of health facility—the hospital, the health centre, and the subcentre (which may be called "health station", "dispensary", etc.). The hospital sector is divided conventionally into district or rural hospitals, regional or provincial hospitals, and national referral or consultant hospitals. In theory, each of these various facilities serves a particular catchment area and is related in hierarchical fashion to the larger facility. In practice, the size of the building often has relatively little to do with the catchment area it actually serves. Although larger buildings may serve somewhat greater population areas than smaller institutions, there is relatively little consistent relationship between the size of a building and the size of the catchment area actually served.

A dispensary may serve a population living within 5–6 km of it reasonably well, while the rural health centre may do the same for a population living up to between 8 and 13 km away. For a hospital, the comparable figures may be 16–32 km. Each facility is serving an area roughly twice as large as the smaller one. However, the costs of building and running the different subcentres, health centres, and regional hospitals may be in the relationship of 1 to 10 to 100 for capital costs and 1 to 5 to 50 for recurrent costs.

Critical decisions have to be taken about the choice of buildings of suitable size, in some combination of the three basic levels mentioned above, as well as their allocation and siting throughout a country. It should be stressed that health service development must be based on realistic possibilities for the referral of patients rather than simply the abstract desirability of such referral. In practice, this means that lower-level institutions must be strengthened so as to be more capable of providing adequate services in the absence of extensive referral possibilities, at least until communications improve sufficiently to justify a reassessment. It is often the case that those who are responsible for hospital development have little real knowledge of the true catchment areas of individual facilities. Surveys to ascertain their extent can be carried out with relatively little difficulty and should be an important part of all planning for health facilities.

In many developing countries, the smallest rural units—subcentres, health stations, dispensaries, or clinics—suffer from manpower and supply problems reflecting the tendency to neglect the development of basic rural health services that was so widespread until recently.

195

At the next level, there is the rural or primary health centre. In some countries, at the time of their original conception, these centres represented a significant departure from the curative orientation of the previously existing hospitals and dispensaries, and it was hoped they would play an ever-increasing role in raising the general standard of health for the majority of people, particularly those in the rural areas. Work in the health centre was to stress the improvement of health standards rather than the treatment of disease. It was intended that a vehicle should be available at all times to permit health centre staff to visit the surrounding villages and dispensaries. It was thought that rural health centre staff would spend as much time out of the centres as in them.

Such centres, in conjunction with their satellite dispensaries or subcentres, can serve a population of between 20 000 and 50 000, depending on the manpower and resources available to them and, in particular, on how well the health workers manning them were trained. One critical factor is that rural health centres must not be allowed to have an ever-increasing number of inpatient beds. In most centres probably 12–18 beds would suffice for the necessary inpatient work and would not detract unnecessarily from the more important preventive and promotive work of the health staff (i.e., primary care, including mobile activities). The few beds available at health centres should be utilized basically for maternity and holding purposes only. Putting a limit to the number of beds available for inpatients should also lead to a significant saving in recurrent costs: in particular the number of bedside nurses required will be limited, as will the service or "hotel" aspect of the health centre. The number of beds required by any given health centre will be affected by the proximity of a hospital to the centre. In general, where hospitals, however inadequate or overcrowded, are close to health centres, less use will be made of the inpatient facilities at the centres. Be that as it may, it is usually the case that the fewer the number of beds assigned to a health centre, the more efficient its operation is likely to be.

These patterns can be observed not only in developing countries but also, for example, in the recently established network of health centres in Finland.

(a) Hospitals

In developing countries, a great variety of institutions carry the name "hospital". They vary from institutions deep in the countryside with 30 or fewer beds to buildings in capital cities with 2000 or more beds. At the simplest level they are generally known as district or rural hospitals: at the next (middle) level come regional or provincial or state hospitals, and at the highest level supraregional or national referral institutions. In addition, there are special facilities for such diseases as tuberculosis, leprosy, and mental illness. The ownership/and management possibilities for these different institutions are very wide. The public sector includes both smaller and larger institutions, often run by different organs of government, i.e., central government and local authorities. In addition, many hospitals are run by mission or church organizations, others are connected to industrial concerns (often in the special insurance sector), yet others are run for the armed forces and police and sometimes for railroad or other special government employees, and some are operated entirely as private profit-making institutions.

Many of these hospitals are used for the teaching of nurses and other paramedical and auxiliary staff. A few of the larger ones are used for the teaching of medical students and sometimes managed as part of the university system. The range of hospitals takes in the simplest rural institutions that still retain the original locally built premises, as well as extremely sophisticated and costly institutions.

Surveys in the African Region have shown that the so-called national referral hospitals may draw 90% or more of their inpatients from the larger cities, in which they are located. Regional or provincial hospitals are likely to draw about half their patients from the medium-sized towns in which they are to be found, and the situation for district hospitals is not dissimilar.

Every urban hospital draws virtually all outpatients from the town in which it is located. The unequal allocation of resources in the health sector results mainly from unequal accessibility of hospitals. This is less true where medical referral rather than self-referral is the norm.

Basically, planning for the construction of additional hospitals must take into account the pattern of the existing lower-level institutions and the possibility of referral from these institutions to the hospitals under consideration. To go ahead with new hospitals in the absence of improved possibilities of referral would only increase the existing investment in the health care of limited urban populations and delay even further the possibility of developing improved health services in the countryside.

Very often considerably more is spent on hospital construction than is warranted. Hospitals are generally built in accordance with one basic standard, with all wards substantially the same, except perhaps for a small intensive care unit. However, most hospital inpatients do not require either sophisticated care or a "grand hotel" standard of accommodation; in fact, most require relatively little care during the major part of their stay in hospital. There is very often a tendency to keep patients in hospital longer than is needed for strictly medical reasons, as it is often not possible to discharge them, even when they are medically fit, if there is no satisfactory place for them to go after leaving the hospital. The same problem arises with regard to a number of patients who need to be near medical care (say, for a daily drug) but do not require a hospital bed as such. Suitable alternatives to conventional hospital wards need to be developed if the present high running costs are to be reduced. One of the most important alternatives is the patient hostel. Such hostels could cater for perhaps 25–50% of all hospital inpatients, especially those who are retained at hospital more for social or administrative convenience than for essentially medical reasons.

Such hostels might or might not supply food to patients, who could in any event prepare it and feed themselves: patients might also be primarily responsible for their own laundry. The staff requirements for such hostels would be negligible. A similar hostel arrangement could be developed for the normal maternity delivery unit which would make use of staff only for assistance at the time of delivery itself, the prospective mothers being responsible for preparing their own food, doing their own laundry, and the like.

The general question of maintenance of equipment is an important one and has been much neglected. The situation with regard to maintenance is difficult enough even in large cities, and in small district hospitals it becomes an especially serious problem. It would be useful for countries to have one or more centres for the maintenance of hospital and health equipment. These could take responsibility for training workers in the maintenance and repair of basic equipment such as that used in hospital kitchens and laundries, as well as X-ray equipment, and other simpler and more robust equipment for use in remoter areas.

(b) *Distribution of hospital beds*

The achievement of a proper balance between inpatient care and other forms of care in overall health service development is essential to successful health planning. With increasing possibilities for referral, i.e., greater geographical and economic accessibility of hospital beds, there is an increasing need to determine more precisely the balance that should be sought between the different levels of health facility. However, the situation in most developing countries at present is that the hospital sector, particularly as regards large hospitals, is already overexpanded relative to other health facilities (although perhaps still not adequate to meet conventional "demand"). At this stage it is necessary in most countries, including the developed ones, to accept existing bed/population ratios and to concentrate further health facility development at the health centre and subcentre levels.

It may be useful to point out that the acceptance of existing bed/population ratios need not make hospital beds less accessible for most or even many of the population. Because a policy of "unlimited" bed development often leads in practice to the extension of the larger urban hospitals, those already enjoying the greatest degree of hospital accessibility are likely to benefit disproportionately from it. However, if a constant bed/population ratio, calculated on a national basis, is accepted for some years to come, it will still be possible to add to the number of hospital beds in a country at a rate of perhaps 2–3% per annum (equivalent to population growth). Most of the additional hospital beds would, in fact, be at smaller district and regional institutions and relatively few, if any, at the larger state and national ones.

Time series data for countries in which 50% of the world's population reside show that the number of hospital beds increased from 8.7 million in 1960 to 11.5 million in 1975, corresponding to bed densities of 43 and 45 per 10 000 population, respectively. There are wide disparities between countries, regions, and continents, as shown in the following table:

Continent or group of countries	Hospital beds per 10 000 population		Percentage of 1975 population included
	1960	1975	
Africa	14	15	77
Americas[a]	61	45	94
Asia	7	10	45
Europe	87	95	98
Oceania	115	118	85
USSR	81	118	100
Developed countries	87	95	89
Developing countries	11	14	56
—least developed countries	7	8	60

[a] The decrease observed in bed density is due to a decrease in the number of beds in long-term hospitals, such as tuberculosis and mental hospitals, in some countries (for instance Canada and the USA).

Very low bed densities are reported for Western Africa and Middle South Asia (fewer than 10 beds per 10 000 population).

In 1975, bed density in all developed countries for which data are available was more than 50; in over half of them the ratio even exceeded 100 per 10 000 population. In two-thirds of the developing countries, on the other hand, bed density was less than 50 per 10 000 population and, in 16 countries, where almost a thousand million people (or 23% of the world's population) live, it was even less than 10.

Bed occupancy rates vary widely from one country to another. In developed countries, the occupancy rates are usually relatively high. In developing countries, however, substantial differences are to be found and, in some instances, surprisingly low occupancy rates are reported (less than 20%). Bed occupancy ratios are largely determined by the availability as well as the accessibility of beds: it is well established that health service supply creates its own demand. Under conditions of bed shortage, it will be possible to admit fewer patients and these will have to remain in hospital for shorter periods than would otherwise be the case. A greater number of beds relative to population (and the accessibility of those beds to the population in both geographical and financial terms) will mean a larger volume of admissions and a greater average stay. In most situations, underutilization of hospital beds results either from a relative excess of beds to population or an unwillingness on the part of the population to utilize the beds for various reasons such as a persistent lack of drugs or of competent staff at the hospital. The picture is similar with regard to the annual number of hospital admissions per 10 000 population. These are usually above 1000 in developed countries (in many of them often considerably more), whereas in developing countries very high rates (more than 2000 per 10 000 population) are found side by side with very low ones (100 or less). Such statistics offer a starting-point for investigations in depth rather than a basis for policy-making. The inadequacy of the numerical information shows the urgent need for a drastic overhaul of traditional statistics.

In selecting the precise sites for new facilities within allotted districts, additional questions arise. Here, too, the principle of equal accessibility should be followed by taking into account the location of populations in relationship to newly planned facilities. At this level it is the district planners who would know best where to site an additional facility, since they would be informed on such matters as local transport possibilities, tribal and linguistic relationships, and seasonal "flooding". The decision to extend new facilities to those living beyond reasonable reach of existing facilities, in terms of travel time, may be made at the cost of greater overcrowding at existing facilities, which may be accessible to a greater number of people than they can comfortably serve. This is an area in which planners at the centre, including geographical experts, can offer technical guidance to those working at district level.

Financial aspects

(a) Expenditure: developed countries

The period under review has been marked by heightened discussion of the relationship between expenditure on health care, the nature of health services, and health status. In the developed countries discussion has centred around the need to contain very rapidly rising health care costs that are apparently unjustified by demographic change. At the same time, there is a growing body of evidence that casts doubt on the likelihood of a positive relationship between further expenditure on health care and improved health status.

Spending on health care in the developed countries is now of the order of 5–9% of the gross national product. In the USA, health care costs, mainly in the form of expenditure on hospitals, have been growing at about twice the rate of national inflation.

Two factors in particular have been singled out as possible cost containment factors: the technology for the delivery of health care, and the methods used to finance health care services. The latter factor will be discussed later. As regards the former, emphasis has been placed on the increased use of various paramedical and auxiliary personnel, the limitation of the overall number of personnel, limitations on the construction of new hospitals, reductions in the actual number of hospital beds, and restraints on the introduction of expensive new equipment, pharmaceutical products, and medical techniques, which might, in any event, be only marginally better than those already in use. In fact, many of these innovations have—usually rather unexpected—negative implications for the overall development of the health services that may overshadow any potential gain.

(b) Expenditure: developing countries

Although some of the same questions have been debated in the developing countries as in the developed ones, notably that of the relationship between increased expenditure on health care and improved health status, the setting is very different, i.e., one in which far less is being spent on health care, both in absolute terms and as a percentage of the national product. Although some developing countries may be spending as much as 4% of their gross national product on health care, 2–3% is far more usual. (These percentages of the gross national product should not, of course, be confused with the national governmental budgets which may show expenditures in the health sector of 10% or more.) It should be noted that the figures just given refer almost entirely to modern "western" types of medical care and do not take expenditure on other types of care, e.g., traditional care, into account.

It is important to note that in a great many countries 2–3% of the gross national product represents as little as US $ 4–6, which, even allowing for a wide difference in purchasing power, is a very small sum indeed.

Because of the very small size of these health budgets in absolute figures, attention in the past tended to concentrate on the lack of resources for health services development. Now, however, it is becoming clear that even a fairly rapid growth in health sector budgets, which is almost certainly required, would only bring them to levels that still could not possibly provide care based on high technology for the majority of the population. For example, if a country in which the equivalent of US $ 5 per capita is now being spent on health care were to increase its health spending in real terms (over and above inflation) by the extremely high rate of 10% per annum, it would in the year 2000 still be spending only around US $ 40 per capita, or less than 5% of the amount spent in the USA two decades earlier (1979–1980).

With growing awareness of the sheer magnitude of the problem of health service resources, increasing attention is being paid to the development of more appropriate means for the delivery of health care. There are two main aspects. One is the reorganization of conventional health care delivery systems so that they will concentrate on the allocation of resources in ways that are consistent with existing limitations. In practice, this means changing the "production function" for the output of units of health care, e.g., carrying out specific health service activities far less expensively through the use of, for example, more appropriate manpower, pharmaceuticals, technology, buildings, and methods of organization, the guiding principle being reasonably complete coverage of the population with the most basic of health service inputs; for example, personal preventive activities such as immunizations, environmental activities relating to clean water and the disposal of wastes, and ambulatory curative care.

The other central issue is the mobilization of the population in the struggle to improve its own health status. This is necessary not only in keeping with worldwide ideas of social justice, but as the most effective means of liberating the vast potential for resource development inherent in community organization everywhere.

(c) Financing health care

The methods by which health services are financed are basic determinants of their quantity, quality, distribution, and, of course, impact on people. The personnel, facilities, and supplies used for the treatment or prevention of disease must be paid for in some way. Methods of financing are highly variable both among and within countries. The most common financing mechanisms are personal payment, charity, payment by employers, voluntary and social insurance, local community self-help efforts, and general government revenues.

Personal payment for health care generally means that health services are distributed, like any other marketable commodity, on the basis of individual purchasing power rather than that of health needs. In general, individuals with greater purchasing power obtain more services. Personal payment for health services exist to some degrees in all countries, even in those with highly socialized economies. Hardly anywhere, however, is this the main method of payment. A major problem with regard to private payments for health care, particularly in developing countries, is that only very limited information is available about its extent and effects.

Charitable donations, often inspired by religious motives, have supported health services for the poor for centuries. Philanthropic and religious foundations continue to offer charitable support for health services, often through the religious missions that exist in many developing countries.

Economic production requires healthy manpower, and large enterprises have therefore found it efficient to provide certain health services for their employees. In industrialized countries, the general health care needs of workers are usually taken care of by the overall health system, and enterprises finance only the care of on-the-job injuries or illnesses, plus work safety programmes. However, when industries are located in isolated areas, for example, mines, lumber companies, or railroad construction projects, general medical care for the workers is often organized by the employers. In developing countries large enterprises, often foreign-owned, provide support for general health services for workers. In socialist countries with centrally planned economies, health services at the place of work have traditionally been provided on a broad scale.

Some countries are trying to promote the maximum self-reliance in local rural communities by creating locally controlled and financed health programmes enjoying the support of the overall national health care system. This approach has been especially effective in promoting preventive programmes as part of the extension of primary health care. Communities can make significant contributions to the construction of health stations, water supply systems, etc., by donating labour and materials. They also provide a basis for locally controlled and managed health services. National examples of this can be found in Bangladesh, India, Niger, and Venezuela. Families sometimes form a health cooperative, contributing funds to a sort of prepaid system. An important feature of these arrangements is that the financial contribution of the local people gives them both the right and the incentive to participate in the running of the programme.

Voluntary insurance supports medical services with funds raised through periodic personal contributions by groups of people before sickness occurs. Sickness insurance or mutual benefit societies rapidly became widespread in Europe in the nineteenth century. In some countries the societies defined eligibility for membership along religious or political lines. Some sickness benefit societies engage one or more doctors to provide care for members for fixed monthly payments. A different pattern emerged in the USA when commercial insurance companies began to sell group life insurance or funeral coverage to all the workers in any particular firm. These insurance policies were sometimes partially financed by the employers. In 1934 the American Hospital Association backed the idea of certain professions pooling small periodic contributions to build a fund (Blue Cross) that would pay the cost of hospitalization for any member who needed it. This pattern of insurance, sponsored by the providers of health care and by private insurance companies, instead of the consumers, has remained unique in the world.

A widely used strategy for increasing the allocation of funds to the health sector has been the introduction of compulsory health insurance. Starting with the industrialized nations of Europe in the nineteenth century, the concept spread to Japan in 1922, to Chile in 1924, and since then to most developing countries in Latin America and the Mediterranean area, and to some other parts of the world. Because funds are raised by new taxes on workers and employers, parliamentary bodies have been generally more favourable to this approach (in spite of the fact that sometimes there is also a considerable government contribution) than to one that would make further claims on the general revenue of the nation. From the workers' point of view, this method of financing ensures the employee, and often the employee's dependants, certain health services as a right rather than a favour dependent upon the generosity of government or charity. In the developed countries of Western Europe, more than 90% of the population is covered. In developing countries, however, there is usually only a small proportion of the national population with regular paid employment and thus with wages subject to social security deductions (about 5–10%). The fraction of the population benefiting from compulsory health insurance programmes has been correspondingly small. With relatively ample funds available, the services provided for insured persons are generally superior in both quantity and quality to those at the disposal of the major part of the population. With occasional exceptions, agricultural workers and peasants are not protected by programmes of this type. The social security approach has accordingly been seriously criticized for failing to achieve equity in the overall distribution of health services. Because this approach reserves extra funds for workers concentrated in the larger cities, it is argued that the maldistribution of resources between urban and rural areas is aggravated and the large rural populations of developing countries are even more handicapped than they were before. For example, it is claimed that it is made more difficult for ministries of health attempting to serve the whole of national populations to recruit the personnel they require. In addition, the entire national health effort may tend to become even more heavily biased towards curative activities. Moreover, in many countries the government is either paying contributions as an employer or subsidizing related social security systems (for example, health insurance schemes for civil servants). In the case of subsidies there is a danger that the burden of government participation may have to be largely borne by the most underprivileged categories of the population in the form of taxes, often indirect ones levied on everyday necessities.

The social security approach can, however, be assessed in other ways. Although population coverage by such schemes in developing countries is essentially small, the tendency is often towards more extended coverage, even though progress to this end may be slow. Social security can add to a nation's stock of hospitals and health centres. In Latin America, where social insurance programmes for medical care have been launched in nearly every country, they have been associated with rapid increases in the output of physicians, nurses, and other health personnel, but particularly in that of physicians. Social security brings extra funds to the health sector and channels them into organized services. One study of 12 Latin American countries with social security programmes has suggested that they in no way weaken the programmes of ministries of health but tend rather to be independent. There is a widespread consensus that social security programmes should be coordinated as closely as possible with the activities of ministries of health and should be planned as part of the overall national system of health care.

General revenues for the support of government health services may come from various forms of taxation—on land, incomes, sales, the profits of companies, imports, or the like. The taxes may be levied by different levels of government: national, provincial, local, or other. In many developed countries there was a tendency, once social insurance systems became well established, to shift the costs increasingly or wholly to general revenues. One of the best known examples of such a shift from national health insurance to a national health service is provided by the United Kingdom, where health insurance for industrial workers was replaced, after the Second World War, by the concept of government responsibility for medical care. Many other developed countries have followed a similar path. In the USSR, funding through social insurance channels continued for many years after the Revolution, and it was only in 1937 that the whole health service began to be financed from general revenue, mostly from the productive industries sector. Today, not only all personal health services, both curative and preventive, but also all building facilities, professional education, and medical research are run by the Government as part of the overall health system. There has been a similar evolution in other socialist countries of Eastern Europe. In Cuba, the voluntary "Mutualista" health insurance programme continued for many years after the 1959 Revolution. Not until about 1970 was the whole Cuban health service brought under a unified system of financing from general revenue. In China, this evolution is not yet complete, and health care is at present financed through a variety of local, compulsory, or voluntary insurance programmes and, in some cases, through private payments. In the developing countries, a substantial share of central government resources are used to finance public hospitals and health centres run by the ministry of health. Some population groups are traditional beneficiaries of health care supported by general revenue, nearly always at the national level, an example being the armed forces. In many countries the military medical services are well above the level of those available to the general population. Another special category of the population consists of persons with diseases deemed to constitute a general threat to the community so that the State feels obliged to finance their care. Serious mental disorders, tuberculosis requiring hospital care, and leprosy usually fall into this category.

Traditionally, general preventive health services are supported by tax funds. In many developing countries there are national government campaigns against malaria, schisto-somiasis, filariasis, cholera, and other infectious diseases. Preventive services in maternal and child health, dealing mainly with the personal health care of expectant mothers and small children, are offered in tax-financed clinics or health stations throughout the world.

Payment mechanisms could determine or control growth of expenditure. Some of the main issues at present under study in many countries are: modes of payment; programme budgeting; price controls; ceilings on the percentage growth of physician incomes, social security incomes, and government subsidies; lists of cheap drugs.

To sum up, it can be stated that there are many variations existing within each of the major methods of financing health care. Although approaches are becoming less indi-vidualistic and fragmented and more organized and cooperative, all the methods listed above are utilized in the majority of countries in providing health services for certain sectors of the population or for dealing with certain diseases, but in greatly varying proportions. On the whole it appears that economic support for health services is becoming more of a publicly organized and supported activity. Private payments are playing a relatively smaller role, whereas social insurance and general tax revenues are playing a relatively larger one.

Information on the volume and sources of governmental and quasigovernmental expenditure on health services is usually available in developing countries, though systematic information is seldom available about the private sector. The information base has to be more refined in industrialized countries than in developing ones, since options for health care development will differ less dramatically in expected costs and benefits. There are considerable variations among countries regarding the proportion of resources made available for health activities in the public sector. In some places, the budget of the ministry of health and other activities dealing with health has been increasing at the same rate as the overall government budget; in others, there is stagnation and even regression. The budget of the ministry of health is often organized in a way that precludes comparisons with national health policies in a number of less developed countries. However, there is one pattern that is valid almost everywhere, namely that of available funds being spent disproportionately in urban areas and for curative services, to the disadvantage of the rural areas and other services, e.g., promo-tive, preventive, and rehabilitative. Medical care funds are mostly committed to the recurrent expenditures of hospitals and only limited amounts can be reallocated to new objectives—for instance, primary health care. Foreign aid is an important source of financing in some countries, notably as regards expenditure on capital development. In many cases, the expenditure patterns are at variance with the expressed goals of national health policy. The provision of funds for new hospitals adds to the problem of meeting the recurrent costs of such institutions. Continuity and regularity are important requirements for foreign aid and, in the absence of medium- or longer-term commitments on the part of donors, national planning becomes more difficult.[1]

A study of the budgets of the ministries of health of 14 African countries showed that in only two of them, between 1970 and 1974, did the health budget grow more rapidly than the overall government budget. In 12 other countries it lagged behind the overall increase in the government budget.

For more effective planning the full range of sources of financing for the health sector would have to be taken into consideration, i.e., not only government expenditure and social security but health funds spent by other national authorities such as those concerned with, for example, public works, education, defence, and prisons; furthermore, private payments made by individuals, charitable donations (including missionary and similar forms of aid), and voluntary health insurance contributions should also be taken into account. There is considerable evidence that, in many developing countries, the private sector—the bulk of which is in traditional medicine—represents more than half of all expenditure on health care. Only if planning is not restricted to the ministry of health's budget, and the private sector is not left to develop in response to unconstrained market forces, have health plans a prospect of success. Several governments and research institutions have realized this fact and started to act on it by initiating studies; other relevant action includes the reorganization by a number of countries of their actual service and planning systems. It is believed that low-cost methods for estimating both sources of financing and expenditure in the health sector can be developed for policy purposes, even with a relatively weak data base. For instance, one such analysis, carried out in connexion with a country health programming exercise, has shown that in Bangladesh in 1975–1976 the health services received 4.3% of total current government expenditure. In Botswana, the total expenditure on health in 1976 came to about 5.3% of the gross domestic product, and the percentage of expenditure on health services as a proportion of total government expenditure increased from 5.9% in 1973–1974 to 7% in 1976–1977.

On the basis of *ad hoc* estimates and financing and expenditure surveys carried out in developing countries, it is believed that information of sufficient reliability can be collected at modest cost, even for the private sector. Such surveys can become part of the regular activities of government planning groups. While new funds should be allocated in accordance with health policies, planners will have to take into account the effects of past methods of financing and expanding health sector resources. The analysis of trends in the sources of financing for health services and the breakdown of expenditure on specific services in different geographical areas constitutes one of the necessary inputs for determining the most effective way of using scanty resources and for mobilizing health resources and activities in other sectors of society.

---

[1] WHO Technical Report Series, No. 625, 1978 (*Financing of health services.* Report of a WHO Study Group), p. 29.

Chapter 5

Research

Introduction

Biomedical and health services research spans a wide range of activities, from funda-mental laboratory research to community field trials, and it represents an important part of the worldwide enterprise of research and development generally, in the context of which certain pertinent generalizations and comparisons can be made.

The total world investment in research and development is estimated at US $150 000 million, and involves 3 million scientists and engineers.[1] The geographical distribution of the investment reflects the worldwide distribution of research and development capability, which in turn closely mirrors the world's distribution of economic power.

The global expenditure on health research is estimated at 7% of the world's total for research and development and follows similar distribution trends. Consequently, in financial terms, about 95% of all health research takes place in the economically developed countries and is primarily geared to the problems of those countries. Nevertheless, the results of such research have also had, and will continue to have, direct and practical implications for the solution of many of the health problems facing mankind as a whole.

Health research is critically important for the achievement of national development goals, and developing countries need to build up a research potential and progressively enhance their research capabilities. Already, there are promising trends which combine research capability-strengthening with goal-oriented health research directed primarily to the major health problems of developing countries. Initiatives of this kind are described below.

Substantial advances have been made through research in the biomedical sciences since the Fifth Report on the World Health Situation, and a large volume of such research continues throughout the world. Detailed information on its nature may very well have special appeal and interest in its own right, and the World Health Organization may therefore need to consider the feasibility and indeed the cost/benefit aspects of taking a more active coordinating role in bringing together data on the scope of worldwide biomedical and health services research. However, for the present World Health Situation Report, attention is focused mainly on trends—trends in the process of

---

[1] NORMAN, C. *Knowledge and power: the global research and development budget,* Worldwatch Paper No. 31, July 1979.

global health research development and trends in a limited number of research areas selected to provide illustrative examples of the implications for the future of world health.

Global health research development

The phenomenal growth in the complexity and scope of biomedical and health services research has had two major implications. First, there is now a compelling necessity for a multidisciplinary team approach to research which demands a high level of organization and coordination; and secondly, the rapidly rising costs of research have increased the need for, and dependence upon, funding from public sources. Consequently, there is a growing demand for health research that is directly relevant to the health problems of society and a pressing challenge to governments and society itself to clarify these problems and establish priorities for their solution.

At the national level, the pattern of health research organization that has evolved in response to these trends naturally varies from country to country. In some cases, one central body is charged with the responsibility of defining objectives and assigning priorities; in other cases, several agencies both governmental and nongovernmental are involved in the process. However, in many other countries, especially in the developing world, there is as yet no effective national organization for the management of health research, though there is a notable trend to develop such mechanisms and to define national focal points for cooperation in international health research.

At the international level similar trends have aroused growing concern over the disparities in the research and development investments between developed and developing countries and have focused attention on the need for coordinated global research efforts that are relevant to worldwide health problems.

Against this background the World Health Organization has reexamined and reorganized its research promotion and development activities and their mechanisms of operation. A network of one global and six regional advisory committees on medical research has been established, comprising a total of about 100 scientists all over the world who have shown their capacity to identify major health research problems and mount appropriate research programmes. Although the level of funding remains modest, there is evidence that this network has had a stimulatory effect on biomedical and health services research.

Through this advisory network a number of priorities, e.g., health services research, nutrition and diarrhoeal diseases, have ben identified for collaborative research on a global scale. In addition, certain research-related topics such as information dissemination, ethics of medical research, and research administration are receiving due attention.

There are, of course, many other areas of health research that are susceptible to the global approach, e.g., cancer epidemiology, mental health research and community-based cardiovascular disease prevention trials. Some of these global activities and trends are reported more fully in the special sections that follow.

The long-term prospects for global health development will ultimately depend on the availability of human as well as financial resources and on the extent to which the developing countries themselves acquire the research capability to meet many of their own health research needs. Basically, both these conditions will require the type of international cooperation that goes somewhat beyond the mere transfer of science and technology; clearly, it must also be concerned with the need to strengthen the local base into which the imported technology is to be adapted, integrated and absorbed and on which indigenous technology is to be developed.

In this connexion, the Guidelines for international scientific cooperation for development prepared by the Pugwash workshop in 1978[1] are pertinent. The recommendations include sections for the guidance of governments and scientists of both developing and developed countries, for funding agencies and governments, and a final section on international cooperation under the auspices of international and regional organizations. The Pugwash Guidelines are based on the consideration that international scientific cooperation for development should involve: (a) the promotion of values and a motivation system conducive to such cooperation; (b) the assumption by the developing countries and developed countries of the responsibility—individually and collectively—to promote conditions which will enable developing countries to follow a self-reliant strategy in science and technology; (c) ensuring that the security of developing countries (political, military, economic, etc.) is not jeopardized; and (d) further strengthening of mutual trust and confidence between developed countries and developing country scientists.

International cooperation in health research in such areas as human reproduction, tropical diseases and diarrhoeal diseases goes far towards fulfilling these criteria.

Trends in global health research

National health problems and support for research to solve them are issues which must ultimately be perceived in the context of national political and social priorities. This is as true for a "war upon cancer" in an industrially developed country as it is for field research to alleviate the health hazards of new irrigation or hydroelectric systems in a developing country. Over US $3000 million have been, and continue to be invested each year in solutions to the priority health problems of the developed world; but at the same time, chloroquine-resistant malaria continues to spread and the prevalence of schistosomiasis continues to increase.

The constraints upon health research in developing countries are compounded by the magnitude of the health problems, the urgent need for action in the social and economic sectors and, above all, by the overall deficiency in research manpower, institutions and funds. And yet the health problems requiring research are staggering, ranging from applied field research to meet the primary health care needs of rural villagers to research into the molecular structure of the membranes of parasites to determine their defences against the immune mechanisms of the host so that vaccines against the disease can be developed. Mechanisms to meet the basic health and nutritional needs of thousands of millions of people must be worked out and methods must be developed to prevent or control such scourges as the tropical diseases, which afflict or threaten over one thousand million of the world's population.

---

[1] Guidelines for international scientific cooperation for development, *Pugwash newsletter*, Vol. 15, No. 4. May 1978.

Recent advances in immunology and molecular biology have stimulated renewed interest in the possibility of developing vaccines against certain tropical diseases. In the immunology of leprosy a strategic plan for the development of a simple immunodiagnostic test and for a vaccine has been drawn up. The research work towards both objectives is being carried out in a network of laboratories spanning a wide geographical area, from Venezuela, through North America, Western Europe, the USSR and Asia to Japan. These scientists are working together on the agreed plan, using standard protocols and jointly producing and sharing the scant supplies of the crude antigen derived from a recently available source in armadillos infected with the disease.[1]

In the field of malaria research, experiments in animal models have indicated that vaccines may be produced from practically all stages of the parasite in man, i.e., sporozoites, schizonts, gametocytes and merozoites. Recent progress in the continuous cultivation of the malarial parasite *Plasmodium falciparum* has given impetus to the possibility of developing a merozoite vaccine. Other experiments indicate that irradiated and formol-killed gametocytes injected into the blood stream can produce changes in gametocytes of infected individuals, so that, when these are taken up by the mosquito, sporogony does not develop and transmission is interrupted. This is an interesting observation but further work is required before it is known whether it will be a practical proposition. The stages of progress of these various approaches to malaria vaccine development vary at the present time and there are still many questions to be answered before a vaccine becomes a practical possibility acceptable for use in human populations.

Drug treatment of tropical diseases has not been neglected and a number of important advances have been made. Schistosomiasis research over the last few years has affected chemotherapy more than any other field and, with the advent of more effective and less toxic drugs, this form of control is playing and will continue to play an increasing role. The most recent and striking advance in this field relates to the use of praziquantel, a drug which possesses most of the desired criteria for the ideal schistosomicide, particularly for *Schistosoma haematobium* infections. This new chemotherapeutic compound is a highly significant advance both in the treatment of the individual patients with any of the three most common forms of schistosomiasis and in the control of the disease in populations of endemic areas.[2]

For the treatment and control of filariasis, trypanosomiasis and leishmaniasis there have been few therapeutic advances recently, but active programmes of chemotherapeutic research and drug screening are in progress.

Research in fertility regulation and infertility

Reproduction is more than a physiological phenomenon: it is conditioned by behavioural, social, and cultural factors and has profound economic and political repercussions. As might be expected, its regulation is equally complex at both personal and societal

[1] *Leprosy: Cultivation of etiologic agent, immunology, animal models*; proceedings of the workshop on future problems in the microbiology of *M. leprae*, Caracas, 12–15 October 1976. Washington DC, Pan American Health Organization, 1977 (Scientific Publication No. 342).

[2] DAVIES, A., & WENGER, D. H. G. Multicentre trials of praziquantel in human schistosomiasis: design and techniques. *Bulletin of the World Health Organization*, **57**: 767–771 (1979).

levels. It is mainly in the past decade that this interaction has gained full recognition and has been reflected in research, which has become increasingly multidisciplinary.

The current main issues in research on fertility regulation and infertility are: the assessment of the safety and efficacy of current methods of fertility regulation; improvement of current methods and the development of new techniques; determination of the extent of the problem of infertility worldwide, and improvement in its prevention, diagnosis and treatment; and appropriate delivery of family planning care.

Safety of current methods of fertility regulation. Experience with modern methods of birth control, such as hormonal contraceptives and intrauterine devices, only extends over a relatively short period of time—less than ten years for most of the preparations and devices currently used—yet they are already employed by hundreds of millions of women and men, if one includes vasectomy. Although their short-term sequelae have been relatively well studied in developed countries, little is known about their effects in developing country populations, who differ in health status, genetic constitution, diet, reproductive patterns, etc. Some problems are specific to developing countries, for instance the effects of contraceptive drugs in the presence of endemic malaria or chronic undernutrition.

Less is known about the long-term sequelae of birth control methods, although some information—for instance, on cardiovascular risks from hormonal contraceptives—have emerged from studies in North America and Europe. The main areas of uncertainty relate to possible risks of congenital malformations in later progeny and to neoplasia.

Research on these issues is being pursued, mainly through medical research councils, in developed countries. In developing countries, a major stimulus has been given to them by the WHO Special Programme of Research, Development and Research Training in Human Reproduction. In this area, as well as those described below, the Programme brings together the talents and skills of scientists from 70 countries, of which 45 are developing countries. A major effort of this Programme also goes into strengthening of the research capabilities of developing countries.

New methods of fertility regulation. Although present birth control technology represents a great improvement over that was available 30 years ago, it has limitations with respect to efficacy, safety and acceptability. Moreover, the choice of methods fails to meet the wide range of individual needs, cultural requirements and service constraints.

Although there is widely expressed demand for better birth control technology, particularly for the primary health care setting, the global effort devoted to this is very small. Industry is relatively inactive because of the long time required for the testing of new methods of fertility regulation, and the high cost of development. This is due to the particularly stringent toxicological requirements for these drugs or devices that are used largely by healthy populations over long periods of time.

Methods at present under development, some at the clinical testing phase, others still at the stage of mission-oriented biological and chemical research, include intrauterine devices and injectable contraceptives that avoid the side-effects of the present devices and drugs, once-a-week and once-a-month pills, long-acting vaginal barrier methods, simple kits for the prediction of the fertile period, drugs for abortion, nonsurgical methods of female sterilization, birth control vaccines and drugs for the control of male fertility.

Family planning care. The large numbers of people for whom family planning care services have to be provided, the newness of these services and the psychological and cultural sensitivities associated with family planning have raised a number of behavioural and managerial issues that require research. These are particularly acute for services in developing countries, with their already overburdened resources.

The need for research is very great, not only because of the variety of questions to be answered, but because it is difficult to extrapolate results from one setting for application in another. The motivation for family planning, and the perceptions of couples about methods, their efficacy and side effects are still largely unknown. The lack of trained personnel in developing countries has stimulated operational studies on the training and supervision of non-physicians for activities such as the insertion of intrauterine devices or even surgical sterilization. Another subject for research is how best to involve the community in decision-making on family planning services.

Infertility is estimated to affect between 5% and 10% of couples all over the world, but in some developing countries its prevalence is alleged to be much higher. There is little sound epidemiological data on its prevalence and etiology. Moreover, infertility remains an aspect of health care that is thwarted by lack of standard definitions and by questionable diagnostic and therapeutic procedures.

Industry is active in the study of new therapeutic drugs, but other aspects of research on infertility are mostly carried out in an *ad hoc* fashion in clinical departments. WHO is launching a major epidemiological and clinical research effort, accompanied by standardization of terms and procedures.

Trends in cardiovascular diseases research

Geographical differences in the prevalence of heart disease and the role of economic, behavioural and other pyschosocial factors in its causation have stimulated the development of international and global efforts in cardiovascular disease research. In the 1970's cardiovascular disease research was characterized by new advances in the understanding of the etiology and pathogenesis of different cardiovascular diseases, and by the strengthening of efforts to apply present scientific knowledge in daily medical practice. Cardiovascular disease prevention and control programmes carried out at the community level—very often integrated in existing systems of health care delivery—became an essential part of the research in most countries active in this field.

Atherosclerosis. In the efforts to elucidate the etiology and pathogenesis of atherosclerosis, significant progress has been made in lipoprotein research. The lipoproteins transport lipids in the blood. Recently, by determining the structure of the protein portion of lipoprotein apoenzymes (apoproteins), it was possible to define how the apoenzymes bind lipids, which may have therapeutic implications for the future.

There is renewed interest in the role of high density lipoproteins (HDL) in the pathogenesis of coronary heart disease. New laboratory, clinical, and specifically epidemiological studies corroborated the evidence that with increasing serum levels of HDL the risk of coronary heart disease decreases. Further, recent research on HDL suggests that this lipoprotein might play a part in the removal of cholesterol from the arterial wall or prevent its deposit there. However, it is still not known whether, by deliberately increasing HDL cholesterol levels, it would be possible to inhibit the eventual

213

development of atherosclerosis in humans. The recent development of a new, noninvasive technique using ultrasound methods to show up atherosclerotic lesions in the arterial wall is an important achievement likely to be of great significance in advancing knowledge through clinical as well as preventive (screening) studies.

There are certain new promising developments in research on atherogenesis related to interaction of blood platelets and arterial wall. Further studies on prostacyclines which, among many other functions, inhibit platelet aggregation, have provided new insight into possibilities of intervention in the atherogenetic process. They strengthen the theory that plaque development starts by injury of the vessel wall. If confirmed, these findings would have great significance in the prevention and control of different cardiovascular diseases.

The epidemiological aspects of atherosclerosis research have not been neglected, and great attention is being paid to studies of atherosclerosis precursors in childhood. However, the following questions need to be answered. How early in life do atherosclerotic lesions develop? Which early lesions progress to give rise to adult atherosclerosis? What are the environmental and genetic determinants that cause such changes? To answer these questions, current research is oriented towards determining the respective roles of breast-feeding and processed baby-foods; serum cholesterol levels in children; obesity; sodium intake; physiological and personal characteristics that are related to increased risks of atherosclerosis; dietary factors; social and cultural factors; parental history of cardiovascular diseases.

Coronary heart disease. Clinical investigations, trials and preventive and control programmes carried out at the community level are being used widely in clarification of the role of diet, thrombosis, high blood pressure and smoking in the etiology and genesis of cardiovascular diseases generally. The possibility of influencing the progress of these diseases is being tested by intervention trials.

Great attention is devoted to the problems related to sudden death, which is responsible for approximately 40% of all mortality due to coronary heart disease. The recent analysis of pathological findings in victims of sudden cardiac death showed that most of them had coronary heart disease; however, in only a very low percentage of the cases could acute thrombosis or recent myocardial infarction be shown. The significance of arrhythmias and "unstable angina" in causing sudden death has been studied; however, results are not conclusive.

The role of "beta-bockers" such as propranolol, used in the treatment of arrhythmias, angina pectoris and hypertension, in preventing sudden death is also being systematically studied; it has been shown that in patients being treated with beta-blockers the incidence of sudden death is substantially lower.

Promising results have been achieved in feasibility studies related to administration of aspirin to men and women who have had at least one acute myocardial infarction with the objective to prevent recurrences. These studies are now being carried out on a much larger scale.

In attempts to prevent coronary heart disease and its complications certain drugs lowering blood lipids have been studied. The results of the clofibrate and nicotinic acid studies show that both drugs had undesirable side effects, and therefore their use is not recommended in primary prevention of coronary heart disease in large population groups.

There are numerous intervention studies being carried out in many countries in different parts of the world, aiming at reducing several coronary heart disease risk factors (mainly hypertension, smoking, high blood cholesterol levels) in high-risk subjects, and assessing the impact of these changes on the incidence of events due to ischaemic heart disease (IHD) or the incidence of stroke. In general, the preliminary results show that it is feasible, through well-planned intervention programmes, to reduce the risk factors in the populations studied. While it is too early to say if this will be followed by a decrease in IHD events, the incidence of stroke has been favourably influenced by successful blood pressure control. In the case of cigarette smoking it has been demonstrated that a person who at the time of an acute heart attack was no longer a smoker has a better chance of surviving the attack than one who was still a smoker.

Hypertension. Research related to the etiology and pathogenesis of essential hypertension, which is the most prevalent cardiovascular disease among all the populations of the world, irrespective of sex and race, concentrates on the role of diet (salt and protein intake), psychosocial factors, and the long-term exposure to unfavourable effects of the environment in the development of essential hypertension. Great attention is also being devoted to the role of genetic factors in the inheritance of arterial hypertension.

Intensive research carried out during the last decade, aiming at control of hypertension at the community level, has already provided valuable results. The studies have shown that control of hypertension in a population is feasible, that it can be carried out through the existing system of health services in different countries, and that the control of blood pressure leads to a decrease of complications of high blood pressure—namely, stroke, heart failure, and renal failure. In some of the projects the incidence of myocardial infarction was also reduced. As a result of these positive findings some countries have decided to start nationwide control programmes in the field of hypertension.

Cardiomyopathies. Research into the etiology and pathogenesis of cardiomyopathies, which comprise 15%–40% of all causes of heart diseases in tropical countries, concentrates on the natural history of the diseases, and specifically, on their early manifestations. Further, the immunological aspects of endomyocardial fibrosis in relation to infectious diseases and environmental or nutritional factors are being considered. Special attention is being given to Chagas' disease (responsible for the most prevalent cardiomyopathy in Latin America) and to control of the reduviid bugs which transmit the parasite to man. Studies are being promoted to identify the possible risk factors such as reinfection, anaemia, malnutrition, physical activity, and the role of other infections in this form of cardiomyopathy.

Rheumatic fever. While most efforts in prevention and control of rheumatic fever and rheumatic heart disease are devoted to secondary prevention, significant advances have been acknowledged recently in the immunology of streptococcal diseases, in particular rheumatic fever and acute glomerulonephritis. The existence of cross-reactive antibodies has been shown, and further advances in this field may be expected.

In developing countries, specific attention is devoted to secondary prevention of rheumatic fever and rheumatic heart disease. These research activities have shown that by proper organization of the programme it is possible to reduce substantially the incidence of recurrences of rheumatic fever in children who have already experienced one or more attacks. Further efforts are designed to make these programmes applicable on a nation-wide scale in countries which still have the problem of rheumatic fever.

Community-based control trials. Special efforts are now being made to operate the control programmes against different cardiovascular diseases at the community level in a comprehensive way. Such comprehensive community programmes for the control of cardiovascular diseases are being integrated with the existing organization of health care in the respective countries or areas, where it is understood that these programmes are the first step in the development of comprehensive noncommunicable disease control programmes. In developing countries, therefore, they are—wherever feasible—linked with primary health care.

One challenge to long-term prevention and control of cardiovascular diseases is the emergence of "risk factors" in populations that have not yet acquired them—an even more fundamental challenge than primary prevention directed against established risk factors, and one which underlines the need for appropriate action to prevent the development of those agricultural, industrial, social and cultural patterns of life that have been shown to predispose communities to a high incidence of cardiovascular diseases.

Trends in cancer research

In the field of environmental carcinogenesis the major advances relate to (*a*) better global characterization of the geographical distribution of cancer and the identification of high-risk groups within countries; (*b*) the realization that most cancers are associated with the environment in the broad sense of the word; (*c*) the distinction between carcinogens and carcinogenic risk factors, which has lead to growing awareness of the importance of and the need to investigate "life-style"; (*d*) the first steps towards systematic evaluation of carcinogenic risk arising from environmental chemicals; and (*e*) a major effort to identify possible human hazards in the absence of human data using long- and short-term tests.

The systematic collection of data on mortality and—though less widely available—on incidence has helped to fill in some of the gaps in the world cancer distribution map, but large parts of Africa and Asia remain blank. For some cancers, such as cancer of the oesophagus, startling contrasts in incidence were shown to occur over rather small areas in France, Iran and Africa; in the United States of America and elsewhere cancer distribution maps have been used to produce causal hypotheses some of which have then been examined. The demonstration of the existence of well defined groups at greater or lesser than average risk of cancer within a given country, such as is seen in those following the precepts of some religions, has proved useful for hypothesis formulation and testing.

In the past five years there has been increasing collaboration between epidemiologists and other disciplines in the investigation of the causes of human cancer. Possibly the greatest influence on epidemiological research has been the realization that for a very large proportion of cancers the risk is strongly influenced by the environment. Unfortunately, environmental influence has been taken by some in the restricted sense of effects due to chemicals of industrial origin, rather than the sum of factors present in air, water and food, as well as life-style, personal habits, work, etc. It has been claimed that much human cancer is due to exposure to hazards at work, but it is evident that an occupational group shares not only such exposure to risks, but also a certain life-style.

Studies in many countries clearly show the harmful effects of cigarette smoking; in several of them some 40% of cancers in males are due to the habit. But while the demonstration that giving up smoking cuts the risk, and that the risk was negligible in nonsmokers, has influenced the smoking habits of professional groups, most other people have not so far abandoned the habit.

The study of the influence of carcinogenic risk factors on the human body has resulted in increased emphasis on what could be termed "metabolic epidemiology." Much of this work has been done on breast cancer, for which the levels of steroid hormones have been measured in groups at greater and lesser risk. The genesis of large bowel cancer, of increasing concern in industrial societies, has been studied to assess the influence of dietary fibre intake, fat and protein consumption on the faecal microflora and steroids, it being postulated that the latter are transformed into carcinogens or act as co-carcinogens. The importance of life-style factors in cancer causation, long recognized, has recently been re-emphasized: they have been estimated to be contributory factors in perhaps 30% of cancer cases in men and 50% in women.

Cohort studies have lead to the recognition of the dangers of exposure, usually at work, to substances such as arsenic, asbestos, or vinyl chloride monomer, or to radiation.

The case-control approach has been increasingly refined as a study method, uncovering two groups of carcinogenic stimuli. The first of these comprises well-defined cultural habits such as betel quid chewing, tobacco smoking and excessive alcohol consumption. The second group comprises factors, often described as carcinogenic risk factors, which are much more difficult to define in objective terms of physics or chemistry, such as age at first full-term pregnancy, age at first coitus, low dietary fibre intake.

The significance of exposure to low levels of carcinogens for the general population is being studied and is still not clear. The impossibility of completely disproving an element of risk, that is, of showing that a given exposure is "safe", remains a barrier. The assessment of the significance of relative risks of the order of 1.2-2.0 to one, which for common exposure and common cancer could be of public health importance, is very difficult. There is an obvious need for the development of methods to assess such low risks.

At the beginning of the period under review it was widely expected that one or more viruses would be shown to be causally linked to a human cancer. The evidence for a viral etiology of breast cancer is now but slight; Burkitt's lymphoma and nasopharyngeal cancer are linked to the ubiquitous Epstein Barr virus, but it has become clear that there is no straightforward relationship of cause and effect; on the other hand a considerable amount of evidence has been accumulated suggesting that hepatitis B virus is one of the etiological factors in hepatocellular carcinoma.

The evaluation of the carcinogenic risk to humans of exposure to chemicals in the environment has been successfully carried out in recent years. A number of industrial chemicals to which humans are exposed because of their occupation have been identified, and the dissemination of such information has been the basis for the establishment of regulatory measures varying from banning the production and the use of certain chemicals to strict codes of practice drastically limiting or totally avoiding human exposure to them.

In addition, the carcinogenic effect of several drugs used in human therapy has been identified. While some of these drugs are currently employed in the therapy of cancer, their use being permitted under strict control and after careful evaluation of the balance between risks and benefits, the use of other carcinogenic drugs has been prohibited, except in the treatment of life-threatening conditions.

The discovery of the possible causal association between liver cancer, which is one of the most common types of cancer in Africa and much of Asia, and the consumption of food contaminated with moulds producing the mycotoxin aflatoxin, has led to the implementation of a control programme.

A major effort has also been made to identify possible carcinogenic factors in areas where human data are lacking, using long-term carcinogenicity tests in rodents and a battery of recently developed short-term tests of which the best known are mutagenicity tests using bacteria. The results of these tests allow the recognition of a possible human hazard from a chemical already present in the environment, and also permit the selection of chemicals for future production. They will only be allowed to enter the environment, however, after the long-term toxicity rating has been ascertained.

In the field of basic research[1] into the biology of cancer cells contemporary efforts have centred mainly on kinetics and genetics.

The immunodeficient, nude (hairless) mouse has been the subject of the experimental transplantation of human tumour cells. These mice lack an efficient mechanism to reject tumour transplants, owing to a hereditary defect of cell-mediated immunity, permitting the propagation of human cells by interspecies tissue transplantation. In addition to providing an *in vivo* system for basic experimentation, tumour transplantation studies with nude mice can provide information on the growth kinetics and drug susceptibility of cancer cells from individual patients. Data gained from studies on nude mice are useful in clinical management because they can be used to predict therapeutic response.

The production of both ectopic hormones such as adrenocorticotropic hormone (ACTH), particularly by the neuroendocrine tumours, and oncofetal proteins such as alphafetoprotein, has been studied extensively. The results have substantially advanced the understanding of their clinical value in management of cancer patients.

Efforts have continued to exploit hormone receptor analysis for therapeutic indications. In general, recent studies have shown that the oestrogen receptor assay is a useful tool in predicting patient response to endocrine ablation or to hormonal therapy. In addition, the assay appears to promise useful applications in predicting recurrence rates and for selecting patients with a high probability of response to antihormone therapy.

Endocrine complications resulting from treatment of neoplasia have also received attention. Earlier reports that pointed to the risks of thyroid cancer developing years after irradiation of the head and neck have led to studies documenting adverse endocrine effects resulting from radiotherapy of these sites. Currently, special efforts are being taken to shield the pituitary gland, hypothalamus and other endocrine organs during therapy in order to avoid subsequent and long-term, endocrine-based complications.

The degree of immunosuppression associated with therapy or poor nutrition is being evaluated in cancer patients. It has long been suspected that the anorexia and cachexia commonly associated with neoplastic diseases have deleterious effects on the immune response of the patient. Recent studies have shown that the administration of concentrated nutrients (hyperalimentation) benefits the patient. These studies have shown that

---

[1] Based on *Clinical oncology* (2nd ed.) International Union against Cancer, Springer-Verlag (1978), Part III.

hyperalimentation generally improves the immune response and the patient's overall status and performance. In addition, the improved nutritional status appears to be reflected in an enhanced response to therapy.

The development of computerized axial tomography (CAT), a remarkable achievement of multidisciplinary cooperative efforts, has had a significant impact on medical oncology in recent years. Although limitations have been found in its efficacy for certain sites, the imaging of lesions in the brain and central nervous system markedly surpasses nondestructive radiological methods previously used to evaluate lesions at these sites. Scans of the liver and retroperitoneum are proving to be a significant aid in locating and determining the stages of secondary lesions.

Recent research developments in diarrhoeal diseases

Intensive research activities stimulated largely by the resurgence of cholera since 1961 have added a considerable new fund of knowledge not only about cholera but also about all types of acute diarrhoeal diseases. Epidemiological enquiries have revealed that a child in a developing country may have from 3 to 5 or even more diarrhoeal episodes in a year during the first five years of life—a fact contributing significantly to malnutrition and childhood mortality. It has been estimated that in 1975 there were at least 500 million episodes of acute diarrhoeas in children less than 5 years old in Africa, Asia and Latin America and that there are at least 6 million deaths a year due to these diseases. One careful study in Latin America has shown that more than one-third of the deaths in children under 5 years of age are due to acute diarrhoeas.

It has now almost definitely been established that while diarrhoeal diseases are more common and more severe in malnourished children, malnutrition is also initiated and aggravated by diarrhoeal episodes due to deprival, refusal and wastage of food.

Treatment. Since the convincing demonstration in 1968 that fluid and electrolyte losses due to acute watery diarrhoea in cholera can be successfully replaced by an optimally constituted oral glucose electrolyte solution, there has been rapid development and application of a highly effective single oral rehydration solution. After demonstration in controlled clinical trials in hospitals, the method of oral rehydration therapy has been successfully used in field conditions to treat acute diarrhoeas of diverse etiologies in all age groups.[1] Proper use of this oral fluid along with better dietetic management has also been shown to help growth of the child by preventing weight loss associated with diarrhoeal episodes. Intravenous fluid is now only required for those who are severely dehydrated or unable to drink.

There has also been considerable interest in the development of drugs, like antisecretory agents, for use in treatment of enterotoxin-mediated diarrhoeas. One such drug, chlorpromazine, has recently been shown in a preliminary trial to reduce intestinal fluid losses in cholera. A number of other drugs are now being evaluated. The limitations and risks of mass or indiscriminate use of antibodies have been demonstrated in treatment of cases and in the control of epidemics.

---

[1] *Treatment and prevention of dehydration in diarrhoeal diseases: a guide for use at primary level.* Geneva, World Health Organization, 1976.

Cause of acute diarrhoea. Major advances have also been made in the understanding of the etiology of diarrhoea. It is now possible to determine the cause of diarrhoea in 70%–80% of cases visiting treatment centres—a reversal of the situation some 10 years ago when 80% of the diarrhoeas were called acute undifferentiated diarrhoea. Rotavirus has emerged as the most important cause of this disease in children aged 6 to 24 months in both the developing and developed countries. *Escherichia coli* has now been found to cause diarrhoeal diseases by producing a heat-labile and/or heat-stable enterotoxin, or by being invasive. The organism is an important cause of diarrhoea in children and adults in developing countries. Although travellers' diarrhoea can be caused by a variety of organisms, recent studies have established that enterotoxigenic *E. coli* is the most common. Two more newly recognized bacterial pathogens, *Yersinia enterocolytica* and *Campylobacter jejuni,* and other viral agents, such as Norwalk agent, have also been found to produce diarrhoea although their relative importance is yet to be determined. Simple laboratory techniques like enzyme-linked immunosorbant assay have been developed for identifying some of the important agents like rotavirus and the enterotoxigenic *E. coli* in moderately equipped laboratories.

Immunity and vaccine development. Considerable advances have been made in the understanding of the antibody-mediated gut-associated immunity, but not much in that of the cell-mediated mechanisms. Vaccine development has received renewed attention following advances in the understanding of the immune mechanisms in the gastrointestinal tract, bacterial genetics and the pathogenesis of some types of infectious diarrhoea. A live oral typhoid vaccine has been developed from a strain deficient in galactose epimerase and shown to be highly efficacious in a field trial in Egypt.

Parenterally administered aluminium-adjuvanted whole-cell cholera vaccines have recently been shown in field trials in India and Indonesia to provide better and longer protection than previous vaccines, especially in children.

The advances in understanding of the structure and the mechanisms of action of the A (active) and B (binding) subunits of cholera enterotoxin have led to the development of live oral vaccines lacking the ability to produce one of the two subunits and also of a natural toxoid (binding component only) vaccine. Combined whole-cell and toxoid vaccine with adjuvants have also been developed for field trials. New knowledge about the importance of colonization factors in the pathogenesis of enterotoxigenic *E. coli* have opened up the possibility of developing more effective *E. coli* vaccine.

Environmental aspects. In the area of environmental health it has clearly been established that environmental control of diarrhoeal diseases cannot be achieved solely through provision of safe water supplies and sanitation facilites. There must also be concern for the attitudes and beliefs of the members of the communities in the design of these provisions if proper acceptance, maintenance and utilization are to be ensured.

Current state of, and priorities for, mental health research

Although major achievements in the control and prevention of the most severe mental health problems are few, the basis of psychiatric, neurological and related research has widened considerably.

In the field of mental disorders, rapid growth in biological research has been stimulated by recent discoveries in the more fundamental disciplines of study of the brain and the nervous system. Significant advances using genetic markers and specific neurotransmitters have been made in the understanding of biochemical mechanisms of depressive disorders, and biochemical classification of the affective illnesses, with important implications for their rational treatment, is almost within reach.

The inroads of biological research in the study of schizophrenic disorders, a group of potentially disabling and prevalent conditions, have been less impressive, but new avenues such as the study of possible viral involvement or investigations into immunological mechanisms have been opened up. Recent discoveries of endogenous opioid peptides in the human brain have indicated a course for investigation of their possible role in schizophrenia, but it is too early to evaluate attempts at such investigation.

A significant discovery has been the demonstration of a naturally occurring receptor in the brain binding the benzodiazepine compounds, potent anti-anxiety agents used in the treatment of neurotic disorders. This basic mechanism is thought to play a role in the development of dependence on a variety of narcotic drugs; a role which, if confirmed, would provide valuable clues to understanding the mechanisms and, possibly. improving the prevention and treatment of conditions of drug dependence.

With regard to neurological disorders, the elucidation of the role of so-called "slow viruses" in the etiology of progressive deteriorating conditions like kuru, and possibly several other related disorders, has been an important step forward. Less dramatic, but a contribution to knowledge offering possibilities for control, have been the advances in the study of cerebral mechanisms of epilepsy (including pharmacological control), stroke, and central nervous complications of tropical and parasitic diseases.

Epidemiological and clinical research in the last decade has been characterized by considerable refinements in research methodologies, including techniques for crosscultural investigations. Although there are wide gaps in knowledge about the incidence and associated ecological factors in many groups of mental disorders, studies in developing countries have furnished for the first time the proof that no community is free from serious mental health problems and that the nature and extent of mental morbidity in developing countries are comparable to those in the developed countries. Diagnostic methods for clinical and epidemiological work have been improved and a sound foundation laid for future field studies focused on the causal and contributory factors involved in mental disorders.

Psychosocial research in mental health has also improved its methodological armamentarium, although the complexity of behavioural issues in various cultures precludes rapid advances of knowledge. Nevertheless, the hypotheses explored in psychosocial research in the last decade have been of a more specific nature than in previous periods. Studies on the social antecedents of depressive illnesses, on the relation of communication of emotion within the family to relapses into psychotic illnesses, on lifestyle characteristics in relation to the risk of ischaemic heart disease and myocardial infarction (including the first demonstration of the feasibility of changing lifestyle components in community trials), have all shown the potential of the behavioural sciences to contribute to the solution of health problems.

In spite of such successes, the overall volume of effort and resources devoted to mental health research continued in most countries to be far below the support provided to other biomedical research. This relative neglect of mental health research is all the more serious

221

in view of the worldwide importance of mental health problems, and is no longer justifiable on grounds of unproven potential of the mental health sciences to make a significant breakthrough in knowledge and applicability of research results. The maturity of research techniques in several important areas in mental health warrants cautious optimism about such a breakthrough and calls for a greater international coordination and concentration of research efforts. The priorities for such expanded research in mental health would include: (a) continued studies on the ecology of mental illness in different human groups and societies; (b) intensified search for biological mechanisms and means of pharmacological control; (c) community trials of lifestyle changes contributing to the overcoming of major health problems; (d) research in service delivery, utilization and evaluation.

Research in nutrition

It is now widely accepted that the etiology of malnutrition, which continues to be one of the major health problems for the majority of the world's population, is interwoven with many facets of poverty and underdevelopment. It is recognized that the ultimate solutions to nutritional problems will be closely associated with overall economic and social development. Experience has shown, however, that socioeconomic development *per se* does not necessarily bring about improvement in nutritional conditions. Furthermore, children who are now dying or becoming seriously handicapped because of malnutrition cannot wait for long-term programmes of socioeconomic development. More urgent initiatives targeted towards nutritional improvement must be undertaken in which the health sector, among others, has important responsibilities.

Past efforts, including those of WHO, have demonstrated that specific nutritional deficiency diseases, such as beri-beri, pellagra, rickets and endemic goitre can yield to control measures even within the constraints of existing socioeconomic conditions. More recent research has made it possible to apply similar procedures to the control of other nutritional diseases, such as the anaemias and vitamin A deficiency.

The understanding of the factors controlling dietary iron absorption and the determination of its bioavailability have greatly increased the possibilities of control of iron deficiency. Biological incorporation of radioactively-labelled iron into food has been used in studies ranging over a wide variety of foodstuffs. Clearly, the absorption of iron from one food can be considerably influenced by the presence of other foodstuffs; for example, meat in the diet increases the absorption or iron from several vegetable sources.

A significant advance was made when it was demonstrated that absorption of dietary iron could basically be considered as occurring from two independent pools, a haem-iron pool and a non-haem-iron pool. Simultaneously, it was shown that the absorption from the two pools can be adequately quantified by the use of extrinsic tags using two differently labelled iron salts. In this way, the total absorption from a given meal is determined accurately. As a result of these methodological advances, it has been possible to calculate with greater precision the levels of iron supplementation necessary to reduce significantly the prevalence of iron deficiency anaemia in population groups. Simultaneously, new techniques of iron supplementation have been developed, and it is now possible to supplement salt, fish sauce, sugar and monosodium glutamate with iron compounds of high biological availability. Large-scale field trials were carried out to test the effectiveness of such techniques in the control of iron deficiency anaemia in Guatemala, India, the Philippines and Thailand.

Two approaches have been studied to control vitamin A deficiency in large population groups. The first one, essentially an emergency measure, involves the periodical distribution (every 4 to 6 months) of a capsule containing 200 000 IU of vitamin A to vulnerable groups and more particularly to children between 6 months and 4–5 years of age. The cost and effectiveness of such a measure are now well understood, following research conducted, notably, in Bangladesh, India, and Indonesia.

The second approach, a long-term one, consists of the supplementing of a staple food or a food consumed especially by children. With the assistance of industry, it has been possible to develop and test the effectiveness of procedures to supplement dry skim milk, sugar and monosodium glutamate with vitamin A. As a result, most preparations of skim milk intended for use in developing countries are now supplemented with vitamin A. In central American countries, almost all sugar for direct human consumption is thus supplemented and in Indonesia and in the Philippines the supplementation of monosodium glutamate, which is widely used a a spice, is being tested.

There is a high prevalence in developing countries of low birth weight; some babies, although born at full term, weigh less than 2.5 kg. Research is therefore being conducted on the prevention of malnutrition of the fetus, since low birth weight constitutes a definite and immediate handicap to the child, with resulting high mortality and morbidity in infancy and during early childhood. Much work has also been done on the effects of severe malnutrition during early childhood on the physical and mental development of the child; this has undoubted important consequences for socioeconomic development.

Considerable attention has also been devoted recently to breastfeeding. Research on the prevalence of breastfeeding and the factors influencing it, as well as on the volume and composition of breast milk, as they are affected by the nutritional status of the mother is being carried out in several parts of the world. The importance of complementary feeding after weaning is well recognized, and developmental work is substantially concerned with improved food formulations, especially home-made formulations, that can be used for this purpose.

Somewhat less progress has been made in attacking the more generalized and more serious problem of undernutrition in which overall intake of food, rather than of specific nutrients, is insufficient or inadequate. However, in recent years significant advances have been made in understanding the nature of this problem. Present knowledge about energy and protein requirements, and ways of satisfying them, appears sufficient to define nutritionally adequate diets based on a variety of foods locally available in different ecological situations and within the economic reach of most populations. This new knowledge derived from basic and clinical research, and supported by epidemiological observations, opens new avenues for effective action in nutrition through the primary health care approach; that is, through operational activities for the prevention of malnutrition at the community level. In taking a fresh look at the problem of malnutrition from this angle one can reasonably expect to find answers in the area of food intake itself rather than in a study of the ill effects of a poor diet. This search has necessarily to be made in the community. Such research strives to identify the potential that exists within the community for self-help and self-care in nutrition. It is concerned not only with why a detected problem exists, but also with how it can be relieved and, most important, in how this new understanding can be transferred to the users and translated into action. The research begins with the people and ends with the people. It does not begin with a nutritional problem and end simply with the report of a laboratory investigation.

The kind of questions for which the new approach is seeking answers include the following: Why is the existing food intake inadequate? What changes would be expected to modify existing practices and improve the food intake? How can these changes be effected within the community setting? How can the experience gained in this sort of investigation and its application be translated and applied in other settings? As a result, generally applicable principles should emerge concerning the determinants of food intake in different ecological, cultural and economic settings, and these may be used in the design of the nutrition component of integrated health care and development programmes. Furthermore, instruments or techniques may become available to health and community workers to diagnose the nature of the problem in specific populations and thereby predict and plan the types of actions that would be beneficial and practicable in improving food intake. In particular, guidance may be expected regarding the extent to which such changes may be effected within the setting of primary health care and using existing resources.

The ultimate objective of this research is to contribute to the improvement and maintenance of health through improvement of the food intake. This is seen as a necessary component of an integrated health care programme which by necessity will include other complementary actions, such as the control of infectious diseases. It is also explicitly recognized that such activities will be part of and supported by overall socioeconomic development at the community and at the national level, which they in turn will be supporting.

Finally it should be mentioned that while substantially greater attention has been given at the international level—and certainly in WHO—to the nutritional problems of developing countries that are related to nutritional deficiencies, evidence is rapidly accumulating regarding the role of the dietary practices of the industrialized countries in the etiology of their major health problems—such as obesity, hypertension and cardiovascular diseases, and some forms of cancer.

The role of proper nutrition as a basic factor for the maintenance of health and the prevention of diseases is becoming more clear as other major environmental causes, particularly of infections, are better understood. In both developed and developing countries, fundamental changes in socioeconomic structures invariably modify dietary and other health-related practices. The possible adverse effects of these changes on overall health are now being recognized. These considerations must be included in intensified research in nutrition if human health is to be protected and actively promoted.

Implications for the future of world health

Predictions about the future of science are very often uncertain and precarious. The implications of present biomedical and health services research for the future of world health are no less uncertain. Yet it is well known that what appears impossible today may be achieved tomorrow; Jenner's prediction in 1801 that smallpox might ultimately be exterminated from the face of the earth was dismissed by a prominent contemporary physician in 1825 as "vain and unfounded". Similar scepticism could have been expressed even a few decades ago; but today, we are witnesses to the realization of Jenner's dream.

Sometimes progress is achieved with less deliberate intention when, after a period of apparent neglect, existing knowledge becomes the means to a major achievement; when, in the early 1900s, Alexis Carrel invented a method of growing animal cells in the laboratory to satisfy his personal curiosity, he had no thought of the practical implications of his discovery. It was not until some 40 years later that Enders and his colleagues made the technical improvements which led to the cultivation of poliovirus and, subsequently, to the development of a vaccine against poliomyelitis.

Occasionally, an unpredictable breakthrough with immense implications for health may occur. However, present trends favour well planned research efforts aimed at solving well defined problems. This approach underlies the current developments in global collaborative health research which may well have significant implications for the future of world health.

What then can be said about tomorrow's health in the light of today's research? The enthusiastic promoter of scientific achievement can quickly conjure up any number of possible "breakthroughs" based on known fact—a new vaccine tomorrow, a new drug the next day. But unfulfilled promises lead to disappointment and may cause scepticism about what science can really do.

In the field of *vaccine research* recent advances have led to the development of new vaccines against pneumococcal pneumonia and meningitis, and improved rabies vaccine, and steady progress in the development of vaccines against hepatitis B and travellers' diarrhoea.

The advances that have led to the development of methods of cultivating parasites *in vitro* and of analysing complex parasite antigens, coupled with the possibilities offered by recombinant DNA research, give specific reasons to believe that production of vaccine against a number of infections, including some parasitic diseases, may become feasible. Vaccines are still a highly cost-effective tool of public health action, and their development or improvement could have an appreciable impact at world level, although certain problems connected with their administration to whole communities have not yet been fully resolved. The reliability of the "cold chain" is one such problem.

Increasing knowledge in the field of *molecular genetics* may well lead to better understanding of cancer etiology and may provide important clues to the problems of bacterial virulence and of drug resistance.

The discovery of special enzyme tools for splitting and joining DNA threads (chromosomes) has given birth to recombinant DNA research (genetic engineering). The possible contribution of this type of research to vaccine development has already been mentioned. Similar approaches have yielded pure human insulin from artificially maintained bacterial cultures. The implications for the health of many diabetic patients are evident, but problems related to commercial production have yet to be solved.

Throughout this chapter, there has been persistent emphasis on the importance not only of new knowledge but of the application of such knowledge. Any forecast must allow a large place for expansion, through research, of the ability to apply the results of scientific investigation. This will mean growing contributions from health services research, the behavioural and social sciences, and other sectors such as organization and management technology, to tackle questions relating to the effectiveness, efficiency and coverage of health care.

Existing knowledge and available research results must be harvested within the next few years if their application is to have a substantial impact on world health by the turn of the century in fulfilment of the social target of health for all set by the International Conference on Primary Health Care at Alma-Ata. There may be spectacular break-throughs, but basically scientific research involves rigorous and repeated testing of hypotheses rather than a series of brilliant flashes of innovation. In any case, "chance favours the prepared mind": Fleming's cultures were not the first to have been contaminated by growth-inhibiting organisms, but Florey had the scientific preparation, as well as the insight, to make inventive use of the observation of an everyday occurrence. The preparation and training for scientific research is therefore an important aspect of strategies to promote research and development, and it is now accepted that institution-strengthening, with the object of broadening the basis of knowledge about scientific approaches and methodology, must be given high priority.

It has been said that 90% of all the scientists who have ever lived are alive today; this bodes well for the development of knowledge. There is no dearth of health problems and no shortage of questions for goal-oriented medical research. However, there is a shortage of appropriately trained men and women to translate research results into economical and feasible measures for health improvement. The philosophy of health research as a spectrum of complementary research activities over a range of disciplines has gained considerable ground in recent years. What is needed now is a purposeful balance between the fundamental and applied aspects of health research and between biomedical and epidemiological and health services research. Ultimately, the implications of health research for the future of world health and for the achievement of the goal of health for all will depend largely on the ability to reconcile, in a practical way, what is known with what is needed, for better health.

Chapter 6

Outlook for the future

Introduction

The need to discern trends in the development of the health situation as they affect socioeconomic development is greater than ever in view of the elaboration of strategies throughout the world for the attainment of an acceptable level of health for all by the 2000. The inadequacy of health information in very many countries makes this task difficult, but it seems that sufficient information exists for the elaboration of strategies based on the concept of primary health care, and as these advance more information should become available for the further planning and operation of the health systems required. The mutual dependency of reliable information and health development activities is clear.

Particularly difficult is the drawing of conclusions from information on demographic and economic development as a basis for projections, even when the information qualifies as "hard fact", so heavily do changes in the demographic or economic situation depend on political and social events. Moreover, information on health status rarely falls in the "hard facts" category. Yet accurate projections in this sphere are essential if the goal of health for all is to be attained; countries must know, at least in terms of orders of magnitude, what the health problems are and what responses to these problems are proving to be useful. Only when countries have analysed their health trends at the national level will it be possible to discern regional and global trends. Good examples of efforts already being made in this area include such studies as those on global health trends and prospects 1950–2000,[1] on child mortality trends in the Americas[2] and on mortality in Europe.[3]

Projections are usually based upon an extrapolation of trends observed over recent years. They are, of course, not predictions—they cannot, for example, take into account all the effects of radical socioeconomic changes, important breakthroughs in health technology and significant developments in health policy which may occur in the future. Thus the validity of a projection is not necessarily best judged by the extent to which it is actually found to be true or false with the passage of time. Simple projections may still provide valid forecasts of what would happen under *status quo*, thereby revealing health gaps to be

---

[1] *World health statistics report*, **27**: 672 (1974).
[2] PUFFER, R. R. & SERRANO, C. V. *Patterns of mortality in childhood*, Washington DC, Pan American Health Organization, 1973 (Scientific Publication No. 262).
[3] *World health statistics report*, **27**: 24 (1974).

filled and the undersirable course of events to be prevented. The reliability of the results, however, inevitably diminishes the longer the period covered. In any case, it is essential that all projections should be evaluated and updated at regular intervals.

The presentation that follows is based primarily on quantitative assumptions about the future as elaborated by national authorities and by the organizations of the United Nations system in the first half of the 1970s.

Demographic prospects

In themselves, population growth and change have an impact on economic and social conditions and therefore on health and well-being. Conversely, evolutions in health also exert significant influences on quantitative changes in the population. From the health planner's point of view the size of the population and its rate of change rank among the primary determinants of health care needs. Population projections nowadays are generally based on the so-called component method, analysing separately each component of population change—fertility, mortality and migration. This method not only provides an improved projection but also helps in identifying factors which have distinct policy implications.

The major changes anticipated by the year 2000 are described below.

(1) World population is expected to increase within the next quarter of a century by almost 60%, exceeding 6000 million by the year 2000. Expected changes in population size by continent or macroregion are shown in Fig. 18, and together with the shifts in the proportional distribution, in Table 21 below (see also Table 2 and the World map of natural increase rates, Fig. 1 in the Annex).

Table 21. Distribution of the world population

Continent or macroregion	Absolute figures (in millions)			Percentage		
	1950	1975	2000	1950	1975	2000
Africa	219	401	814	9	10	13
America	330	561	916	13	14	15
Asia	1368	2256	3637	55	57	58
Europe	392	473	540	16	12	9
Oceania	13	21	33	0	0	0
USSR	180	255	315	7	7	5
World*	2501	3968	6254	100	100	100

* Apparent discrepancies in totals are due to rounding.
Source: Population by sex and age for regions and countries, 1950–2000, as assessed in 1973 (document ESA/P/WP.60). United Nations Population Division, Department of Economic and Social Affairs.

In 1975 about 70% of the world's population lived in what are today considered as developing countries; the proportion in these countries will grow to almost 80% by the turn of the century.

(2) Rates of natural increase, i.e., the difference between birth and death rates are expected gradually to slow down, mainly as a consequence of increasing acceptance of family planning and an associated decline in fertility in developing countries and—to a

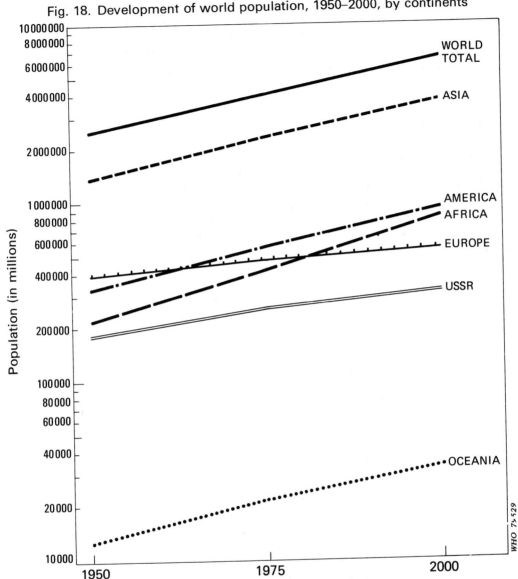

Fig. 18. Development of world population, 1950–2000, by continents

Source: Selected World Demographic Indicators by Countries, 1950–2000 (document ESA/P/QP.55). United Nations Population Division, Department of Economic and Social Affairs.

lesser extent—as a consequence of slowing down of decreases in crude death rates. The African continent is a major exception as no reduction in the growth rate is anticipated there (see Table 22 below). In assessing the significance of the rates of natural growth for development planning, one has to bear in mind that an average annual growth of 20 per 1000 population implies an increase of the population of 64% within a quarter of a century while a growth rate of 30 per 1000 leads to a doubling of the population within less than 25 years.

Table 22.   National increase by continent or macroregion, 1950–2000.

Continent or macroregion	Rates of natural increase (per 1000 population)			Birth rates (per 1000 population)			Death rates (per 1000 populations)		
	1950–1954	1970–1974	1995–1999	1950–1954	1970–1974	1995–1999	1950–1954	1970–1974	1995–1999
Africa	21	27	28	48	46	39	27	20	11
America	21	19	18	33	28	25	12	9	7
Asia	17	21	16	40	35	25	23	14	9
Europe	9	6	5	20	16	15	11	10	10
Oceania	15	16	13	28	25	21	12	9	8
USSR	17	10	7	26	18	16	9	8	10
World	17	19	16	36	32	25	19	13	9

Source: Selected world demographic indicators by countries, 1950–2000 (document ESA/P/WP.55). United Nations Population Division, Department of Economic and Social Affairs.

(3) The composition of a population by sex and age is one of its most fundamental features. Factors such as educational level, attitudes, physiological capabilities, occupation, income, consumption patterns, vary accordingly. For the health planner the age, sex and structure of the population is of crucial importance as the disease spectrum, and the consequent needs in health care, vary with sex and age. Requirements for the development of social services for children and the elderly (here defined as population under 15 years of age and those aged 65 years and older, respectively) are to a substantial extent conditioned by the numerical size of these groups. In short, planning for socioeconomic development has to be based on knowledge of the future age and sex composition of the population. The changes to be expected in the age structure of the population are shown in condensed form in Table 23 below (for details, see Table 2 in the Annex).

Table 23.   Population by age group, developed and developing countries, 1975 and estimates for the year 2000.

Age group (years)	Developed countries Absolute population (in millions)		Percentage		Developing countries Absolute population (in millions)		Percentage	
	1975	2000	1975	2000	1975	2000	1975	2000
<15	283	307	25	23	1145	1718	41	35
15–44	497	581	44	43	1224	2278	43	46
45–64	233	304	20	22	359	670	13	14
65–79	100	137	9	10	97	201	3	4
≥80	19	31	2	2	11	26	0	1
Total	1132	1360	100	100	2836	4894	100	100

Source: Population by sex and age for regions and countries, 1950–2000, as assessed in 1973 (document ESA/P/WP.60). United Nations Population Division, Department of Economic and Social Affairs.

In assessing the relevance of the age structure for health policy considerations three indicators are used, namely the total dependency ratio, the child dependency ratio and the old age dependency ratio.[1]

---

[1] *Total dependency ratio*: population aged <15 years + population ≥65 years per 100 population aged 15 to <65 years (i.e., the population of working age);
   Child dependency ratio: population aged <15 years per 100 population aged 15 to <65 years; and
   Old age dependency ratio: population aged ≥65 years per 100 population aged 15 to <65 years.

These dependency ratios calculated from the above table are as follows:

	Child dependency ratio		Old age dependency ratio		Total dependency ratio	
	1975	2000	1975	2000	1975	2000
Developed countries	39	35	16	19	55	54
Developing countries	72	58	7	8	79	66
World	62	53	10	10	72	63

The anticipated implications of these changes are reviewed below.

(4) The total dependency ratio will remain practically unchanged in the developed countries at a level of about 55, while in the developing countries it will register a marked drop from 79 to 66.

The increase in the population of working age relative to the dependent population in the developing countries as described above will constitute a great potential for productive work but will also present a serious challenge to development planners. The ILO has estimated[1] that the world's labour force (i.e., employed and unemployed persons) is expected to increase from almost 1650 millions in 1975 to 2550 millions by the year 2000, i.e., about 900 millions more jobs will have to be absorbed by the world economy (see also Table 4 in the Annex). The corresponding figures for developed and developing countries are:

	Labour force (in millions)		Change	
	1975	2000	Absolute	%
Developed countries	520	640	+120	+23
Developing countries	1125	1910	+755	+70
World	1645	2550	+905	+55

Two additional factors are worth mentioning, namely (a) the growing concern in a number of developed countries for the aging of their labour force, i.e., a rising proportion of those in the higher brackets of the working age; and (b) the shift of steadily growing numbers of workers from agriculture to manufacturing and service industries in developing countries. This redistribution of the labour force as a result of "modernization" has obvious implications for the protection of the health of the working population and the development or strengthening of appropriate legislation and services.

(5) The anticipated sharp decline of the child dependency ratio in developing countries from 72 in 1975 to 58 in 2000 reflects decreases in fertility. It should be noted, however, that as the course of fertility is very difficult to project, the projection is marked by a margin of uncertainty greater than the one to be attached to the projection of the numbers of population of working age and of old people.

In spite of the expected decline in fertility, the world child population will grow from 1428 million in 1975 to 2025 million in 2000, i.e., an increase of about 600 million, and will still constitute a large segment of the total population. In developing countries in

---

[1] 1950–2000 Labour Force, Volume V, World Summary. 2nd ed. Geneva, International Labour Office, 1977.

particular, more than a third of the population will be under 15 years of age in the year 2000. Two factors combine to lessen the impact of anticipated declines of fertility on the child population, namely the projected increase in the number of women of child-bearing age (see below, section (6)) and the projected decreases of infant and child mortality (see page 239). The protection of child health will therefore remain as an important concern of the community.

Because of the continuous increase in the child population, the problem of education will pose a formidable task to many of the developing countries. According to a projection of illiteracy made by UNESCO[1], the proportion of the illiterate among those aged 15 to <20 years, which is the age group reflecting the outcome of primary education, will decrease only gradually, if the current rate of progress is maintained. Illiterates will be found almost entirely in developing countries and the rate among women will remain high, as seen from the following table:

	Sex	1975	2000
Developed countries	Male	1	1
	Female	1	1
	Both sexes	1	1
Developing countries	Male	26	16
	Female	42	23
	Both sexes	34	19

In absolute terms, however, the number of illiterates of age 15 to >20 years has been projected to rise from 69 to 76 million. (For adult literacy rates, see Annex, Table 8.)

(6) Important for maternal and child health care are projections of the number of women of child-bearing age (here defined as women aged 15 to <45 years). Relevant figures are given below:

	Females aged 15 to <45 years				
	Absolute numbers (in millions)			Index (1950 = 100)	
	1950	1975	2000	1975	2000
Developed countries	203	247	286	122	141
Developing countries	350	601	1120	171	320
World	553	848	1406	153	254

---

[1] UNESCO (1978) Estimates and projections of illiteracy (document CSR-E-29).

In the developing countries the number of women of child-bearing age is expected to roughly double by the end of this century; compared to 1950, the projected course implies a trebling of the number within 50 years. Together with information on projected trends in fertility and family planning practices, data on the population of child-bearing age provide an indispensable foundation for the planning of maternal and child health services.

(7) In both developed and developing countries the elderly (aged 65 and older) will comprise a higher share of the total dependency, a trend which is not without its own complexities. In fact, the rapid and unprecedented growth of the elderly population in absolute numbers is a distinguishing feature of world population and must receive greater attention in the future throughout the world. Between 1975 and the year 2000 the world's elderly are expected to increase from 227 million to 395 million, an increase of 168 million or 75% within the 25-year period. This rate of increase exceeds by far that of any other age segment of the population. More than 70% of this increase will be found in the developing countries. In 1975 more than half of the world's elderly lived in developed countries; by the year 2000 the balance will have shifted and it is the developing countries that will have almost three-fifths of the total.

The relevance of this trend to the health sector is demonstrated by the fact that in some developed countries the elderly occupy more than half of the non-psychiatric hospital beds, although their share in the population is below 15%. One can anticipate an even greater strain to be put on services used by the elderly, such as hospital geriatric services and other institutional care, home nursing and home help, in those countries, particularly as the elderly population itself will age. The projected increase in the number of people aged 80 and older from 19 to 31 million between 1975 and 2000 suggests a grave and growing challenge as regards the provision of geriatric community care. It has been argued that a fundamental revision of the value system of the health care organization towards the needs of the chronically ill is overdue. A similar trend towards aging will also gradually require the attention of developing countries, particularly if coupled with profound changes in cultural patterns and urbanization, including the disintegration of tradition family systems which until now provided the framework for the care of the aged. In short, the great increase in the number of older persons poses potentially serious socioeconomic and cultural problems of a national, regional and global nature. The recognition of these problems should alert the health and social systems to ways of overcoming them. For instance, the maintenance of traditional cultural patterns may play a vital role in ensuring the health and welfare of the aged in developing countries.

As women outlive men by several years on the average, the psychosocial environment of elderly widows is an important aspect of the problems of aging (the number of males per 1000 females will change in the age group 65 and older between 1975 and 2000 from 896 to 887 in the developing countries; in the developed countries the corresponding values are 641 and 687 respectively, the improvement reflecting the gradual disappearance of the disturbances in the balance of the sexes caused by the Second World War.

(8) By the year 2000 the proportion of the population residing in urban areas will—according to United Nations estimates[1]—have increased from 39% in 1950 to 50%,

---

[1] Selected world demographic indicators by countries, 1950–2000 (document ESA/P/WP.55). United Nations Population Division, Department of Economic and Social Affairs.

i.e., half of the population of the world will live in urban areas; the proportion will rise between 1950 and 2000 from 69% to 81% in the developed countries and from 27% to 41% in the developing countries (see Table 3 in the Annex). In absolute term the picture is as follows:

	Urban population (in millions)			Rural population (in millions)		
	1975	2000	Change	1975	2000	Change
Developed countries	783	1107	+324	349	254	−95
Developing countries	775	1996	+1221	2060	2896	+836
World	1558	3103	+1545	2409	3150	+741

Though the proportion of the population residing in rural areas will decline markedly, in actual numbers it will increase by almost 750 million (this increase being attributable mainly to the developing countries), underlining the continuous importance of providing health care to the rural population.

The trend towards urbanization will be characterized by rapid growth of the population in many metropolitan areas. Fig. 19 shows the impressive rate of growth of the population in the first 15 cities in the world according to population projections for the year 2000. The implications of this anticipated development for the physical and psychosocial environment will have to be given careful attention.

Social and economic aspects[1]

In this time of social change, unprecedented in its extent, scope, and pace, there are many forces at work that have a crucial bearing on the future. One of the most important factors to emerge over the past few years is the search for a new interpretation of "development", involving a critical reassessment of ideals, goals, and conceptions about the future. A determined effort to achieve a new order of individual and national dignity is anticipated. Some of the major factors for change which will have a considerable impact in the future are:

—promotion of social equity within and among countries, particularly to guarantee fulfilment of basic human needs to everybody;
—protection of minorities and disadvantaged groups;
—equal rights of men and women and protection of children;
—changes in societal structures, family patterns, and life styles;
—wider participation in decision-making.

The new perception of people's health needs and the new goal of "Health for all by the year 2000" will constitute an integral part of this changing process; the aim is to enable all people of the world to attain an acceptable level of health and to lead a socially and economically productive life. As was emphasized in Section III of the Declaration of

---

[1] This section is primarily based on: *1978 Report on the world social situation*, New York, United Nations, 1979; The World Bank. *World development report, 1978*, New York, Oxford University Press, 1978; and LEONTIEF, W. ET AL. *The future of the world economy*, New York, United Nations, 1977.

Fig. 19. World's fifteen largest agglomerations ranked by population size projected for the year 2000

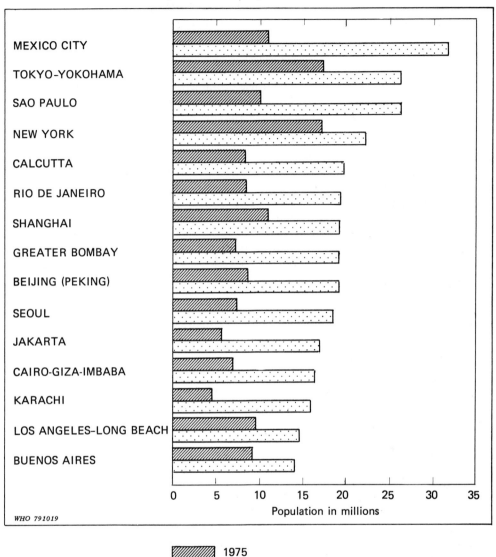

Alma-Ata, "Economic and social development, based on a New International Economic Order, is of basic importance to the fullest attainment of health for all and to the reduction of the gap between the health status of the developing and developed countries. The promotion and protection of the health of the people is essential to sustained economic and social development and contributes to a better quality of life and to world peace".

Many of the developed and developing countries alike continue, however, to devote substantial proportions of their national income to armaments. Efforts for an international agreement on disarmament, stimulated by the United Nations, have so far had little effect; "The annual spending of US $250–260 billion (in constant 1973 dollars) for military purposes can be compared to the US $83 million spent over a 10-year period by WHO to eradicate smallpox".[1] As pointed out in Section X of the Declaration of Alma-Ata, "An acceptable level of health for all the people of the world by the year 2000 can be attained through a fuller and better use of the world resources. A genuine policy of independence, peace, détente and disarmament could and should release additional resources that could well be devoted to peaceful aims and in particular to the acceleration of social and economic development...".

Forecasts of changes in the number of absolutely poor people depend on assumptions about patterns of economic growth and social redistribution. According to World Bank projections, the number of persons with an income of less than US $200 per annum (in 1970 dollars) will decline from about 800 million to 600 million by the year 2000, but almost all of them will be living in developing countries. Though these projections do not take into account any possibility for radical socioeconomic changes and are subject to a number of qualifications, they do provide a useful background for social policy planning. For instance, they underline the importance of developing approaches which would guarantee access to adequate health care to all social strata of the population at a cost that the community and country could afford at every stage of their development.

Although the developing countries were virtually self-sufficient in food in the 1950s, by 1970 they had to import 15 to 20 million tonnes of major staple foods annually. According to World Bank estimates, by 1985 the total production of the developing countries, with the exception of Latin America where a food surplus is expected, will fall short of their demand by about 45 million tonnes. These countries will then need to import about 11% of their consumption demand. The Thirtieth World Health Assembly in 1977 adopted resolution WHA30.51 on development of national and international food policies and plans in order to express its concern "at the inadequate attention and commitments being given by the health and other sectors in a greater number of countries to improve this critical situation". The World Bank forecast also confirms the strategic importance of proposed structural and institutional changes such as land reforms in the agricultural sector with a view to promoting more rapid increases in agricultural production and more equitable distribution in the developing countries. This problem was the crucial issue at the World Conference on Agrarian Reform and Rural Development, held in Rome in the summer of 1979.

The above reflections on the world food situation reinforce the emphasis being placed on stimulation of permanent multisectoral coordination of food and nutrition policies and programmes in order to derive the greatest nutritional benefit from available food.

A United Nations study which prepared a set of alternative projections on the economic and environmental states of the world, as well as demographic projections for 1980, 1990 and 2000, makes it clear that "development" cannot be interpreted in terms of economic growth only, even though economic growth is an indispensable component of a strategy aimed at improving living conditions throughout the world. Indeed economic growth and

---

[1] *1978 Report on the world social situation*, New York, United Nations, 1979, p. 3.

social equity should not be viewed separately or in isolation but as mutually reinforcing goals. At the same time, it will be necessary for developing countries to profit from the experience of the developed countries so as to avoid certain undesirable aspects of development such as air, water and soil pollution, and energy problems, with which a number of countries are currently struggling.

The various studies of prospective economic trends undertaken by the organizations of the United Nations system draw attention to the economic constraints under which the health sector may have to operate in the next decades.

In addition to overall economic trends in a country there is also the specific area of health economics itself. The "cost explosion" of health expenditure that has characterized the developments in the last decades in many developed and developing countries alike, has been generally recognized. This has often led to a thorough review of national and international health development strategies and the realization of the necessity to adopt efficient low-cost approaches. A crucial point, and one of steadily growing importance, concerns the need to reconcile two basic principles, namely (a) provision of health care to all segments of the population, and (b) containment of the costs of health care within reasonable limits and in accordance with national capabilities.

In the coming decades a number of factors will combine to increase health care costs. They include growing health consciousness, producing a vocal public demand for high quality treatment services; extension of coverage of health care so as to remove all physical and financial barriers to its ready access and utilization; introduction of environmental control measures to eliminate or at least reduce potential health hazards; progress in biomedical research and advanced health technology.

However there will also be a growing awareness of the need to scrutinize expenditure for health services more closely than in the past and to apply rigorous scientific methods to the establishment of priorities and allocation of resources in the health budget. The new emphasis on the application of scientific management and operational research to the health sector, tempered by a sound scepticism concerning the achievements and limitations of high-cost sophisticated medical technology will—together with the emphasis on self-reliance and participation of the general public—be among the factors which will exercise a constraining influence. Though more resources than hitherto will have to be allocated to the health sector for drastic improvements in the health status of the world's deprived people in order to reduce inequities among as well as within countries, it would hardly seem realistic to rely exclusively on such additional resources. The tremendous challenge will also tax ingenuity in developing low-cost approaches, better utilization of available resources and their redistribution within the health sector.

Health status trends

Mortality and life expectancy

Numerical projections of changes in health status have up to now largely been limited to projections of mortality. The focus has been on mortality as a determinant of population change, rather than as an indicator of health status of the population. It is sometimes argued that such mortality projections are only of limited usefulness for health planners, particularly in countries with already relatively low mortality levels. However, a considerable body of evidence is gradually emerging to suggest that in low mortality countries mortality statistics can often be used as a proxy indicator of morbidity. Certainly for conditions such as mental disorders, chronic arthritis, dental ill-health, or conditions of pregnancy, which consume considerable amounts of health resources in a number of countries, mortality statistics provide hardly any guide to morbidity. Nevertheless, a clear perception of the use to be made of mortality-based projections of health status and their interpretation in a circumspect manner have proved to be useful for estimating requirements for non-psychiatric inpatient services and related problems.

The usefulness of mortality projections would be greatly enhanced if details by broad cause-of-death groups were available. Unfortunately, cause-specific projections of mortality, either as a methodological tool for improving the projection of total mortality or solely for use in the health sector, have only rarely been attempted. However, a distinct tendency to pay more attention to this hitherto neglected area is now discernible. Cause-specific projections of mortality invariably require assumptions to be made about the probable impact of detection, prevention, and therapeutic programmes.

Evaluation studies of national mortality projections carried out in developed countries in the 1950s and 1960s[1,2] showed that the available information has often not been adequately used. Death rates at the older ages have proved least predictable.

Generally speaking, the projections have failed to allow for the emergence of a new structure of mortality in developed countries, particularly as regards male adult and old-age mortality. This new structure is characterized particularly by a very marked slow-down in the reduction of male death rates in some age groups, and occasionally even increases in others. Among the explanations put forward are (a) that with a decline in infectious and parasitic diseases, less tractable diseases such as cardiovascular diseases and cancer now have an increasing effect on the level of "all-causes" mortality; and (b) the effect of remissions achieved by the application of new treatments to patients who are still comparatively young.[2]

Life expectancy at birth, despite its limitations, has time and again been proved to be the most important single measure of the level of health of a population, particularly when viewed from the broader perspective of socioeconomic development strategy. A study[3] made by the United Nations Research Institute for Social Development has found that life expectancy was closely correlated with the "general development index" devised by the Institute, and much more substantially so than any other available health status indicators. Even in developed countries the correlation between gross national product per capita, used as a proxy indicator of economic development, and life expectancy at birth is still highly significant.[4]

---

[1] PRESTON, S. H.: An evaluation of postwar mortality projections in Australia, Canada, Japan, New Zealand and the United States. *World health statistics report*, **27**: 719–745 (1974).

[2] PRESSAT, R.: Mortality projections and actual trends. A comparative study. *World health statistics report*. **27**: 516–539 (1974).

[3] McGRANAHAN, P. V. ET AL. *Contents and measurement of socio-economic development*, United Nations Research Institute for Social Development, United Nations, New York, 1972.

[4] For a more detailed review, see *inter alia*: Health Trends and Prospects 1950–2000, *World health statistics report*, **27**: 688 (1974), and HANSLUWKA, H.: Cancer mortality in Europe 1970–74. *World health statistics quarterly*, **31**: 160 (1978).

A recent WHO survey of national mortality projections revealed that, in the developed countries, by the year 2000 life expectancy at birth is estimated to be in the range of 75–80 years and infant mortality will be 10 per 1000 liveborn, or less. The majority of countries anticipated no significant improvements at ages other than infancy; whenever minor reductions of the age-specific death rates were projected, these tended to be limited to females. In developing countries it may be anticipated, barring unforeseen developments, that by the year 2000 the majority of their populations will have a mean life expectancy at birth of at least 65 years, and the infant mortality will only rarely be in excess of 50 per 1000 liveborn. Thus the present gap in life expectancy at birth between developed and developing countries, which is estimated to be of the order of 15–18 years, will be almost halved by the end of this century, provided that satisfactory progress is made in all those social, economic, and politico-institutional areas that influence mortality.

A condensed picture of these changes in life expectancy at birth between 1950 and 1975 and the projected values for 2000 is shown in the table below.

Life expectancy at birth

	Developed countries	Developing countries	Difference (in years)
c. 1950	65	42	23
c. 1975	72	55	17
c. 2000	75–80	65–70	10

According to past experience in a number of countries, the projected level of life expectancy for developing countries, namely 65–70 years, would be compatible with the above-mentioned expected level for an infant mortality of 50 per 1000 liveborn. It should be borne in mind, however, that today the gap in life expectancy at birth between the group of the least developed countries and the remainder of the developing countries is of a magnitude of about 10 years. The least developed countries, will, therefore, have to achieve much greater gains if current inequalities are to be drastically reduced.

In assessing these estimates one has to bear in mind that for some developing countries evidence about the direction and pace of change of mortality, particularly in the late 1960s and first half of the 1970s, is based on weak and occasionally inconsistent data. Efforts are currently under way on the national as well as international level (United Nations in collaboration with WHO) to obtain more reliable data and to make more judicious use of available data for trend analysis. However, with these reservations in mind, the above estimates are reasonably close to the truth and permit broad policy conclusions.

However, for social policy it is of considerable importance that the anticipated changes in mortality will significantly shape the survivorship pattern[1] of future generations. For instance, in developed countries the proportion of survivors to age 65 can be estimated at close to 90%, and almost every second person will be able to celebrate his or her eightieth birthday if these assumptions for the year 2000 hold (the corresponding values for the mid-1970s are about 80% and 40%, respectively). To put it differently: death will strike only relatively rarely before the age of 65, and the age distribution of deaths as derived

---

[1] See also the information in the section on Demographic prospects (page 228), concerning changes in the age structure of the population.

from the projection for the year 2000 would be approximately as follows:

Age in years	% of deaths
<65	10
65–<80	40
≥80	50

With the progressive reduction of premature deaths the numbers in special morbidity and disability risk groups will increase, particularly those of the disabled, the mentally retarded and the chronically ill. "If the needs of these populations are to be met, the values of the health care system will have to be changed. 'Care' will have to be raised to the same level of importance as 'cure' before sufficient attention is paid to the needs of many populations with chronic or intractable illnesses".[1] These developments also have obvious implications for the priority to be given to the training of health professions specializing in care of the aged.

In developing countries the proportion of those who are going to live to be 65 in the year 2000 can be estimated at approximate 70% (compared to about 45% now) and one out of three can be expected to celebrate his or her eightieth birthday, as compared to one out of seven under 1975 mortality conditions. Here, too, the figures emphasize that problems concerning the provision of social services for the elderly can no longer be considered to be issues for the distant future. In many developing countries the time is rapidly approaching when the gradual institution of relevant social policy measures—in line with their cultural tradition and economic capability—will require urgent attention.

Morbidity

Few attempts have been made to project morbidity and disability, either as total load to the community or as disease-specific estimates. Development in this area has been hampered by deficiencies in the population-based data, as morbidity statistics currently available in many countries are institution-based. It is hoped that with the major emphasis on improvements in primary health care, data generated for its management will also improve in both quality and quantity so as to provide a basis for projections of morbidity and disability in the population.

Among the few recent examples of morbidity projections, those for cancer and mental disorders can be singled out to illustrate applications of national priorities, control programmes and intervention strategies. In Finland, for instance, projections of cancer incidence[2] were made by primary site for each hospital district, as a basis for the planning of oncological facilities by the National Board of Health and the allocation of services and resources. More recently, trends in male lung cancer incidence were projected until the year 2000. It was concluded that direct extrapolations of past trends in cancer incidence may lead to grossly erroneous results. The age-adjusted lung cancer incidence rate among

---

[1] LALONDE, M. *A new perspective on the health of Canadians*, Ottawa, Department of National Health and Welfare, 1974, p. 41.

[2] HAKAMA, M. Projections of cancer incidence: experience and some results in Finland. *World health statistics quarterly*, **33** (1980) (in press).

Finnish males for instance would increase from a level of about 70 per 100 000 males in 1975 to over 100 in the year 2000 if the extrapolation were made on the basis of data covering the 20 years 1956–1975. However, if the extrapolation were based on data for the quinquennium 1971–1975 only, the age-adjusted incidence rate would fall below 40 per 100 000 males.

The growing importance being attached to the provision of better services for the mentally ill and mentally handicapped is reflected in the literature. In a study of the effect of population changes between 1975 and 2000 on selected indices of mental disorders, it is concluded that, all other things being equal, increases of 60% to 125% in the number of annual new cases of mental disorders in the developing countries can be expected, owing to the evolution of the age structure of the population.

In England, the Department of Health and Social Security recently reviewed the inadequacies of services for the mentally ill and mentally handicapped and set forth the implications for health policy. It found that the number of residential care places (per 100 000 population) should be increased from 17 for adults and 4 for children in 1974 to 60 and 10 respectively by 1991, and the number of places per 100 000 population in adult training centres from 68 in 1976 to 150 in 1991. To meet these targets "a deliberate decision" to give mental health services high priority in the allocation of resources was recommended.

In general, an increasing preoccupation with projections of disease-specific morbidity has become apparent in a number of developed countries in recent years. However, projections of disease frequency should prove useful in all countries, particularly for the planning and evaluation of disease control programmes and the assessment of their potential social effects.

In the coming decades, many of the developing countries will continue their struggle against infectious and parasitic diseases and accord them first priority. However, health problems now typical in the developed countries—such as cancer, cardiovascular diseases, mental health and accidents—may well become of major concern to the developing countries as they move along the path of socioeconomic development. In addition, environmental health problems which will arise with rapid urbanization and industrialization will have to be tackled (see also the section on Demographic prospects, pages 228 and 234–235).

The lessons of the recent past have impressively demonstrated that the dangers posed by certain infectious and parasitic diseases should not be underestimated. The conquest of diseases such as malaria, schistosomiasis and onchocerciasis will be a long and arduous task, challenging personal ingenuity and political determination. Success will depend very heavily on changes in the socioeconomic setting and in the political climate; a significant breakthrough in improving the health status of the world's population cannot be expected unless the main causes of poverty and underdevelopment, such as obsolete socioeconomic structures, can be removed.

An important part will be played by national and international efforts to attain the goals set by the United Nations Water Conference in Mar del Plata in 1977, and by WHO's Expanded Programme on Immunization, namely to provide by 1990 (a) safe drinking-water and sanitation for the entire world population; and (b) immunization for all the children of the world against the main infectious diseases.

Last but not least, changes in behavioural patterns, eating habits, smoking, alcohol consumption, use of drugs, physical exercise and driving have an important bearing on health prospects; much will depend on whether health education can reach the public more effectively than in the past.

Health manpower supply and demand

The 1978 International Conference on Primary Health Care held in Alma-Ata suggested that in many developed and developing countries a fundamental reorientation in the organization of health services may be anticipated. Among the crucial issues were: emphasis on primary health care; expansion of health protection to the whole population as part of a strategy aimed at more social equity within and among countries; review of health technology, including the controversy about sophisticated and costly medical technology, with special reference to its importation into developing countries; delegation of responsibilities and functions from highly specialized to multipurpose professional and auxiliary staff; an appeal to the general public to participate in health programmes and encouragement of self-reliance on a personal as well as a collective national basis. All this will have profound implications for the planning of health manpower.

Several case studies of national health manpower projections of density per 100 000 population have been published. These studies cover different periods, involve different sets of assumptions about increments and losses and refer to various categories of health manpower. Some also project health manpower demand and state whether a surplus of deficit may be expected in the future, on the basis of the gap between projected supply and demand. Table 24 gives a range of projections from two developed and four developing countries.

The use of projections for target-setting with respect to health manpower planning has been illustrated *inter alia* in a study of world trends in medical manpower from 1950 to 1970.[1] This showed, for instance, that in Africa medical manpower density increased between 1960 and 1970 by 25%. The implications of the projected increase in the population of Africa for physician requirements based on a number of physicians in 1970 approximate to 47 000, correspond to two different targets: the number of physicians required in the year 2000 (*a*) to maintain the 1970 level of 14 per 100 000 population, which gives a total of 110 000; and (*b*) to improve the physician/population ratio by 25% (1960–1970 rate) per decade, and obtain a ratio of 27 per 100 000 in the year 2000, which would raise it to 215 000. To put these figures into proper perspective, it must be borne in mind that the ratio of 27 physicians per 100 000 population would raise the average for the continent to the level attained by Mauritius in 1970, and would require the number of physicians to increase by more than 350% in 30 years.

These computations demonstrate convincingly that for the provision of adequate health care to the population, the health manpower profile typical of the developed countries requires substantial modifications under the conditions prevailing in many developing countries. New approaches must be developed, including better use and training of local health manpower resources, particularly of traditional medicine and of auxiliary staff. Comprehensive reviews of the roles and functions of different types of health personnel

---

[1] BUI DANG HA DOAN. World trends in medical manpower, 1950–1970. *World health statistics report,* **27:** 84–108 (1974).

Table 24. Selected national health manpower supply projections

Country	Period	Categories of manpower[a]	Major assumptions	Projected density (per 100 000 population)	Supply/demand predictions[b]
United States of America	1970–1990	1,2,3,4,5,6, 7,8,9	Federal funding will follow a certain pattern. Health man-power migration will follow same trends as in 1970.	Physicians, high (1990): 254.2; low (1990): 220.2.	Demand not measured in this study.
France[d]	1969–1985	1	Two different assump-tions on health man-power migration	Physicians, high (1985): 227; low (1985): 183	Demand not measured in this study.
India[e]	1971–2001	1,3,5,8,10	Rates of change in 1951–1969 extrapolated for 1971–2001.	Physicians (2001): 29.1; nurses, 71.1	Demand projected separately. No shortage shown for physicians. Shortages of trained pharmacists and trained nurses.
Kenya[f]	1967–2001		No emigration expected.	Physicians high, (2000): 8.6; low (2000): 5.4.	Demand not measured in this study.
Peru[g]	1964–1984	1,3,5,8,9,10	Manpower retained in the system at either present (1964), im-proved, or maxi-mum rates	Physicians, high, (1984): 62.5; low (1984): 58.8.	Demand projected separately. No shortage shown for physicians. Shortages of trained pharmacists and trained nurses.
Turkey[h]	1964–1977	1,8,9,10	(1) Present annual increment; (2) Additional medical schools; (3) Additional medical schools and/or slower decrease in medical schools.	Total numbers only. Population not projected.	Demand projected. Shortages of physicians, nurses and rural midwives.

[a] 1 = Physicians; 2 = Medical specialists (M.D.S.); 3 = Dentists; 4 = Optometrists; 5 = Pharmacists; 6 = Podiatrists; 7 = Veterinarians; 8 = Nurses; 9 = Other health occupations; 10 = Midwives.

[b] "No shortage" refers only to total numbers and not to distribution between geographical areas or by specialization within the profession.

[c] Source: United States Department of Health, Education, and Welfare, The supply of health manpower. 1970 profiles and projections to 1990. Washington, DC, 1975 (Publication No. (HRA) 75–38).

[d] Source: BUI DANG HA DOAN. Le corps médical français en 1985. Concours médical, 92: 388 (1970).

[e] Source: WAHEED, M. Health manpower planning in a developing economy: India. A case study. Indian journal of public health, 17: 5 (1973).

[f] Source: WHEELER, M. Medical manpower in Kenya. A projection and some of its implications. East African medical journal, 46: 93 (1969).

[g] Source: HALL, T. L. Health manpower in Peru. A case study in planning. Baltimore, Johns Hopkins University Press, 1969.

[h] Source: TAYLOR, C. E. ET AL. Health manpower planning in Turkey. Baltimore, Johns Hopkins University Press, 1967.

may help to correct imbalances in the supply, particularly for the pressing needs of primary health care.

World health policies

The implications of the aspects treated in the aforegoing sections of this chapter for world health policies are that countries, as part of their strategies for the attainment of health for all by the year 2000, will have to take into account—to paraphrase resolution WHA23.59 adopted by the Twenty-third World Health Assembly in 1970—the analysis and evaluation of information on the state of health of their population and on factors affecting environmental health. It will be necessary to identify general trends in the health situation, and to evolve the most promising strategies for developing programmes for the better implementation of health services and application of health technology. WHO, in fulfilling its constitutional function as the coordinating authority on international health work and in implementing the above resolution, will also have to pay greater attention to the development of health trend analysis for use by countries and by the Organization. It will have to present more succinct yet clear analyses of health trends to ensure that the selected strategies truly deal with the most important and widespread world health problems. This is a great challenge; it is hoped that the meeting of this challenge will provide good subjects for presentation in forthcoming reports by WHO, and in particular in the seventh and subsequent reports on the world health situation.

Successful implementation of these proposed developments is an essential ingredient of the technical support required to make a reality of the overall objective of the attainment of an acceptable level of health for all by the year 2000, which was established by the Thirtieth World Health Assembly in 1977 by resolution WHA30.43, and recognized in the Declaration of Alma-Ata elaborated by the International Conference on Primary Health Care in September 1978.

Annex Tables
and Figures

TABLE 1. POPULATION, RATE OF INCREASE, BIRTH AND DEATH RATES, SURFACE AREA AND DENSITY FOR THE WORLD, CONTINENTS AND GEOGRAPHICAL REGIONS (SELECTED YEARS)

Continents, geographical regions	Estimates of mid-year population (in millions)							Birth rate (per 1000) 1965-77	Death rate (per 1000) 1965-77	Annual rate of population increase (%)		Surface area (km²) (thousands) 1977	Density (per km²) 1977
	1950	1955	1960	1965	1970	1976	1977			1965-77	1970-77		
WORLD TOTAL	2 501	2 722	2 986	3 288	3 610	4 044	4 124	31	13	1.9	1.9	135 830	30
AFRICA	219	243	273	309	352	412	424	46	20	2.7	2.7	30 319	14
Eastern Africa	62	69	77	88	100	118	121	48	21	2.7	2.8	6 338	19
Middle Africa	26	29	32	36	40	46	48	44	21	2.4	2.3	6 613	7
Northern Africa	52	58	66	74	86	101	104	43	15	2.8	2.8	8 525	12
Southern Africa	14	16	18	21	24	28	29	43	16	2.9	2.8	2 701	11
Western Africa	65	72	80	90	102	119	122	49	23	2.6	2.7	6 142	20
AMERICA	330	370	415	461	509	572	584	28	9	2.0	2.0	42 082	14
LATIN AMERICA	164	188	216	247	283	333	342	37	9	2.7	2.8	20 566	17
Caribbean	17	18	20	22	25	28	28	32	9	1.9	2.0	238	119
Middle America	36	42	49	57	67	81	84	42	9	3.3	3.3	2 496	34
Temperate South America	25	28	31	33	36	39	40	24	9	1.5	1.4	3 726	11
Tropical South America	86	100	116	134	155	185	190	38	9	3.0	2.9	14 106	13
NORTHERN AMERICA	166	182	199	214	226	239	242	17	9	1.0	0.9	21 515	11
ASIA	1 368	1 492	1 644	1 824	2 027	2 304	2 355	34	13	2.2	2.2	27 580	85
East Asia	675	729	788	854	926	1 021	1 037	26	10	1.6	1.6	11 756	88
South Asia	693	763	856	970	1 101	1 283	1 318	41	16	2.6	2.6	15 825	83
Eastern South Asia	173	192	217	248	283	333	342	42	15	2.7	2.7	4 498	76
Middle South Asia	475	520	581	656	742	860	882	41	17	2.5	2.5	6 785	130
Western South Asia	44	51	58	67	77	91	93	43	15	2.9	2.9	4 542	21
EUROPE	392	408	425	445	459	476	478	16	10	0.6	0.6	4 937	97
Eastern Europe	89	93	97	100	103	107	108	17	10	0.6	0.6	990	109
Northern Europe	72	74	76	79	80	82	83	15	11	0.4	0.4	1 636	51
Southern Europe	109	113	118	123	128	133	134	18	9	0.7	0.7	1 315	102
Western Europe	122	128	135	143	148	153	154	15	11	0.6	0.5	995	155
OCEANIA	12.6	14.1	15.8	17.5	19.3	21.7	22.2	23	10	2.0	2.0	8 510	3
Australia and New Zealand	10.1	11.4	12.7	14.0	15.4	17.1	17.4	19	9	1.8	1.8	7 956	2
Melanesia	1.8	2.0	2.2	2.5	2.8	3.2	3.3	41	17	2.5	2.5	524	6
Polynesia and Micronesia	0.7	0.8	0.9	1.0	1.2	1.4	1.4	34	7	2.6	2.6	30	47
UNION OF SOVIET SOCIALIST REPUBLICS	180	196	214	231	243	258	260	18	8	1.0	1.0	22 402	12

Source: United Nations Demographic Yearbook, 1977.

247

TABLE 2. POPULATION BY CONTINENTS, GEOGRAPHICAL REGIONS, SEX, AND MAJOR AGE GROUPS, 1950, 1975, 2000 (IN THOUSANDS)

Continents, geographical regions	Year	Total	Sex		Sex Ratio	Absolute numbers					Percentages					Dependency ratio
			Male	Female		0-14	15-44	45-64	65-79	80+	0-15	15-44	45-64	65-79	80+	
WORLD TOTAL	1950	2 501 213	1 250 496	1 250 718	100.0	874 185	1 112 372	377 596	121 485	15 572	35.0	44.5	15.1	4.9	0.6	67.4
	1975	3 967 864	1 987 516	1 980 348	100.4	1 428 261	1 721 572	591 357	196 628	30 045	36.0	43.4	14.9	5.0	0.8	71.6
	2000	6 254 377	3 145 059	3 109 318	101.1	2 025 831	2 859 253	973 274	338 413	57 605	32.4	45.7	15.6	5.4	0.9	63.2
More developed regions	1950	857 305	409 316	447 989	91.4	239 303	387 415	165 969	56 381	8 238	27.9	45.2	19.4	6.6	1.0	54.9
	1975	1 131 684	547 337	584 348	93.7	283 032	497 402	232 759	99 540	18 951	25.0	44.0	20.6	8.8	1.7	55.0
	2000	1 360 245	668 911	691 334	96.8	307 403	580 849	303 763	137 028	31 203	22.6	42.7	22.3	10.1	2.3	53.8
Less developed regions	1950	1 643 908	841 180	802 728	104.8	634 882	724 957	211 627	65 104	7 334	38.6	44.1	12.9	4.0	0.5	75.5
	1975	2 836 180	1 440 179	1 396 001	103.2	1 145 229	1 224 170	358 598	97 088	11 094	40.4	43.2	12.6	3.4	0.4	79.2
	2000	4 894 133	2 476 148	2 417 985	102.4	1 718 428	2 278 404	669 511	201 385	26 402	35.1	46.6	13.7	4.1	0.5	66.0
AFRICA	1950	218 803	108 741	110 063	98.8	93 939	93 384	24 125	6 727	628	42.9	42.7	11.0	3.1	0.3	86.2
	1975	401 314	199 497	201 817	98.9	177 396	168 602	43 705	10 510	1 100	44.2	42.0	10.9	2.6	0.3	89.0
	2000	813 681	405 261	408 420	99.2	350 150	349 530	87 246	24 126	2 629	43.0	43.0	10.7	3.0	0.3	86.3
Eastern Africa	1950	61 878	30 447	31 431	96.9	27 173	26 123	6 612	1 811	157	43.9	42.2	10.7	2.9	0.3	89.0
	1975	114 498	56 757	57 741	98.3	51 480	47 703	12 261	2 807	248	45.0	41.7	10.7	2.5	0.2	90.9
	2000	239 861	119 157	120 704	98.7	107 646	100 643	24 236	6 641	694	44.9	42.0	10.1	2.8	0.3	92.1
Middle Africa	1950	26 258	12 609	13 649	92.4	10 917	11 277	3 034	941	88	41.6	43.0	11.6	3.6	0.3	83.5
	1975	45 310	22 189	23 120	96.0	19 315	19 476	5 222	1 182	114	42.6	43.0	11.5	2.6	0.3	83.5
	2000	87 732	43 411	44 322	97.9	37 969	37 001	9 775	2 705	282	43.3	42.2	11.1	3.1	0.3	87.6
Northern Africa	1950	51 806	26 096	25 710	101.5	21 785	22 120	6 026	1 722	152	42.1	42.7	11.6	3.3	0.3	84.1
	1975	98 185	49 222	48 963	100.5	43 437	40 721	10 784	2 908	335	44.2	41.5	11.0	3.0	0.3	90.6
	2000	191 824	96 530	95 294	101.3	73 821	88 203	22 455	6 565	781	38.5	46.0	11.7	3.4	0.4	73.4
Southern Africa	1950	14 324	7 178	7 146	100.4	5 629	6 196	1 846	598	55	39.3	43.3	12.9	4.2	0.4	78.1
	1975	27 853	13 735	14 117	97.3	11 455	11 969	3 343	948	140	41.1	43.0	12.0	3.4	0.5	81.9
	2000	56 231	27 904	28 326	98.5	23 407	24 288	6 358	1 921	256	41.6	43.2	11.3	3.4	0.5	83.5
Western Africa	1950	64 538	32 411	32 127	100.9	28 434	27 667	6 606	1 656	175	44.1	42.9	10.2	2.6	0.3	88.3
	1975	115 469	57 593	57 875	99.5	51 710	48 734	12 097	2 665	263	44.8	42.2	10.5	2.3	0.2	80.8
	2000	238 034	118 259	119 775	98.7	107 307	99 393	24 424	6 294	616	45.1	41.8	10.3	2.6	0.3	92.3
AMERICA	1950	329 998	165 382	164 616	100.5	111 733	146 250	53 853	16 472	2 651	33.9	44.3	16.0	5.0	0.8	65.7
	1975	560 933	278 052	282 882	98.3	196 596	241 299	86 504	30 282	6 255	35.0	43.0	15.4	5.4	1.1	71.1
	2000	916 128	456 037	460 091	99.1	299 988	413 501	142 735	49 025	10 877	32.7	45.1	15.6	5.4	1.2	64.7
LATIN AMERICA	1950	163 925	82 532	81 393	101.4	66 680	72 047	19 529	4 912	757	40.7	44.0	11.9	3.0	0.5	79.0
	1975	324 092	162 220	161 872	100.2	136 231	136 665	38 744	10 990	1 463	42.0	42.2	12.0	3.4	0.5	84.8
	2000	619 929	310 746	309 183	100.5	232 487	281 578	77 903	24 094	3 865	37.5	45.4	12.6	3.9	0.6	72.5
Caribbean	1950	16 725	8 425	8 299	101.5	6 579	7 431	2 057	576	81	39.3	44.4	12.3	3.4	0.5	76.3
	1975	27 116	13 544	13 572	99.8	11 042	11 187	3 504	1 206	177	40.7	41.3	12.9	4.4	0.7	84.6
	2000	44 504	22 332	22 172	100.7	15 442	20 608	5 994	2 063	396	34.7	46.3	13.5	4.6	0.9	67.3

TABLE 2. POPULATION BY CONTINENTS, GEOGRAPHICAL REGIONS, SEX, AND MAJOR AGE GROUPS, 1950, 1975, 2000 (IN THOUSANDS)
(continued)

Continents geographical regions	Year	Total	Sex Male	Sex Female	Sex Ratio	Absolute numbers 0–14	15–44	45–64	65–79	80+	Percentages 0–15	15–44	45–64	65–79	80+	Dependency ratio
Middle America	1950	35 835	17 947	17 888	100.3	15 417	15 140	4 109	1 036	133	43.0	42.3	11.5	2.9	0.4	86.2
	1975	78 652	39 555	39 096	101.2	35 973	32 210	7 789	2 308	372	45.7	41.0	9.9	2.9	0.5	96.6
	2000	172 670	87 123	85 548	101.8	72 268	76 453	17 968	5 085	898	41.9	44.3	10.4	2.9	0.5	82.9
Temperate South America	1950	25 437	12 952	12 485	103.7	8 176	12 011	4 137	981	132	32.1	47.2	16.3	3.9	0.5	57.5
	1975	38 747	19 313	19 434	99.4	11 773	17 001	7 141	2 443	389	30.4	43.9	18.4	6.3	1.0	60.5
	2000	52 078	25 776	26 303	98.0	13 515	23 720	9 947	4 005	891	26.0	45.6	19.1	7.7	1.7	54.7
Tropical South America	1950	85 928	43 208	42 721	101.1	36 507	37 463	9 226	2 320	411	42.5	43.6	10.7	2.7	0.5	84.0
	1975	179 578	89 808	89 770	100.0	77 443	76 266	20 311	5 034	525	43.1	42.5	11.3	2.8	0.3	85.9
	2000	350 676	175 516	175 160	100.2	131 262	160 797	43 995	12 942	1 680	37.4	45.9	12.6	3.7	0.5	71.2
NORTHERN AMERICA	1950	166 073	82 850	83 223	99.6	45 093	74 203	33 324	11 560	1 894	27.2	44.7	20.1	7.0	1.1	54.5
	1975	236 841	115 832	121 010	95.7	60 365	104 634	47 760	19 292	4 792	25.5	44.2	20.2	8.2	2.0	55.4
	2000	296 199	145 291	150 908	96.3	67 501	131 923	64 832	24 931	7 012	22.8	44.5	21.9	8.4	2.4	50.5
ASIA	1950	1 367 737	702 541	665 196	105.6	511 060	607 803	184 315	58 116	6 446	37.4	44.4	13.5	4.2	0.5	72.6
	1975	2 256 173	1 150 079	1 106 094	104.0	868 724	987 289	304 659	85 460	10 042	38.5	43.8	13.5	3.8	0.4	74.6
	2000	3 637 327	1 847 405	1 789 922	103.2	1 172 905	1 721 040	548 129	171 860	23 395	32.2	47.3	15.1	4.7	0.6	60.3
East Asia	1950	674 821	347 624	327 197	106.2	233 919	301 428	103 434	32 203	3 839	34.7	44.7	15.3	4.8	0.6	66.7
	1975	1 006 380	511 286	495 094	103.3	329 284	458 676	160 472	51 500	6 448	32.7	45.6	16.0	5.1	0.6	62.5
	2000	1 370 061	689 371	680 690	101.3	343 500	646 401	272 817	92 427	14 916	25.1	47.2	19.9	6.8	1.1	49.1
South Asia	1950	692 916	354 917	337 999	105.0	277 141	306 375	80 881	25 913	2 607	40.0	44.2	11.7	3.7	0.4	78.9
	1975	1 249 793	638 793	611 000	104.6	539 440	528 613	144 187	33 960	3 594	43.2	42.3	11.5	2.7	0.3	85.8
	2000	2 267 266	1 158 034	1 109 232	104.4	829 405	1 074 639	275 312	79 433	8 479	36.6	47.4	12.1	3.5	0.4	68.0
Eastern South Asia	1950	173 228	85 728	87 500	98.0	70 384	77 463	19 140	5 648	594	40.6	44.7	11.0	3.3	0.3	79.3
	1975	323 836	161 295	162 542	99.2	141 248	136 481	36 544	8 702	861	43.6	42.1	11.3	2.7	0.3	87.2
	2000	591 622	296 315	295 307	100.3	215 765	282 463	70 516	20 710	2 169	36.5	47.7	11.9	3.5	0.4	67.6
Middle South Asia	1950	475 345	246 723	228 623	107.9	188 923	209 558	56 123	18 853	1 890	39.7	44.1	11.8	4.0	0.4	78.9
	1975	837 799	432 868	404 931	106.9	360 195	355 571	97 493	22 121	2 418	43.0	42.4	11.6	2.6	0.3	84.9
	2000	1 501 213	773 715	727 498	106.4	546 298	712 847	184 370	52 211	5 486	36.4	47.5	12.3	3.5	0.4	67.3
Western South Asia	1950	44 343	22 466	21 876	102.7	17 833	19 352	5 618	1 415	123	40.2	43.6	12.7	3.2	0.3	77.6
	1975	88 158	44 630	43 528	102.5	37 997	36 561	10 149	3 136	315	43.1	41.5	11.5	3.6	0.4	88.7
	2000	174 432	88 005	86 427	101.8	67 344	79 330	20 424	6 511	824	38.6	45.5	11.7	3.7	0.5	74.9
EUROPE	1950	391 968	188 355	203 613	92.5	99 500	173 766	84 598	29 724	4 380	25.4	44.3	21.6	7.6	1.1	51.7
	1975	473 098	230 628	242 470	95.1	113 093	200 020	101 673	49 388	8 926	23.9	42.3	21.5	10.4	1.9	56.8
	2000	539 500	267 317	272 182	98.2	119 001	224 420	123 129	59 766	13 181	22.1	41.6	22.8	11.1	2.4	55.2
Eastern Europe	1950	88 500	41 992	46 508	90.3	23 628	40 088	18 562	5 522	700	26.7	45.3	21.0	6.2	0.8	50.9
	1975	106 267	51 619	54 648	94.5	24 547	47 215	22 263	10 661	1 580	23.1	44.4	21.0	10.0	1.5	53.0
	2000	121 437	60 077	61 360	97.9	26 341	50 415	28 745	13 502	2 435	21.7	41.5	23.7	11.1	2.0	53.4

TABLE 2. POPULATION BY CONTINENTS, GEOGRAPHICAL REGIONS, SEX, AND MAJOR AGE GROUPS, 1950, 1975, 2000 (IN THOUSANDS)
(continued)

Continents, geographical regions	Year	Sex			Sex Ratio	Absolute numbers					Percentages					Dependency ratio
		Total	Male	Female		0–14	15–44	45–64	65–79	80 +	0–15	15–44	45–64	65–79	80 +	
Northern Europe	1950	72 477	35 395	37 082	95.5	17 021	31 445	16 542	6 428	1 041	23.5	43.4	22.8	8.9	1.4	51.0
	1975	81 975	40 137	41 838	95.9	19 472	32 738	18 716	9 210	1 839	23.8	39.9	22.8	11.2	2.2	59.3
	2000	91 320	45 045	46 275	97.3	20 864	38 328	20 214	9 239	2 675	22.9	42.0	22.1	10.1	2.9	56.0
Southern Europe	1950	108 552	52 637	55 915	94.1	30 198	50 073	20 263	6 942	1 078	27.8	46.1	18.7	6.4	1.0	54.3
	1975	132 354	64 580	67 774	95.3	33 711	55 9?	28	12.166	2.174	25.5	42.3	21.4	9.2	1.6	57.1
	2000	155 685	76 621	79 064	96.9	35 833	65 139	33 440	17 676	3 597	23.0	41.8	21.5	11.4	2.3	57.9
Western Europe	1950	122 439	58 331	64 108	91.0	28 654	52 161	29 233	10 832	1 561	23.4	42.6	23.9	8.9	1.3	50.4
	1975	152 503	74 292	78 210	95.0	35 304	64 097	32 420	17 350	3 332	23.2	42.0	21.3	11.4	2.2	58.0
	2000	171 058	85 575	85 483	100.1	35 965	70 540	40 731	19 350	4 473	21.0	41.2	23.8	11.3	2.6	53.7
OCEANIA	1950	12 632	6 424	6 208	103.5	3 758	5 602	2 336	812	126	29.8	44.4	18.5	6.4	1.0	59.1
	1975	21 308	10 812	10 496	103.0	6 703	9 203	3 825	1 328	247	31.5	43.2	18.0	6.2	1.2	63.6
	2000	32 715	16 577	16 138	102.7	9 541	14 757	5 832	2 148	438	29.2	45.1	17.8	6.6	1.3	58.9
Australia and New Zealand	1950	10 127	5 103	5 024	101.6	2 734	4 494	2 060	724	115	27.0	44.4	20.3	7.2	1.1	54.5
	1975	16 840	8 493	8 347	101.7	4 822	7 272	3 306	1 205	235	28.6	43.2	19.6	7.2	1.4	59.2
	2000	24 512	12 368	12 144	101.8	6 493	10 965	4 790	1 861	404	26.5	44.7	19.5	7.6	1.7	55.6
Melanesia	1950	1 827	966	861	112.2	725	818	211	67	7	39.7	44.8	11.6	3.4	0.4	77.6
	1975	3 126	1 628	1 498	108.7	1 325	1 330	374	90	8	42.4	42.5	12.0	2.9	0.3	83.5
	2000	5 847	3 011	2 836	106.2	2 280	2 653	695	193	21	39.0	45.5	11.9	3.3	0.4	74.3
Micronesia and Polynesia	1950	678	355	323	109.9	299	290	65	20	4	44.1	42.8	9.6	3.0	0.6	91.0
	1975	1 341	691	651	106.1	555	602	145	33	4	41.4	44.9	10.8	2.5	0.3	79.5
	2000	2 356	1 197	1 159	103.3	770	1 133	348	93	13	32.7	48.1	14.8	3.9	0.6	59.1
UNION OF SOVIET SOCIALIST REPUBLICS	1950	180 075	79 053	101 022	78.3	54 156	85 571	29 374	9 633	1 341	30.1	47.5	16.3	5.3	0.7	56.7
	1975	255 038	118 448	136 589	86.7	65 749	115 158	50 992	19 663	3 475	25.8	45.2	20.0	7.7	1.4	53.5
	2000	315 027	152 461	162 566	93.8	74 246	136 008	66 201	31 487	7 085	23.6	43.2	21.0	10.0	2.3	55.8

Source: Population by sex and age for regions and countries, 1950, 2000, as assessed in 1973 (ESA/P/WP.60) United Nations Population Division, Department of Economic and Social Affairs.

TABLE 3. POPULATION BY URBAN/RURAL RESIDENCE, CONTINENTS AND GEOGRAPHICAL REGIONS, 1950, 1975, 2000 (IN THOUSANDS)

Continents, geographical regions	1950 Total	1950 Urban	1950 Rural Absolute numbers	1950 Rural %	1975 Total	1975 Urban	1975 Rural Absolute numbers	1975 Rural %	2000 Total	2000 Urban	2000 Rural Absolute numbers	2000 Rural %
WORLD TOTAL	2 501 243	714 681	1 786 562	71.4	3 967 005	1 557 685	2 409 320	60.7	6 253 135	3 103 214	3 149 921	50.4
More developed regions	857 305	457 339	399 966	46.7	1 131 715	785 582	349 133	30.8	1 360 557	1 106 942	253 615	18.6
Less developed regions	1 643 938	257 342	1 386 596	84.3	2 835 290	775 103	2 060 187	72.7	4 892 579	1 996 272	2 896 307	59.2
AFRICA	218 833	28 878	189 955	86.8	401 138	98 059	303 079	75.6	813 119	306 780	506 339	62.3
Eastern Africa	61 878	3 291	58 587	94.7	114 498	14 034	100 464	87.7	239 861	53 358	186 503	77.8
Middle Africa	26 258	2 121	24 137	91.9	45 310	11 126	34 184	75.4	87 732	38 914	48 818	55.6
Northern Africa	51 806	12 032	39 774	76.8	98 185	38 774	59 411	60.5	191 824	106 045	85 779	44.7
Southern Africa	14 354	5 240	9 114	63.5	27 678	12 795	14 883	53.8	55 669	33 699	21 970	39.5
Western Africa	64 538	6 194	58 344	90.4	115 469	21 330	94 139	81.5	238 034	74 764	163 270	68.6
AMERICA	329 998	172 742	157 256	47.7	560 933	377 066	183 867	32.8	916 128	719 668	196 460	21.4
LATIN AMERICA	163 925	67 039	96 886	59.1	324 092	195 809	128 283	39.6	619 929	463 736	156 193	25.2
Caribbean	16 725	5 513	11 212	67.0	27 116	13 068	14 048	51.8	44 504	28 175	16 329	36.7
Middle America	35 835	14 155	21 680	60.5	78 652	44 916	33 736	42.9	172 670	124 511	48 159	27.9
Temperate South America	25 437	15 987	9 450	37.2	38 747	31 314	7 433	19.2	52 078	46 912	5 166	9.9
Tropical South America	85 928	31 384	54 544	63.5	179 578	106 512	73 066	40.7	350 676	264 137	86 539	24.7
NORTHERN AMERICA	166 073	105 703	60 370	36.4	236 841	181 257	55 584	23.5	296 199	255 932	40 267	13.6
ASIA	1 367 737	219 284	1 148 453	84.0	2 255 458	595 268	1 660 019	73.6	3 636 335	1 385 689	2 250 646	61.9
East Asia	674 821	111 696	563 125	83.4	1 005 665	308 376	697 289	69.3	1 369 069	591 336	777 733	56.8
South Asia	692 916	107 588	585 328	84.5	1 249 793	286 892	962 901	77.0	2 267 266	794 353	1 472 913	65.0
Eastern South Asia	173 228	23 220	150 008	86.6	323 836	71 567	252 269	77.9	591 622	207 076	384 546	65.0
Middle South Asia	475 345	74 055	401 290	84.4	837 799	176 797	661 002	78.9	1 501 213	481 469	1 019 744	67.9
Western South Asia	44 343	10 313	34 030	76.7	88 158	38 528	49 630	56.3	174 432	105 809	68 623	39.3
EUROPE	391 968	214 751	177 217	45.2	473 128	317 700	155 428	32.9	539 812	424 996	114 816	21.3
Eastern Europe	88 500	37 348	51 152	57.8	106 297	60 165	46 132	43.4	121 749	87 266	34 483	28.3
Northern Europe	72 477	51 281	21 196	29.2	81 975	61 529	20 446	24.9	91 320	76 055	15 265	16.7
Southern Europe	108 552	48 765	59 787	55.1	132 354	78 425	53 929	40.7	155 685	113 479	42 206	27.1
Western Europe	122 439	77 357	45 082	36.8	152 503	117 581	34 922	22.9	171 058	148 196	22 862	13.4
OCEANIA	12 632	8 142	4 490	35.5	21 308	15 262	6 046	28.4	32 715	25 584	7 131	21.8
Australia and New Zealand	10 127	7 966	2 161	21.3	16 840	14 403	2 437	14.5	24 512	22 456	2 056	8.4
Melanesia	1 827	36	1 791	98.0	3 126	429	2 697	86.3	5 847	2 041	3 806	65.1
Micronesia and Polynesia	678	140	538	79.4	1 341	430	911	67.9	2 356	1 086	1 270	53.9
UNION OF SOVIET SOCIALIST REPUBLICS	180 075	70 884	109 191	60.6	255 038	154 330	100 708	39.5	315 027	240 498	74 529	23.7

Source: Trends and prospects in urban and rural population 1950–2000, as assessed in 1973–74 (ESA/WP.51), United Nations Population Division, Department of Economic and Social Affairs.

251

TABLE 4. LABOUR FORCE ESTIMATES BY SEX AND AGE, CONTINENTS AND GEOGRAPHICAL REGIONS, 1950, 1975, 2000
A. Absolute numbers (in thousands)

Continents, geographic regions		Sex	All ages	Age groups 15–64	10–14	15–44	45–64	65≤I
WORLD TOTAL	1950		1 100 150	994 347	57 105	750 515	243 831	48 698
		M	755 824	683 602	35 840	512 101	171 501	36 382
		F	344 326	310 745	21 265	238 415	72 329	12 316
	1975		1 645 575	1 537 881	54 717	1 147 900	389 982	52 977
		M	1 069 870	999 480	32 630	742 859	256 621	37 759
		F	575 705	538 400	22 086	405 039	133 361	15 218
	2000		2 545 857	2 442 672	37 342	1 817 998	624 675	65 843
		M	1 668 029	1 598 039	22 529	1 183 288	414 751	47 461
		F	877 829	844 634	14 813	634 709	209 924	18 382
More developed regions	1950		397 436	373 841	5 526	269 383	104 458	18 069
		M	251 711	236 604	3 293	167 269	69 335	11 814
		F	145 725	137 237	2 233	102 114	35 123	6 255
	1975		520 082	504 457	1 549	350 167	152 290	16 076
		M	313 366	301 767	972	210 203	91 565	10 627
		F	206 715	200 689	577	139 965	60 726	5 449
	2000		638 514	619 712	921	414 712	204 999	17 881
		M	378 165	366 018	577	242 736	123 282	11 570
		F	260 348	253 692	344	171 975	81 717	6 312
Less developed regions	1950		702 714	620 506	51 579	481 133	139 373	30 629
		M	504 113	446 998	32 547	344 832	102 165	24 568
		F	198 601	173 508	19 032	136 301	37 208	6 061
	1975		1 125 493	1 035 424	53 168	797 732	237 692	36 901
		M	756 504	697 714	31 658	532 657	165 056	27 132
		F	368 989	337 711	21 509	265 076	72 636	9 769
	2000		1 907 344	1 822 961	36 421	1 403 285	419 675	47 962
		M	1 289 864	1 232 021	21 952	940 551	291 469	35 891
		F	617 480	590 941	14 469	462 734	128 207	12 070
AFRICA	1950		94 698	82 718	8 042	64 930	17 788	3 938
		M	63 533	55 404	5 242	43 476	11 927	2 887
		F	31 165	27 314	2 800	21 454	5 860	1 051
	1975		152 142	137 856	9 641	108 559	29 297	4 645
		M	102 777	93 337	6 087	73 536	19 801	3 353
		F	49 366	44 519	3 555	35 022	9 495	1 292
	2000		284 246	267 120	10 076	211 182	55 938	7 050
		M	194 067	182 636	6 303	144 472	38 166	5 128
		F	90 178	84 482	3 774	66 711	17 772	1 922
Eastern Africa	1950		28 634	24 645	2 843	19 424	5 221	1 146
		M	18 145	15 556	1 824	12 373	3 184	765
		F	10 489	9 088	1 020	7 051	2 036	381
	1975		48 332	42 852	3 995	33 980	8 872	1 485
		M	31 237	27 757	2 486	22 209	5 549	994
		F	17 095	15 095	1 509	11 771	3 323	491
	2000		90 322	82 979	4 796	65 685	17 294	2 547
		M	59 798	55 087	2 979	43 933	11 154	1 732
		F	30 524	27 893	1 816	21 753	6 140	815
Middle Africa	1950		12 603	11 094	972	8 585	2 509	537
		M	7 703	6 748	555	5 189	1 559	400
		F	4 899	4 345	417	3 396	949	137
	1975		18 826	17 161	1 088	13 465	3 696	577
		M	11 742	10 728	591	8 403	2 326	423
		F	7 084	6 433	497	5 062	1 371	154
	2000		31 737	30 017	924	23 478	6 539	796
		M	20 104	18 992	518	14 799	4 194	594
		F	11 632	11 023	406	8 679	2 345	203
Northern Africa	1950		16 213	14 192	1 279	11 105	3 087	742
		M	15 087	13 299	1 080	10 399	2 900	708
		F	1 126	893	198	706	187	35
	1975		26 557	24 202	1 495	18 909	5 293	860
		M	24 157	22 114	1 236	17 237	4 876	807
		F	2 400	2 089	258	1 672	417	53
	2000		54 084	51 590	1 287	40 997	10 592	1 207
		M	47 901	45 803	982	36 232	9 573	1 116
		F	6 182	5 786	305	4 768	1 018	91
Southern Africa	1950		5 562	5 035	262	3 924	1 112	265
		M	4 248	3 828	206	2 939	889	214
		F	1 314	1 207	56	985	222	51

252

TABLE 4. LABOUR FORCE ESTIMATES BY SEX AND AGE, CONTINENTS AND GEOGRAPHICAL REGIONS, 1950, 1975, 2000 (continued)
A. Absolute numbers (in thousands)

Continents, geographical regions	Year	Sex	All ages	Age groups 15–64	10–14	15–44	45–64	65≤
	1975		10 612	10 172	165	8 047	2 126	275
		M	6 884	6 565	110	5 044	1 521	209
		F	3 728	3 607	55	3 002	604	66
	2000		21 028	20 507	151	16 500	4 007	370
		M	12 983	12 595	102	9 899	2 694	286
		F	8 045	7 913	48	6 601	1 312	84
Western Africa	1950		31 686	27 752	2 686	21 893	5 860	1 248
		M	18 349	15 971	1 577	12 577	3 395	801
		F	13 337	11 781	1 109	9 316	2 465	447
	1975		47 816	43 468	2 899	34 159	9 309	1 449
		M	28 756	26 172	1 663	20 643	5 530	921
		F	19 059	17 295	1 236	13 516	3 780	528
	2000		87 076	82 028	2 919	64 521	17 507	2 129
		M	53 281	50 160	1 721	39 609	10 550	1 400
		F	33 795	31 868	1 198	24 911	6 957	729
AMERICA	1950		128 018	119 062	3 246	87 362	31 701	5 710
		M	97 709	90 465	2 528	66 115	24 350	4 715
		F	30 309	28 597	718	21 248	7 350	994
	1975		206 256	195 917	3 656	142 981	52 937	6 683
		M	144 493	136 803	2 700	100 233	36 570	4 990
		F	61 763	59 114	956	42 747	16 367	1 693
	2000		346 869	336 101	2 587	248 665	87 435	8 181
		M	234 063	226 378	1 652	167 279	59 099	6 033
		F	112 806	109 722	935	81 385	28 336	2 149
LATIN AMERICA	1950		57 464	52 205	3 031	41 317	10 888	2 228
		M	47 130	42 883	2 367	33 642	9 241	1 880
		F	10 334	9 322	664	7 677	1 646	348
	1975		102 022	95 654	3 278	75 245	20 409	3 090
		M	79 269	74 207	2 447	57 498	16 708	2 615
		F	22 753	21 447	831	17 746	3 701	475
	2000		207 320	200 683	2 296	160 119	40 563	4 341
		M	150 601	145 521	1 460	113 318	32 203	3 620
		F	56 719	55 161	836	46 800	8 360	722
Caribbean	1950		6 575	6 046	237	4 705	1 341	292
		M	4 750	4 374	152	3 357	1 016	224
		F	1 825	1 672	85	1 348	325	68
	1975		9 110	8 558	223	6 493	2 065	329
		M	6 437	6 049	132	4 523	1 526	256
		F	2 673	2 510	91	1 971	540	72
	2000		16 173	15 583	189	12 193	3 389	401
		M	11 261	10 849	110	8 405	2 443	302
		F	4 912	4 734	79	3 789	945	99
Middle America	1950		11 751	10 463	736	8 240	2 224	552
		M	10 195	9 078	637	7 127	1 952	480
		F	1 555	1 384	99	1 113	272	72
	1975		23 073	21 361	793	17 199	4 161	919
		M	18 874	17 430	657	13 900	3 530	787
		F	4 200	3 932	136	3 299	631	132
	2000		53 264	51 422	615	41 896	9 527	1 227
		M	40 463	38 990	444	31 140	7 849	1 029
		F	12 803	12 433	171	10 755	1 678	197
Temperate South America	1950		10 141	9 560	243	7 212	2 348	338
		M	8 025	7 567	167	5 579	1 988	291
		F	2 116	1 994	76	1 633	361	46
	1975		14 247	13 636	202	10 022	3 615	409
		M	10 635	10 159	133	7 270	2 890	343
		F	3 611	3 475	70	2 751	725	66
	2000		20 041	19 438	127	14 366	5 071	476
		M	14 225	13 753	82	9 850	3 902	390
		F	5 816	5 685	45	4 516	1 169	86
Tropical South America	1950		28 997	26 136	1 815	21 161	4 975	1 046
		M	24 160	21 864	1 411	17 579	4 285	885
		F	4 838	4 273	404	3 582	690	161

253

TABLE 4. LABOUR FORCE ESTIMATES BY SEX AND AGE, CONTINENTS AND GEOGRAPHICAL REGIONS, 1950, 1975, 2000 (continued)
A. Absolute numbers (in thousands)

Continents, geographical regions		Sex	All ages	Age groups				
				15–64	10–14	15–44	45–64	65≤
	1975		55 593	52 100	2 060	41 531	10 568	1 433
		M	43 324	40 570	1 525	31 805	8 764	1 229
		F	12 269	11 531	534	9 725	1 804	204
	2000		117 843	114 240	1 365	91 664	22 576	2 238
		M	84 652	81 931	823	63 923	18 008	1 898
		F	33 191	32 310	541	27 741	4 568	340
NORTHERN AMERICA	1950		70 554	66 857	215	46 045	20 813	3 482
		M	50 579	47 582	161	32 473	15 109	2 836
		F	19 975	19 275	54	13 571	5 704	646
	1975		104 234	100 263	378	67 736	32 528	3 593
		M	65 224	62 596	253	42 735	19 862	2 375
		F	39 010	37 667	125	25 001	12 666	1 218
	2000		39 549	135 418	291	88 546	46 872	3 840
		M	83 462	80 857	192	53 961	26 896	2 413
		F	56 087	54 561	99	34 585	19 976	1 427
ASIA	1950		596 224	528 752	41 257	407 202	121 552	26 215
		M	423 330	376 853	25 479	288 277	88 576	20 998
		F	172 894	151 898	15 779	118 923	32 975	5 217
	1975		940 859	868 083	40 453	660 320	207 763	32 324
		M	618 394	571 738	23 281	430 977	140 761	23 376
		F	322 466	296 348	17 171	229 346	67 002	8 947
	2000		1 503 475	1 438 089	24 139	1 082 857	355 233	41 247
		M	998 057	953 485	14 266	713 557	239 927	30 306
		F	505 418	484 604	9 873	369 298	115 305	10 941
East Asia	1950		292 722	264 152	15 576	198 460	65 693	12 994
		M	211 193	191 219	9 393	142 878	48 342	10 581
		F	81 529	72 933	6 183	55 582	17 351	2 413
	1975		472 770	444 291	9 941	330 863	113 426	18 538
		M	293 237	275 160	5 631	202 418	72 743	12 446
		F	179 532	169 130	4 310	128 446	40 684	6 092
	2000		660 942	636 279	3 409	449 492	186 787	21 255
		M	404 463	387 914	1 979	269 469	118 445	14 570
		F	256 480	248 366	1 430	180 023	68 342	6 684
South Asia	1950		303 502	264 599	25 682	208 742	55 859	13 221
		M	212 138	185 635	16 086	145 400	40 234	10 417
		F	91 365	78 965	9 596	63 341	15 623	2 804
	1975		468 090	423 794	30 511	329 457	94 335	13 785
		M	325 156	296 576	17 650	228 559	68 018	10 930
		F	142 933	127 217	12 861	100 900	26 318	2 855
	2000		842 532	801 810	20 730	633 364	168 446	19 992
		M	593 594	565 571	12 287	444 088	121 482	15 736
		F	248 939	236 240	8 443	189 276	46 964	4 256
Eastern South Asia	1950		77 658	68 987	5 739	54 834	14 153	2 932
		M	49 292	44 154	3 082	35 095	9 060	2 056
		F	28 366	24 833	2 657	19 738	5 093	876
	1975		125 156	114 606	7 154	89 607	24 999	3 396
		M	79 842	73 757	3 775	57 309	16 448	2 310
		F	45 314	40 850	3 379	32 297	8 551	1 085
	2000		228 953	218 789	4 880	174 282	44 508	5 284
		M	150 432	144 249	2 575	114 956	29 293	3 608
		F	78 521	74 540	2 305	59 325	15 215	1 676
Middle South Asia	1950		207 295	179 083	18 623	141 136	37 948	9 589
		M	149 785	129 826	12 102	101 257	28 569	7 857
		F	57 511	49 257	6 521	39 879	9 378	1 733
	1975		312 747	281 954	21 656	218 683	63 271	9 137
		M	222 722	202 309	12 740	155 381	46 929	7 673
		F	90 025	79 645	8 916	63 302	16 342	1 464
	2000		556 032	528 134	14 746	415 720	112 415	13 152
		M	400 250	380 371	8 953	296 958	83 412	10 926
		F	155 783	147 765	5 792	118 761	29 003	2 226
Western South Asia	1950		18 549	16 530	1 320	12 773	3 758	699
		M	13 061	11 655	902	9 049	2 606	504
		F	5 488	4 875	418	3 723	1 153	195

254

TABLE 4. LABOUR FORCE ESTIMATES BY SEX AND AGE, CONTINENTS AND GEOGRAPHICAL REGIONS, 1950, 1975, 2000 (*continued*)
A. Absolute numbers (in thousands)

Continents, geographical regions		Sex	All ages	Age groups				
				15–64	10–14	15–44	45–64	65≤
	1975		30 187	27 233	1 701	21 167	6 066	1 253
		M	22 592	20 510	1 135	15 868	4 641	947
		F	7 595	6 724	566	5 300	1 424	305
	2000		57 547	54 885	1 105	43 362	11 523	1 557
		M	42 912	40 951	759	32 175	8 777	1 202
		F	14 635	13 934	346	11 188	2 746	355
EUROPE	1950		181 971	170 571	3 060	119 517	51 054	8 340
		M	122 015	114 089	1 911	78 381	35 709	6 015
		F	59 956	56 482	1 149	41 138	15 344	2 325
	1975		210 305	201 727	817	137 827	63 899	7 761
		M	134 181	128 595	477	87 127	41 468	5 109
		F	76 124	73 131	341	50 700	22 431	2 652
	2000		245 231	237 382	403	157 243	80 138	7 446
		M	151 985	147 009	233	95 822	51 186	4 743
		F	93 247	90 373	171	61 422	28 952	2 703
Eastern Europe	1950		45 872	43 389	357	30 390	12 999	2 126
		M	26 626	25 129	194	17 357	7 772	1 303
		F	19 246	18 260	163	13 033	5 228	823
	1975		56 195	53 243	89	36 548	16 696	2 863
		M	30 885	29 147	47	20 142	9 004	1 691
		F	25 310	24 096	42	16 404	7 691	1 172
	2000		65 139	62 221	41	40 211	22 010	2 877
		M	35 050	33 489	22	21 467	12 021	1 539
		F	30 090	28 734	19	18 744	9 989	1 337
Northern Europe	1950		33 627	32 154	54	22 201	9 952	1 419
		M	23 510	22 356	29	14 975	7 383	1 125
		F	10 116	9 797	25	7 229	2 569	294
	1975		37 213	35 949	14	22 895	13 055	1 250
		M	23 671	22 796	8	14 401	8 395	867
		F	13 542	13 153	6	8 495	4 659	383
	2000		42 940	41 859	7	27 073	14 785	1 074
		M	26 167	25 443	4	16 387	9 056	720
		F	16 773	16 416	3	10 687	5 730	354
Southern Europe	1950		46 367	41 840	2 186	31 044	10 796	2 341
		M	34 814	31 485	1 415	22 861	8 622	1 914
		F	11 553	10 356	771	8 182	2 174	426
	1975		51 075	48 691	504	34 217	14 474	1 880
		M	36 687	34 952	294	23 912	11 039	1 441
		F	14 388	13 739	210	10 304	3 435	439
	2000		60 109	58 080	217	40 833	17 246	1 812
		M	41 697	40 176	125	27 443	12 734	1 395
		F	18 412	17 903	93	13 390	4 512	416
Western Europe	1950		56 105	53 188	463	35 881	17 308	2 454
		M	37 065	35 120	273	23 188	11 933	1 672
		F	19 040	18 069	190	12 694	5 375	781
	1975		65 821	63 843	210	44 168	19 676	1 768
		M	42 938	41 701	127	28 672	13 029	1 110
		F	22 883	22 142	83	15 497	6 647	658
	2000		77 044	75 223	138	49 126	26 097	1 683
		M	49 071	47 902	82	30 526	17 376	1 087
		F	27 972	27 320	56	18 599	8 721	596
OCEANIA	1950		5 449	5 134	118	3 804	1 331	197
		M	4 039	3 802	72	2 724	1 079	165
		F	1 410	1 332	46	1 080	252	32
	1975		9 076	8 705	149	6 298	2 407	222
		M	6 147	5 885	86	4 142	1 743	176
		F	2 929	2 819	64	2 156	664	46
	2000		14 192	13 758	137	9 999	3 759	297
		M	9 298	8 988	76	6 375	2 612	234
		F	4 894	4 770	61	3 625	1 146	63
Australia, New Zealand	1950		4 203	4 042	16	2 926	1 115	145
		M	3 242	3 108	10	2 172	938	124
		F	961	933	7	756	178	21

255

TABLE 4. LABOUR FORCE ESTIMATES BY SEX AND AGE, CONTINENTS AND GEOGRAPHICAL REGIONS, 1950, 1975, 2000 (*continued*)
A. Absolute numbers (in thousands)

Continents, geographical regions		Sex	All ages	Age groups				
				15–64	10–14	15–44	45–64	65≤
	1975		7 099	6 921	14	4 896	2 024	164
		M	4 869	4 729	8	3 244	1 486	132
		F	2 230	2 190	7	1 652	540	33
	2000		10 655	10 435	14	7 385	3 050	206
		M	7 017	6 845	7	4 721	2 125	165
		F	3 638	3 589	7	2 664	925	42
Melanesia	1950		1 020	889	89	712	177	42
		M	603	520	51	412	109	32
		F	417	369	38	300	68	10
	1975		1 541	1 372	121	1 072	301	48
		M	922	821	66	634	188	35
		F	619	552	55	439	113	12
	2000		2 658	2 467	116	1 946	522	75
		M	1 628	1 510	63	1 176	334	55
		F	1 030	958	52	770	189	20
Micronesia and Polynesia	1950		226	203	13	165	38	10
		M	194	174	11	141	33	9
		F	33	30	2	25	6	1
	1975		436	412	14	330	81	10
		M	356	335	12	265	69	9
		F	80	77	2	66	10	1
	2000		879	856	7	670	186	16
		M	652	632	6	478	154	14
		F	226	222	2	191	32	2
UNION OF SOVIET SOCIALIST REPUBLICS	1950		93 790	88 110	1 382	67 702	20 407	4 298
		M	45 197	42 988	608	33 130	9 859	1 601
		F	48 593	45 122	774	34 572	10 549	2 697
	1975		126 935	125 592	—	91 914	33 680	1 343
		M	63 878	63 123	—	46 845	16 278	755
		F	63 058	62 470	—	45 067	17 402	588
	2000		151 845	150 223	—	108 050	42 172	1 622
		M	80 560	79 542	—	55 782	23 760	1 018
		F	71 285	70 681	—	52 268	18 412	604

Source: Labour Force, Vol. V, World summary 1950–2000, International Labour Office, 1977.

TABLE 4. LABOUR FORCE ESTIMATES BY SEX AND AGE, CONTINENTS AND GEOGRAPHICAL REGIONS, 1950, 1975, 2000 (*continued*)
B. Percentage of total population

Continents, geographical regions		Sex	All ages	Age groups				
				15–64	10–14	15–44	45–64	65≤
WORLD TOTAL	1950		43.9	66.7	21.8	67.5	64.4	35.4
		M	60.4	91.9	26.9	91.5	93.1	58.4
		F	27.5	41.6	16.5	43.1	37.2	16.4
	1975		41.5	56.0	12.6	66.7	66.0	23.3
		M	53.8	72.3	14.8	85.0	89.1	38.7
		F	29.1	39.5	10.4	47.8	44.0	11.8
	2000		40.7	54.6	5.8	63.6	64.2	16.6
		M	53.0	70.6	6.9	81.4	85.7	27.1
		F	28.2	38.2	4.7	45.1	42.9	8.3
More developed regions	1950		46.4	67.6	7.0	69.5	62.9	28.0
		M	61.5	90.7	8.3	90.5	91.4	44.0
		F	32.5	46.9	5.7	50.4	39.0	16.6
	1975		46.0	69.1	1.6	70.4	65.4	13.6
		M	57.3	84.6	1.9	83.9	86.3	23.0
		F	35.4	53.7	1.2	56.7	48.0	7.5
	2000		46.9	70.1	0.9	71.4	67.5	10.6
		M	56.5	82.6	1.1	82.4	82.9	16.9
		F	37.7	57.5	0.7	60.1	52.7	6.3

TABLE 4. LABOUR FORCE ESTIMATES BY SEX AND AGE, CONTINENTS AND GEOGRAPHICAL REGIONS, 1950, 1975, 2000 (*continued*)
B. Percentage of total population

Continents, geographical regions		Sex	All ages	Age groups				
				15–64	10–14	15–44	45–64	65≤
Less developed regions	1950		42.7	66.2	28.2	66.4	65.5	41.9
		M	59.8	92.5	34.8	92.0	94.3	69.3
		F	24.7	38.1	21.2	38.9	35.6	16.1
	1975		39.7	65.4	15.9	65.2	66.3	34.0
		M	52.5	86.6	18.6	85.5	90.7	52.9
		F	26.4	43.4	13.1	44.1	41.2	17.1
	2000		39.0	61.8	6.8	61.6	62.7	21.1
		M	52.1	82.5	8.0	81.2	86.9	33.6
		F	25.5	40.6	5.5	41.3	38.3	10.0
AFRICA	1950		42.8	69.6	31.3	69.4	70.3	49.5
		M	57.7	93.8	40.8	93.1	96.6	78.5
		F	28.0	45.7	21.8	45.8	45.2	24.6
	1975		37.9	65.0	19.7	64.3	67.3	38.8
		M	51.6	89.1	24.8	87.9	93.9	61.8
		F	24.4	41.4	14.6	41.2	42.4	19.8
	2000		34.8	61.0	10.0	60.3	63.9	26.6
		M	47.8	84.2	12.4	82.7	90.4	42.8
		F	22.0	38.2	7.5	38.0	39.2	13.3
Eastern Africa	1950		46.2	75.4	39.0	74.9	77.2	54.5
		M	59.2	96.6	50.2	96.2	97.9	81.0
		F	33.5	54.8	27.9	54.0	57.9	33.0
	1975		42.2	71.3	29.0	70.6	74.2	48.1
		M	55.0	93.7	36.1	93.0	96.4	71.6
		F	29.6	49.6	21.9	48.6	53.6	28.9
	2000		37.3	65.9	15.7	64.8	70.2	35.9
		M	49.8	88.5	19.5	87.3	93.4	53.6
		F	25.0	43.8	11.9	42.6	48.3	21.1
Middle Africa	1950		46.5	74.6	32.1	75.1	72.9	47.7
		M	57.9	92.7	36.9	92.1	94.7	77.4
		F	35.6	57.2	27.3	58.5	52.9	22.5
	1975		41.6	69.5	20.7	69.4	70.0	40.0
		M	52.7	88.7	22.6	87.8	92.5	66.0
		F	30.8	51.0	18.8	51.4	49.6	19.2
	2000		36.3	64.5	8.7	63.9	66.4	26.8
		M	46.5	82.9	9.7	81.4	88.6	44.4
		F	26.3	46.6	7.6	46.8	45.9	12.4
Northern Africa	1950		31.3	50.4	21.1	50.2	51.2	39.6
		M	57.8	93.7	35.3	93.0	96.6	80.1
		F	4.4	6.4	6.6	6.5	6.2	3.5
	1975		27.0	47.0	12.0	46.4	49.1	26.5
		M	49.1	86.4	19.5	84.9	92.2	53.1
		F	4.9	8.1	4.2	8.2	7.6	3.1
	2000		28.2	46.6	5.6	46.5	47.2	16.4
		M	49.6	82.4	8.4	80.9	88.5	34.0
		F	6.5	10.5	2.7	11.0	8.8	2.2
Southern Africa	1950		38.8	62.5	16.6	63.2	60.2	40.4
		M	59.1	93.7	26.1	92.9	96.4	71.1
		F	18.4	30.4	7.1	32.4	24.0	14.4
	1975		38.1	66.4	4.9	67.2	63.6	25.3
		M	50.1	87.0	6.5	85.7	91.9	44.3
		F	26.4	46.4	3.3	49.3	35.7	10.8
	2000		37.4	66.9	2.2	68.0	62.9	17.0
		M	46.5	83.3	3.0	82.1	88.3	28.3
		F	28.4	51.0	1.4	54.1	39.6	7.2
Western Africa	1950		48.0	79.2	34.7	78.7	81.1	56.7
		M	55.9	91.8	41.0	90.7	96.3	77.8
		F	40.1	66.7	28.6	66.8	66.6	38.2
	1975		41.4	71.7	20.7	70.5	76.6	46.7
		M	50.3	87.6	23.8	86.0	94.1	65.5
		F	32.6	56.2	17.6	55.2	60.3	31.1
	2000		36.5	66.1	9.7	64.6	72.2	31.0
		M	45.0	82.0	11.4	80.1	90.4	44.7
		F	28.1	50.6	7.9	49.5	55.3	19.5

257

TABLE 4. LABOUR FORCE ESTIMATES BY SEX AND AGE, CONTINENTS AND GEOGRAPHICAL REGIONS, 1950, 1975, 2000 (*continued*)

B. Percentage of total population

Continents, geographical regions		Sex	All ages	Age groups				
				15–64	10–14	15–44	45–64	65 ≤
AMERICA	1950		38.8	59.8	10.5	59.7	60.0	29.9
		M	59.1	90.8	16.0	90.4	91.8	52.3
		F	18.4	28.8	4.7	29.1	27.9	9.8
	1975		36.8	59.8	5.9	59.3	61.2	18.3
		M	52.0	84.1	8.6	83.0	87.4	31.9
		F	21.8	35.8	3.1	35.5	36.6	8.1
	2000		37.9	60.4	2.7	60.1	61.3	13.6
		M	51.3	81.5	3.4	80.3	85.0	23.6
		F	24.5	39.4	2.0	39.7	38.7	6.3
Latin America	1950		35.1	57.0	16.2	57.3	55.8	39.3
		M	57.1	92.9	25.0	92.5	94.2	71.8
		F	12.7	20.5	7.2	21.5	16.9	11.4
	1975		31.5	54.5	8.3	55.1	52.7	24.8
		M	48.9	84.8	12.2	84.1	87.6	45.7
		F	14.1	24.4	4.2	26.0	18.8	7.1
	2000		33.4	55.8	3.2	56.9	52.1	15.5
		M	48.5	80.9	4.0	79.9	84.3	28.5
		F	18.3	30.7	2.4	33.5	21.1	4.7
Caribbean	1950		39.3	63.7	12.5	63.3	65.2	44.4
		M	56.4	91.5	15.8	90.6	94.5	71.8
		F	22.0	35.5	9.1	36.2	33.1	19.7
	1975		33.6	58.2	6.5	58.0	58.9	23.8
		M	47.5	83.3	7.6	82.0	87.3	37.9
		F	19.7	33.8	5.4	34.8	30.7	10.2
	2000		36.3	58.6	3.9	59.2	56.5	16.3
		M	50.4	81.3	4.4	80.4	84.4	26.8
		F	22.2	35.7	3.3	37.3	30.5	7.4
Middle America	1950		32.8	54.4	17.5	54.4	54.1	47.2
		M	56.8	94.4	30.0	93.7	96.8	87.3
		F	8.7	14.4	4.7	14.8	13.0	11.6
	1975		29.3	53.4	7.8	53.4	53.4	34.3
		M	47.7	93.9	12.7	85.8	92.8	63.2
		F	10.7	19.7	2.7	20.6	15.8	9.2
	2000		30.8	54.5	2.9	54.8	53.0	20.5
		M	46.4	82.0	4.1	80.5	88.7	37.2
		F	15.0	26.5	1.6	28.5	18.4	6.1
Temperate South America	1950		39.9	59.2	10.0	60.0	56.7	30.4
		M	62.0	91.3	13.7	91.2	91.4	55.7
		F	16.9	25.4	6.4	27.7	18.4	7.8
	1975		36.8	56.5	5.3	58.9	50.6	14.4
		M	55.1	84.2	6.9	84.8	82.7	26.9
		F	18.6	28.8	3.7	32.6	19.9	4.2
	2000		38.5	57.7	2.8	60.6	51.0	9.7
		M	55.2	81.6	3.6	82.2	80.2	18.9
		F	22.1	33.8	2.0	38.5	23.0	3.0
Tropical South America	1950		33.7	56.0	17.9	56.5	53.9	38.3
		M	55.9	93.1	27.4	92.8	94.4	71.7
		F	11.3	18.4	8.0	19.3	14.7	10.8
	1975		31.0	53.9	9.3	54.5	52.0	25.8
		M	48.2	84.3	13.6	83.4	87.4	48.7
		F	13.7	23.8	4.8	25.5	17.5	6.7
	2000		33.6	55.8	3.4	57.0	51.3	15.3
		M	48.2	80.2	4.0	79.3	83.5	28.1
		F	18.9	31.5	2.7	34.6	20.4	4.3
Northern America	1950		42.5	62.2	1.7	62.1	62.5	25.9
		M	61.0	89.0	2.6	88.3	90.4	44.3
		F	24.0	35.7	0.9	36.3	34.3	9.2
	1975		44.0	65.8	1.7	64.7	68.1	14.9
		M	56.3	83.3	2.2	81.6	87.3	23.9
		F	32.2	48.7	1.1	47.8	50.6	8.6
	2000		47.1	68.8	1.2	67.1	72.3	12.0
		M	57.4	82.5	1.6	81.0	85.9	18.8
		F	37.2	55.2	0.9	53.0	59.6	7.5
ASIA	1950		43.6	66.8	27.6	67.0	65.9	40.6
		M	60.3	92.0	33.2	91.5	93.7	66.9
		F	26.0	39.7	21.6	40.6	36.7	15.7

B. Percentage of total population

Continents, geographical regions		Sex	All ages	Age groups				
				15–64	10–14	15–44	45–64	65≤
	1975		41.7	67.2	15.7	66.9	68.2	33.8
		M	53.8	86.5	17.7	85.3	90.7	51.8
		F	29.2	46.9	13.7	47.6	44.8	17.8
	2000		41.3	63.4	6.4	62.9	64.8	21.1
		M	54.0	82.5	7.4	81.1	86.8	33.0
		F	28.2	43.5	5.3	43.9	42.4	10.6
East Asia	1950		43.4	65.2	22.8	65.8	63.5	36.1
		M	60.8	91.7	26.2	91.3	92.8	62.7
		F	24.9	37.2	19.0	38.4	33.8	12.6
	1975		47.0	71.8	9.7	72.1	70.7	32.0
		M	57.4	86.7	10.8	85.8	89.5	46.8
		F	36.3	56.0	8.5	57.7	51.4	19.4
	2000		48.2	69.2	3.0	69.5	68.5	19.8
		M	58.7	83.5	3.5	82.5	85.7	29.2
		F	37.7	54.7	2.6	56.3	50.8	11.6
South Asia	1950		43.8	68.3	31.6	68.1	69.1	46.4
		M	59.8	92.4	39.2	91.7	94.9	71.8
		F	27.0	42.4	23.8	42.9	40.6	20.0
	1975		37.5	63.0	19.7	62.3	65.4	36.7
		M	50.9	86.4	22.2	84.8	92.0	58.8
		F	23.4	38.6	17.1	38.9	37.5	15.0
	2000		37.2	59.4	7.8	58.9	61.2	22.7
		M	51.3	81.8	9.0	80.3	87.9	37.6
		F	22.4	35.9	6.5	36.3	34.3	9.2
Eastern South Asia	1950		44.8	71.4	26.6	70.8	73.9	47.0
		M	57.5	90.8	29.2	90.0	94.0	66.6
		F	32.4	51.8	24.2	51.3	53.6	27.8
	1975		38.7	66.2	17.8	65.7	68.4	35.5
		M	49.5	86.5	18.5	85.1	91.6	53.0
		F	27.9	46.5	17.1	46.7	46.0	20.9
	2000		38.7	62.0	7.0	61.7	63.1	23.1
		M	50.8	81.8	7.3	80.4	87.4	35.1
		F	26.6	42.2	6.7	42.5	41.1	13.3
Middle South Asia	1950		43.6	67.4	34.0	67.3	67.6	46.2
		M	60.7	92.8	43.5	92.2	95.1	73.3
		F	25.2	39.1	24.2	40.0	36.0	17.3
	1975		37.3	62.2	20.8	61.5	64.9	37.2
		M	51.5	86.3	23.6	84.6	92.2	61.0
		F	22.2	36.4	17.7	36.8	35.1	12.2
	2000		37.0	58.9	8.4	58.3	61.0	22.8
		M	51.7	81.9	9.9	80.3	88.1	38.8
		F	21.4	34.1	6.8	34.6	32.3	7.5
Western South Asia	1950		41.8	66.2	26.0	66.0	66.9	45.4
		M	58.1	92.8	34.0	92.1	95.6	72.1
		F	25.1	39.3	17.3	39.1	39.9	23.2
	1975		34.2	58.3	16.1	57.9	59.8	36.3
		M	50.6	86.7	21.1	85.6	91.0	57.5
		F	17.4	29.2	10.9	29.4	28.2	16.9
	2000		33.0	55.0	5.2	54.7	56.4	21.2
		M	48.8	81.5	7.1	80.1	87.2	35.3
		F	16.9	28.1	3.3	28.6	26.5	9.0
EUROPE	1950		46.4	66.0	9.5	68.8	60.3	24.5
		M	64.8	92.6	11.7	93.0	91.9	41.3
		F	29.4	41.8	7.2	46.0	33.5	11.9
	1975		44.5	66.9	2.1	68.9	62.8	13.3
		M	58.2	86.2	2.4	85.8	86.9	21.7
		F	31.4	48.0	1.8	51.5	41.6	7.6
	2000		45.5	68.3	1.0	70.1	65.1	10.2
		M	56.9	83.7	1.2	83.8	83.4	15.4
		F	34.3	52.6	0.9	55.8	46.9	6.4
Eastern Europe	1950		51.8	74.0	4.5	75.8	70.0	34.2
		M	63.4	91.8	4.9	91.2	93.1	49.6
		F	41.4	58.4	4.2	61.9	51.2	22.9
	1975		52.9	76.6	1.1	77.4	75.0	23.4
		M	59.8	85.6	1.2	84.5	88.1	33.7
		F	46.3	68.0	1.1	70.1	63.9	16.2

259

B. Percentage of total population

Continents, geographical regions		Sex	All ages	Age groups				
				15–64	10–14	15–44	45–64	65≤
	2000		53.6	78.6	0.5	79.8	76.6	18.1
		M	58.3	84.0	0.5	83.7	84.7	22.9
		F	49.0	73.1	0.4	75.7	68.6	14.5
Northern Europe	1950		46.4	67.0	1.1	70.6	60.2	19.0
		M	66.4	95.1	1.2	95.0	95.2	35.2
		F	27.3	40.0	1.0	46.1	29.2	6.9
	1975		45.4	69.9	0.2	69.9	69.8	11.3
		M	59.0	88.6	0.2	86.5	92.4	19.6
		F	32.4	51.2	0.2	52.8	48.4	5.8
	2000		47.0	71.5	0.1	70.6	73.1	9.0
		M	58.1	86.0	0.1	84.1	89.7	15.1
		F	36.2	56.7	0.1	56.7	56.6	5.0
Southern Europe	1950		42.7	59.5	21.8	62.0	53.3	29.2
		M	66.1	93.1	27.8	93.6	91.8	55.6
		F	20.7	28.4	15.7	31.9	20.0	9.3
	1975		38.6	57.8	4.4	61.1	51.2	13.1
		M	56.8	84.6	5.1	85.6	82.6	23.9
		F	21.2	32.0	3.8	36.8	23.0	5.3
	2000		38.6	58.9	1.8	62.7	51.6	8.5
		M	54.4	81.6	2.1	83.1	78.6	15.4
		F	23.3	36.3	1.6	41.7	26.2	3.4
Western Europe	1950		45.8	65.3	4.9	68.8	59.2	19.8
		M	63.5	91.4	5.7	92.5	89.3	31.6
		F	29.7	42.1	4.1	46.9	33.9	11.0
	1975		43.2	66.1	1.7	68.9	60.7	8.5
		M	57.8	86.6	2.0	86.6	86.7	13.7
		F	29.3	45.8	1.4	50.0	38.2	5.2
	2000		45.0	67.6	1.1	69.6	64.1	7.1
		M	57.3	84.0	1.3	84.5	83.3	10.7
		F	32.7	50.3	0.9	54.0	43.9	4.4
OCEANIA	1950		43.1	64.7	11.6	67.9	57.0	21.0
		M	62.9	93.7	13.8	94.5	91.9	37.4
		F	22.7	34.3	9.2	39.7	21.7	6.4
	1975		42.6	66.8	7.0	68.4	62.9	14.1
		M	56.9	88.0	7.9	87.1	90.3	25.4
		F	27.9	44.4	6.2	48.5	35.1	5.2
	2000		43.4	66.8	4.4	67.8	64.5	11.5
		M	56.1	85.3	4.8	84.3	88.0	19.9
		F	30.3	47.4	4.0	50.4	40.0	4.5
Australia, New Zealand	1950		41.5	61.7	2.2	65.1	54.1	17.3
		M	63.5	93.6	2.7	94.7	91.2	32.0
		F	19.1	28.9	1.9	34.3	17.2	4.6
	1975		42.2	65.4	0.9	67.3	61.2	11.4
		M	57.3	87.5	1.0	86.6	89.6	21.1
		F	26.7	42.4	0.9	46.9	32.8	4.0
	2000		43.5	66.2	0.7	67.4	63.7	9.1
		M	56.7	85.1	0.6	84.1	87.4	16.2
		F	30.0	46.5	0.7	49.8	39.2	3.4
Melanesia	1950		55.8	86.6	42.6	87.0	84.3	56.0
		M	62.4	94.7	46.8	94.3	97.3	80.0
		F	48.4	77.0	38.4	78.5	69.4	28.6
	1975		49.3	80.6	31.8	80.6	80.5	49.0
		M	56.6	91.7	33.5	90.8	95.4	70.0
		F	41.3	68.3	30.1	69.6	64.2	25.0
	2000		45.5	73.6	16.1	73.2	75.1	35.0
		M	54.1	87.0	17.1	85.7	92.3	51.9
		F	36.3	59.2	14.9	59.9	56.6	18.5
Micronesia and Polynesia	1950		33.3	57.2	16.5	56.9	58.5	41.7
		M	54.6	93.0	27.5	92.2	97.1	64.3
		F	10.2	17.9	5.1	18.2	19.4	10.0
	1975		32.5	55.2	7.9	54.8	55.5	26.3
		M	51.5	86.6	13.2	85.5	90.8	47.4
		F	12.3	21.2	2.4	22.5	14.5	5.3
	2000		37.3	57.8	2.8	59.1	53.4	15.1
		M	54.5	83.8	4.8	82.6	87.5	28.0
		F	19.5	30.6	1.7	34.5	18.6	3.6

TABLE 4. LABOUR FORCE ESTIMATES BY SEX AND AGE, CONTINTENTS AND GEOGRAPHICAL REGIONS, 1950, 1975, 2000 (*continued*)
B. Percentage of total population

Continents, geographical regions		Sex	All ages	Age groups				
				15–64	10–14	15–44	45–64	65≤
UNION OF SOVIET	1950		52.1	76.7	6.3	79.1	69.5	39.2
SOCIALIST REPUBLICS		M	57.2	89.0	5.5	88.5	90.6	49.0
		F	48.1	67.7	7.0	71.8	57.0	35.0
	1975		49.8	75.6	—	79.8	66.0	5.8
		M	53.9	81.1	—	81.5	80.1	10.6
		F	46.2	70.7	—	78.2	56.8	3.7
	2000		48.2	74.3	—	79.4	63.7	4.2
		M	52.8	79.2	—	81.1	75.0	7.2
		F	43.8	69.5	—	77.7	53.4	2.5

TABLE 5. DISTRIBUTION OF COUNTRIES BY LIFE EXPECTANCY AT BIRTH AND PER CAPITA GROSS NATIONAL PRODUCT (US $) AROUND 1975

Life expectancy, both sexes (years)	Total No. of countries	Number of countries with a per capita GNP of:						
		≤150	151–280	281–550	551–1135	1136–2500	2501–5000	5001≤
35–44	44	24	12	6	2	—	—	—
45–54	35	12	6	12	2	1	2	—
55–64	20	1	3	12	4	—	—	—
65≤	57	1	—	7	15	16	17	1
	156	38	21	37	23	17	19	1

Source: World population data sheet 1975, Population Reference Bureau, Inc.

TABLE 6. DISTRIBUTION OF COUNTRIES BY LIFE EXPECTANCY AT BIRTH AND KILOCALORIES PER PERSON PER DAY, AROUND 1975

Life expectancy (years)	Total countries	Number of countries with kilocarbons of:				
		≤1740	1750–1990	2000–2490	2500–2990	3000≤
35–44	36	1	5	28	2	—
45–54	28	2	2	19	5	—
55–64	19	2	9	6	2	—
65≤	44	—	—	8	12	24
	127	5	16	61	21	24

Source: World population data sheet, 1975, Population Reference Bureau, Inc.

TABLE 7. DISTRIBUTION OF WORLD POPULATION BY LIFE EXPECTANCY AT BIRTH IN 1960/65 AND 1970/75 (BOTH SEXES)

Life expectancy at birth	Number of countries		Population (in thousands)[*]		Percentage distribution of population	
	1960/65	1970/75	1960/65	1970/75	1960	1975
WORLD						
<35	4	—	10 143	—	0.3	—
35–44	50	45	824 341	406 841	27.6	10.3
45–54	31	30	313 868	1 103 073	10.5	27.8
55–64	25	23	877 285	1 285 305	29.4	32.4
65≤	44	56	959 357	1 170 438	32.1	29.5
	154	154	2 984 994	3 965 657	100	100
More Developed Countries						
<35	—	—	—	—	—	—
35–44	—	—	—	—	—	—
45–54	—	—	—	—	—	—
55–64	4	1	36 453	10 253	3.7	0.9
65≤	32	35	938 932	1 120 998	96.3	99.1
	36	36	975 385	1 131 251	100	100
Less Developed Countries						
<35	4	—	10 143	—	0.5	—
35–44	50	45	824 341	406 841	41.0	14.4
45–54	31	30	313 868	1 103 073	15.6	38.9
55–64	21	22	840 832	1 275 052	41.8	45.0
65≤	12	21	20 425	49 440	1.0	1.7
	118	118	2 009 609	2 834 406	100	100

Source: Selected world demographic indicators by countries, 1950–2000 (ESA/P/WP.55), United Nations Population Division, Department of Economic and Social Affairs.

[*] In general no data have been given separately for small countries or areas which had 250 000 population or less in mid–1970.

TABLE 8. SELECTED DEMOGRAPHIC, SOCIOECONOMIC, AND HEALTH INDICATORS BY COUNTRIES, AROUND 1975

Continents, regions, countries	Population (in thousands)	Area in km² (thousands)	Density (per km²)	Birth rate (per 1000)	Death rate (per 1000)	Gross reproduction rate	Net reproduction rate	Life expectancy at birth Male	Life expectancy at birth Female	GNP per capita (US $) 1976	Kilocalories per capita, per day	Adult literacy rate	Medical team density per 100 000
WORLD TOTAL	3 967 005	135 830	29	31.5	12.8	2.13	1.68	53.9	56.6	1 650	2 470	...	349.6
AFRICA	401 138	30 319	13	46.3	19.8	3.10	2.09	43.5	46.6	440	2 250	...	101.2
Eastern Africa	114 498	6 338	18	48.1	20.7	3.18	2.11	42.2	45.4	210	2 240	...	59.0
Burundi	3 765	27.8	135	48.0	24.7	3.10	1.87	37.5	40.6	120	2 040	10	22.6
Comoros	306	2.2	141	46.6	21.7	3.00	1.94	40.9	44.1	180	...	...	63.2
Ethiopia	27 975	1 221.9	23	49.4	25.8	3.30	1.95	36.5	39.6	100	2 160	7	6.2
Kenya	13 251	582.6	23	48.7	16.0	3.30	2.44	48.3	51.7	240	2 360	40	146.8
Madagascar	8 020	587.0	14	50.2	21.1	3.30	2.18	41.9	45.1	200	2 530	40	49.7
Malawi	4 916	118.5	41	47.7	23.7	3.00	1.89	39.4	42.6	140	2 210	25	35.0
Mauritius	899	2.0	440	24.4	6.8	1.59	1.43	63.7	67.4	680	2 360	...	207.0
Mozambique	9 239	783.0	12	43.1	20.1	2.80	1.85	41.9	45.1	170	2 050	...	32.4
Réunion	501	2.5	220	31.2	8.5	2.13	1.87	61.2	64.9	1 920	...	...	480.4
Rwanda	4 200	26.3	159	50.0	23.6	3.40	2.13	39.4	42.6	110	1 960	23	27.3
Somalia	3 170	637.7	5	47.2	21.7	3.00	1.89	39.4	42.6	110	1 830	50	39.7
Southern Rhodesia	6 276	390.6	16	47.9	14.4	3.25	2.46	49.8	53.3	550	2 660	...	189.1
Uganda	11 353	236.0	48	45.2	15.9	3.00	2.22	48.3	51.7	240	2 130	25	46.7
United Republic of Tanzania	15 438	945.1	16	50.2	20.1	3.30	2.22	42.9	46.1	180	2 260	63	...
Zambia	5 022	752.6	7	51.5	20.3	3.40	2.28	42.9	46.1	440	2 590	43	80.5
Middle Africa	45 310	6 613	7	44.4	21.7	2.86	1.83	40.3	43.5	230	2 120	...	59.0
Angola	6 353	1 246.7	5	47.2	24.5	3.20	1.91	37.0	40.1	330	2 000	...	71.7
Central African Republic	1 790	623.0	3	43.4	22.5	2.70	1.70	39.4	42.6	230	2 220	...	20.4
Chad	4 023	1 284.0	3	44.0	24.0	2.60	1.55	37.0	40.1	120	2 110	...	28.7
Congo	1 345	342.0	4	45.1	20.8	2.85	1.89	41.9	45.1	520	2 260	15	200.9
Equatorial Guinea	310	28.1	11	36.8	19.7	2.50	1.65	41.9	45.1	330	...	50	87.1
Gabon	526	267.7	2	32.2	22.2	2.00	1.26	39.4	42.6	2 590	2 220	...	203.6
United Republic of Cameroon	6 398	475.4	13	40.4	22.0	2.70	1.70	39.4	42.6	290	2 410	12	73.3
Zaire	24 485	2 354.4	10	45.2	20.5	2.90	1.92	41.9	45.1	140	2 060	15	50.0
Northern Africa	98 185	8 825	12	43.3	15.2	3.05	2.27	50.6	53.4	650	2 240	15	137.6
Algeria	16 792	2 381.7	7	48.7	15.4	3.50	2.66	51.7	54.8	990	1 730	35	112.2
Egypt	37 543	1 001.4	37	37.8	14.0	2.53	1.89	51.2	53.6	280	2 500	40	177.1
Lybian Arab Republic	2 255	1 759.5	1	45.0	14.7	3.34	2.52	51.4	54.5	6 310	2 570	...	409.8
Morocco	17 504	446.6	39	46.2	15.7	3.44	2.60	51.4	54.5	540	2 220	26	59.2
Sudan	18 268	2 505.8	7	47.8	17.5	3.40	2.39	47.3	49.9	290	2 160	15	120.0
Tunisia	5 747	163.6	35	40.0	13.8	3.04	2.34	52.5	55.7	840	2 250	55	126.1
Southern Africa	27 678	2701	10	43.0	16.2	2.76	2.06	48.9	52.4	1 240	2 720	...	377.3
Botswana	691	600.4	1	45.6	23.0	2.90	1.92	41.9	45.1	410	2 040	...	113.5
Lesotho	1 148	30.4	38	39.0	19.7	2.50	1.73	44.4	47.6	170	...	40	155.1
Namibia	708	824.3	1	45.5	23.2	3.00	1.89	39.4	42.6	980	...	...	...
South Africa	24 663	1 221.0	20	42.9	15.5	2.75	2.08	49.8	53.3	1 340	2 740	...	398.7
Swaziland	468	17.4	27	49.0	21.8	3.20	2.11	41.9	45.1	470	...	...	185.4
Western Africa	115 469	6 142	19	48.7	23.0	3.24	2.03	39.4	42.5	350	2 220	...	65.8
Benin	3 074	112.6	27	49.9	23.0	3.30	2.08	39.4	42.6	130	2 260	10	45.3
Cape Verde	295	4.0	73	32.8	13.7	2.00	1.48	48.3	51.7	260	...	...	63.0

263

TABLE 8. SELECTED DEMOGRAPHIC, SOCIOECONOMIC, AND HEALTH INDICATORS BY COUNTRIES, AROUND 1975 (Continued)

Continents, regions, countries	Population (in thousands)	Area in km² (thousands)	Density (per km²)	Birth rate (per 1000)	Death rate (per 1000)	Gross reproduction rate	Net reproduction rate	Life expectancy at birth Male	Female	GNP per capita (US $) 1976	Kilocalories per capita, per day	Adult literacy rate	Medical team density per 100 000
Gambia	509	11.3	45	43.3	23.1	2.80	1.73	38.5	41.6	180	2 490	⋮	48.7
Ghana	9 873	238.5	41	48.8	21.9	3.30	2.18	41.9	45.1	580	2 320	25	95.7
Guinea	4 416	246.0	18	46.6	22.9	3.05	1.92	39.4	42.6	150	2 200	⋮	73.1
Guinea–Bissau	525	36.1	15	40.1	25.1	2.60	1.56	37.0	40.1	140	⋮	⋮	189.7
Ivory Coast	4 885	322.5	15	45.6	20.6	3.05	2.01	41.9	45.1	610	2 430	20	74.4
Liberia	1 708	111.4	15	43.6	20.7	2.80	1.85	41.9	45.1	450	2 170	15	79.4
Mali	5 697	1 240.0	5	50.1	25.9	3.30	1.95	36.5	39.6	100	2 060	10	42.6
Mauritania	1 283	1 030.7	1	44.8	24.9	2.90	1.73	37.0	40.1	340	1 970	10	70.0
Niger	4 592	1 267.0	4	52.2	25.5	3.50	2.08	37.0	40.1	160	2 080	⋮	21.1
Nigeria	62 925	923.8	68	49.3	22.7	3.30	2.07	39.4	42.6	380	2 270	⋮	68.6
Senegal	4 418	196.2	23	47.6	23.9	3.10	1.91	38.5	41.6	390	2 370	10	90.0
Sierra Leone	2 983	71.7	42	44.7	20.7	2.90	1.91	41.9	45.1	200	2 280	15	44.4
Togo	2 248	56.0	40	50.6	23.3	3.30	2.08	39.4	42.6	260	2 330	12	44.4
Upper Volta	6 032	274.2	22	48.5	25.8	3.20	1.89	36.5	39.6	110	1 710	⋮	27.1
AMERICA	560 933	42 081	13	28.3	9.2	1.93	1.72	62.7	68.7	3 950	2 860	⋮	⋮
Latin America	324 092	20 566	16	36.9	9.2	2.57	2.23	59.2	63.7	1 100	2 530	⋮	⋮
Caribbean	27 116	238	114	32.8	9.1	2.27	1.97	61.4	64.8	1 060	2 320	⋮	237.3
Barbados	245	0.4	569	21.6	8.9	1.50	1.43	66.7	71.6	1 550	⋮	⋮	468.6
Cuba	9 481	114.5	83	29.1	6.6	1.97	1.83	68.1	71.5	860	2 700	⋮	300.7
Dominican Republic	5 118	48.7	105	45.8	11.0	3.38	2.78	55.9	59.7	780	2 120	51	130.8
Guadeloupe	354	1.8	199	29.3	6.4	2.25	2.13	67.4	71.4	1 500	⋮	⋮	351.7
Haiti	4 552	27.8	164	35.8	16.3	2.42	1.73	49.0	51.0	200	1 730	20	30.0
Jamaica	2 029	11.0	185	33.2	7.1	2.65	2.51	67.9	71.2	1 070	2 360	86	231.6
Martinique	363	1.1	330	29.7	6.7	2.25	2.13	67.4	71.4	2 350	⋮	⋮	424.0
Puerto Rico	2 902	8.9	326	22.6	6.8	1.37	1.33	69.7	74.7	2 430	⋮	⋮	475.8
Trinidad and Tobago	1 009	5.1	197	25.3	5.9	1.65	1.57	67.9	71.2	2 240	2 380	90	224.4
Windward Islands	372	2.1	177	35.9	8.9	2.79	2.56	63.5	67.6	⋮	⋮	⋮	⋮
Other Caribbean	690	16.6	41	30.0	7.3	2.06	1.93	66.1	69.6	⋮	⋮	⋮	⋮
Middle America	78 652	2 496	32	42.2	9.4	3.11	2.67	59.7	63.3	1 000	2 490	⋮	127.5
Costa Rica	1 994	50.7	39	33.4	5.9	2.27	2.09	66.5	69.9	1 040	2 610	89	240.9
El Salvador	4 108	21.0	192	42.2	11.1	3.02	2.48	56.0	59.7	490	1 930	63	107.1
Guatemala	6 129	108.9	56	42.8	13.7	2.96	2.25	52.2	53.7	630	2 130	47	91.6
Honduras	3 037	112.1	27	49.3	14.6	3.55	2.71	52.1	55.0	390	2 140	61	115.6
Mexico	59 204	1 972.5	30	42.0	8.6	3.15	2.76	61.3	65.2	1 090	2 580	76	126.0
Nicaragua	2 318	130.0	18	48.3	13.9	3.38	2.61	51.2	54.6	750	2 450	57	169.6
Panama	1 678	75.7	22	36.2	7.1	2.47	2.22	65.0	68.2	1 310	2 580	82	146.0
Temperate South America	38 747	3 726	10	23.3	8.9	1.54	1.42	63.5	69.7	1 400	2 940	⋮	304.2
Argentina	25 384	2 766.9	9	21.8	8.8	1.45	1.36	65.2	71.4	1 550	3 060	93	329.1
Chile	10 253	756.9	14	27.9	9.2	1.80	1.58	59.5	65.7	1 050	2 670	90	279.2
Uruguay	3 108	177.5	18	20.4	9.3	1.43	1.35	66.9	72.8	1 390	2 880	91	179.2
Tropical South America	179 578	14 106	13	38.3	9.2	2.64	2.29	58.1	63.0	1 090	2 470	⋮	122.6
Bolivia	5 410	1 098.6	5	43.7	18.0	3.00	2.08	45.7	47.9	390	1 900	40	75.6
Brazil	109 730	8 512.0	13	37.1	8.8	2.51	2.22	58.5	64.4	1 140	2 620	64	104.7
Colombia	25 890	1 138.9	23	40.6	8.8	2.87	2.49	59.2	62.7	630	2 200	⋮	106.7

TABLE 8. SELECTED DEMOGRAPHIC, SOCIOECONOMIC, AND HEALTH INDICATORS BY COUNTRIES, AROUND 1975 (Continued)

Continents, regions, countries	Population (in thousands)	Area in km² (thousands)	Density (per km²)	Birth rate (per 1000)	Death rate (per 1000)	Gross reproduction rate	Net reproduction rate	Life expectancy at birth — Male	Life expectancy at birth — Female	GNP per capita (US $) 1976	Kilocalories per capita, per day	Adult literacy rate	Medical team density per 100 000
Ecuador	7 090	283.6	25	41.8	9.5	3.07	2.61	58.2	61.2	640	2 010	69	114.9
Guyana	791	215.0	4	32.4	5.9	2.22	2.10	65.3	70.6	540	2 390	...	122.1
Paraguay	2 647	406.8	7	39.8	8.9	3.03	2.63	60.3	63.6	640	2 740	81	147.8
Peru	15 326	1 285.2	12	41.0	11.9	2.83	2.30	53.9	57.5	800	2 320	72	97.6
Suriname	422	163.3	3	41.6	7.5	3.20	2.95	63.3	67.8	1 370	2 450	...	180.0
Venezuela	12 213	912.1	13	36.1	7.0	2.58	2.32	62.9	66.7	2 570	2 430	82	354.0
NORTHERN AMERICA	236 841	21 515	11	16.5	9.3	1.08	1.05	67.7	75.3	7 850	3 320	...	853.3
Canada	22 801	9 976.1	2	18.6	7.7	1.16	1.13	69.4	75.4	7 510	3 180	98	961.4
United States of America	213 925	9 363.1	23	16.2	9.4	1.07	1.04	67.5	75.3	7 890	3 330	99	842.1
ASIA	2 255 458	27 581	81	34.8	13.6	2.39	1.83	53.8	55.6	...	2 160	...	231.2
East Asia	1 005 665	11 756	86	26.2	9.8	1.75	1.55	60.7	64.3	350	2 220	...	399.1
China	975 230*	9 597.0	102*	6.3*	18.3*	...	...	...	...	...	...	...	257.2
Japan	111 120	372.3	294	19.6	6.6	1.05	1.03	70.6	76.2	4 910	2 510	99	474.3
Other East Asia	55 742	1 786	31	30.2	8.7	2.09	1.82	59.3	63.0	...	...	90	...
Hong Kong	4 225	1.0	4 043	19.4	5.5	1.47	1.41	67.0	73.2	2 110	...	...	280.0
Korea, Democratic People's Republic of	15 852	120.5	132	35.7	9.4	2.53	2.19	58.8	62.5	470	2 520	...	...
Korea, Republic of	33 949	98.5	345	28.7	8.8	1.94	1.68	58.8	62.5	670	2 520	92	147.5
Mongolia	1 446	1 565.0	1	38.8	9.3	2.73	2.35	59.1	62.3	860	2 380	...	863.0
SOUTH ASIA	1 249 793	15 825	79	41.9	16.7	2.92	2.07	48.4	48.7	...	2 120	...	...
Eastern South Asia	323 836	4 498	72	42.4	15.4	2.85	2.14	49.1	52.1	330	2 070	...	97.0
Burma	31 240	676.6	46	39.5	15.8	2.70	2.01	48.6	51.5	120*	2 210	67	109.0
Democratic Kampuchea	8 110	181.0	45	46.7	19.0	3.25	2.24	44.0	46.9	...	2 430	...	79.0
East Timor	672	14.9	45	44.3	23.0	3.00	1.83	39.2	40.7	...	1 790	...	...
Indonesia	136 044	1 491.6	71	42.9	16.9	2.70	1.93	46.4	48.7	240	2 110	62	37.6
Lao People's Democratic Republic	3 303	236.8	14	44.6	22.8	3.00	1.87	39.1	41.8	90	2 460	...	45.9
Malaysia	12 093	329.7	37	38.7	9.9	2.78	2.37	57.5	61.3	860	1 940	...	126.5
Philippines	44 437	300.0	148	43.8	10.5	3.10	2.60	56.9	60.0	410	...	87	126.6
Singapore	2 248	0.6	3 869	21.2	5.2	1.35	1.29	67.4	71.8	2 700	...	75	369.7
Thailand	42 093	514.0	82	43.4	10.8	3.10	2.63	55.4	60.8	380	2 560	82	103.7
Viet Nam	43 451	329.6	131	41.5	20.5	3.00	2.03	43.2	46.0	...	...	...	211.9
Middle South Asia	837 799	6 785	124	41.7	17.0	2.94	2.05	48.4	47.6	220	2 070	...	80.7
Afghanistan	19 280	647.5	30	49.2	23.8	3.35	2.06	39.9	40.7	160	1 970	14	12.1
Bangladesh	73 746	144.0	517	49.5	28.1	3.52	1.95	35.8	35.8	110	1 840	23	49.5
Bhutan	1 173	47.0	25	43.6	20.5	3.00	1.99	42.2	45.0	70	...	...	...
India	613 217	3 287.6	187	39.9	15.7	2.80	1.99	50.1	48.8	150	2 070	36	80.6
Iran	32 923	1 648.0	20	45.3	15.6	3.35	2.47	50.7	51.3	1 930	2 300	50	101.6
Nepal	12 572	141.0	89	42.9	20.3	3.00	1.99	42.2	45.0	120	2 080	19	24.5
Pakistan	70 560	803.9	88	47.4	16.5	3.50	2.53	49.9	49.6	170	2 160	21	112.1
Sri Lanka	13 986	65.6	213	28.6	6.3	2.05	1.89	66.3	69.3	200	2 170	78	189.9
Western South Asia	88 158	4 542	20	42.8	14.3	3.08	2.35	52.3	55.4	1 730	2 760	...	157.3
Cyprus	673	9.3	73	22.2	6.8	1.36	1.27	69.5	73.4	1 480	2 670	...	402.4

* The totals for East Asia and Asia, the world total, and the related indicators do not take into account these latest figures for China.

TABLE 8. SELECTED DEMOGRAPHIC, SOCIOECONOMIC, AND HEALTH INDICATORS BY COUNTRIES, AROUND 1975 (continued)

Continents, regions, countries	Population (in thousands)	Area in km² (thousands)	Density (per km²)	Birth rate (per 1000)	Death rate (per 1000)	Gross reproduction rate	Net reproduction rate	Life expectancy at birth Male	Life expectancy at birth Female	GNP per capita (US $) 1976	Kilocalories per capita, per day	Adult literacy rate	Medical team density per 100 000
Iraq	11 067	434.9	25	48.1	14.6	3.45	2.60	51.2	54.3	1 390	2 160	26	108.8
Israel	3 417	20.8	165	26.4	6.7	1.78	1.73	69.4	72.6	3 920	2 960	84	685.1
Jordan	2 688	97.7	28	47.6	14.7	3.45	2.62	51.7	54.8	610	2 430	62	168.8
Kuwait	1 085	17.8	61	47.1	5.3	3.50	3.26	65.3	69.2	15 480	...	55	611.1
Lebanon	2 869	10.4	276	39.8	9.9	3.05	2.64	61.4	65.1		2 280	68	166.4
Saudi Arabia	8 966	2 149.7	4	49.5	20.2	3.50	2.32	44.2	46.5	4 480	2 270	15	117.9
Syrian Arab Republic	7 259	185.2	39	45.4	15.4	3.45	2.65	52.4	55.7	780	2 650	...	90.7
Turkey	39 882	780.6	51	39.4	12.5	2.84	2.28	55.2	58.7	990	3250	55	150.8
Yemen	6 668	195.0	34	49.6	20.6	3.50	2.30	43.7	45.9	250	2 040	10	21.6
Yemen, Democratic	1 660	333.0	6	49.6	20.6	3.50	2.30	45.8	48.3	280	2 070	10	98.2
Other Western South Asia	1 331	307.6	4	49.6	18.7	3.50	2.39			...	...	...	...
EUROPE	473 128	4 937	96	16.1	10.4	1.12	1.07	68.4	74.2	4 420	3 150	...	575.7
Eastern Europe	106 297	990	107	16.6	10.2	1.07	1.02	67.1	72.6	2 820	3 240	...	635.5
Bulgaria	8 793	110.9	79	16.2	9.1	1.05	1.02	69.8	74.0	2 310	3 290	...	757.3
Czechoslovakia	14 757	127.9	115	16.9	11.2	1.05	1.00	65.8	73.1	3 840	3 180	...	880.1
German Democratic Republic	17 193	108.2	159	13.9	12.4	1.02	1.00	70.0	75.3	4 220	3 290	...	371.5
Hungary	10 534	93.0	113	15.2	11.5	0.97	0.93	66.7	72.5	2 280	3 280	98	695.5
Poland	33 841	312.7	108	16.8	8.5	1.02	0.98	67.2	73.2	2 860	3 280	98	572.3
Romania	21 178	237.5	89	19.3	10.3	1.27	1.18	65.1	69.5	1 450	3 140	98	537.2
Northern Europe	81 975	1 636	50	15.8	11.2	1.14	1.10	69.5	75.6	4 910	3 140	...	667.7
Denmark	5 026	43.1	117	14.0	10.1	0.93	0.91	71.3	76.6	7 450	3 240	99	800.3
Finland	4 652	337.0	14	13.2	9.3	0.82	0.80	66.7	74.2	5 620	3 050	100	984.2
Iceland	216	103.0	2	19.2	7.7	1.27	1.25	70.9	77.2	6 100	...	...	778.6
Ireland	3 131	70.3	45	22.1	10.4	1.81	1.74	69.5	74.2	2 560	3 410	98	718.6
Norway	4 007	324.2	12	16.7	10.1	1.19	1.16	71.5	77.8	7 420	2 960	99	925.6
Sweden	8 291	450.0	18	14.2	10.5	0.97	0.94	72.1	77.1	8 670	2 810	99	963.7
United Kingdom	56 427	244.0	231	16.1	11.7	1.17	1.13	69.1	75.3	4 020	3 190	98	566.6
Southern Europe	132 354	1 315	101	17.7	9.2	1.22	1.15	68.3	73.6	2 620	2 990	...	438.2
Albania	2 482	28.7	86	33.4	6.5	2.37	2.20	67.2	69.9	540	2 390	...	554.9
Greece	8 930	131.9	68	15.4	9.4	1.10	1.03	69.7	74.0	2 590	3 190	82	402.3
Italy	55 023	301.2	183	16.0	9.8	1.11	1.07	69.2	75.3	3 050	3 180	98	542.5
Malta	329	0.3	1 042	17.5	9.0	1.00	0.96	68.5	73.2	1 390	2 820	98	885.0
Portugal	8 762	92.1	95	18.4	10.0	1.26	1.16	64.9	71.3	1 690	2 900	70	334.2
Spain	35 433	504.8	70	19.5	8.3	1.40	1.32	69.6	74.7	2 920	2 600	94	338.2
Yugoslavia	21 322	255.8	83	18.2	9.2	1.14	1.03	65.4	69.7	1 680	3 190	85	371.9
Western Europe	152 503	995	153	14.6	11.1	1.04	1.01	68.9	75.2	6 900	3 230	...	604.6
Austria	7 538	83.8	90	14.7	12.2	1.08	1.04	67.9	74.7	5 330	3 310	99	587.4
Belgium	9 846	30.5	323	14.8	11.2	1.08	1.06	70.1	75.8	6 780	3 380	99	393.1
France	52 913	547.0	97	17.0	10.6	1.20	1.16	69.4	75.9	6 550	3 210	99	711.1
Germany, Federal Republic of	61 682	248.6	248	12.0	12.1	0.89	0.86	67.6	73.7	7 380	3 220	99	581.0
Luxembourg	342	2.6	132	13.5	11.7	0.98	0.95	67.8	74.1	6 460	3 380	...	470.3
Netherlands	13 599	40.8	333	16.8	8.7	1.11	1.09	70.9	76.8	6 200	3 320	99	488.4
Switzerland	6 535	41.3	158	14.7	10.0	0.96	0.94	69.8	75.1	8 880	3 190	99	547.6

TABLE 8. SELECTED DEMOGRAPHIC, SOCIOECONOMIC, AND HEALTH INDICATORS BY COUNTRIES, AROUND 1975 (*continued*)

Continents, regions, countries	Population (in thousands)	Area in km² (thousands)	Density (per km²)	Birth rate (per 1000)	Death rate (per 1000)	Gross reproduction rate	Net reproduction rate	Life expectancy at birth Male	Life expectancy at birth Female	GNP per capita (US $) 1976	Kilocalories per capita, per day	Adult literacy rate	Medical team density per 100 000
OCEANIA	21 308	8 510	3	24.8	9.3	1.66	1.50	63.6	68.2	4 730	3 270	...	579.3
Australia and New Zealand	16 840	7 956	2	21.2	8.1	1.40	1.37	69.2	75.3	...	...	...	687.8
Australia	13 809	7 686.8	2	21.0	8.1	1.39	1.35	69.3	75.6	6 100	3 280	100	672.7
New Zealand	3 031	268.7	11	22.3	8.3	1.48	1.45	68.9	75.2	4 250	3 200	99	751.4
Melanesia	3 126	524	6	40.7	16.6	2.93	2.07	48.2	48.6	...	...	...	155.5
Papua New Guinea	2 716	461.7	6	40.6	17.1	2.93	2.04	47.7	47.6	490	...	...	131.3
Other Melanesia	411	...	1	41.2	13.6	2.93	2.30	51.8	55.0	...	...	...	...
Micronesia and Polynesia	1 341	30	44	32.9	7.4	2.23	1.97	61.2	64.5	...	...	...	262.9
Micronesia	306	...	77	35.9	9.0	2.50	2.20	60.0	63.5	...	...	...	...
Polynesia	1 036	...	39	32.0	7.0	2.16	1.90	61.6	64.8	...	...	...	...
Fiji	577	18.3	32	25.0	4.3	1.55	1.47	68.5	71.7	1 150	...	...	...
Other Polynesia	459	...	56	40.9	10.4	3.05	2.54	56.2	59.3	...	...	...	207.7
UNION OF SOVIET SOCIALIST REPUBLICS	255 038	22 402	11	17.8	7.9	1.18	1.13	66.5	74.3	2 760	3 280	99	1 116.5

Sources: United Nations Demographic Yearbook 1977; Population by sex and age for regions and countries, 1950, 2000, as assessed in 1973 (ESA/P/WP.60), United Nations Population Division, Department of Economic and Social Affairs; World population data sheet, 1975, 1978, Population Reference Bureau, Inc.; World Development Report, 1978, World Bank (1978); WHO questionnaires.

TABLE 9. HEALTH MANPOWER BY OCCUPATION AND RATE PER 100 000 POPULATION AROUND 1975, AVAILABILITY OF DATA AND POPULATION COVERED BY THE DATA

Health occupation	World*					Developed countries					Developing countries				
		Rate per 100 000 population	Availability of data				Rate per 100 000 population	Availability of data				Rate per 100 000 population	Availability of data		
	Number		Number of countries or areas	Population covered (in thousands)	% of world population	Number		Number of countries or areas	Population covered (in thousands)	% of world population	Number		Number of countries or areas	Population covered (in thousands)	% of world population
Physicians	3 037 674	76.86	193	3 952 295	99	2 089 319	190.65	39	1 095 899	100	948 355	33.18	154	2 858 307	99
Medical assistants	676 016	82.00	56	824 436	21	624 609	168.96	8	369 687	34	51 407	11.31	48	454 699	16
Multipurpose health auxiliaries	1 820 134	160.24	20	1 135 911	29	—	—	—	—	—	1 820 134	160.24	20	1 135 911	40
Midwives and assistant midwives	790 145	29.31	161	2 695 448	68	484 579	59.87	33	809 400	74	305 566	16.87	128	1 811 667	63
Nurses and assistant nurses	6 904 613	174.75	193	3 951 132	99	5 035 582	459.52	39	1 095 841	100	1 869 031	65.46	154	2 855 291	99
Traditional medical practitioners	596 967	33.61	14	1 776 308	45	3 715	6.01	1	61 832	6	593 252	34.60	13	1 714 476	60
Dentists	551 211	18.64	188	2 957 702	75	437 372	42.09	38	1 039 153	95	113 839	5.93	150	1 918 349	67
Dental operating auxiliaries and dental hygienists	55 398	5.30	61	1 045 448	26	51 363	11.64	15	441 145	40	4 036	0.67	46	604 310	21
Dental laboratory technicians	95 886	9.04	79	1 060 908	27	91 553	13.92	16	657 838	60	3 284	0.81	63	403 070	14
Pharmacists	691 873	23.39	178	2 958 038	75	518 439	47.97	37	1 080 708	99	173 434	9.24	141	1 877 330	65
Pharmaceutical assistants	297 045	20.42	114	1 454 452	37	240 364	40.36	25	595 564	55	56 681	6.60	89	858 888	30
Laboratory technicians and assistant technicians	476 622	16.81	176	2 835 121	71	418 385	47.31	31	884 307	81	58 237	2.99	145	1 950 814	68
X-ray technicians and assistant technicians	211 226	7.95	162	2 658 210	67	174 968	19.88	28	879 902	81	36 258	2.04	134	1 778 308	62
Sanitarians and assistant sanitarians	153 527	6.80	156	2 256 924	57	73 474	12.41	25	591 906	54	80 053	4.81	131	1 665 018	58

Sources: WHO questionnaires; United Nations Demographic Yearbook

* Excluding Bhutan and Democratic People's Republic of Korea. Data for China were provided by the State Statistical Bureau and the Ministry of Public Health, Beijing, and relate to 1978.

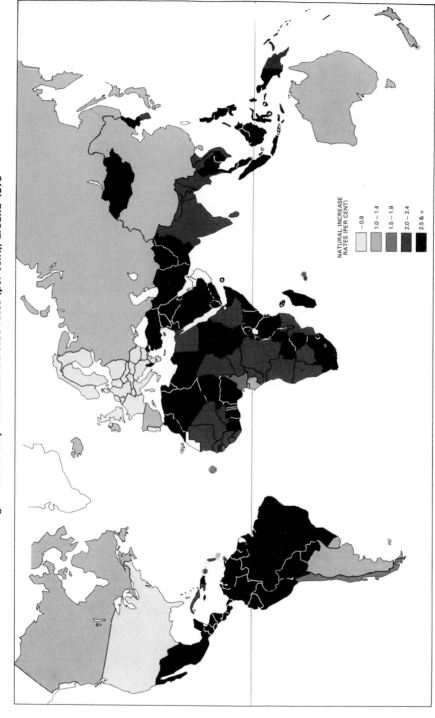

Fig. 1. World map of natural increase rates (per cent), around 1975

NATURAL INCREASE
RATES (PER CENT)

- 0.9
1.0 — 1.4
1.5 — 1.9
2.0 — 2.4
2.5 & +

Source: Selected world demographic indicators by countries, 1950–2000 (ESA/P/WP.55). United Nations Population Division, Department of Economic and Social Affairs.

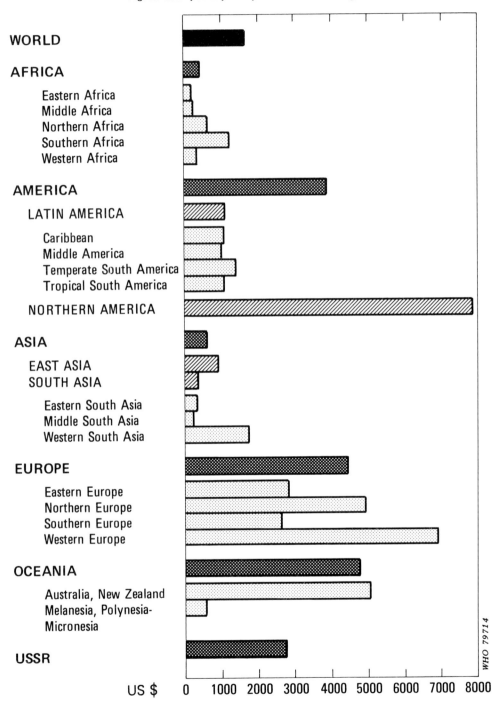

Fig. 2. GNP per capita by continents and regions

US $

270

Fig. 3. Primary education enrolment by continents and regions, around 1975

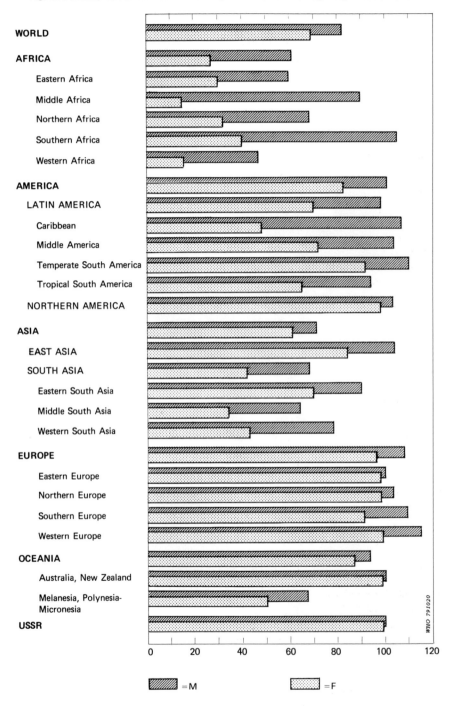

WORLD
AFRICA
 Eastern Africa
 Middle Africa
 Northern Africa
 Southern Africa
 Western Africa
AMERICA
 LATIN AMERICA
  Caribbean
  Middle America
  Temperate South America
  Tropical South America
 NORTHERN AMERICA
ASIA
 EAST ASIA
 SOUTH ASIA
  Eastern South Asia
  Middle South Asia
  Western South Asia
EUROPE
 Eastern Europe
 Northern Europe
 Southern Europe
 Western Europe
OCEANIA
 Australia, New Zealand
 Melanesia, Polynesia-Micronesia
USSR

0   20   40   60   80   100   120

WHO 791020

▨ = M   ▨ = F

271

Fig. 4. World food map: dietary energy supply (per capita), around 1975

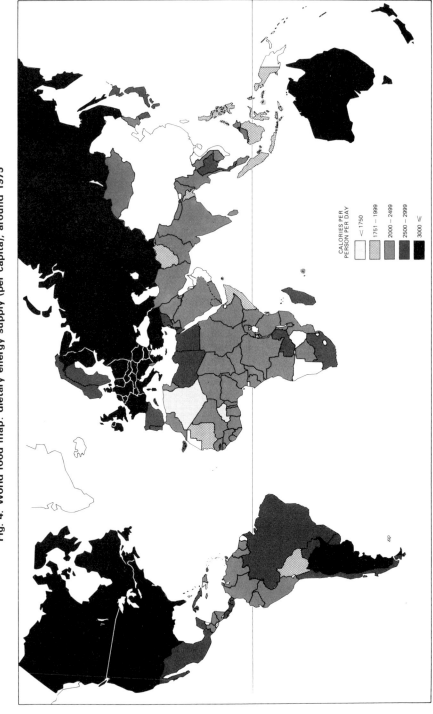

CALORIES PER
PERSON PER DAY

< 1750
1751 − 1999
2000 − 2499
2500 − 2999
3000 ≤

Source: World population data sheets, 1975 and 1978, Population Reference Bureau, Inc.
Note: No official data available for China.

Fig. 5. World population net reproduction rates, around 1975

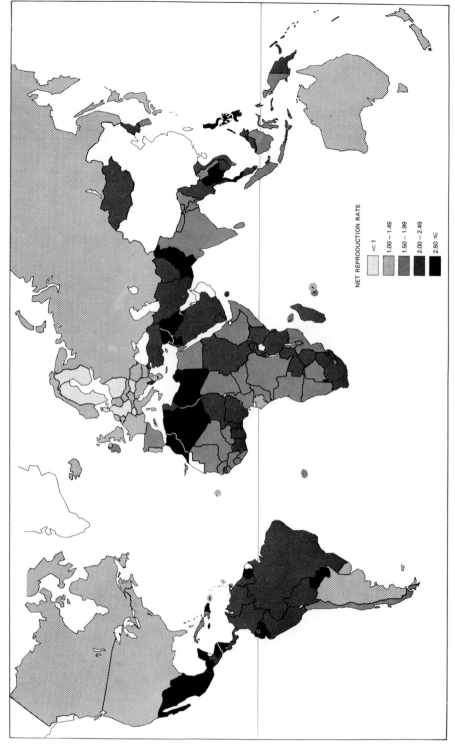

NET REPRODUCTION RATE

< 1
1.00 — 1.49
1.50 — 1.99
2.00 — 2.49
2.50 ≤

Source: Selected world demographic indicators by countries, 1950–2000 (ESA/P/WP.55). United Nations Population Division, Department of Economic and Social Affairs.

Fig. 6A. Life expectancy at birth, around 1975

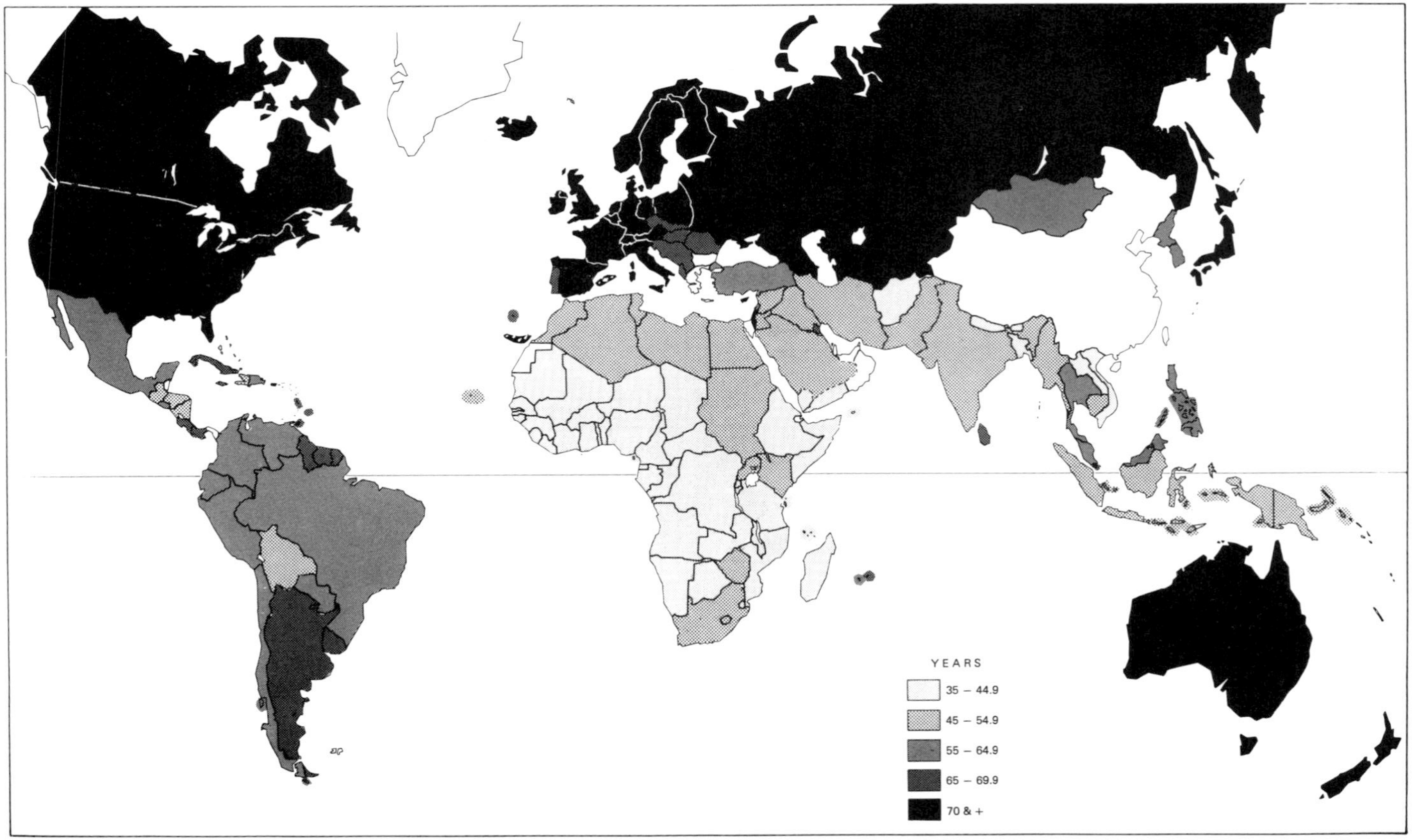

YEARS

35 – 44.9
45 – 54.9
55 – 64.9
65 – 69.9
70 & +

Source: Selected world demographic indicators by countries, 1950–2000 (ESA/P/WP.55). United Nations Population Division, Department of Economic and Social Affairs.
Note: No official data available for China.

274

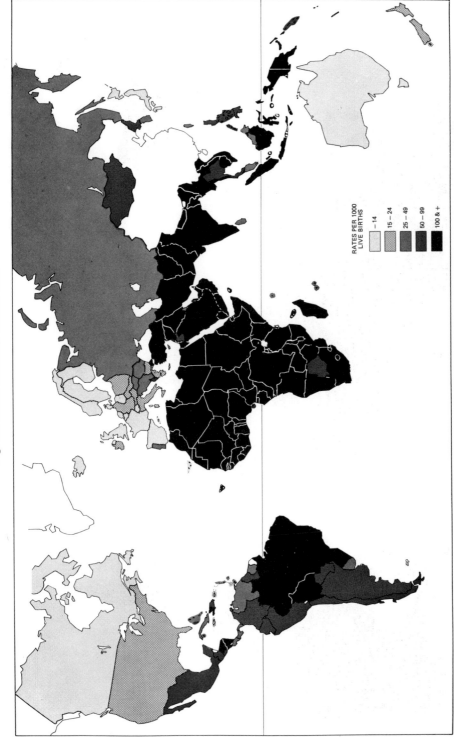

Fig. 6B. Infant mortality, around 1975

RATES PER 1000
LIVE BIRTHS

– 14
15 – 24
25 – 49
50 – 99
100 & +

Source: World population data sheets, 1975 and 1978, Population Reference Bureau, Inc.
Note: For China, the urban infant mortality rate is 12 and the rural rate 15–30 per 1000 live births.

275

Fig. 7. Density of certain health occupations, around 1975

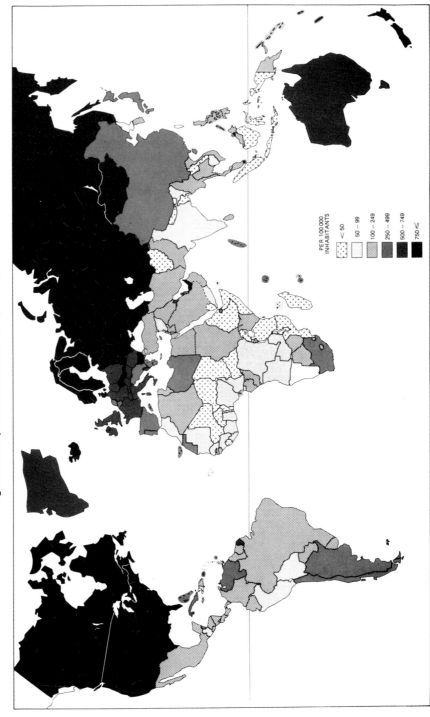

PER 100 000
INHABITANTS

< 50
50 – 99
100 – 249
250 – 499
500 – 749
750 ≤

Source: WHO questionnaires.
[1] Includes: physicians, medical assistants, multipurpose health auxiliaries (barefoot doctors, village health auxiliaries, etc.), professional midwives, assistant midwives, traditional birth attendants, professional nurses, assistant nurses, traditional medical practitioners.

276

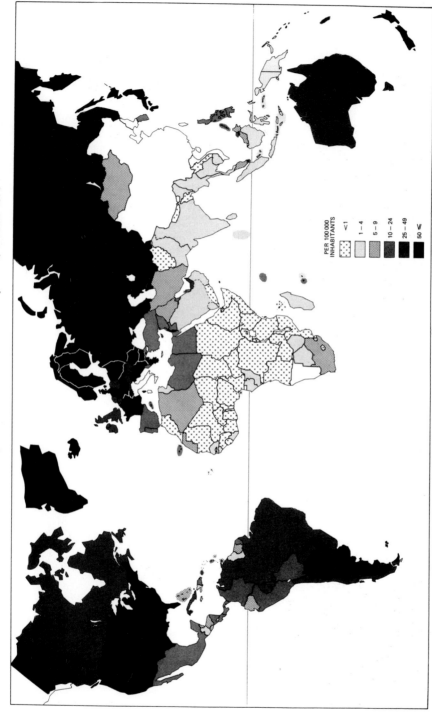

Fig. 8. Density of certain dental health occupations, around 1975

PER 100 000
INHABITANTS

<1
1 – 4
5 – 9
10 – 24
25 – 49
50 ≤

Source: WHO questionnaires.
¹ Includes: Dentists (dental surgeons, stomatologists), dental operating auxiliaries (dental therapists, school dental nurses), dental hygienists, dental laboratory technicians.
Note: No official data available for China.

277

Index

Abortion, 128, 139–140
Accidents, 44–45, 132, 146–147, 150
  prevention and control, 173–178
Adolescence, health in, 133–134, 141, 156–157
Agriculture, development, 19, 32
  workers' health, 147–148
Alcohol-related problems, 158–160
Arthritis, see Chronic rheumatic diseases
Atherosclerosis, 213–214

Behavioural factors, health-related, 28–33, 133
Biologicals, 173
Blindness, 97–98

Cancer, 29, 32, 104–111
  data processing, 109–110
  epidemiology, 110–111, 216–218
  organization of services, 107
  prevention, screening and early detection, 106–108
  research, 215–218
  therapy, 108–109
Cardiovascular diseases, 29, 32, 33, 99–104
  community action, 102–103, 216
  prevention and control, 102–103
  research, 213–216
Cerebrospinal meningitis, 92
Chagas' disease, 87, 121, 210
Chemicals, control of hazards, 123–124, 216–218
  see also Occupational health
Children, immunization, 93–94, 140
  mental health, 156–157
  mortality and morbidity, 41–42, 49, 129–133
Cholera, 87–89, 219, 220
Chromosomal disorders, 112–113
Chronic rheumatic diseases, 114–115
Cirrhosis of liver, 158–159
Communicable diseases, 45–46, 111–112
  prevention and control, 82–97
  susceptibility (genetic markers), 113
Community participation in health programmes, 102–103, 122, 124, 215, 223–224
Community water supply and wastes disposal, 119
Coronary heart disease, 214–215
Country health programming, 55–57

Demographic prospects, see Population . . . trends
Dental health, see Oral health
Diabetes, 114, 128, 143
Diarrhoeal diseases, 87–89, 131
  research, 219–210
Differentials of health status, 37–50

Diphtheria, 93–94, 140
Disasters and natural catastrophes, 178–179
Disease prevention and control, 82–117
Drinking-water, 119
Drug dependence and abuse, 133, 141, 160–162
Drugs, see Prophylactic, diagnostic and therapeutic substances
Dust, see Agriculture, workers' health
Dysentery, 89

Econometrics, health, see Differentials
Economic and social development, evaluation of progress and data needs, 33–34, 55
  general considerations, health aspects, 8–9, 121, 129, 142–143, 151–153, 227–228
  policy issues, 34–36, 50, 51–54, 118–119, 243
  social changes, 22–23, 125–126, 234–237
  legislation, 141–142
Economic trends, 23–25, 234–237
Education, 19–22
  see also Health manpower
Elderly, care of, 156, 162, 233
  see also Life expectancy, trends
Employment, 25–26, 231
Enteric infections, 87–90
Environmental health, 118–124, 216–217, 220
  new approaches (monitoring and management), 122–123

Families and households as units in health studies, 15–17
Family health, 124–142
Family planning, 136, 139–140
  research, 212–213
Fertility regulation, research, 211–213
Filariasis, 87, 99
Financing of health care, see Health expenditure
Food and nutrition, 18–19, 142–144
  research, 222–224
Food production, 20, 142
Food safety, 124, 218
Foodborne diseases, 95–96

Gastroenteritis, 88–89
Genetics, human, 112–113
  molecular, research, 225
Gonococcal infections, 96–97

Haemoglobinopathies and allied disorders, 112
Haemorrhagic fever, viral, 95

Health care, delivery systems, 63–78
  administration and management, 73–78
  financing, 201–205
  integration, organization and regionalization, 66–70
  private sector, role of, 72–73
  referral, 70–72
  see also Hospitals; Maternal and child health, organization of care and services
Health education, 117, 140, 141, 144–146
Health expenditure, 77–78, 199–205, 236
Health legislation, 57–63, 124, 141–142, 167–168
Health manpower, 55, 179–195
  education and training, 186–190
    dental manpower, 116–117, 182
    maternal and child health manpower, 137
  management, 190–195
    systems, 183–184
  planning, 184–186, 242–244
Health status, differentials, 37–50
  trends, 237–242
Heart disease, 32, 33, 100–101, 213–214
Hepatitis, viral, 95
Hereditary diseases, 112
Hospitals, health centres and dispensaries, 196–200
  distribution of beds, 198–199
Housing, human settlements and, 119–122
Human genetics, 112–113
Human reproduction, research, 209–210, 211–213
Hypertension, 32, 101
  research, 215

Illiteracy, 8, 232
Immunization, 93–94, 140
  research on vaccines, 220, 225
Industrialization, 32, 150–151
Infant mortality, 41–42, 129–132
Infertility, 129, 140
  research, 211–213
Influenza, 94–95
Information systems, 75–77
  see also Cancer, data processing; Health manpower, management, systems

Legislation, *see* Health legislation
Leishmaniasis, 87
Leprosy, 91–92
  research, 211
Life expectancy, trends, 38–41, 237–240
Liver diseases, *see* Cirrhosis ; Hepatitis

Malaria, 82–86, 121, 128
  research, 211
Malnutrition, 18–19, 99, 130–131, 132, 142–144, 157–158, 222–224

Maternal and child health, 126–132, 133–142, 149
  organization of care and services, 135–142
Maternal mortality and morbidity, 127–129
Measles, 94, 132, 140
Medical schools, 187–188
Meningitis, cerebrospinal, 92
Mental health, 121, 150–151, 153–168
  control and treatment, 163–165
  organization of services, 165–167
  research, 220–222
Mental retardation, 132, 157
Midwives, *see* Health manpower
Migrant workers' health, 149–150
Migration, 15, 32, 163
  of health personnel, 192–193
Mortality rates and health status, *see* Health status, differentials
Motor-vehicle accidents, 175, 177
Myocardial infarction, 32, 33, 100
  research, 214

Neurological disorders, 157–158
Noncommunicable diseases, prevention and control, 99–111, 111–117, 153–168
Nurses, *see* Health manpower
Nutrition, 18–19, 142–144
  research, 222–224

Occupational health, 146–153
Onchocerciasis, 87, 98
Oral health, 115–117, 143

Paediatrics, *see* Children; Maternal and child health
Parasitic diseases, 45–46, 82–89
Pertussis, 94, 140
Pharmaceuticals, *see* Prophylactic, diagnostic and therapeutic substances
Pharmacists, *see* Health manpower
Planning, 54–57
  see also Country health programming
Pneumonia, *see* Respiratory diseases
Poisoning, *see* Occupational health
Policies for health and economic and social development, 34–36, 51–54, 118–119, 168, 243–244
Poliomyelitis, 94, 140
Pollution, environmental, control, 123–124
Population, composition, size and growth, trends, 9–17, 228–234
Poverty, 18–19, 26–28, 143–144
  see also Economic and social development, general considerations
Pregnancy risks and delivery services, 127–128, 130, 134, 138–139
Primary health care, 78–82, 124

Prophylactic, diagnostic and therapeutic substances, 168–173
  drug policies and management, 172
  quality and safety control, 170–172, 217–218
  selection, procurement and utilization, 169–170
  supply systems, 168–169
  see also Biologicals; Immunization
Psychiatry, 153–154, 163–165, 220–221
Psychosocial factors, 32–33, 162–163
  at work, 149–150
  research, 220–222

Radiation protection, 106, 123–124, 217
Refugees, 15
  see also Disasters
Research, 206–226
  general development and financing, 206–209
    international cooperation, 209–210
  implications, 224–226
  training, 209–210
  see also under subjects
Respiratory diseases, 111–112, 131, 146, 147, 148
  see also Smoking
Rheumatic fever, 101, 102–103
  research, 215–216
Rheumatic heart disease, 99, 101, 103
Rheumatism, see Chronic rheumatic diseases
Road (motor-vehicle) accidents, 174, 175, 177–178

Sanitation, see Housing; Community water supply and wastes disposal
Schistosomiasis, 86–87
  research, 211
Schizophrenia, 154–155, 163–164
School health, 141
Sexually transmitted diseases, 96–97, 129, 133
Smallpox, 92–93
Smoking, 28–32, 104, 106, 111, 128, 133, 215, 217
Social security, see Economic and social development, social changes; Health care, financing

Socioeconomic development, see Economic and social development
Special Programme of Research, Development and Research Training in Human Reproduction, 209–210
Special Programme for Research and Training in Tropical Diseases, 209, 210–211
Sterility, see Infertility
Stroke, 101, 103
Suicide, 162, 176

Tetanus, 94, 131, 140
Trachoma, 98
Treponematoses, endemic, 97
Tropical diseases, research, 209, 210–211
Trypanosomiasis, 87, 121, 210
Tuberculosis, 89–91, 140

United Nations system, coordination, see Economic and social development, policy issues
Urbanization, 14–15, 32, 233–234

Vaccines, see Biologicals; Immunization; Prophylactic, diagnostic and therapeutic substances
Vector biology and control, see Parasitic diseases; Zoonoses
Veterinary public health, 95–96
Viral diseases, 94–95, 217

Water supply and wastes disposal, 119, 120, 121
Women, in health and development, 124–125, 138, 141–142, 192
  see also Maternal and child health
Working populations, health of, 146–153, 231
  epidemiological studies, 151
  in small industries, 148–149
  see also Employment

Zoonoses, 95–96, 147

Acknowledgements

A number of experts either assisted in drafting individual sections or in providing extensive comments for Part I of the *Sixth Report on the World Health Situation*. Particular gratitude is owed to Professor D. Jakovljević, Vice-President of the Executive Council of the Assembly of the Socialist Autonomous Province of Vojvodina, Novi Sad, Yugoslavia, and Professor O. Gish, School of Public Health, Department of Health Planning and Administration, University of Michigan, Ann Arbor, Michigan, United States of America, for their advice on the overall design of the Report.

A draft manuscript for Part I was reviewed in May 1979 in Geneva by a group of experts who provided valuable guidance for the finalization of the Report. This group consisted of:

Dr J. H. Bryant, Deputy Assistant Secretary for International Health, Department of Health, Education, and Welfare, Rockville, Maryland, United States of America.

Dr Dora Galego Pimentel, Chief, Department of International Organizations, Ministry of Public Health, Havana, Cuba.

Dr A. S. Hassoun, Director of International Health Affairs, Ministry of Health, Baghdad, Iraq.

Mr A. A. Kiselev, Counsellor, Permanent Representative of the USSR to the United Nations and Other International Organizations at Geneva, Switzerland.

Dr P. Mocumbi, Provincial Director of Health of Sofala, Secretariat for International Cooperation, Ministry of Health, Maputo, Mozambique.

Dr A. Mukhtar, Under-Secretary, Ministry of Health, Khartoum, Sudan.

Professor Wai-Onn Phoon, Professor and Head, Department of Social Medicine and Public Health, University of Singapore, Singapore.

The work was conducted in the WHO Division of Health Statistics (Mr K. Uemura, Director).

SIXTH REPORT ON THE
WORLD HEALTH SITUATION, 1973–1977

Part II: Review by country and area

CORRIGENDUM

Page 9, second column, third paragraph, first line
delete 1965
insert 1975

Page 11, first column, table
delete Natural increase (%) 24.9
insert Natural increase (%) 2.5

Page 84, second column, last paragraph
delete 5.6 per 1000 births in 1974 to 4.3 in 1977
insert 0.56 per 1000 births in 1974 to 0.43 in 1977

Page 87, first column, fourth paragraph, penultimate line
delete 6%
insert 60%

Page 108, first column, third paragraph, last line
delete ₲ 080 457 117
insert ₲ 1 080 457 117

Page 136, second column, under (*f*)
delete per 100 live births
insert per 1000 live births

Page 163, first column, fourth paragraph, fourth line
delete 6.4%
insert 6.4 per thousand

Page 163, second column, last line
delete 609
insert 60.9

Page 165, second column, third paragraph, third line
delete Narna
insert Varna

Page 177, table
delete number of beds 12 105
insert number of beds 13 105

Page 224, table
    delete number of deaths (1–4 years) 18
    insert number of deaths (1–4 years) 184

Page 225, first column, last paragraph, first line
    delete 190
    insert 189

Page 225, second column, table
    delete Rehabilitation hospitals 197 586
    insert Rehabilitation hospitals 197 566

Page 227, second column, fourth paragraph, second, third and fourth lines
    delete 19.1%, 9.0%, 10.1%
    insert 19.1 per thousand, 9.0 per thousand, 10.1 per thousand

Page 232, first column, second paragraph
    delete 20.8%, 20.8%, 10.4%, 10.8%,38.9%, 58.0%, 0.43%, 0.73%
    insert 20.8 per thousand, 20.8 per thousand, 10.4 per thousand, 10.8
          per thousand, 38.9 per thousand, 58.0 per thousand, 0.43 per
          thousand, 0.73 per thousand

Page 235, second column, last table
    delete (rates per 1 000 population)
    insert (rates per 100 000 population)

Page 235, second column, last table
    delete Viral hepatitis 269.7
    insert Viral hepatitis 265.7

Page 266, second column, table
    delete Birth rate per 1000 population 17.1
    insert Birth rate per 1000 population 17.6

Page 283, first table
    delete Faculties of dentistry 400
    insert Faculties of dentistry 408

Page 289, first column, second paragraph, second line
    delete 78%
    insert 70%

Page 289, second column, fourth paragraph, first line
    delete 7 640 674
    insert 7 640 675

Page 290, second column, first table
insert Paediatric hospitals 14

Page 306, last table
delete Infant mortality rate (per 1000 live births) 23.6
insert Infant mortality rate (per 1000 live births) 13.6

Page 307, first column, second paragraph, ninth line
delete poliomyelitis (20)
insert poliomyelitis (30)

Page 311, first column, second paragraph, second line
delete 70
insert 90

Page 319, first column, second paragraph, fourteenth line
delete (5.9%
insert (5.8%

Page 355, first column, first paragraph, first line
delete 23 April
insert 26 April

Page 355, first column, third paragraph, second line
delete 1677
insert 1685

Page 383, table
delete Community health posts 5 785
insert Community health posts 5 786

Page 384, second table
delete Obstetrical examinations 1 678 140
insert Obstetrical examinations 1 678 164

Page 391, second column, second table
delete Sanitary engineers 18
insert Sanitary engineers 2

Page 398, first column, fourth paragraph
delete The maternal and child health centre in the first *arrondissement* has recently been completed with financing by the Fonds d'Aide et de Coopération and the World Lutheran Federation, but is not yet open.
insert The maternal and child health centre in the first *arrondissement* and a psychiatric in the fifth have recently been completed with financing respectively by the Fonds d'Aide et de Coopération and the World Lutheran Federation, but are not yet open.

Page 398, second column, fourth paragraph, first line
delete 40
insert 49

Page 399, first column, table
delete Pharmacists 4
insert Pharmacists 5

Page 399, first column, table
After State-qualified nurses
insert Certified nurses 195   195   296   296   108

Page 399, first column, table
delete Auxiliary midwives   17   17   . . .   .
insert Auxiliary midwives   17   17   . . .

Page 400, first column, third paragraph, third line
delete 5 000 beds
insert 500 beds

Page 400, first column, third paragraph, point (7), third line
delete 5 500
insert 5 590

Page 401, second column, first paragraph, seventh line
delete 155
insert 153

Page 403, table
delete Pagouda 5 639
insert Pagouda 5 689

Page 404, first column, fourth paragraph, fourth line
delete 40 407
insert 40 487

Page 404, table

	1973	1977	1978
delete General budget	3 434 166	55 280 829	60 593 000
insert General budget	13 434 166	55 200 829	60 598 000

WHO publications may be obtained, direct or through booksellers, from:

ALGERIA	Société Nationale d'Edition et de Diffusion, 3 bd Zirout Youcef, ALGIERS
ARGENTINA	Carlos Hirsch SRL, Florida 165, Galerias Güemes, Escritorio 453/465, BUENOS AIRES
AUSTRALIA	*Mail Order Sales:* Australian Government Publishing Service, P.O. Box 84, CANBERRA A.C.T. 2600; *or over the counter from:* Australian Government Publishing Service Bookshops *at:* 70 Alinga Street, CANBERRA CITY A.C.T. 2600; 294 Adelaide Street, BRISBANE, Queensland 4000; 347 Swanston Street, MELBOURNE, VIC 3000; 309 Pitt Street, SYDNEY, N.S.W. 2000; Mt Newman House, 200 St. George's Terrace, PERTH, WA 6000; Industry House, 12 Pirie Street, ADELAIDE, SA 5000; 156–162 Macquarie Street, HOBART, TAS 7000 — Hunter Publications, 58A Gipps Street, COLLINGWOOD, VIC 3066
AUSTRIA	Gerold & Co., Graben 31, 1011 VIENNA I
BANGLADESH	The WHO Programme Coordinator, G.P.O. Box 250, DACCA 5 — The Association of Voluntary Agencies, P.O. Box 5045, DACCA 5
BELGIUM	Office international de Librairie, 30 avenue Marnix, 1050 BRUSSELS — *Subscriptions to World Health only:* Jean de Lannoy, 202 avenue du Roi, 1060 BRUSSELS
BRAZIL	Biblioteca Regional de Medicina OMS/OPS, Unidade de Venda de Publicações, Caixa Postal 20.381, Vila Clementino, 04023 São PAULO, S.P.
BURMA	*see* India, WHO Regional Office
CANADA	*Single and bulk copies of individual publications (not subscriptions):* Canadian Public Health Association, 1335 Carling Avenue, Suite 210, OTTAWA, Ont. K1Z 8N8. *Subscriptions: Subscription orders, accompanied by cheque made out to the* Royal Bank of Canada, Ottawa, Account World Health Organization, *should be sent to the* World Health Organization, P.O. Box 1800, Postal Station B, OTTAWA, Ont. K1P 5R5. *Correspondence concerning subscriptions should be addressed to the* World Health Organization, Distribution and Sales, 1211 GENEVA 27, Switzerland
CHINA	China National Publications Import Corporation, P.O. Box 88, BEIJING (PEKING)
COLOMBIA	Distrilibros Ltd., Pio Alfonso Garcia, Carrera 4a, Nos 36–119, CARTAGENA
CYPRUS	Publishers' Distributors Cyprus, 30 Democratias Ave Ayios Dhometious, P.O. Box 4165, NICOSIA
CZECHO-SLOVAKIA	Artia, Ve Smeckach 30, 111 27 PRAGUE 1
DENMARK	Munksgaard Ltd., Nørregade 6, 1165 COPENHAGEN K
ECUADOR	Libreria Cientifica S.A., P.O. Box 362, Luque 223, GUAYAQUIL
EGYPT	Nabaa El Fikr Bookshop, 55 Saad Zaghloul Street, ALEXANDRIA
EL SALVADOR	Libreria Estudiantil, Edificio Comercial B No 3, Avenida Libertad, SAN SALVADOR
FIJI	The WHO Programme Coordinator, P.O. Box 113, SUVA
FINLAND	Akateeminen Kirjakauppa, Keskuskatu 2, 00101 HELSINKI 10
FRANCE	Librairie Arnette, 2 rue Casimir-Delavigne, 75006 PARIS
GERMAN DEMOCRATIC REPUBLIC	Buchhaus Leipzig, Postfach 140, 701 LEIPZIG
GERMANY, FEDERAL REPUBLIC OF	Govi-Verlag GmbH, Ginnheimerstrasse 20, Postfach 5360, 6236 ESCHBORN — W. E. Saarbach, Postfach 101 610, Follerstrasse 2, 5000 COLOGNE 1 — Alex. Horn, Spiegelgasse 9, Postfach 3340, 6200 WIESBADEN
GHANA	Fides Enterprises, P.O. Box 1628, ACCRA
GREECE	G.C. Eleftheroudakis S.A., Librairie internationale, rue Nikis 4, ATHENS (T. 126)
HAITI	Max Bouchereau, Librairie "A la Caravelle", Boîte postale 111-B, PORT-AU-PRINCE
HONG KONG	Hong Kong Government Information Services, Beaconsfield House, 6th Floor, Queen's Road, Central, VICTORIA
HUNGARY	Kultura, P.O.B. 149, BUDAPEST 62 — Akadémiai Könyvesbolt, Váci utca 22, BUDAPEST V
ICELAND	Snaebjørn Jonsson & Co., P.O. Box 1131, Hafnarstraeti 9, REYKJAVIK
INDIA	WHO Regional Office for South-East Asia, World Health House, Indraprastha Estate, Ring Road, NEW DELHI 110002 — Oxford Book & Stationery Co., Scindia House, NEW DELHI 110001; 17 Park Street, CALCUTTA 700016 (*Sub-agent*)
INDONESIA	M/s Kalman Book Service Ltd., Jln. Cikini Raya No. 63, P.O. Box 3105/Jkt, JAKARTA
IRAN	Iranian Amalgamated Distribution Agency, 151 Khiaban Soraya, TEHERAN
IRAQ	Ministry of Information, National House for Publishing, Distributing and Advertising, BAGHDAD
IRELAND	The Stationery Office, DUBLIN 4
ISRAEL	Heiliger & Co., 3 Nathan Strauss Street, JERUSALEM
ITALY	Edizioni Minerva Medica, Corso Bramante 83–85, 10126 TURIN; Via Lamarmora 3, 20100 MILAN
JAPAN	Maruzen Co. Ltd., P.O. Box 5050, TOKYO International, 100–31
KOREA, REPUBLIC OF	The WHO Programme Coordinator, Central P.O. Box 540, SEOUL
KUWAIT	The Kuwait Bookshops Co. Ltd., Thunayan Al-Ghanem Bldg, P.O. Box 2942, KUWAIT
LAO PEOPLE'S DEMOCRATIC REPUBLIC	The WHO Programme Coordinator, P.O. Box 343, VIENTIANE
LEBANON	The Levant Distributors Co. S.A.R.L., Box 1181, Makdassi Street, Hanna Bldg, BEIRUT

A/1/80

WHO publications may be obtained, direct or through booksellers, from:

LUXEMBOURG	Librairie du Centre, 49 bd Royal, LUXEMBOURG
MALAWI	Malawi Book Service, P.O. Box 30044, Chichiti, BLANTYRE 3
MALAYSIA	The WHO Programme Coordinator, Room 1004, Fitzpatrick Building, Jalan Raja Chulan, KUALA LUMPUR 05-02 — Jubilee (Book) Store Ltd, 97 Jalan Tuanku Abdul Rahman, P.O. Box 629, KUALA LUMPUR 01-08 — Parry's Book Center, K. L. Hilton Hotel, Jln. Treacher, P.O. Box 960, KUALA LUMPUR
MEXICO	La Prensa Médica Mexicana, Ediciones Científicas, Paseo de las Facultades 26, Apt. Postal 20-413, MEXICO CITY 20, D.F.
MONGOLIA	*see* India, WHO Regional Office
MOROCCO	Editions La Porte, 281 avenue Mohammed V, RABAT
MOZAMBIQUE	INLD, Caixa Postal 4030, MAPUTO
NEPAL	*see* India, WHO Regional Office
NETHERLANDS	N.V. Martinus Nijhoff's Boekhandel en Uitgevers Maatschappij, Lange Voorhout 9, THE HAGUE 2000
NEW ZEALAND	Government Printing Office, Mulgrave Street, Private Bag, WELLINGTON 1. *Government Bookshops at:* Rutland Street, P.O. 5344, AUCKLAND; 130 Oxford Terrace, P.O. Box 1721, CHRISTCHURCH; Alma Street, P.O. Box 857, HAMILTON; Princes Street, P.O. Box 1104, DUNEDIN — R. Hill & Son Ltd, Ideal House, Cnr Gillies Avenue & Eden Street, Newmarket, AUCKLAND 1
NIGERIA	University Bookshop Nigeria Ltd, University of Ibadan, IBADAN — G. O. Odatuwa Publishers & Booksellers Co., 9 Benin Road, Okirigwe Junction, SAPELE, BENDEL STATE
NORWAY	J. G. Tanum A/S, P.O. Box 1177 Sentrum, OSLO 1
PAKISTAN	Mirza Book Agency, 65 Shahrah-E-Quaid-E-Azam, P.O. Box 729, LAHORE 3
PAPUA NEW GUINEA	The WHO Programme Coordinator, P.O. Box 5896, BOROKO
PHILIPPINES	World Health Organization, Regional Office for the Western Pacific, P.O. Box 2932, MANILA — The Modern Book Company Inc., P.O. Box 632, 926 Rizal Avenue, MANILA
POLAND	Składnica Księgarska, ul Mazowiecka 9, 00052 WARSAW *(except periodicals)* — BKWZ Ruch, ul Wronia 23, 00840 WARSAW *(periodicals only)*
PORTUGAL	Livraria Rodrigues, 186 Rua do Ouro, LISBON 2
SIERRA LEONE	Njala University College Bookshop (University of Sierra Leone), Private Mail Bag, FREETOWN
SINGAPORE	The WHO Programme Coordinator, 144 Moulmein Road, G.P.O. Box 3457, SINGAPORE 1 — Select Books (Pte) Ltd, 215 Tanglin Shopping Centre, 2/F, 19 Tanglin Road, SINGAPORE 10
SOUTH AFRICA	Van Schaik's Bookstore (Pty) Ltd, P.O. Box 724, 268 Church Street, PRETORIA 0001
SPAIN	Comercial Atheneum S.A., Consejo de Ciento 130-136, BARCELONA 15; General Moscardó 29, MADRID 20 — Libreria Diaz de Santos, Lagasca 95, MADRID 6; Balmes 417 y 419, BARCELONA 6
SRI LANKA	*see* India, WHO Regional Office
SWEDEN	Aktiebolaget C.E. Fritzes Kungl. Hovbokhandel, Regeringsgatan 12, 10327 STOCKHOLM
SWITZERLAND	Medizinischer Verlag Hans Huber, Länggass Strasse 76, 3012 BERNE 9
SYRIAN ARAB REPUBLIC	M. Farras Kekhia, P.O. Box No. 5221, ALEPPO
THAILAND	*see* India, WHO Regional Office
TUNISIA	Société Tunisienne de Diffusion, 5 avenue de Carthage, TUNIS
TURKEY	Haset Kitapevi, 469 Istiklal Caddesi, Beyoglu, ISTANBUL
UNITED KINGDOM	H.M. Stationery Office: 49 High Holborn, LONDON WC1V 6HB; 13a Castle Street, EDINBURGH EH2 3AR; 41 The Hayes, CARDIFF CF1 1JW; 80 Chichester Street, BELFAST BT1 4JY; Brazennose Street, MANCHESTER M60 8AS; 258 Broad Street, BIRMINGHAM B1 2HE; Southey House, Wine Street, BRISTOL BS1 2BQ. *All mail orders should be sent to P.O. Box 569, LONDON SE1 9NH*
UNITED STATES OF AMERICA	*Single and bulk copies of individual publications (not subscriptions):* WHO Publications Centre USA, 49 Sheridan Avenue, ALBANY, N.Y. 12210. *Subscriptions: Subscription orders, accompanied by check made out to the Chemical Bank, New York, Account World Health Organization, should be sent to the* World Health Organization, P.O. Box 5284, Church Street Station, NEW YORK, N.Y. 10249; *Correspondence concerning subscriptions should be addressed to the* World Health Organization, Distribution and Sales, 1211 GENEVA 27, Switzerland. *Publications are also available from the* United Nations Bookshop, NEW YORK, N.Y. 10017 *(retail only)*
USSR	*For readers in the USSR requiring Russian editions:* Komsomolskij prospekt 18, Medicinskaja Kniga, Moscow — *For readers outside the USSR requiring Russian editions:* Kuzneckij most 18, Meždunarodnaja Kniga, Moscow G-200
VENEZUELA	Editorial Interamericana de Venezuela C.A., Apartado 50.785, CARACAS 105 — Libreria del Este, Apartado 60.337, CARACAS 106 — Libreria Médica Paris, Apartado 60.681, CARACAS 106
YUGOSLAVIA	Jugoslovenska Knjiga, Terazije 27/II, 11000 BELGRADE
ZAIRE	Librairie universitaire, avenue de la Paix N⁰ 167, B.P. 1682, KINSHASA 1

Special terms for developing countries are obtainable on application to the WHO Programme Coordinators or WHO Regional Offices listed above or to the World Health Organization, Distribution and Sales Service, 1211 Geneva 27, Switzerland. Orders from countries where sales agents have not yet been appointed may also be sent to the Geneva address, but must be paid for in pounds sterling, US dollars, or Swiss francs.

Price: Sw. fr. 20.—   Prices are subject to change without notice.

NOTES

NOTES

NOTES

NOTES

NOTES

NOTES